Lexical Challenges in a Multilingual Europe

DUISBURGER ARBEITEN ZUR SPRACH- UND KULTURWISSENSCHAFT

DUISBURG PAPERS ON RESEARCH IN LANGUAGE AND CULTURE

Herausgeben von /edited by
Ulrich Ammon, René Dirven und /and Martin Pütz

Band/Volume 99

PETER LANG
EDITION

Gerhard Stickel/Tamás Váradi (eds.)

Lexical Challenges in a Multilingual Europe

Contributions to the Annual Conference 2012 of EFNIL in Budapest

PETER LANG
EDITION

Bibliographic Information published by the Deutsche Nationalbibliothek
The Deutsche Nationalbibliothek lists this publication in the Deutsche Nationalbibliografie; detailed bibliographic data is available in the internet at http://dnb.d-nb.de.

Library of Congress Cataloging-in-Publication Data

European Federation of National Institutions for Language. Conference (2012 : Budapest)
Lexical challenges in a multilingual Europe : contributions to the Annual Conference 2012 of EFNIL in Budapest / Gerhard Stickel, Tamás Váradi (eds.). -- PL Edition.
pages cm. -- (Duis ; Band/Volume 99)
Chiefly in English, with contributions is in French, German, and Spanish.
"European Federation of National Institutions for Language10th Annual Conference, Budapest 25-26 October 2012: Lexical challenges in a Multilingual Europe Host: Research Institute for Linguistics, Hungarian Academy of Sciences."
ISBN 978-3-631-64394-5
1. Language and languages--Study and teaching--Europe--Congresses. 2. Lexicography--Europe--Congresses. 3. Multilingualism--Europe--Congresses. I. Stickel, Gerhard, editor of compilation. II. Váradi, Tamás, editor of compilation. III. Title.
P57.E9E958 2012
418.0071'04--dc23
2013024304

ISSN 0934-3709
ISBN 978-3-631-64394-5 (Print)
E-ISBN 978-3-653-03492-9 (E-Book)
DOI 10.3726/978-3-653-03492-9

Peter Lang Edition is an Imprint of Peter Lang GmbH.
Peter Lang – Frankfurt am Main · Bern · Bruxelles · New York · Oxford · Warszawa · Wien

www.peterlang.de

Preface

We proudly present in this volume the contributions to the tenth annual conference of EFNIL. This time our network of the central language institutions of the EU states and other European countries again chose for its general meeting a thematic field that is of special importance for the languages of the individual countries and for communication in multilingual Europe. The conference in Budapest was about words and so is this book: about the various methods for collecting and describing words of the individual languages and for confronting words of different languages and about the media in which lexical information is made available and used. Besides traditional lexicographic methods and products, modern methods and media of monolingual and multilingual lexicography are dealt with, this also from the special perspectives of the possible and real use of available lexicographic results.

After the opening contributions, several experts offer their general reflections and overview of lexicography in Europe in the past and present. Reports of the representatives of various member institutions of EFNIL on remarkable lexicographic projects in their countries follow. The *Budapest Resolution*, presented in the official languages of most member states of the European Union and several other European countries completes the volume. This resolution underlines the special importance of monolingual and multilingual lexicography for the European languages and the interlingual communication in Europe. It points out the insufficient support of lexicographic work in some European countries and specifically calls for more promotion of bilingual and multilingual lexicography in the interest of Europe.

We thank again Ulrich Ammon and his colleagues for also accepting this volume for their series. And we thank Joachim Hohwieler and Mark Newson for their efficient help in preparing the book for the printers.

Vorwort

Wir freuen uns, in diesem Band die Beiträge zur zehnten Jahrestagung von EFNIL vorlegen zu können. Auch diesmal hat unser Netzwerk der zentralen Sprachinstitutionen der EU-Staaten und anderer europäischer Länder für seine Hauptversammlung einen Themenbereich gewählt, der eine besondere Bedeutung für die Sprachen der einzelnen Länder wie auch für die Kommunikation im vielsprachigen Europa hat. Es ging bei der Tagung in Budapest und geht in diesem Band um Wörter: um die verschiedenen Verfahren, mit denen Wörter einzelner Sprachen gesammelt und beschrieben sowie Wörter verschiedener Sprachen konfrontiert werden, und um die Medien, in denen lexikalische Informationen verfügbar gemacht und genutzt werden. Behandelt werden neben traditionellen lexikographischen Verfahren und Produkten moderne Methoden und Medien ein- und mehrsprachiger Lexikographie. Dies auch unter dem besonderen Aspekt der Nutzungsmöglichkeiten und tatsächlichen Nutzung verfügbarer lexikographischer Ergebnisse.

Nach den Eröffnungsbeiträgen bieten mehrere Experten ihre generellen Überlegungen und Überblicksdarstellungen der Lexikographie in Europa in Vergangenheit und Gegenwart an. Es folgen Berichte von Beauftragten verschiedener Mitgliedsinstitute von EFNIL über bemerkenswerte lexikographische Arbeiten in ihren jeweiligen Ländern. Der Band wird abgeschlossen von einer *Budapester Resolution*, die in den offiziellen Sprachen der meisten Mitgliedsstaaten der Europäischen Union und mehrerer weiterer europäische Länder präsentiert wird. Diese Resolution unterstreicht die besondere Bedeutung der ein- und mehrsprachigen Lexikographie für die europäische Sprachen und für die interlinguale Verständigung in Europa. Sie weist nachdrücklich auf die unzureichende öffentliche Förderung lexikographischer Arbeiten in mehreren Staaten hin und fordert im europäischen Interesse insbesondere eine stärkere Unterstützung zwei- und mehrsprachiger lexikographischer Projekte.

Wieder einmal danken wir Ulrich Ammon und seinen Kollegen für die Aufnahme auch dieses Bandes in ihre Reihe. Joachim Hohwieler und Mark Newson danken wir für ihre tatkräftige Hilfe bei der Einrichtung des Buchs für den Druck.

Előszó

Örömmel adjuk közre ebben a kötetben az EFNIL tizedik éves konferenciáján tartott előadások gyűjteményét. A tagállamok és a többi európai ország központi nyelvi intézeteit tömörítő szervezet a korábbi évekhez hasonlóan az idén is olyan témát választott az éves ülése tárgyául, amelynek különleges jelentősége van az egyes országok és az európai többnyelvi kommunikáció szempontjából. A budapesti konferencia a szókészletről szólt, és ez a jelen kötetnek is a tárgya: az egyes nyelvek szókincsének gyűjtése és leírása, a különböző nyelvek szókészletbeli eltéréseinek a kezelése, és a lexikai információk megjelenítésének és használatának a médiuma. A hagyományos lexikográfiai módszereken és termékeken túl a kötet bemutatja a modern egy- és többnyelvű lexikográfia módszereit és eszközeit, mindezt az elért lexikográfiai eredmények tényleges és lehetséges használatának a szemszögéből.

A bevezető előadásokat az európai lexikográfia múltját és jelenét áttekintő általános témájú előadások követik, melyek után az egyes EFNIL tagintézmények kéviselőinek beszámolóját olvashatjuk az országukban folyó lexikográfiai projektekről. A kötetet a konferencián elfogadott Budapesti Határozat zárja, melyet az EFNIL tagországok és számos más európai ország hivatalos nyelvére fordított változatban találhatjuk. A Határozat rámutat arra, hogy bizonyos európai országokban nem elégséges szintű a lexikográfiai munkálatok támogatása és egyben sürgeti a két- és többnyelvű lexikográfia erőteljesebb támogatását Európa érdekében.

Ismét köszönjük Ulrich Ammon úr és kollégáinak, hogy befogadták a jelen kötetet a sorozatba. Köszönettel tartozunk Joachim Hohwielernek és Mark Newsonnak a kötet nyomdai előkészítéséhez nyújtott hathatós segítségükért.

Mannheim / Budapest

Gerhard Stickel / Tamás Váradi

Contents

a) Opening

b) General reflections

c) Reports on different countries

a) Opening

Istvan Kenesei

Welcome address

Ladies and Gentlemen!

Welcome to this magnificent neo-Renaissance building on the bank of the Danube, the seat of the Hungarian Academy of Sciences, which was inaugurated in 1862, exactly 150 years ago. It is fitting for this 10th Annual Conference of EFNIL on Lexical Challenges in a Multilingual Europe to be held at this venue, since the Academy owes its foundation in a very large part to endeavours to create a dictionary.

As with so many nations in the early 19th century, such as the Germans and Italians in particular, perhaps the most important instrument of the national revival of Hungarians was language. The Kingdom of Hungary at the time was part of the sprawling Hapsburg Empire, whose official language was of course German, and the Emperor was always decreed to be the ruler of Hungary, though not always crowned as its king. Parliament had some sovereignty in internal affairs but all bills passed had to be signed into law by the Emperor. National identity was the order of the day and one possible avenue to declare it was through the vernacular. After years of fruitless debates in Parliament on how to move forward, a wealthy young aristocrat who had travelled the world, Count István Széchenyi, stood up at the Diet in 1825 in Pozsony (Pressburg, today's Bratislava), and offered a year's income of his estate to establish the "Hungarian Science Society". His example was followed on the spot by a number other rich noblemen present, and the Academy was soon enacted.

The Society's primary function was to promote the case of Hungarian as the language of sciences, and in order to achieve this aim, members were asked in its very first session in 1831 "to collect ancient and current Hungarian technical terms from 782 Hungarian books so as to be read by members, each one as appertained to his own department", and thus the "Great Hungarian Word-Book" was to be created. But even at that time the Society was aware that "to gather every Hungarian word for the Great Word-Book many years' work will be necessary," though they cannot have predicted that after almost 200 years only four volumes would have been published.

But these four tomes of the Comprehensive Dictionary of Hungarian, as published by the Research Institute for Linguistics (RIL) of the Hungarian Academy of Sciences, and comprising the letters *A* and *B* as well as a companion volume with the sources and technical information, rely on an extensive corpus and the most up-to-date technology available, thus, in effect, turning the delay into an advantage, and providing for an easily augmentable database. Ever since its foundation in 1949, RIL has been the most prolific producers of dictionaries of the Hungarian language of various sizes and subjects, from etymologies to loanwords to poets' vocabularies, to list just a few.

The lexicographic activities of RIL are, however, not limited to monolingual dictionaries. Although it is not within our sphere of interest to publish bilingual "paper" dictionaries, having recognized the need emerging from the predicament that bilingual dictionaries of two languages each with less than a certain number of speakers are commercially not viable, on the one hand, and fostering the cause of machine translation between a wide range of European languages, on the other, we have embarked upon developing language technologies that have made promising advances in both areas, as will surely be discussed by my colleagues during this conference.

On behalf of the host organisation allow me to thank you for coming to Budapest and to this opening session of the Conference and I wish you have an excellent time whether as speakers or as audience.

Claude Durand

Intervention de M. Claude Durand à la conférence annuelle de l'EFNIL – Budapest, 25 octobre 2012

Monsieur le Directeur de l'Institut,

Monsieur le Président de l'EFNIL,

Mesdames et Messieurs,

Au nom de mon Directeur General, M. Benedetti, je voudrais en premier lieu vous adresser le salut de la Commission Européenne, et notamment de la DG Interprétation, qui avec la DG EAC et la DGT est tout particulièrement chargée de faire vivre le multilinguisme dans les échanges européens. Je précise qu'au sein de la DG Interprétation j'exerce la fonction de Chef de l'unité Multilinguisme qui entre autres gère un vaste programme de coopération avec les universités européennes.

Multilinguisme – le mot est lâché – il s'agit à la fois d'une valeur fondamentale au respect de laquelle l'institution que je représente est profondément attachée et d'une réalité opérationnelle – peut être imparfaite mais une réalité tout de même – vécue au jour le jour au sein des institutions européennes et que nous, managers du plus grand service d'interprétation d'Europe et du monde sommes chargés de faire fonctionner aussi harmonieusement que possible afin de faciliter la communication et la prise de décision à l'échelon européen.

Permettez-moi de dire quelques mots sur ces deux dimensions du concept de multilinguisme, la dimension politique au sens noble du terme, et la dimension opérationnelle telle qu'elle se traduit dans la pratique quotidienne de notre service d'interprétation.

La dimension politique, voire philosophique, tout d'abord. La Commission européenne, gardienne de Traités, est profondément attachée à l'idée même du multilinguisme, qui est constitutif de l'ADN de l'UE. Le président de votre fédération européenne s'en souviendra tout aussi bien que moi puisqu'il était présent à Chypre lors de la récente conférence organisée par la Commission du 26 au 28 septembre à Limassol à l'occasion de la journée européenne des langues: Mme Vassiliou, commissaire chargée de l'Education, de la Culture, de la Jeunesse et du Multilinguisme a souligné une fois de plus combien pour la Commission européenne le multilinguisme est le reflet même de la diversité qui caractérise notre continent.

Le projet européen, aujourd'hui tout autant qu'hier, vise à mobiliser et à rassembler les citoyens européens et leurs responsables politiques autour de la recherche de solutions à des problèmes communs, sans pour autant tenter de gommer les spécificités et les identités des peuples qui composent ce grand ensemble, bien au contraire. C'est un lieu commun que de rappeler la belle devise des pères fondateurs de l'Europe, "l'unité dans la diversité".

Les linguistes que vous êtes savent pertinemment que le génie de chaque langue traduit un angle de vision, un mode de penser la réalité et le monde qui est original. Or, dans cette période de crise et de mutations rapides que nous traversons, les Européens ont plus que jamais besoin de confronter à partir de leur patrimoine linguistique et culturel, leurs idées et leurs aspirations, en tentant d'en faire une synthèse, afin d'être capables d'imaginer de nouvelles pistes pour l'avenir, et cela dans tous les domaines où les enjeux dépassent de loin le cadre national, qu'il s'agisse de l'économie ou du social, de l'environnement et des ressources énergétiques, de l'éducation ou de la culture, pour ne citer que les exemples les plus évidents.

En autres termes, le multilinguisme est un remarquable antidote à la pensée unique, il faut donc cesser de le considérer comme un obstacle et comme une charge, voyons-le résolument comme un atout, comme un générateur d'idées pour les Européens.

Maintenant, quittons le plan des concepts et analysons pendant quelques instants la pratique du multilinguisme telle qu'elle est vécue quotidiennement par la DG Interprétation, en nous attardant sur les défis terminologiques (plutôt que “lexicaux”) auxquels nos interprètes ont à faire face.

Pour camper le décor: la DG Interprétation, ce sont près de 600 interprètes permanents et plus de 3.000 freelance, et 11 à 12.000 réunions organisées chaque année, dans des régimes linguistiques à géométrie variable, allant de 2 à 23 langues officielles (voire davantage), en passant par toutes sortes de combinaisons intermédiaires, des régimes asymétriques, etc, bref un appareil de communication complexe au service des décideurs européens.

Nos interprètes possèdent de toute évidence de vastes connaissances linguistiques mais l'éventail des sujets traités dans les réunions européennes est si étendu qu'ils doivent s'adapter rapidement et quotidiennement à des questions et à des jargons souvent très techniques. Ces termes trouvent en partie leur place dans des dictionnaires bilingues ou multilingues plus ou moins spécialisés et élaborés par d'éminents lexicographes et des spécialistes du domaine. Ces dictionnaires existent pour beaucoup en version électronique et peuvent être consultés sur DVD ou en ligne au moment de la préparation des réunions par nos professionnels.

La phase de préparation est en effet capitale pour la qualité du service que rendra l'interprète au moment de la réunion, après avoir fait un travail de repérage des concepts et de la terminologie utilisés dans la documentation fournie par l'organisateur de l'évènement, documents de séance ou documents contextuels.

Documentation et terminologie sont en fait inséparables et c'est pourquoi la DG Interprétation a mis au point sur son Intranet une plateforme électronique intitulée MEDATA, à laquelle ont accès tous nos professionnels et où figurent à la fois les documents et les glossaires spécialisés correspondant à la réunion à laquelle les interprètes sont affectés.

Ces glossaires très pointus sont parfois issus de publications officielles, internes ou externes, ils émanent aussi d'une base de données “maison” appelée LITHOS, qui résulte d'un travail collectif réalisé par les interprètes eux-mêmes grâce à leur expérience des réunions européennes, et dont les termes ne sont pas tous validés mais correspondent néanmoins à l'usage du moment dans les domaines considérés; actuellement, cette base de données contient près de 178.000 termes puisés pour la plupart dans 895 glossaires spécialisés. Cette base est actualisée à un rythme mensuel, elle peut être téléchargée intégralement par nos interprètes pour un usage hors ligne, et l'utilisateur peut définir à l'avance le profil de recherche en fonction de ses besoins propres, qui peuvent varier suivant la réunion à laquelle il est affecté.

Les interprètes s'appuient également fortement sur les travaux terminologiques effectués par la DGT, qui alimente régulièrement la base terminologique IATE, dont il existe également une version ouverte au public (près de 27 millions de consultations en 2011). Je pourrai difficilement être exhaustif dans la citation des sources auxquelles recourent nos interprètes, mais je me permettrai de singulariser QUEST, outil de recherche terminologique interinstitutionnel très rapide, qui puise simultanément dans 26 sources terminologiques mais pas seulement puisque elles comprennent aussi des sources documentaires telles que EURAMIS Concordance, DGT Vista et EUR-LEX.

Je le répète, la consultation de ces sources intervient principalement lors de la phase de préparation elle peut se faire aussi – puisque l'ordinateur portable et la tablette trouvent aujourd'hui de plus en plus souvent leur place dans la cabine d'interprétation simultanée – entre les interventions traduites par l'interprète lorsque son collègue reprend à son tour ou lorsque le déroulement de la réunion et la répartition des langues parlées lui offrent le loisir de procéder à cette recherche sans interférer négativement dans ses prestations au micro.

Je pourrais parler encore longuement des défis terminologiques que j'ai eu à relever au cours des 30 années où j'ai exercé la profession d'interprète, mais je ne voudrais pas abuser de votre temps. Je voudrais surtout moi-même écouter ce que les ardents artisans de la lexicographie que vous êtes apportent à la cause de la diversité et du multilinguisme qui constituent une richesse pour nous Européens.

Je vous remercie de votre attention et souhaite plein succès à votre conférence annuelle.

Claude Durand

Chef de l'unité Multilinguisme et Assistance à la formation d'interprètes
DG Interprétation
Commission européenne

Gerhard Stickel

Introduction

Hölgyeim és uraim, kedves kollégák és vendégek!

Engedjék meg, hogy az EFNIL nevében meleg és őszinte hálámat fejezzem ki magyar barátainknak e konferencia előkészítéséért és megrendezéséért. Nagyon örülünk, hogy itt lehetünk Budapesten. A meleg vendégszeretet, amely körülvesz minket, nagyszerű környezet az EFNIL tagok tizedik plenáris konferenciájához. Egyben arra ösztönöz minket, hogy elmélyedjünk az idei év általános témájában és kicseréljük véleményünket és tapasztalatainkat a lexikográfia helyzetéről.[1]

Dear colleagues and guests,

Let me hope for your leniency and understanding for my clumsy attempt to thank our Hungarian friends in their own language for their hospitality. I also thank our friend and colleague Istvan Kenesei, the director of the hosting institute, for the stimulating opening of this session. We are glad to have a representative of the European Commission with us. Thank you very much, Monsieur Durand, for conveying the greetings of your director general and for contributing to our general topic with a report on the practice of interpretation for the Commission. I welcome Uwe Mohr, the president of EUNIC and the Civil Society Platform for European Multilingualism. I consider his visit to our conference as an answer to the engagement of our delegates Bessie Dendrinos and Johan Van Hoorde in the activities of the Civil Society Platform. I also welcome the representative of Meta-Net, Georg Rehm, and thank him for his brief introduction to the activity programme of Meta-Net that in several respects coincides with the aims of EFNIL. When I attended the Meta-Forum in Brussels last June, I said in my plenary address that because of our interrelated aims and activities I could not decide whether Meta-Net could be considered as a technological arm of EFNIL or EFNIL as a linguistic branch of Meta-Net. Of course, I also welcome our guest speakers and the guests from the local academic scene and from abroad. And last, but by no means least, let me welcome all the delegates of our member institutions. This is somehow a confusion of addressees, since I am myself one of the EFNIL delegates. However, I only want to express how glad I am that you all have come to the 10th annual conference of EFNIL. It is indeed the 10th one if we count our founding conference in Stockholm in 2003 as the first one. Our 10th anniversary, however, cannot be celebrated before next year.

Please, allow me to use the opening of the conference for a brief comment on this year's general theme: *Lexical Challenges in Multilingual Europe*. The attribute *lexical* sug-

[1] Ladies and gentlemen, dear colleagues and guests!
On behalf of EFNIL, I want to give my warm and sincere thanks to our Hungarian friends for preparing and organizing this conference. We are all glad to be here now in Budapest. The generous hospitality that is being offered to us is a pleasant context for the 10th plenary meeting of the members of EFNIL. It is also an incentive for us to get deeply involved in this year's general theme and to exchange our views and experiences in the field of lexicography.

gests that the conference will be mainly concerned with lexical units, with words, words of the various European languages. Why should we care about words? Why are words important? I hesitate to answer with the first sentence of St. John's gospel: *In initio erat verbum. In the beginning was the Word.* This would lead to theological arguments that a simple linguist like myself could not meet. Let me instead make use of another classical quote. In one of the scenes of Shakespeare's tragedy *Hamlet* (II, 2), Polonius asks the prince who is reading a book: “What do you read, my Lord?” Hamlet answers: “Words, words, words.” He could have answered even more generally: *a text* or *a book*, because Hamlet does not want to be interrogated by the old bore Polonius and, therefore, meets the question evasively by a generality. However, Hamlet's answer is in its general sense true, because everything that we speak and hear, that we write and read consists of words.

I will not enter a long discussion of what words are in a strict sense of modern linguistics. There are various attempts to come to a definition of words as units somewhere between the structural levels of morphology and syntax. Distinctions are made between lexical words and grammatical words, between autosemantic and synsemantic words, between phonological and graphematical words, between simple and compound words, between indigenous words and loan words, between the various word classes and so on and, of course, between words of different languages. Distinctions like this must be made and observed by grammarians and, more important in our present context, by lexicographers. For my brief deliberations, however, it suffices to look at words from the perspective of a language user as the units of speech or writing that native speakers of a language usually regard as the smallest isolable meaningful elements of the language. More naively, words can be seen as items that can be looked up in a dictionary, provided there is a dictionary.

The repetition of isolated words is the beginning of the language acquisition of a child. The use of single words and, perhaps, our hands are the first steps to communicate in a foreign language. Structural linguistics considered syntax as the core of a language. However, syntactic structures by themselves convey little meaning. Lexical units, words, are always needed to make an utterance meaningful.

Since ancient times, the collection of the words of a language in a list or a wordbook was an important means to stabilize a language, to establish and codify a standard variety of the language. A dictionary was, therefore, often considered as a linguistic treasure, a metaphor still used, for instance, for the modern *Tresor de la langue française.* In German, we use the expression *Wortschatz* (treasure of words) when we refer to the vocabulary of a language. These days, one of our member institutes, the Accademia della Crusca in Florence, celebrates the 400th anniversary of its *Vocabolario degli Accademici della Crusca* of 1612, a lexical treasure that became a model for similar authoritative dictionaries of other European languages.

While a wordbook of an individual language, that is, a monolingual dictionary, is especially important for the cultivation and preservation of the language of an ethnic group or a nation; bilingual and multilingual dictionaries that confront the words of two or more languages are aids for the learning of other languages, for understanding foreign texts and for the communication between speakers of different languages. Bilingual glossaries and dictionaries are historically even older than monolingual ones.[2] Within the context of EFNIL and especially under the heading of this conference, we emphasize that bilingual and multilingual dictionaries are indispensable tools to overcome the borders between the different European languages and to maintain the linguistic diversity of Europe. For some people, dictionaries are even tools to enjoy this diversity. Dictionaries are indispensable for translators and interpreters, for teachers and learners of foreign languages, for the authors of textbooks and other learning material, for the scholar, scientist, or engineer who tries to understand a foreign text as well as for the tourist in a foreign country who wants to know what a sign or a public warning is about.

The importance of words as essential elements of our various languages and the undisputable benefit that our languages and their speakers have from dictionaries were the motives for EFNIL to put this year's general conference under the title *Lexical Challenges in Multilingual Europe*. I use the word *dictionary* not only for printed books but as a cover term for collections of words in all media in which lexical data are being presented nowadays.

I would like to distinguish between three interrelated kinds or aspects of lexical challenges. The first challenge is directed as ever towards the lexicographers in our institutes and publishing houses in our countries to produce and to present reliable information on the words of our language and their use. More than in the past, the linguistic diversity in present Europe demands, however, that the vocabulary of each individual language is not only described for itself and by itself but also within the context of other European languages.

A challenge in a second sense is directed towards the participants of this conference. We should feel challenged to learn from each other about modern methods and aims of lexicographic projects in the various countries and forward this knowledge and experience to our own language institutions and publishers in order to stimulate and improve their lexicographic activities. This exchange of information on theoretical concepts, practical methods, and experiences should not be limited to the ways of extracting lexical units from corpora and other sources and ordering and analyzing them but should also include, beside traditional ways of publication, modern means and media of presenting and distributing lexical information. This again should presuppose the study of the actual needs people have and the ways they use dictionaries and other lexical sources: What kind of words do people look up, and what information on words do they want? How and for what purposes do they use dictionaries in conventional forms or digital media? The challenge to us to learn from each other about modern developments and experiences in lexicography will be at the core of this conference.

We should, however, not forget a third kind of challenge, a challenge directed towards the authorities in our countries and on the European level. It is more a demand than a challenge which should be felt and accepted by the addressees. In current international discussions, the compilation of dictionaries in various media and their distribution is usually subsumed under the term of *language industries*. This suggests that dictionary

[2] The oldest known dictionary consists of tablets with bilingual Sumerian-Akkadian wordlists, dated roughly 2300 BC.

making is a commercial industry, a business like many others. However, the financial gain that can be made by selling dictionaries is in most cases very small in relation to the amount of research and lexicographic efforts invested in their production. In some countries, the production of standard dictionaries of the national language or languages is, fortunately, not considered as a profit-oriented business but as a cultural task and is, therefore, financially supported by the governments or other public institutions. This is not the case for dictionary projects on all our official languages. Some lexicographic projects are left solely to the care of publishing houses that, of course, live on the profit they can make with their products. The development of a comprehensive or even authoritative dictionary of one of the so called smaller languages does not offer much profit. The economical situation is especially difficult for the production of bilingual dictionaries, not to speak of multilingual dictionaries. Governments and other public institutions may feel obliged to support dictionaries of their own national language but have little interest in supporting projects in bi- or multilingual lexicography.

Here, the support of the European authorities must come in. If multilingualism is still on the agenda of the European Union – and an impressive conference in Cyprus last month seemed to confirm this – the Union should give more support for the development of modern bilingual and multilingual dictionaries in all appropriate media as tools for us Europeans to cope with the diversity of our languages and to preserve this linguistic and cultural wealth. Special support is needed for lexicographic enterprises on languages and language pairs, the results of which are not economically rewarding but necessary to enable and ease interlingual communication in Europe. Our own project EFNILEX is a modest attempt to develop an exemplary model for this kind of dictionaries. One of the results of this conference that I hope for could be an appeal addressed to our national governments and to the European authorities to increase the support for current lexicographic projects and to provide the necessary funds for the development of a European lexicographic infrastructure. This is one of the issues the General Assembly of EFNIL will discuss tomorrow.

Well, let us get to work now! As stated in the announcement of the conference, we will at first hear overview descriptions and general discussions of international developments in modern lexicography by several experts in this field. In advance, let me thank Patrick Hanks and Willy Martin for their contributions. Thanks in advance also to Gábor Prószéky for contributing to the panel. Representatives of several member institutes of EFNIL or specialists of their choice will give a series of reports on important lexicographic projects in their countries. The thematic part of the conference will end tomorrow with a panel discussion on central questions concerning present lexicography in Europe. I appeal to all speakers and chairpersons to allow some time for the other participants to ask questions or contribute their ideas on the various topics. Altogether, I am confident that we will hear informative and stimulating papers and have lively discussions over these two days.

Thank you for your attention!

Vielen Dank!

Merci beaucoup!

Köszönöm szépen!

b) General reflections

Patrick Hanks

Lexicography and technology in the Renaissance and now

Abstract

The development of lexicography has always been closely integrated with and dependent on technological developments. In this paper, I draw attention to some parallels between lexicography in the Renaissance and the present day.

In 16th-century Europe, the character of lexicography underwent a radical change as a result of two inventions: printing from movable type and metal type-founding. It was also profoundly affected by the so-called 'rebirth of learning'. Part 1 of this paper discusses the technology and philosophy of Renaissance lexicography.

In the 21st century, computer technology and developments in scholarship are beginning to have a comparable radical effect on lexicography. It is too early to say where this will lead, but one thing is already certain: traditional printed dictionaries, after five hundred years of unparalleled success, are a thing of the past. The business model according to which a publisher pours huge sums of money over many years into developing a dictionary in the hope of reaping rich rewards from sales of the dictionary as a printed book each year is dead. Dictionary users nowadays, seeking information about the spelling, use, or meaning of a word, do not turn to a printed book: they turn instead to a web site. Whether they are well served or ill served by such web sites is a matter for debate.

At the same time, there has been a revolution in cognitive and philosophical understanding of the nature of language, and in particular the role of lexis, which lexicographers have been slow to come to terms with. Traditional Leibnizian models of word meaning and phraseology have been superseded by the work of philosophers such as Wittgenstein and Putnam, anthropologists such as Rosch and Tomasello, and linguists such as Sinclair.

A third revolution has taken place in the collection of lexicographical evidence. Traditional lexicographers relied on extremely time-consuming and inefficient reading programmes for the collection of evidence, or (following the lead of generative linguists) simply invented the evidence by introspection. It has been said that linguistics of this kind is the only 'scientific' discipline in which it is regarded as acceptable first to invent evidence, then to explain what has been invented, then to claim that something of general validity has been 'discovered'. A modern alternative approach – empirical linguistics –, particularly relevant to lexicography, is to collect large quantities of data (e.g. an electronic corps of texts or speech) and investigate how people actually use words with the aid of various kinds of computational and statistical methods. Generative linguists, defending their use of introspection to create evidence, sometimes raise a counter-accusation that empirical linguistics has no role for introspection and intuitions. Some unthinking empirical linguists even agree. But this is self-evidently not true. There is a role for intuitions in empirical linguistics, namely the *interpretation* of data. The empiricists' true objection is to the invention of evidence.

In Part 2 of this paper, I present one of many possible new approaches to lexicography, namely Corpus Pattern Analysis (CPA). This picks up a theme promulgated by the late John Sinclair, that "many meanings depend for their realization on the presence of more than one word" (Sinclair 1998). It is a truism that meaning very often depends on context, yet much modern lexicography ignores context. And what is meant by 'context' anyway? I discuss some of the many problems that are lying in wait for lexical analysts who seek to adopt a phraseological approach to lexicography. Nevertheless, I shall conclude that lexicography needs to pay more attention to phraseology than is currently customary.

A third revolution has taken place in the collection of lexicographical evidence. Traditional lexicographers relied on unbelievably time-consuming reading programmes for the collection of evidence, or simply invented the evidence by introspection (navel-gazing). It has been said that linguistics (generative linguistics) is the only 'scientific' discipline in which it is regarded as acceptable first to invent evidence, then to explain what has been invented, then to claim that something of general validity has been 'discovered'. A modern alternative approach, empirical linguistics (including various approaches to lexical analysis), is to collect large quantities of data (e.g. an electronic corps of texts or speech), followed by explanation of what has been collected using various kinds of large-scale computational and statistical analysis. Generative linguists, defending their use of introspection to create evidence, sometimes claim that empirical linguistics has no role for introspection and intuitions. But this is self-evidently not true. There is a role for intuitions in empirical linguistics, namely the *interpretation* of data. The empiricists' objection is to the use of intuitions to invent evidence, not (of course) to the use of intuitions to interpret it.

1. Renaissance lexicography and printing technology

1.1 Dictionaries in England and Europe before Cawdrey

Surveys of English lexicography, starting with Murray (1900), give the impression that the first English dictionary was Robert Cawdrey's *Table Alphabeticall*, published in 1604. This little book is a dictionary of hard words, mostly 'inkhorn terms' – learned words that were introduced in profusion from Latin into English by scholars during the 16th century. Cawdrey's book is addressed mainly to women – who, in the 16th and 17th centuries were rarely fortunate enough to receive a Latin education and as a result tended to be excluded from intellectual discourse and in some cases could not even understand the Latinate English words (known as 'inkhorn terms') addressed to them in sermons. Apart from this, the *Table Alphabeticall* is a historical curiosity of comparatively little intellectual or cultural interest. It had no ambition to be a 'complete' inventory of the lexicon. The notion that a dictionary should serve as an inventory of the lexicon of a language was not an innovation of English lexicographers, but was a goal that had been pursued (for Latin) by several important lexicographical works in Continental Europe in the 16th century.

The prominence assigned to Cawdrey's *Table Alphabeticall* by Murray (1900) and by subsequent Anglocentric writers such as Starnes and Noyes (1946) had the unfortunate effect of deflecting attention from the rich lexicographic tradition of the European Renaissance in the 16th century, in which English was only one of several participant languages – a rather minor one, as we shall see. Starnes (1963) tried to correct the false impression given by his earlier work, but apparently in vain. Landau (1984, 2001) describes *Cawdrey's Table Alphabeticall* as a seminal work, adding that it is "the least inspiring of all seminal works". The *Table Alphabeticall* is indeed uninspiring, but it is not a seminal work.

The word ***dictionary*** itself came into English as an inkhorn term in the mid 16th century. The *Oxford English Dictionary* (OED) shows that the Medieval Latin word *dictionarium* was coined as early as 1225 and was used to denote a collection of Latin words arranged according to subject, rather than in alphabetical order. More exotic synonyms such as *glossarium* 'glossary', *cornucopia* 'horn of plenty', *elucidarius* 'elucidator', and *thesaurus* 'treasure house' also became widespread.

OED comments:

> Dictionaries proper are of two kinds: those in which the meanings of the words of one language or dialect are given in another (or, in a polyglot dictionary, in two or more languages), and those in which the words of a language are treated and illustrated in this language itself. The former were the earlier. (OED second edition, s.v. *dictionary*)

So what were these Renaissance dictionaries before Cawdrey? What did they consist of, how and where did they originate, who compiled them, and what was their purpose?

Scholarly studies by Starnes/Talbert (1955), Starnes (1963), Considine (2008), and an excellent chapter by Bately (2009) in Cowie's monumental *Oxford History of English Lexicography* have gone some way towards correcting the misleading impression perpetuated by Landau and others. Bately shows how lexicography developed as a scholarly and cultural activity during the 16th century. She observes that lexicographers both of Latin-English dictionaries and of other foreign language-English dictionaries turned to the continent for models and sources.

> So, when, in 1538, Thomas Elyot [...] produced his unidirectional Latin-English *Dictionary*, the authorities he cited included French, Dutch, and Italian contemporaries, who, like him, were seeking to provide the linguistic tools demanded by the 'New Learning'. It was the monolingual Latin *Dictionarium* of 'Calepinus' – Augustinian friar Ambrogio Calepino of Bergamo –, first published in 1502, that was his chief source. And when Elyot's dictionary was reissued in 1542 as the *Bibliotheca Eliotae – Eliotis librarie*, it was from the *Dictionarium Latino-Gallicum* (1538) of French printer Robert Estienne [...] that much of its new material was derived.

More will be said about Calepino below. And it should be noted here, at the outset, that Estienne was much more than a printer in the modern sense. He was a classical scholar, an editor, a publisher, and a Humanist thinker, conversing on equal terms with the leading Parisian intellectuals of his day.

1.2 The development of printing and typography

The development of lexicography in 16th-century Europe was dependent on the development of printing technology and the associated crafts of punch-cutting and typefounding. Dictionary-like compilations pre-dated printing, but dictionaries as products for widespread general use only became available because of the rapid reproduction of identical copies that printing made possible. Collections of words with glosses were created in monasteries as manuscripts throughout Europe in the later Middle Ages. Mostly, these works consisted of collections of Latin words glossed into vernacular languages, for the benefit of young novices learning to read Latin texts. Sometimes the Latin words arranged (more or less roughly) in alphabetical order, sometimes thematically. For propagation each manuscript had to be laboriously copied out by hand, and each act of copying could produce only one copy at a time, each with its own idiosyncrasies and copying errors. The invention of printing by Johannes Gutenberg in about 1440 in Strasbourg (subsequently moved to Mainz) changed everything, not only for lexicography but for all other fields of knowledge, as discussed by Eisenstein (1979). Suddenly, rapid replication and massive dissemination of identical copies of a text – including large and complex texts such as dictionaries – became possible.

Three components contributed to and are intertwined with the development of lexicography and with each other: 1) the invention of printing, 2) the rediscovery of classical Latin literature, philosophy, and art (including lettering), and 3) the development of challenging thinking that constituted the Reformation. The history of all these events has been intensively studied, but their interaction bears re-examination, for an understanding of it will crucially affect our appreciation of the early history of European lexicography. Let us first look at the relationship between printing and lexicography.

After Gutenberg, a key figure is Nicolas Jenson, a man of German extraction who was born in 1420 in Sommevoire, France (about half-way between Paris and Strasbourg). By the 1450s, Jenson had risen to become controller of the French royal mint at Tours. In 1458 he moved to Mainz, where he evidently became fascinated by the technology of printing with movable type, recognizing its potential for the rapid dissemination of knowledge. To this technology, he devoted the rest of his life. After a few years as a printer and publisher in Mainz and Frankfurt, Jenson moved to Italy, where, in Venice in 1468, he set up shop as a printer, publisher, and typographer. Between 1468 and his death in 1480 he edited and printed about 150 books, mostly editions of Latin theological tracts, but also some Latin classics, some Greek, an Italian guide to medicinal herbs, and miscellaneous other works. Jenson was not the only printer and typographer in Venice in the 1470s, but he is surely the most important of them.

Let us look a little more closely at his typographic principles, which were to play such an important role in the development of lexicography in subsequent decades, not only in Venice, but also as far afield as Paris, Lyons, Frankfurt, and Geneva. Jenson's type styles were based on the clean lines and subtle distinctive serifs of the lettering on monumental inscriptions that had been created by anonymous Roman stonemasons and other craftsmen a millennium and a half earlier. An important part of Jenson's contribution to the Renaissance was his replacement of the heavy black lettering style of medieval manuscripts, which had served Gutenberg for a model, with the more sharply defined letters of the ancient Roman alphabet.

A key principle of early Venetian typographers, in particular Jenson, was legibility. A generic term for this style of typography is Antiqua, in contrast to the Germanic Black-Letter style. As far as we know, Jenson designed, cut, and founded his own type. No doubt his experience of overseeing working in metal at the French Royal Mint stood him in good stead. According to an advertisement issued by his firm shortly after his death, Jenson's typographic symbols, “do not hinder the reader's eyes, but rather help them and do them good. Moreover, the characters are so intelligently and carefully elaborated that the letters are neither smaller, larger, nor thicker than reason or pleasure demand”.

A comparison of a sample of Gutenberg’s Black Letter (Figure 1) with Jenson’s Venetian Old Style (Figure 2) is instructive. At first glance, the two seem to have almost nothing in common. The letters look as if they might even represent different alphabets. Gutenberg’s style is a version of the letters in medieval manuscripts. Jenson’s is completely different: to a modern reader, it looks uncannily familiar, because it established typographical principles that are still relevant today. It is astonishingly, even shockingly modern – a design achievement worthy of the 20th-century Bauhaus at its best. It was the foundation of almost all subsequent type-founding and design in the Roman alphabet down to the present day, with the exception of German Fraktur, which owes more to the tradition of Gutenberg and medieval manuscripts and which, even in 19th-century Germany, was recognized to be unsuitable for printing dictionaries, not least because it is uneconomical in terms of space on the page and its potentially ambiguous when used in a small size. Typefaces based on medieval manuscript lettering are designed to be read slowly and sequentially. Medieval reading was slow. By contrast, the legibility of Jenson's type style enabled fast, non-sequential skimming and dipping, of a kind characteristic of dictionary use.

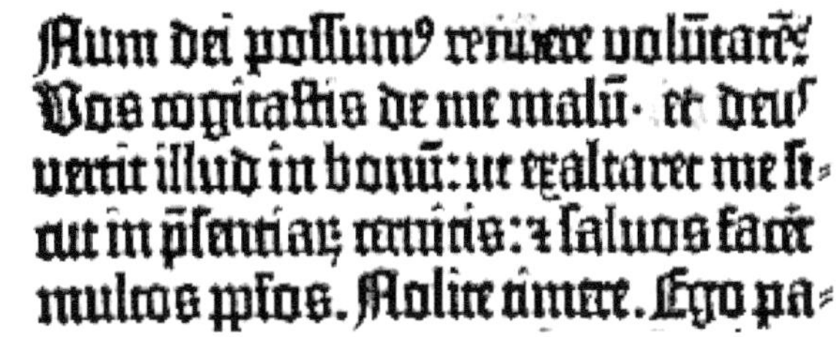

Figure 1: The Gutenberg Bible (c. 1455): sample from the *Book of Exodus*

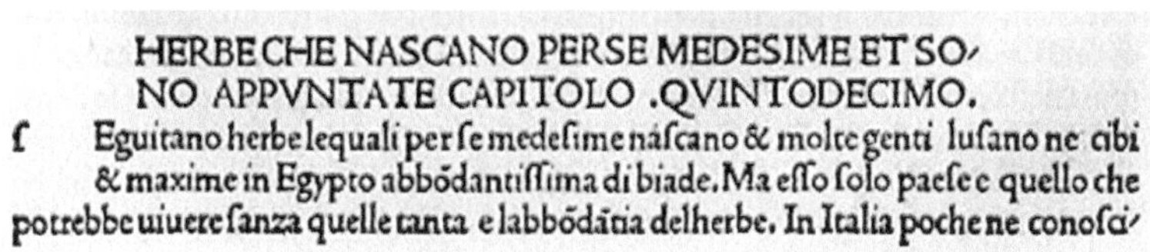

Figure 2: Sample of Jenson's typography (from the Wikipedia entry for 'Jenson')

It takes a modern reader all of thirty seconds to become familiar with what can now be seen as the idiosyncrasies of Jenson's Venetian Old Style. These are:

- representation, in certain contexts, of the letters ***n*** and ***m*** as a superscript bar over a preceding vowel (suggesting nasalization of the vowel rather a full-quality consonant),
- two forms of the letter *s*, long and short, whose uses are contextually determined,
- two short forms of Latin words meaning 'and': the symbol '&', which is still used today in certain contexts, and 'q:' for the bound morpheme *–que*, which has gone out of use.

In all other respects, Antiqua type styles are recognizably the same as their modern equivalents. Other great type designers and punch-cutters of 16th-century Europe (Graffo, Bembo, Garamond, Baskerville, and others) would design typographical symbols that share most of their fundamental characteristics with those of Jenson, although it has to be said that they do not share the same classic simplicity. Jenson's typographical principles have survived unchanged through the centuries and through various more recent technological revolutions for over 500 years. This is all the more remarkable when we consider the idiosyncrasies of conventional handwriting styles of the Renaissance, which require many hours of training in paleography before they can be read with fluency.

An important aspect, from the point of view of lexicography, of Jenson's contribution was that his typographic principles made it possible for printers to put many more words on the page without sacrificing legibility. This was to be an important contribution to the herculean lexicographic efforts that were to come. In a big text (and Renaissance dictionaries were big), more words on the page means fewer pages, which in turn means a more manageable product.

Fourteen years after Jenson's death, his printing and publishing business in Venice was inherited (in 1494), through marriage, by a man who was to play a pivotal role in the Italian Renaissance. Teobaldo Manucci, better known as Aldus Manutius (1450-1515), was a scholar with a passion for Ancient Greek philosophy and classical literature. Aldus was a man of means as well as scholarship. He devoted himself to using the technology of typesetting and printing to disseminating as many classical works as he could, rescuing them from obscurity, and to preventing further losses. He commissioned the typographer Francesco Griffo to create additional typefaces, including Greek (though the Greek typefaces have many cursive features and are less legible than the Roman ones designed by Jenson). Aldus acquired ancient Greek manuscripts from all over the Levant and the eastern Mediterranean region and employed Greek-speaking editors and compositors to collate and edit these manuscripts and get the texts typeset and printed. Venice was well placed for this activity, as the Venetian Republic during the 15th and 16th century held sway politically over some of the islands of Greece (Naxos, Crete, and the Ionian islands), so he had access to Greek-speaking scholars and workers.

Another important figure must now be briefly mentioned. In 1508 the Humanist scholar Erasmus came to stay in Venice as a guest of Aldus Manutius. Here, he compiled his *Adagia*, a sort of dictionary of quotations from Classical authors. As he readily acknowledged, Erasmus received much help from the scholars and editors in Aldus's workshop, including Aldus himself. The *Adagia* is not merely a collection of quotations and proverbs, but also contains discursive articles on certain selected key words and concepts. It is a precursor of the lexicographical insistence on supporting definitions and explanations with citations.

1.3 Printing in 15th-century England

Printing was introduced to England in the 1470s by William Caxton. Caxton took up printing only towards the end of his life; he was an extremely energetic man with many other business, artistic, and literary interests: a highly respected and successful merchant as well as a writer, translator, printer, and publisher. After a period spent living and working in Bruges and elsewhere, he established himself as an importer of velvet, silk, and other luxurious fabrics, eventually rising to be governor of the Company of Merchant Adventurers of London. It was not until 1475-1476, when he was over sixty years old, that he established the business on which his present-day fame rests. He set up a printing press, at first in Bruges and later in London, in imitation of one that he had observed in Cologne, and began to print books in English. The output of Caxton's press was prolific. Among its most famous publications were Chaucer's *Canterbury Tales* and Mallory's *Morte d'Arthur*.

Caxton and his business partner Wynkyn de Worde (an Alsatian whom he had met in Bruges) did not publish any dictionaries apart from a very modest French-English glossary. The earliest printed dictionary in England was the *Promptorium Parvulorum* ('Young People's Storeroom'), an English-Latin word list, printed in 1499 by Richard Pynson. This work had been compiled about sixty years earlier by Galfridus Anglicus (alias Galfridus Grammaticus 'Geoffrey the Grammarian'), a Dominican friar who lived in Norfolk. Its 10,000 entries (words and phrases) had already been laboriously copied out by hand several times – the only means of dissemination possible until the invention of printing – before Pynson set it in type and printed it (Figure 3). Both Caxton and Pynson used type styles that were based on those of Gutenberg. Neither had been able to learn about or benefit from the streamlined, economical character of contemporary Venetian typography. Indeed, principles of typographical clarity analogous to those of 15th century Venice were not really introduced into England for another 300 years. Over a hundred years after Pynson, Cawdrey's printer still used black-letter type for glosses, and English typography of the 17th and 18th centuries is full of unnecessary flourishes and ligatures. It looks cluttered and fussy compared with the clean lines and legibility of Jenson and Aldus Manutius.

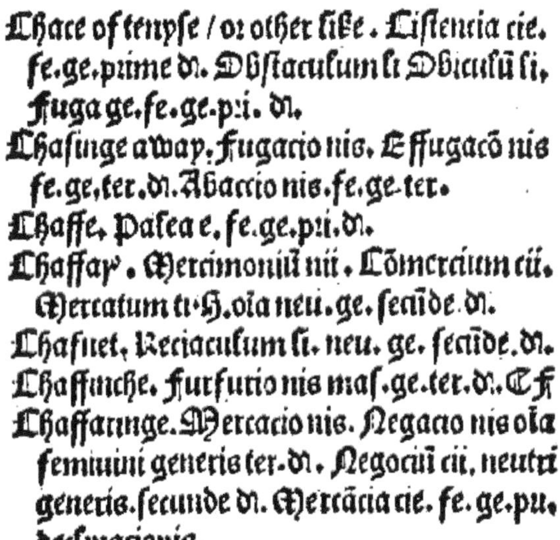
Chace of tenyse / or other like. Cisiencia cie.
fe.ge.prime dn. Obstaculum li Obicculū li.
Fuga ge.fe.ge.p'i. dn.
Chasinge away. Fugacio nis. Effugacō nis
fe.ge.ter.dn. Abaccio nis.fe.ge.ter.
Chaffe. Palea e. fe.ge.pri.dn.
Chaffay. Mercimoniū nii. Cōmercium cii.
Mercatum ti. .oīa neu.ge. secūde.dn.
Chafnet. Reciaculum li. neu. ge. secūde.dn.
Chaffinche. Furfurio nis mas.ge.ter.dn. Cf
Chaffaringe. Mercacio nis. Negacio nis oīa
feminini generis ter.dn. Negociū cii. neutri
generis.secunde dn. Mercācia cie. fe.ge.pu.
declinacionis.

Figure 3: Extract from Pynson's printing of *Promptorium Parvulorum*, 1499

1.4 The Estienne family of Paris and Geneva

If we compare the first printing of *Promptorium Parvulorum* (1499) with the Latin dictionaries compiled, edited, and printed in Paris by Robert Estienne in the 1530s, we see a quantum leap in both technology and scholarship. *Promptorium Parvulorum* is a practical work for students struggling to express themselves in Latin, i.e. it is designed for encoding use. It is printed in heavy black-letter type and even though it was using the latest technology for printing, its typography makes it look old-fashioned. By contrast, the *Dictionarium, seu Thesaurus Linguae Latinae* (1531) of Robert Estienne is a decoding aid. It is a work for scholarly use by people reading the Latin texts of classical antiquity, many of which were printed by Estienne himself. In his authoritative study of Renaissance lexicography, Considine (2008) argues that preservation of "heritage" was an important part of the goal of Renaissance lexicographers such as Estienne and his sons. Early lexicographers were not merely producing practical tools for language learners or translators; they were contributing to the Renaissance programme of preserving and indeed reviving the classical heritage.

The type of Estienne's *Dictionarium* was designed, cut, and cast by Claude Garamond, one of several type cutters with whom Estienne had a business relationship. Garamond's elegant type style owes more to the Venetian Antiqua school of typography than to Gutenberg, though it is embellished by the occasional flourish which Jenson would surely have regarded as superfluous. Nevertheless, Estienne's *Dictionarium* is both a work of scholarship and a triumph of elegance in the printer's art – an aesthetic pleasure to peruse as well as a scholarly inventory of the vocabulary of classical literature. This is also true, though to a lesser extent, of the *Thesaurus Linguae Graecae* (1572), which was compiled, edited, printed, and published forty years later by Robert's son Henri Estienne II.

If we look at an entry from Estienne's 1531 *Dictionarium* – I have chosen, more or less at random, the entry for *conclamo* (Figure 4) – we can see immediately that this is not a bilingual French-Latin dictionary. It is a monolingual dictionary of Latin, with a French gloss (in this case, "Crier") appended. The rest of the text of the entry is taken up with morphological information, a monolingual gloss in Latin ("simul clamare"), and a great wealth of citations from Latin authors, on the basis of which Estienne offers collocational norms, some of which are glossed or explained in Latin (not French).

The French glosses in Estienne's *Thesaurus Linguae Latinae* play a comparatively minor role. More striking is the large number of citations and references. Estienne was concerned not merely to say what the meaning of each Latin word is, but to record where the word is used in the classical Latin texts that he had available to him. This is in essence very similar to the lexicographical principles adopted for the academy dictionaries of the 17th century to the present day.

Estienne's work is part of the true foundation of European lexicography. Following Starnes (1963), we may regard Robert Estienne's Latin dictionary of 1531 as a seminal work, but this does not mean that it had no predecessors or that he and his team of lexicographers were working in a vacuum. He was an early part of a highly productive accretive continuum of European lexicography. Other Latin dictionaries had appeared even earlier, in particular that of Ambrogio Calepino (1502), of which more later. It is clear that the scholars in Estienne's workshop made use of these works, just as OED built on the foundations laid by Johnson (1755) and other earlier lexicographers.

Among the factors that distinguish Estienne's 1531 dictionary from its predecessors are its meticulous scholarship, the systematic inclusion of citations from works of classical literature (many of which were also printed by Estienne), a concern with semantic differentiation and phraseology, and reliance on readable typography.

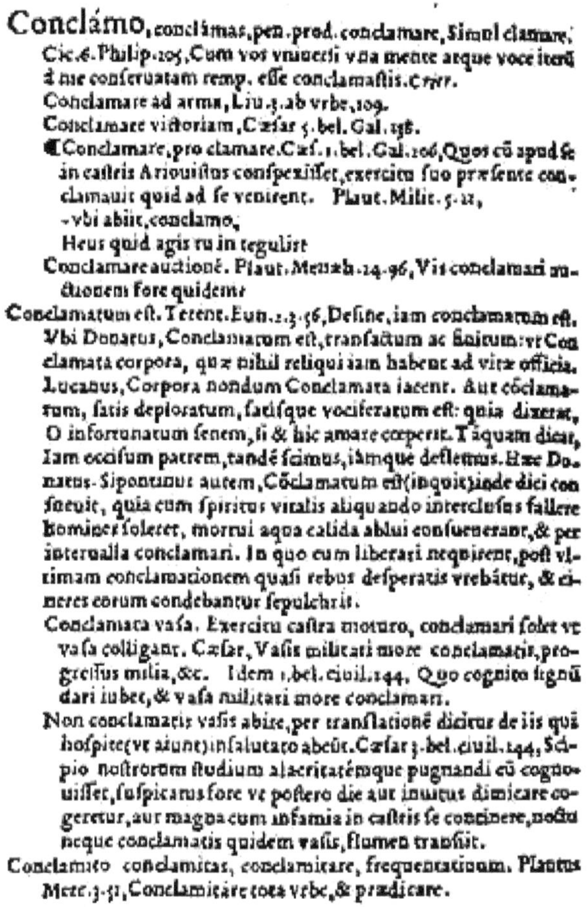
Conclámo, conclámas, pen. prod. conclamare, Simul clamare.
Cic. 6. Philip. 105, Cum vos vniuersi vna mente atque voce iterũ a me conseruatam remp. esse conclamastis. Cretr.
Conclamare ad arma, Liu. 3. ab vrbe, 109.
Conclamare victoriam, Cæsar 5. bel. Gal. 138.
¶ Conclamare, pro clamare. Cæs. 1. bel. Gal. 106, Quos cũ apud se in castris Ariouistus conspexisset, exercitu suo præsente conclamauit quid ad se venirent. Plaut. Milit. 5. 12,
- vbi abiit, conclamo,
Heus quid agis tu in tegulis?
Conclamare auctionẽ. Plaut. Menæch. 24. 96, Vis conclamari auctionem fore quidem?
Conclamatum est. Terent. Eun. 2. 3. 56, Desine, iam conclamatum est. Vbi Donatus, Conclamatum est, transactum ac finitum: vt Conclamata corpora, quæ nihil reliqui iam habent ad vitæ officia. Lucanus, Corpora nondum Conclamata iacent. Aut cõclamatum, satis deploratum, satisque vociferatum est: quia dixerat, O infortunatum senem, si & hic amare cœperit. Tãquam dicat, Iam occisum patrem, tandẽ scimus, iamque deflemus. Hæc Donatus. Sipontinus autem, Cõclamatum est (inquit) inde dici consueuit, quia cum spiritus vitalis aliquando interclusus fallere homines soleret, mortui aqua calida ablui consueuerant, & per interualla conclamari. In quo cum liberari nequirent, post vltimam conclamationem quasi rebus desperatis vrebãtur, & cineres eorum condebantur sepulchris.
Conclamata vasa. Exercitu castra moturo, conclamari solet vt vasa colligant. Cæsar, Vasis militari more conclamatis, progressus milia, &c. Idem 1. bel. ciuil. 144. Quo cognito signũ dari iubet, & vasa militari more conclamari.
Non conclamatis vasis abire, per translationẽ dicitur de iis qui hospite (vt aiunt) insalutato abeũt. Cæsar 3. bel. ciuil. 144, Scipio nostrorum studium alacritatẽmque pugnandi cũ cognouisset, suspicatus fore vt postero die aut inuitus dimicare cogeretur, aut magna cum infamia in castris se continere, noctu neque conclamatis quidem vasis, flumen transiit.
Conclamito conclamitas, conclamitare, frequentatiuum. Plautus Merc. 3. 51, Conclamitare tota vrbe, & prædicare.

Figure 4: R. Estienne, *Dictionarium*, 1531, entry for ‘conclamo’

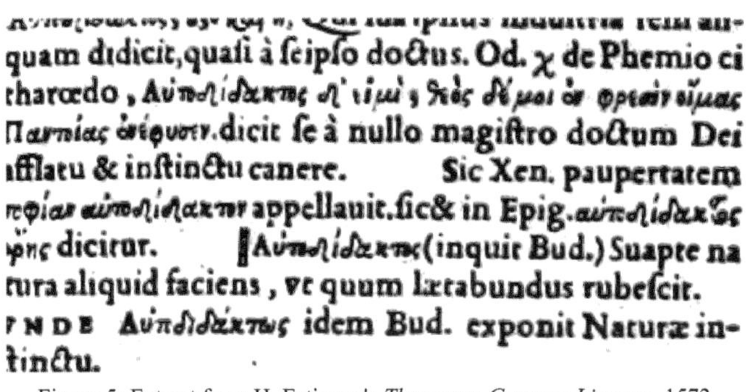
quam didicit, quasi à seipso doctus. Od. χ de Phemio citharœdo, Αὐτοδίδακτος δ' εἰμί, θεὸς δέ μοι ἐν φρεσὶν οἴμας Παντοίας ἐνέφυσεν. dicit se à nullo magistro doctum Dei afflatu & instinctu canere. Sic Xen. paupertatem σοφίαν αὐτοδίδακτον appellauit. sic & in Epig. αὐτοδίδακτος ...ρης dicitur. ‖ Αὐτοδίδακτος (inquit Bud.) Suapte natura aliquid faciens, vt quum lætabundus rubescit. YNDE Αὐτοδιδάκτως idem Bud. exponit Naturæ instinctu.

Figure 5: Extract from H. Estienne's *Thesaurus Graecae Linguae*, 1572

There can be no doubt that Considine (2008) is right that the main purpose of Robert Estienne's 1531 *Dictionarium* was to contribute to the preservation of the heritage of classical literature, and the same is true of the equally ambitious and equally monumental *Thesaurus Graecae Linguae*, published by his son Henri Estienne in 1572 (Figure 5).

Two other important dictionaries of Robert Estienne show a different side of this great lexicographer. As we have seen, his main concern in 1531 was to cater to the needs of scholars and literati by preserving the heritage of the classical Latin language. But he was also sensitive to the needs of more humble students and language learners. The *Dictionnaire francoislatin* of 1539 (Figure 6) is a practical work explicitly aimed at students wishing to express themselves in Latin. A noticeable feature is the large number of idiomatic French phrases for which Latin equivalents are offered. For example, *l'ordre et collocation des mots* is glossed as 'verborum constructio'. Robert Estienne placed considerable emphasis on phraseology and context: it is perhaps not too fanciful to believe that he would have been sympathetic to modern theories of collocation and construction grammar.

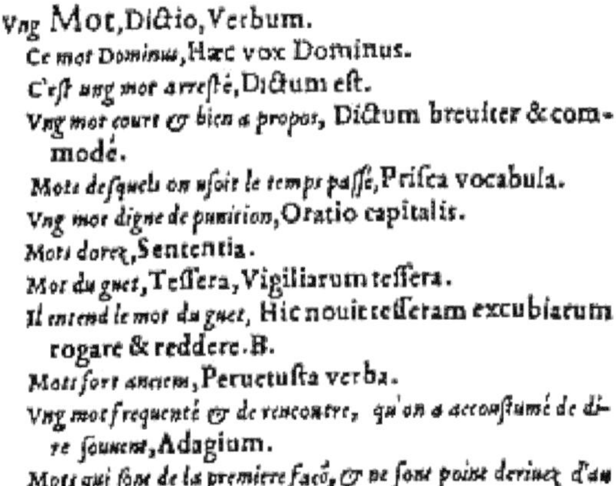
Vng Mot, Dictio, Verbum.
Ce mot Dominus, Haec vox Dominus.
C'est ung mot arresté, Dictum est.
Vng mot court & bien a propos, Dictum breuiter & commodé.
Mots desquels on usoit le temps passé, Prisca vocabula.
Vng mot digne de punition, Oratio capitalis.
Mots dorez, Sententia.
Mot du guet, Tessera, Vigiliarum tessera.
Il entend le mot du guet, Hic nouit tesseram excubiarum rogare & reddere. B.
Mots fort anciens, Peruetusta verba.
Vng mot frequenté & de rencontre, qu'on a accoustumé de dire souuent, Adagium.
Mots qui sont de la premiere facō, & ne sont point deriuez d'autres, Natiua verba.
C'est ung mot qui a esté bien dict, Prendre exemple a autruy, Hoc scitum est, Periculum ex aliis facere, tibi quod ex vsu siet.
Mots transposez l'ung pour l'autre, Inuersa verba.
L'ordre & collocation des mots, Verborum constructio.
Plein de mots dorez, Sententiosus.
A mon mot, Meo pretio.
Reciter de mot a mot, Totidem verbis recitare, Ad verbū.
Trāscrire ung lieu de mot a mot, Locū ad literam subiicere.

Figure 6: R. Estienne, *Dictionnaire francoislatin*, 1539, entry for 'mot'

A complementary (and equally practical) work, published by Robert Estienne in 1552, is the *Dictionarium Latino-Gallicum* (Figure 7). This is not a revised version of his 1531 work. Instead, it is a practical guide whose aim is to help students decode the meanings of Latin words and Latin texts into their native French. As can be seen in Figure 8, there are many more French glosses on the Latin words and phrases than in the 1531 work (though they are still, by modern standards, sparse). The 'principle parts' of verbs are given at the start of the entry ("conduco, conducis, conduxi, co[n]ductum, conducere"), which is helpful for both decoding and encoding use to anyone studying Latin. Citations from literature have been replaced by short phrases, often with a gloss. The authority of a classical author for phraseology is invoked in abbreviated form, generally without a full citation. Thus, the Latin phrase 'nimium magno conducere' is included on the authority of Cicero and glossed as 'Acheter trop cher', i.e. in English, 'to buy too dear'. This is information of a kind that is particularly useful for students learning to read and understand Latin texts, as opposed to scholars who were already fluent in Latin. It is also, coincidentally, of potential interest to modern scholars studying the cultural persistence of conventional metaphors and idiomatic phrases in European languages going back to classical Latin.

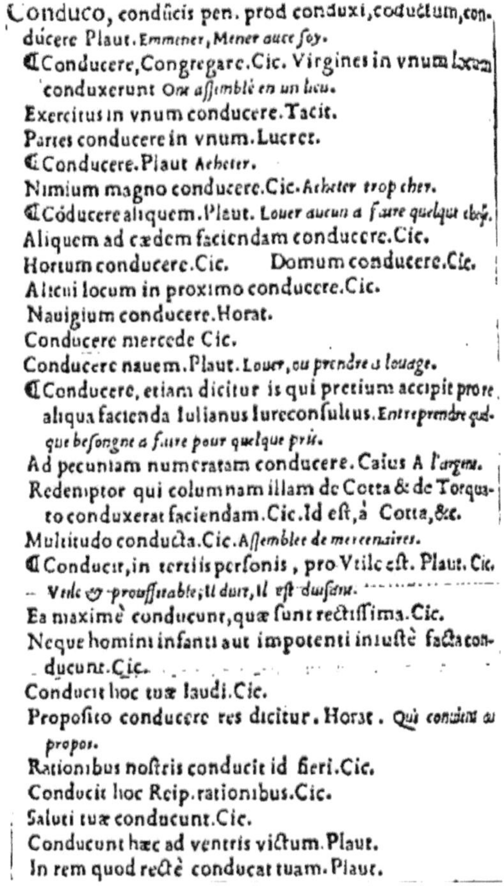
Conduco, condūcis pen. prod conduxi, coductum, conducere Plaut. *Emmener, Mener auec soy.*
¶Conducere, Congregare. Cic. Virgines in vnum locum conduxerunt *Ont assemblé en un lieu.*
Exercitus in vnum conducere. Tacit.
Partes conducere in vnum. Lucret.
¶Conducere. Plaut *Acheter.*
Nimium magno conducere. Cic. *Acheter trop cher.*
¶Códucere aliquem. Plaut. *Louer aucun a faire quelque chose.*
Aliquem ad cædem faciendam conducere. Cic.
Hortum conducere. Cic. Domum conducere. Cic.
Alicui locum in proximo conducere. Cic.
Nauigium conducere. Horat.
Conducere mercede Cic.
Conducere nauem. Plaut. *Louer, ou prendre a louage.*
¶Conducere, etiam dicitur is qui pretium accipit pro re aliqua facienda Iulianus Iureconsultus. *Entreprendre quelque besongne a faire pour quelque pris.*
Ad pecuniam numeratam conducere. Caius *A l'argent.*
Redemptor qui columnam illam de Cotta & de Torquato conduxerat faciendam. Cic. Id est, à Cotta, &c.
Multitudo conducta. Cic. *Assemblee de mercenaires.*
¶Conducit, in tertiis personis, pro Vtile est. Plaut. Cic. *Vtile & prouffitable; Il duit, Il est duisant.*
Ea maximè conducunt, quæ sunt rectissima. Cic.
Neque homini infanti aut impotenti iniustè facta conducunt. Cic.
Conducit hoc tuæ laudi. Cic.
Proposito conducere res dicitur. Horat. *Qui conuient au propos.*
Rationibus nostris conducit id fieri. Cic.
Conducit hoc Reip. rationibus. Cic.
Saluti tuæ conducunt. Cic.
Conducunt hæc ad ventris victum. Plaut.
In rem quod rectè conducat tuam. Plaut.

Figure 7: R. Estienne, *Dictionarium Latino-Gallicum*, 1552, entry for 'conduco'

Trench (1858) rightly describes lexicographers as "the inventory clerks of language", but these great Renaissance lexicographers were very much more than mere inventory clerks. They were scholars, compilers, definers, printers, and publishers. The Estienne firm was founded by Henri Estienne (c. 1460-1520), who had married the widow of a printer in 1502 and expanded the business. Three sons and two grandsons became printers. There can be no doubt that Robert Estienne (1503-1559) was the greatest of the family, even though his son Henri II was to successfully tackle the even more challenging task of compiling a scholarly dictionary of classical Greek. Part of the greatness of Robert lies in his evident concern for students as well as scholars and the range of the different dictionaries that he and his staff compiled and published, a range that would have been quite impractical without the recent innovations in the technology of printing and typesetting.

In addition to his remarkable achievements in scholarly and practical lexicography, Robert Estienne also ran a successful printing business, publishing editions of major classical texts and other works. According to his biography (Armstrong 1954), he printed and published on average 18 books a year in Paris, as well as undertaking his massive lexicographic projects. He ran a lively and polyglot workshop. According to his son Henri II, "There sat down to table daily a staff of ten assorted nationalities, together with family and guests, all speaking Latin, including the servants" (Armstrong 1954, 15). She estimates, on the basis of contemporary records, that in its heyday the firm employed a staff of 50 (2 type-founders, 18 compositors, 5 proof-readers, 21 printers, 3 apprentices, and one shop boy), in addition to the master himself and his family. Estienne was on intimate terms with the greatest Parisian scholars and intellectuals of his day. He styled himself "printer to the king" but eventually, as an outspoken Protestant, in or before 1550 he found it prudent to remove himself to Geneva, where his output dropped to about six books a year.

1.5 Polyglot and bilingual dictionaries during the Renaissance

The most important and innovative bilingual dictionary of the early 16th century was compiled in English. It is Palsgrave's ambitious *Lesclaircissement de la langue francoyse* (1530). Palsgrave had been tutor at the English court to Henry VIII's sister Princess Mary, who in 1515 became Queen of France. His guide to the French language is not only a bilingual dictionary but also a grammar. The dictionary part contains 18,890 English-French equivalents. Black Letter type is used for English, Antiqua for French. The arrangement is alphabetical by part of speech; i.e., each part of speech is given a separate "table". The table of substantives consists mostly of single-word equivalents, with disambiguation of polysemous words, e.g. there are two entries for ***meale: meale of corne*** is glossed as 'farine', ***meale of meate*** is glossed as 'repast'. The table of verbs pays more attention to phraseology (see Figure 8). Each sense of each English verb is first embedded in an English phrase (or given an English gloss), and then the target word and/or the phrase as a whole is translated into French.

Palsgrave was a true comparative linguist as well as a pioneering lexicographer. However, rather surprisingly, his fine example was not followed: his work did not serve as a model for other bilingual dictionaries of vernacular languages – at least, not for another sixty years. Instead, the standard lexicographical tool used for translation during the Renaissance was a polyglot dictionary based on Latin. It is time to examine how this came about.

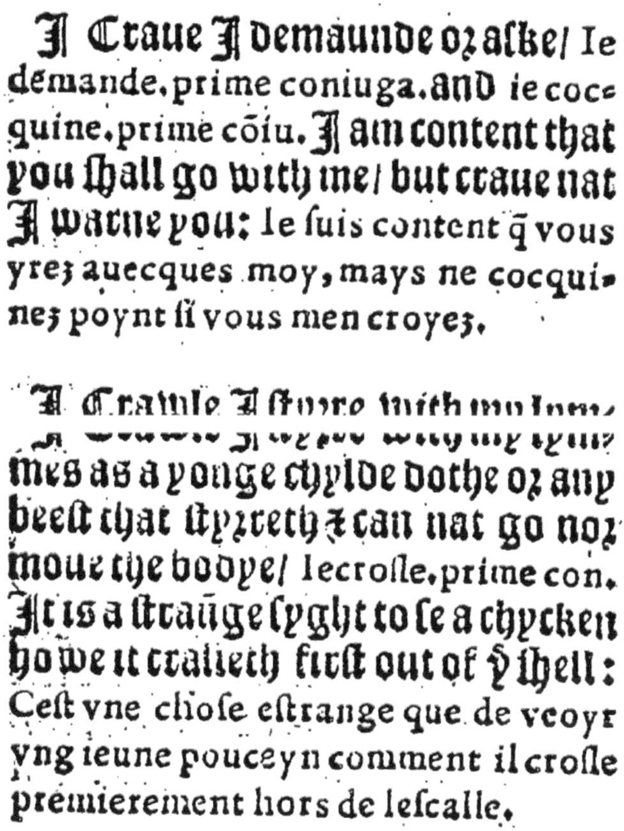
I Craue I demaunde or aſke/ Ie demande, prime coniuga. and ie cocquine, prime cõiu. I am content that you ſhall go with me/ but craue nat I warne you: Ie ſuis content q̃ vous yrez auecques moy, mays ne cocquinez poynt ſi vous men croyez.

I Crawle I ſtere with my lymmes as a yonge chylde dothe or any beeſt that ſtyrreth & can nat go nor moue the bodye/ Iecroſle, prime con. It is a ſtraunge ſyght to ſe a chycken howe it craweth firſt out of ỹ ſhell: Ceſt vne choſe eſtrange que de veoyr vng ieune pouceyn comment il croſle premierement hors de leſcalle.

Figure 8: Extract from Palsgrave's *Lesclaircissement de la langue francoyse* (1530)

By 1490, many cities in Italy, Germany, and the Netherlands had a printing press, many of which produced dictionaries, vocabularies, and word lists of one sort or another – some in thematic order, others in more or less exact alphabetical order. Most of these were monolingual Latin dictionaries, the demand for them reflecting the status of Latin as the language of knowledge, culture, and international communication. The first Greek-Latin lexicon was compiled and published by a Carmelite monk, Giovanni Crastone of Piacenza (1497).

As for vernacular languages, there blossomed in the early 16th century a fine crop of monolingual Italian dictionaries, as described by Alonge (2006). This is a clear indication of the confidence of Italians in their language as a literary medium rivaling Latin, distinguishing it in status from other vernaculars of Renaissance Europe.

Surprisingly, though, there were few bilingual dictionaries of vernacular languages at this stage. Everything was mediated through Latin, which functioned as a sort of interlingua. As shown by Kramer (2006) and Schoonheim/Pijnenburg (2006), in the German-speaking lands and the Netherlands, early Latin-German and German-Latin lexicographic works appeared, notably Van der Schueren (1477), Dasypodius (1535-1536), and Maaler (1561). The complex relationships among European languages of this period are well described in Burke (2002).

The seminal work in the development of European multilingual lexicography was the *Dictionarium* of Ambrogio Calepino. Calepino's original edition (1502) was a Latin alphabetical vocabulary book, with glosses in Latin supported by citations, together with encyclopedic entries for the figures of classical mythology. In a second edition, glosses in Italian and French were added. By a process of accretion, the vocabularies of other languages, starting with Greek and Hebrew, were gradually added to successive editions of Calepino's original. In the words of Fried (2007, 231), "it evolved into the first polyglot dictionary". By 1580, a dozen different editions, containing glosses in up to eleven different languages, all attributed to Calepino, were in print, published in locations as far apart as Reggio nell'Emilia, Venice, Paris, Strasbourg, Hagenau, Lyon, and Rome. In Paris alone, five competing editions appeared between 1524 and 1541. The 1573 edition printed and published in Venice includes the following comment in its front matter, quoted and translated by Freed:

> *In hac postrema editione, ut hoc dictionarium commodius exteris nationibus inservire possit, singulis vocibus latinis italicas, gallicas, & hispanicas interpretationes inseri curavimus.*
>
> In this latest edition, in order that this dictionary might more fully serve foreign nations, we have taken care to insert Italian, French, and Spanish definitions among the lone Latin entries.

By this time, Ambrogio Calepino himself (1450-1510) was long dead and his book had become common property. Stathi (2006) argues that the popularity of the many 'Calepinos' was due, not to its etymologies, but to its explanations of meanings and the inclusion of examples of word use. The extraordinarily complex bibliographical history of this work and its derivatives was traced by Labarre (1975). This shows that multilingual editions really began to take off in the 1550s (Figure 9); by the 1580s it had come to include lexical items in up to 11 languages – not only Latin, Greek, Hebrew, Italian, French, and Spanish, but also 'outlandish' tongues such as German, English, Polish, and Hungarian. By the end of the century, a Latin-Portuguese-Japanese 'Calepino' had appeared, supporting the missionary work of the Portuguese Jesuits who were at that time attempting to Christianize Japan.

It has been said (with what justice I know not) that Calepino's work is deficient in scholarly precision. Moreover, the polyglot works that bore his name are great, cumbersome things, not very suitable for carrying around on a tour of Europe and not particularly user-friendly. Nevertheless, they seem to have been the principal works that served the practical translation needs of Europeans in the 16th century.

Not only did Calepino's work become the common property of Europeans in many different editions; his very surname also passed into the vocabulary of Italian, French, English, and other languages. In the 16th and 17th centuries, Italian ***calepino*** and English ***calepin*** were used as generic terms for a dictionary. In French, ***calepin*** was further extended to mean a notebook or a compilation of rare and unusual linguistic facts, and was used in various colloquial expressions such as *mettez cela sur votre calepin* 'add that to your calepin'. Watson (1908) and Starnes (1955) show that a 'calepin' was a widely available – and widely used – resource in schools and universities throughout England in the 16th century. ***Calepine*** was also adopted by Edmund Spenser as a proper name for an allegorical character in the *Faerie Queene*, the significance of which is discussed by Fried (2007) in an article that contains a remarkably illuminating account of Renaissance lexicography.

Conclamo, as, are, a.p. Simul clamare, clamare. *συμβοᾶν.* { Ital. *Gridare inſieme, gridare.* Gall. *Crier enſemble, s'eſcrier.* Hiſp. *Llamar dando uoces.* Germa. *Mitſchreien, zůſamen ſchreien.* } Cic. 6. Phil. Quum uos uniuerſi una mente atq; uoce iterum à me conſeruatam eſſe Rempub. conclamaſtis. Tacit. lib. Conclamant patres, corpus ad rogum humeris Senatorum ferendum. ¶ Conclamare, pro ſimplici Clamare. Cæſar 1. bel. Gallic. Quos quum apud ſe in caſtris Ariouiſtus conſpexiſſet, exercitu ſuo præſente conclamauit quid ad ſe uenirent. ¶ Conclamare uaſa, militaris eſt locutio, pro denunciare inter milites, ut uaſa colligant: quod fiebat quum exercitus moturus erat caſtra. *ἀναζυγὴν σημαίνειν.* Cæſar lib. 1. bell. Ciu. Quo cognito, ſignum dari iubet, & uaſa militari more conclamari. ¶ Cōclamatum eſt, hoc eſt, tranſactum & finitum eſt. *πέπρακται.* { Ital. *Egli è finito.* Gall. *Tout eſt feit.* Hiſp. *Le coſa eſta acabada.* Germ. *Die ſach iſt ſchon uber hin, es iſt ſchon beſchehen.* } Quod locutionis genus ab ijs tractum putatur, qui morientibus aſſiſtūt. Solent enim illi cadauerum recens exanimatorum faciem identidem frigida abluere, nomenq; eorum clara uoce inclamare, ne fortè ſyncope correptos pro mortuis funerarent. Nam qui animi deliquium patiuntur, mortuis ſimilimi ſunt: unde & nonnullos pro mortuis claros, & à rogo relatos accepimus. Quum itaq; affuſa ſubinde frigida, nomineq; ſæpius inclamato nihil proficeretur, poſt ultimam conclamationem re iam deſperata comburebātur. ¶ Hinc corpora conclamata dicuntur, hoc eſt, deplorata, quibuſq; extremum hoc conclamationis præſtitum eſt officium. Luca. -corpora nondum Conclamata iacent.

Conclamatio, onis, uerbale *καταβοὴ, καταβόησις.* { Ital. *Crido di piu genti.* Gall. *Cri de pluſieurs gens.* Hiſpan. *Aquello llamado con bozes.* Ger. *Das zůſammen ſchreien viler.* } Clamor multorum. Seneca quum aliqua conclamatio eſt quomodo exeat, non quid efferat, quærit.

Figure 9: Extract from a 1550 Basel edition of Calepino

There were some exceptions to all this polyglottalism. As we have already noted, Caxton printed a short, practical French-English vocabulary in 1480, although this is a comparatively minor work. An Italian-German thematic dictionary, *Introito e porta*, was compiled by Adam von Rottweil as early as 1477. It stands at the head of a long tradition, ultimately comprising 89 separate publications between 1477 and 1636.

1.6 Dictionaries in 16th-century England

The Renaissance dictionaries discussed in the preceding sections bore rapid fruit in England, in the first place as a source for the first printed Latin-English dictionary in England, the *Dictionary* of Sir Thomas Elyot (1538) (Figure 10). Unlike *Promptorium Parvulorum*, this was a work for decoding use, as was its most important successor, the *Dictionarium Linguae Latinae et Anglicanae* (1587), compiled and printed by Thomas Thomas, printer to the University of Cambridge (Figure 11). This latter work enjoyed tremendous success for several decades. It is admirably succinct and practical. The English glosses in it are full and informative. As printer to the University of Cambridge, Thomas Thomas was well aware of the needs of students and was at pains to provide them with help in the form of systematic but succinct glosses in their own native tongue.

Typographically, Elyot's work is very obviously indebted to the medieval tradition of Pynson, Caxton, and Gutenberg, whereas Thomas's work of fifty years later is very much more legible. It owes much to the Renaissance typographical tradition of Estienne, Aldus Manutius, and Jenson – though it must be said that it seems sadly debased compared with the beautiful clean lines of Jenson's original Venetian Old Style. Neither the Parisians of the 16th century nor the Elizabethans in England could resist a flourish – literary or typographical.

Finally, in this brief survey of Renaissance lexicography, we must mention the evolution of bilingual dictionaries proper. Two such works are well known to students of Shakespeare: John Florio's *Italian and English Dictionary* of 1598 and John Minsheu's *Dictionarie in Spanish and English* of 1599. Both of these are practical works for the emerging modern world and what was eventually to become the European Enlightenment. They are designed as aids for translation between contemporary vernacular languages, rather than being mediated through Latin. Minsheu's work was an expanded version of an earlier work called *Bibliotheca Hispanica* (1591), compiled by Richard Percyvall. Along with Palsgrave for English-French, these are the precursors of modern bilingual dictionaries.

Minsheu was to go on to compile *The Guide into Tongues* (*Ductor in linguas*, 1617), an ambitious polyglot work in eleven languages. It would no doubt be an interesting research topic to determine the debt of Minsheu to Calepino. This, however, lies outside the period and the scope of the present study.

Despite the efforts of Palsgrave (1530), it was not until the 1590s that the European intelligentsia accepted that it was not necessary to use Latin as an interlingua or reference point in order to translate words and phrases of one vernacular language into those of another. The first French-German/German-French dictionary was published in 1596 by

Levinus Hulsius in Nürnberg. He also compiled the first Italian-German/German-Italian dictionary. Other bilingual dictionaries of vernacular languages were to follow thick and fast during the 17th century.

These dictionaries contributed, albeit somewhat belatedly, to the internationalization of European culture, making the literature and culture of countries such as Italy and France accessible to speakers of remoter northern languages such as English.

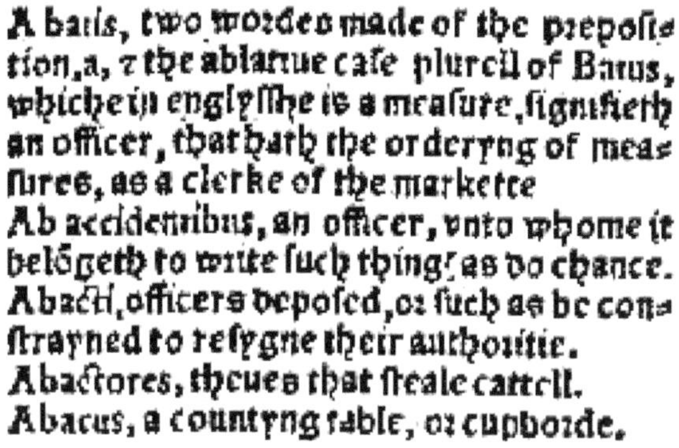
A batis, two wordes made of the preposition, a, & the ablatiue case pluræll of Batus, whiche in englyshe is a measure, signifieth an officer, that hath the orderyng of measures, as a clerke of the markette

Ab accidentibus, an officer, vnto whome it belongeth to write such thinges as do chance.

Abacti, officers deposed, or suche as be constrayned to resygne their authoritie.

Abactores, theues that steale cattell.

Abacus, a countyng table, or cupborde.

Figure 10: Extract from the *Dictionarium* of Sir Thomas Elyot, 1538

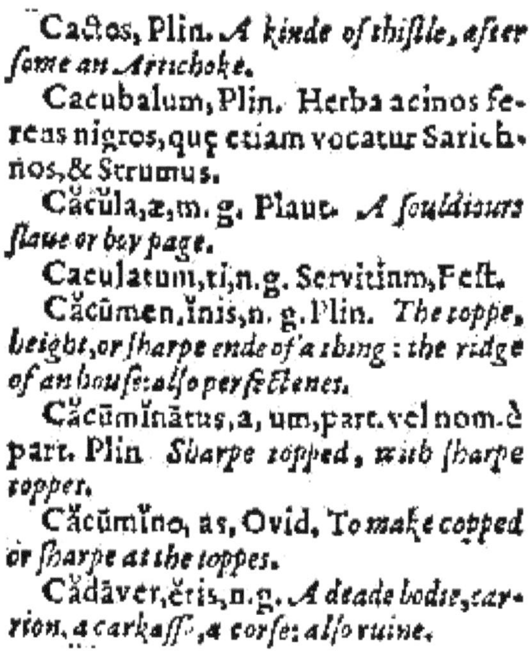
Cactos, Plin. *A kinde of thistle, after some an Artichoke.*

Cacubalum, Plin. Herba acinos fereas nigros, quę etiam vocatur Sarichinos, & Strumus.

Căcŭla, æ, m. g. Plaut. *A souldiours slaue or boy page.*

Caculatum, ti, n. g. Servitium, Fest.

Căcūmen, ĭnis, n. g. Plin. *The toppe, height, or sharpe ende of a thing: the ridge of an house: also perfectenes.*

Căcūmĭnātus, a, um, part. vel nom. è part. Plin. *Sharpe topped, with sharpe toppes.*

Căcūmĭno, as, Ovid. *To make copped or sharpe at the toppes.*

Cădāver, ĕris, n. g. *A deade bodie, carrion, a carkasse, a corse: also ruine.*

Figure 11: Extract from Thomas Thomas' *Dictionarium Linguae Latinae et Anglicanae*, 1589

to Accent, sing tunably or pronounce truly, vide Accentuár.
Accenting or true pronouncing, vide Accénto.
an Accent ouer a letter, vide Accénto.
to Accept or take in good part, vide Acetár, Aceptár.
Acceptable, vide Aceptáble.
Acceptance, vide Aceptación.
Acceptation, vide Acéto, Acépto,
Accepted, vide Aceptádo.
Accepting, vide Aceptación.
to haue Accesse vnto, vide Allegár.
Accessarie to a fault or culpable, vide Accessório.
that is Accessarie, vide Accessório.
an Accessarie, vide Accessór.
Accessarily, vide Accessoriaménte.
an Accidence, or booke so called, an Accidence or Grammar, vide la Gramática.
an Accident, or that which chaunceth or happeneth, vide Acaccimiénto, Acontecimiénto, Succésso.
to Accompanie or goe with one, vide Acompañár.
Accompanied, vide Acompañádo.
an Accompanying, vide Acompañamiénto.

Figure 12: Extract from Minsheu, 1599

1.7 A 21st century analogy with the Renaissance

In this first part of the paper I have identified three themes in Renaissance lexicography: the preservation and dissemination of the classical heritage; the creation of practical tools for students of Latin and Greek; and the emergence of bilingual dictionaries as practical aids for translation among vernacular languages. None of this would have been possible without the invention of printing technology and the creation of type fonts that make economic and elegant use of space on the page.

I have argued that histories of English lexicography such as Landau (2001) should pay more attention to the formative influences of the great Latin dictionaries of the 16th century. Studies by scholars such as Armstrong, Bately, and Considine provide an important perspective. A curious fact is that much 16th-century European lexicography used Latin as an interlingua, so that it took several decades for genuine bilingual lexicography to emerge, apart from a few pioneering works such as Palsgrave (1530).

A modern analogue now suggests itself, namely that of the development of computer technology in the second half of the 20th century, which could have (or should have) an impact on present-day lexicography that is as profound as was the development of printing technology in the 15th century. The full possibilities are only just beginning to be worked out. There are at least four aspects:

1. **Evidence.** Just as the Renaissance programme of collecting, printing, and publishing the texts of classical antiquity led to major, technologically innovative dictionaries of Greek and Latin, so the advent of electronic corpora and internet search engines have opened up possibilities for new lexicographic descriptions of phraseology and meaning in contemporary languages.
2. **Resources.** For Renaissance lexicographers, newly printed copies of classical texts served as resources to be quarried for the lexis of Latin and Greek. At present, a plethora of electronic resources, of variable quality and accuracy, for NLP and AI applications are being developed for modern languages. One only needs to look at the Global WordNet Programme, to see an example. It remains to be seen who will be the Robert Estienne of the 21st century and how he or she will present the lexicon of a modern language (presumably English) for a new generation of users, which will include machines as well as humans.
3. **Compilation.** In the 16th century, the index card was invented and used to compile lexicographical information and sort data into alphabetical order. Now, the computer has freed lexicographers from the tyranny of having to work in alphabetical order. Any entry in any part of the alphabet can be compiled, edited, improved, and expanded at any time.
4. **Dissemination.** The invention of printing enabled the rapid reproduction of large numbers of copies of large, complex texts in legible print. This was to be an essential component of lexicography for the ensuing 500 years. At the present time, this whole technology is being superseded by on-line dissemination of information. The waters are muddy and a business model has not yet clearly emerged. But the potential is tremendous. It has hardly begun to be tapped.

2. Lexicography and technology in the 21st century

2.1 Corpus evidence

The single most important technological development in the 20th century, as far as lexicography is concerned, was the development of the electronic corpus. Nowadays, it is commonplace for corpus linguists to stuff billions of words of text into a computer, tokenize them, tag them in various ways (usually starting by assigning a part of speech to each token), lemmatize them, and analyse them in various ways for various purposes. This technology is a central component of all reputable modern lexicographical research. Before publication of the Cobuild Dictionary in 1987, lexicographers were reliant on two source of evidence:

1. vastly slow and expensive reading programmes, such as that which made the OED possible at the end of the 19th century;
2. introspection – consulting one's intuitions in order to invent example of word uses in sense that the lexicographer already believed to exist.

Dictionaries that are not supported by a vast budget cannot afford either the time or the money for a reading programme that can be relied on to collect examples of all uses of all words in a language. As regards reading programmes, the fact is that a reading programme has a built-in tendency to distort. This is because citation readers tend, very naturally, to select citations for rare, unusual, and 'interesting' uses. They do not send in citations for words and uses that may be presumed to have already been collected from other sources. James Murray recognized this problem in 1878, at the very beginning of his work as editor of the work that was to become the OED, when he had just begun to sort the 'slips' on which citations collected by the reading programme were copied out:

> The editor and his assistants have to spend precious hours searching for examples of common everyday words. Thus, in the slips we have 50 examples of ***abusion,*** but of ***abuse*** not five. (Murray 1878)

As regards the second source of evidence, introspection, it has gradually become clear from corpus-driven studies of lexis that introspection is a flawed source of evidence. In the first place, it is conducive to self-fulfilling prophecies. The lexicographer or linguist believes that a word has a certain meaning or use, and invents an example to support that belief. In the second place, it encourages linguists and lexicographers alike to ignore facts that even casual corpus analysis can make blindingly obvious. Despite being sanctioned by generative linguists and cognitive linguists alike, reliance on invented examples and introspective judgements of acceptability has led to a situation in which all the research findings based on such examples (that is to say, much of the linguistic research of the past seventy years) must be regarded as suspect. Such findings need to be confirmed, not only by the acceptability judgements of a peer group, but also by empirical evidence of actual usage. Corpus-driven lexicography has a role to play in this wholesale re-evaluation of linguistic research.

One type of finding that is often overlooked by evidence based on citations collected in reading programmes and examples invented by introspection is the relative frequency of different uses or meanings of words.

I will discuss in some detail a very simple example, from which much follows. Some years ago, in conversation with an eminent American linguist who shall be nameless, I was surprised to discover that, in his deep introspection-based analysis of the verb *hazard*, there was no place for the possible meaning 'say tentatively'. If we ask, "How is the English verb *hazard* normally used?" corpus evidence confirms the introspectively obvious answer: in normal usage, "People hazard guesses" accounts for over half the English sentences containing this not very common verb.

As soon as a reader sees this answer, it seems obviously plausible. In this case, the corpus evidence and our intuitions are in accord.

But then counterexamples may start springing to mind. Maybe you can hazard an idea. Is an idea a kind of guess? It also seems plausible that you can hazard your money or your life – but *money* and *life* are certainly not kinds of guesses. What is going on here? Let us enjoy the new-found luxury of consulting corpus evidence, and look and see what other uses of the verb *hazard* can be found in readily accessible actual data. Looking at the BNC-50 corpus (consisting of 50 million words, half the British National Corpus) here is a summary of what I found.

The part-of-speech tagger used by the Sketch Engine corpus search tool (Kilgarriff et al. 2004) finds 50 verb uses of hazard in this half-corpus. Six of them turn out to be tagging errors: they are nouns or modifiers, not verbs. For example, the expressions *hazard assessment*, *hazard control*, and *hazard studies* are all modifier + noun, not verb + noun. These are mistakes – but they are not unreasonable and not unusual. An error rate of 12% in part-of-speech tagging is about par for the course using the CLAWS tagger.

Of the 44 verb uses in this half-corpus, 23 take the word *guess* or *guesses* as a direct object. In other words, the expression *hazard a guess* is a prototypical norm of English usage, accounting for around 50% of all uses of the verb.

```
1.   loving friendship with Justin. Guesses are hazarded, and are quoted from
2.  experience and technical background. And, I hazard a guess, more logged
3.being a builder, nor an architect, I can only hazard a guess. During construction in
4. Punter. What's it all about? I can only (hap)hazard a guess. BAY CITY ROLLERS The
5.   such mindless, moronic abuse, one can only hazard a guess. Thank goodness Ronnie
6.mining industry? Would my hon. Friend care to hazard a guess about how many fewer
7.   had hair and eyes like her mother. I would hazard a guess and say she would be
8.   all, can result in lost profits. When staff hazard a guess as to the price of
9.   party. No one at this stage is prepared to hazard a guess at the outcome of the
10.          What the connection is we can only hazard a guess at but it confirms all
11. ceived virtually no recognition? I can only hazard a guess at what it must have
12.  replied, `But off the top of my bonce I'll hazard a guess how many have
13.   away from the wall. Stifling a giggle, she hazarded a guess that the wardrobe
14.  rs to them as Part I and Part 2. One might hazard a guess that Part I was
15. UTIONS Where do your art materials live? We hazard a guess that they're lurking
16. ipatory excitement than others, and I would hazard a guess that, even if they've
18.     command line to begin restoring. But I'd hazard a guess that if you restore the
19.   to work OK once you boot from a floppy I'd hazard a guess that the MS-DOS system
20. passengers in those stations' heyday, but I hazard a guess that considerably more
21. raiser to the day's racing. In fact I would hazard a guess that one, if not both
22. me movies age and some movies date. I would hazard the guess that The Graduate
23. ntity of the farmer is not revealed; we may hazard the guess that he was William
24.  agent of society itself. Indeed, one could hazard a further [ ] observation
25.   is becoming proficient. Perhaps we can now hazard an attempt at defining `a go
26.   the North American standards. He does not hazard any opinions on how
27.   6.1 The Phillips curve. Although Phillips hazarded some theoretical conjectures
28. succeeding shapes and colours from which we hazard the inference that a leaping
29.  about his achievement, such as it was, and hazarded the opinion that he might
30.part of the tour's organiser -- and, I would hazard, a severe case of under-
31.   odd name--`Chicken'. `Not Hen Chicken?' I hazarded, as this humorous
32. e demand. Some critics of the NAIRU concept hazarded that, if there was any
33. gh in parliament, and it seemed sensible to hazard that a man of this standing
34. ultimate, supreme grade of evil'. It may be hazarded that it was this inevitable
35. ffect. To take the British example, I would hazard that the ratio of real balance
36. tleman, in his stable costume, would rather hazard his neck four-in-hand, than
37. would have been lost and commandos were not hazarded in foolish risks, although
38. objective, and a principle strong enough to hazard lives for, America cannot hope
39.marvelled at the readiness of the British to hazard so much in company with Franc
40. ted making references to `underwater rocks' hazarding the goodwill of his visit.
41. one may from time to time admire people who hazard their entire company on one
42.  d who wish the King [] well, who would not hazard their estates for him".
43. save my life I know you would, some of you, hazard your own. And yet will not
44. e morals and eternal welfare of numbers are hazarded and ruined for want of an
```

Figure 13: Some uses of the verb *hazard*: concordance from BNC50

But what about the remaining uses of this verb? Lines 24-35 can be classified as exploitations of the most normal use of the verb, whereas 36–44 are examples of a completely different norm for the same verb. Why should we say this? On what facts in the texts is this assertion based?

In 24-29 the direct object has the same semantic type as the prototypical direct object, *guess*. *Conjecture*, for example, is a near synonym of *guess*. Both words denote speech acts or mental events in the mind of the speaker. Likewise, an *observation*, an *attempt at defining*, *opinions*, and *inferences*, are kinds of speech act or thought act. A *that*-clause (as in 32-35) represents a speech act or a proposition underlying a speech act, while direct speech (as in 30-31) is an overt expression of a proposition. The words *I hazarded* are, it seems, deliberately chosen in 31 (rather than the more neutral expression *I said*) in order to imply that what is said is a matter of guesswork rather than a simple factual statement. It can be seen that in 24-35 the semantic values gradually move outward from the prototypical norm *hazard a guess*. Some speakers of American English assert that for them direct speech with the verb *hazard*, as in 30 and 31, is unidiomatic. Be that as it may, even in British English this is a comparatively rare way of exploiting the norm, though arguably all the more effective because of its rarity. By contrast, in 36-44 the direct objects belong to a completely different semantic type and activate a different sense of the verb, one that is a close synonym of *risk*. Further examination of corpus evidence shows that people hazard not only their lives and their companies or business enterprises but also their wealth, their reputation, and other valued entities. Here, what is hazarded is an object of value, and the purpose of hazarding it is to try to obtain some benefit. The two norms are not entirely independent. As a matter of historical fact, the notion of hazarding a speech act developed as an exploitation of the notion of hazarding or gambling money or an object of value in a game of dice. A person's ability to say true things is, in social terms, an object of value. But this is irrelevant to the meaning and use of the word in modern English. Very often, a modern sense of a word develops as an exploitation of an earlier sense. Sometimes the two senses coexist peacefully for centuries. In other cases, the new sense elbows the older one out of existence.

The point of this analysis is not to show that *hazard a guess* is an idiomatic phrase of English, but to illustrate how normal phraseology works. Instead of trying to draw boundaries encompassing all possible uses of a word, lexicographers of the future, with the benefit of corpus evidence at their fingertips, will seek to identify the prototypical phraseological norms with which each meaning of each word is associated. Needless to say, most cases will turn out to be a lot more complex than *hazard*, but careful examination and sorting of very large quantities of data for each word will generally reveal phraseological prototypes around which each sense is grouped. The lexicographer's art is then required to decide where to draw a line on the continuum between normal uses and exploitations of norms.

2.2 Lexical sets and semantic types

Few verbs are associated as strongly as the one we have just discussed (*hazard*) with just one noun as the typical direct object. However, almost all verbs are associated with one or more prototypical groups of nouns, and these different groups often pick out different senses of the verb. This is explained in more detail in Hanks (2012), using the example of the verb *shower*. That essay also goes on to show how a rather different apparatus is needed for the corpus analysis of nouns, using the noun *spider* as well as *shower* used as as a noun. There is no need to repeat that detailed analysis here. The associations between phraseological norms and meanings of English verbs are being explored by corpus pattern analysis in the AHRC-funded DVC project ("Disambiguation of Verbs by Collocation"), being conducted at the Research Institute of Information and Language Processing at the University of Wolverhampton, UK, with support from corpus linguists at the Faculty of Informatics, Masaryk University, Brno, Czech Republic. The results of the analyses (800 verbs so far analysed) are posted at http://deb.fi.muni.cz/pdev/.

Natural language is a puzzling mixture of logical and analogical processes. Until the availability of large quantities of corpus evidence, the analogical side was largely neglected. Corpus-driven studies of lexis (e.g. Sinclair 1964, 1991, 1998, 2004; Stubbs 2001) have provided ample evidence that the cognitive prototypes identified by Rosch (1973), Geeraerts (2010), and others are matched by phraseological prototypes that shape everyday usage in natural languages such as English.

Unfortunately for the lexical analyst, prototypical phraseology often consists of groups of words associated with other groups of words, rather than individual lexical items. Hanks/Pustejovsky (2005) and Hanks/Jezek (2008) discuss both the merits and some of the problems of grouping words together in lexical sets according to a shared semantic type. A well-known example concerns the idiom *to be shaking in one's shoes* (meaning to be frightened), which can also appear as *shivering in one slippers, quaking in one's boots, quivering in one's sandals*, and various other phraseological permutations and exploitations.

These are examples of the issues with which the empirical lexicographers of the future will grapple, if they are to achieve an accurate representation of the relationship between word use and word meaning.

2.3 Exploiting phraseological norms

The central argument of Hanks (2013) is that a natural language is indeed rule-governed behaviour, as so many thinkers have observed, but that there is not just one gigantic monolithic system of rules governing such behaviour. Instead there are two interlinked rule systems: one governing the normal, conventional, grammatical uses of words; the other governing creative exploitations of normal word use, in metaphors, metonymy, ellipsis, anomalous arguments, etc. The business of lexicography is with the first of these; bad lexicography often results from a failure to make a distinction between normal word use and creative exploitations, as in the case of the American dictionary that defines *newspaper*, not only as a noun, but also as a verb, with the sense "to do newspaper work (as running a newspaper or reporting or editing news)". This is a clear case of failing to recognize a linguistic exploitation for what it is. I argue that such uses do not belong in a dictionary unless there is clear evidence that they have established themselves as conventions of the language. Unfortunately, the dividing line between norms and exploitations is not clear-cut, not least because some imaginative creative uses of words tend to catch on and become part of the norm. Today's exploitation may become tomorrow's norm. Part of the job of lexicography is to monitor the gradual establishment of particular exploitations as new secondary norms.

Continuing the discussion of the verb *hazard*, let us conclude by looking at a clear case of an exploitation, in order to see how this aspect of meaning in language works.

1. I hazarded various Stuartesque destinations like Florida, Bali, Crete and Western Turkey.

Many readers – especially computational linguists and other people with a logical orientation – coming to this sentence out of context like this judge it to be crazy, meaningless, unidiomatic, or uninterpretable. But this fact merely underlines the unnatural nature of what linguists and logicians do in general and what corpus linguists do in particular. No normal reader takes a sentence from the middle of a text and pores over it, asking what it might mean, without reference to what has gone before. Texts have a beginning, a middle, and an end. Example 1 comes from Julian Barnes's 1991 novel *Talking It Over*. Barnes is a writer admired for his stylistic elegance – The Complete Review, for example, when reviewing this novel called him "a very fine stylist" – so our problems with interpreting this sentence are unlikely to be due to infelicity or ignorance on the part of the writer. In fact, when the sentence is put back into context, it makes unremarkable good sense, in a way that can only be explained in terms of exploitations of norms. The extended context is given in 2.

> Stuart needlessly scraped a fetid plastic comb over his cranium. 'Where are you going? You know, just in case I need to get in touch.' 'State secret. Even Gillie doesn't know. Just told her to take light clothes.' He was still smirking, so I presumed that some juvenile guessing game was required of me. I hazarded various Stuartesque destinations like Florida, Bali, Crete and Western Turkey, each of which was greeted by a smug nod of negativity. I essayed all the Disneylands of the world and a selection of tarmacked spice islands; I patronised him with Marbella, applauded him with Zanzibar, tried aiming straight with Santorini. I got nowhere.

At least two kinds of linguistic exploitation are present here. The first is ellipsis. Having just said that "some juvenile guessing game was required," the speaker does not need to repeat the word *guess*. This particular exploitation rule (ellipsis) is then promptly repeated in five subsequent clauses, in each of which a noun denoting a location or type of location (Disneylands, spice islands, Marbella, Zanzibar, Santorini) is (in its particular context) elliptical for a speech act (a guess) referring to that location. Moreover, a secondary exploitation of considerable complexity is involved in "tried aiming straight": normally, you aim a gun straight at something, you aim (or fire) a question at someone; you don't aim straight at a destination. However, it is noteworthy that, once the scenario has been set up, these stylistic complexities do not distract from the comprehensibility of the text. No ordinary human reader puzzles over what was being essayed or aimed at.

The second directly relevant kind of exploitation that enables a reader to understand Barnes's sentence is lexical creativity involving a combining form. Nowhere else in the novel, nowhere else in the BNC, have I been able to find the word *Stuartesque*. It is used occasionally in texts found on the Internet, with the meaning 'characteristic of Stuart', referring in each case to a completely different Stuart. But that does not make it meaningless or (in context) hard to understand. Stuart is the name of a character in the novel, and in English the combining form *-esque* is regularly affixed to a proper name to form an adjective meaning 'resembling the person or place named, typically in respect of certain noticeable and even eccentric or bizarre characteristics': *Kafkaesque*, *Bergmanesque*, *Monroesque*, *Hollywoodesque*, *Dylanesque*, *Jaggeresque*, *Caravaggesque* are just a few of the examples of such creations attested in the Oxford English Corpus.

There are many other kinds of exploitation, notably freshly created figurative language, that cannot be discussed here. It can be hoped that this brief discussion will be sufficient to illustrate the kinds of challenges that lie in wait for lexicographers of the future, if they decide to take seriously the need to investigate the relationship between phraseology and word meaning.

3. Acknowledgements

This paper is an expanded version of an invited talk given at the 10th Annual EFNIL conference (European Federation of National Institutions for Language) in Budapest, Hungary, 2012. An earlier version of Part I was presented at the 14th International Congress of Euralex (European Association for Lexicography) in Leeuwarden, Netherlands, 2010.

The research was funded in part by the Czech Ministry of Education (MSM 0021620838) and the Czech Science Foundation (P406/2010/0875) as part of a series of studies in lexicography at the Faculty of Informatics, Masaryk University, Brno and the Institute of Formal and Applied Linguistics of the Charles University in Prague.

I am grateful to John Considine and Gilles-Maurice de Schryver for comments on an earlier draft of Part I. Thanks are also due to Anne Urbschat for help in the selection and preparation of the illustrations. Illustrations of original printed entries from the Estienne dictionaries cited are shown by courtesy of the Librarians of All Souls College, Oxford and Christ Church, Oxford. For electronic versions of Renaissance dictionaries, acknowledgment is due to the magnificent Lexicon of Modern English (LEME) database of the University of Toronto: http://leme.library.utoronto.ca/.

4. References

4.1 Dictionaries

Calepino, A. (1502): *Dictionarium*. Very many subsequent editions and multilingual elaborations, compiled by various hands and printed in various European cities. Reggio nell'Emilia.

Cawdrey, R. (1604): *A table alphabeticall of hard usual English words*... London.

Dasypodius, P. (Peter Hasenfus) (1535-1536): *Dictionarium latinogermanicum et vice versa germanicolatinum*. Strasbourg.

Elyot, Sir T. (1538): *Dictionary* [Latin-English Dictionary]. London: Printed by Thomas Berthelet.

Estienne, R. (1531): *Dictionarium, seu Thesaurus Linguae Latinae*. Paris.

Estienne, R. (1539): *Dictionnaire francoislatin*. Paris.

Estienne, R. (1552): *Dictionarium Latino-Gallicum.* Geneva.

Estienne, H. II. (1572): *Thesaurus Linguae Graecae*. Paris.

Florio, J. (1598): *A worlde of wordes, or most copious and exact dictionary in Italian and English*. London: printed by Arnold Hatfield for Edw. Blount.

Galfridus Anglicus (alias Galfridus Grammaticalus; Geoffrey the Grammarian) (c1440): *Promptorium Parvulorum* ['The Young Person's Storeroom']. Printed in 1499 by Richard Pynson and subsequently by others.

Hulsius, L. (Levin van Hulse) (1596): *Dictionaire* [sic] *François-Allemand* [French-German dictionary]. Nürnberg.

Maaler, J. (1561): *Die Teütsch Sprach: Dictionarium latinogermanicum novum.* Zürich.

Minsheu, J. (1599): *Dictionarie in Spanish and English.* London.

Palsgrave, J. (1530): *Lesclaircissement de la langue francoyse*. London.

Rottweil, A. v. (1477): *Introito e porta.* [Italian-German thematic dictionary].

Sinclair, J./Patrick, H. (eds.) (1987): *Collins Cobuild English language dictionary*. London/ Glasgow: Collins.

Thomas, T. (1587): *Dictionarium linguae Latinae et Anglicanae*. Cambridge.

Torrentius, H. (Hermann van Beck) (1498): *Elucidarius carminum et historiarum vel vocabularius poeticus.* Deventer.

Van der Schueren, G. (1477): *Vocabularius qui intitulatur theuthonista vulgariter dicendo Duytschlender.* [Dutch-Latin, Latin-Dutch glossary]. n.p.

4.2 Other works

[Anon] (1554): *A very profitable book to learn the manner of reading, writing and speaking English and Spanish.* London.

Armstrong, E. (1954): *Robert Estienne, Royal Printer: an historical study of the elder Stephanus*. Cambridge: Cambridge University Press.

Bately, J. (2009): Bilingual and multilingual dictionaries of the Renaissance and early seventeenth century. In: Cowie, A. (ed.): *The Oxford history of English lexicography*, vol. 1. Oxford: Oxford University Press.

Burke, P. (2002): *Languages and communities in early modern Europe.* (= The Wiles Lectures, Queen's University, Belfast). Cambridge: Cambridge University Press.

Considine, J. (2008): *Dictionaries in early modern Europe: Lexicography and the making of heritage*. Cambridge: Cambridge University Press.

Cowie, A (ed.) (2009): *The Oxford history of English lexicography.* Oxford: Oxford University Press.

Eisenstein, E.L. (1979): *The printing press as an agent of change: Communications and cultural transformations in early-modern Europe.* Cambridge: Cambridge University Press.

Fried, D. (2007): Defining courtesy: Spenser, Calepine, and Renaissance lexicography. In: *Review of English Studies* 58, 229-244.

Firth, J.R. (1957): *Papers in Linguistics 1934-1951*. Oxford: Oxford University Press.

Geeraerts, D. (2010): *Theories of Lexical Semantics.* Oxford: Oxford University Press.

Halliday, M.A.K. (1961): Categories of the theory of grammar. In: *Word* 17 (3), 241-292.

Hanks, P. (1994): Linguistic norms and pragmatic explanations, or why lexicographers need prototype theory and vice versa. In: Kiefer, F./Kiss, G./Pajzs, J. (eds): *Papers in Computational Lexicography: Complex '94*. Budapest: Research Institute for Linguistics, Hungarian Academy of Sciences.

Hanks, P. (2004): Corpus pattern analysis. In: Williams, G./Vessier, S. (eds.): *Proceedings of the Eleventh Euralex International Congress.* Lorient: Université de Bretagne-Sud, 87-98.

Hanks, P. (2010): Nine issues in metaphor theory and analysis. In: *International Journal of Corpus Linguistics* 15 (1), 133-150.

Hanks, P. (2013): *Lexical Analysis: Norms and Exploitations*. Cambridge, MA: MIT Press.

Hanks, P./Jezek, E. (2008): Shimmering lexical sets. In Bernal, E./De Cesaris, J. (eds.): *Proceedings of the XIII EURALEX International Congress.* Barcelona: Universitet Pompeu Fabra, 391-402.

Hanks, P./Pustejovsky, J. (2005) A pattern dictionary for natural language processing. In: *Revue Française de Linguistique Appliquée* 10 (2), 63-82.

Hausmann, F.-J. (1984): Das erste französisch-deutsch Wörterbuch: Levinus Hulsius' *Dictionnaire* von 1596-1607. In: *Zeitschrift für romanische Philologie* 100/3-4.

Jezek, E./Hanks, P. (2010): What lexical sets tell us about conceptual categories. In: *Lexis* 4, 7-22. Internet: http://screcherche.univ-lyon3.fr/lexis/IMG/pdf/Lexis_4.pdf (last visited: 17/05/2013).

Kilgarriff, A./Rychly, P./Smrz, P./Tugwell, D. (2004): The Sketch Engine. In: Williams, G./ Vessier, S. (eds): *Proceedings of the Eleventh Euralex International Congress*. Lorient: Université de Bretagne-Sud, 105-116.

Korshin, P.J. (1974): Johnson and the Renaissance dictionary. In: *Journal of the History of Ideas* 35: 2, 300-312.

Kramer, U. (2006): German lexicography. In: Brown, K. (ed.): *Encyclopedia of language and linguistics*. 2nd edition. Amsterdam: Elsevier, vol. 5, 45-52.

Labarre, A. (1975): *Bibliographie du Dictionarium d'Ambrogio Calepino*. (= Bibliotheca bibliographica Aureliana 26). Baden-Baden: Koerner.

Lancashire, I. (2006): Computing the lexicons of early modern English. In: Renouf, A./Kehoe, A. (eds.): *The changing face of Corpus Linguistics*. (= Language and Computers 55). Amsterdam: Rodopi, 45-62.

Landau, S.I. (2001): *Dictionaries: The art and craft of lexicography*. 2nd edition. Cambridge: Cambridge University Press.

Murray, J.A.H. (1878): *Presidential address.* The Philological Society.

Murray, J.A.H. (1900): *The evolution of English lexicography.* (= The Romanes Lecture). Oxford: Clarendon Press.

Pustejovsky, J. (1995): *The generative lexicon*. Cambridge, MA: MIT Press.

Pustejovsky, J./Hanks, P./Rumshisky, A. (2004): Automated induction of sense in context. In: *Proceedings of the 20th international conference on Computational Linguistics*. Internet: http://acl.ldc.upenn.edu/C/C04/C04-1133.pdf (last visited: 17/05/2013).

Putnam, H. (1970): Is semantics possible? In: *Metaphilosophy* 1 (3), 187-201.

Putnam, H. (1975a): The meaning of "meaning". In: *Minnesota Studies in the Philosophy of Science* 7, 131-193.

Putnam, H. (1975b): *Mind, language, and reality: Philosophical papers.* Cambridge: Cambridge University Press.

Rosch, E. (1973a): Natural categories. In: *Cognitive Psychology* 4 (3), 328-350.

Rosch, E. (1973b): On the internal structure of perceptual and semantic categories. In: Moore, T. (ed.): *Cognitive development and the acquisition of language.* New York: Academic Press, 111-144.

Schoonheim, T.H./Pijnenburg, W.J.J. (2006): Dutch and Flemish lexicography. In: Brown, K. (ed.): *Encyclopedia of language and linguistics.* 2nd edition. Amsterdam: Elsevier, vol. 4, 20-23.

Sinclair, J. (1966): Beginning the study of lexis. In: Bazell, C./Catford, J./Halliday, M./Robins, R. (eds.): *In Memory of J.R. Firth.* London: Longman, 410-431.

Sinclair, J. (ed.) (1987): *Looking up: An account of the COBUILD project in lexical computing.* London: Collins ELT.

Sinclair, J. (1991): *Corpus, concordance, collocation.* Oxford: Oxford University Press.

Sinclair, J. (1998): The lexical item. In: Weigand, E. (ed.): *Contrastive Lexical Semantics.* (= Amsterdam Studies in the Theory and History of Linguistic Science: Ser. 4, Current Issues in Linguistic Theory 171). Amsterdam: John Benjamins, 1-24.

Sinclair, J. (2004) *Trust the text: Language, corpus and discourse.* London: Routledge.

Starnes, DeWitt T. (1963): *Robert Estienne's influence on lexicography.* Austin: Texas University Press.

Starnes, DeWitt T./Noyes, G.E. (1946): *The English dictionary from Cawdrey to Johnson.* Chapel Hill: University of North Carolina Press.

Starnes, DeWitt T./Talbert, E.W. (1955): *Classical myth and legend in Renaissance dictionaries.* Chapel Hill: University of North Carolina Press.

Stathi, E. (2006): Latin lexicography. In: Brown, K. (ed.): *Encyclopedia of language and linguistics.* 2nd edition. Amsterdam: Elsevier, vol. 6, 723-724.

Stubbs, M. (2001): *Words and phrases: corpus studies of lexical semantics.* Oxford: Blackwell.

Tesnière, L. (1959): *Éléments de syntaxe structurale.* Paris: Klincksieck.

Trench, R.C. (1858): On some deficiencies in our English dictionaries. In: *Proceedings of the Philological Society.*

Watson, F. (1908 [1968]): *The English Grammar Schools to 1660: their curriculum and practice.* London: Cass (Reprint 1968).

Gábor Prószéky

How "truly electronic dictionaries" of the 21st Century should look like?

Abstract

The first part of the presentation follows the main points of Atkins (2002) paper on the future of bilingual dictionaries. More than ten years ago she claimed that – besides the still existing printed dictionaries – the future should produce "truly electronic dictionaries" enriched with new types of information. But what sorts of new information have appeared in our dictionaries in the last decade? We try to enumerate the most important features which make today's traditions really different from those of the past. With the help of these features the basic design of our near future's electronic dictionaries is sketched out. Various new aspects must be taken into consideration if the dictionaries of the 21st century are to be better usable than the ones of the previous ages. In the second part of the presentation we show some methods of how new functions of a dictionary appear in the reality.

1. What sorts of new information have appeared in our dictionaries in the last decade?

In 1996, at the EURALEX Congress Sue Atkins gave a speech on the future of bilingual dictionaries. This keynote address was published in a festschrift in her honor six years later, followed by a series of other papers about the same topic (Corréard 2002). One of Atkins's claims formalized a general truth, namely "Change is not something that people tend to associate with dictionaries" (Atkins 1996). Electronic dictionaries, however, are part of the fast changing electronic world, thus, in the last decade several new features have appeared in them.

In the electronic world it is common sense that hypertext functionality eliminates linear text restrictions and opens the way to new types of information by offering new ways of presenting them. In the dictionary world, the first consequence of being electronic is that there are no space constraints, that is, we don't need to follow the well-known dictionary formats, which is a sort of consequence of the Gutenberg-galaxy. Our dictionaries can be disengaged from the shortcomings of being printed. The entries don't need to follow any order, alphabetic or other, the hits for any query can be sorted according to the actual user needs. There can be alternative ways of presenting information: it is not bound to the nature of the paper. There are a lot of opportunities for user customization: for example, if the user likes the more traditional view of dictionary entries with tilde signs, he or she can see the dictionary content according to this, but if other, non-traditional views are preferred, it can be done without changing the dictionary's internal database representation. There are other new options as well: lexicographers are not obliged to insert various examples into the entries, because of the rapid access to large amounts of lexicographical data in available mono- or bilingual corpora showing the actual use of the word or expression in context, with or without translation.

There are other consequences of being electronic: e.g. intelligent dictionary production which is an important branch of computational lexicography of the corpus linguistic age. Starting from corpora ("corpus-based lexicography") many dictionaries have been developed in the past years with the help of statistical and linguistic analyses and other extended corpus-linguistic technologies ("corpus-driven lexicography"). Unfortunately, the detailed description of these methods falls outside of the scope of present paper as does dictionary making with the help of sophisticated electronic tools based on current software technology. In the next sections, however, some existing solutions will be shown of how language technology can be combined with dictionaries – mostly along the basic ideas of Sue Atkins.

2. Towards "intelligent" dictionary lookup

Atkins (1996) claims that dictionaries can be used in two different ways: in look-up mode and browsing mode. Look-up mode is where the user is in a quick search of a specific piece of information and browsing mode is where a more relaxed process of reading of dictionary entries takes place. In the traditional dictionary look-up entries are in alphabetic order and the computer search relying on indexing of headwords can be either full or partial string matching. This means that electronic dictionaries using this querying method are very close to the traditional paper dictionaries, only the search in the alphabetic register is much faster in them. As Atkins (1996) says: "The dictionary of the present is at heart little different from the dictionary of the past". Using an analogy: the first electronic dictionaries are similar to the first automobiles where the engine was put in the place of horses, and many decades have been needed to reach the current form of cars which is mostly determined by wind channels. The new, language technology based look-up relies on stemming (that is, the stem of the actual running word is looked up in the dictionary. The new look-up should use some sort of spelling to find information also with misspelled input. There are experimental look-up technologies that use semantic similarity while searching (Segond et al. 2000). A very important difference between paper or paper-like electronic dictionaries and the dictionary look-up using new technologies is that the latter is able to use more than a single source while searching. In other words, parallel lookup in many sources can be done, thus for the end-user it is much less important whether the needed information is found in a single source or in various sources that are currently available for the multi-dictionary look-up system.

3. "Intelligent" dictionary visualization

Visualization is another issue which plays a role in the design of future dictionaries. Alternative formats may be needed in various situations. An example of this is when dictionaries use the '~'-sign for the headword in the body of the entries to minimize the size of the paper dictionary, but this is useless in electronic dictionaries. Some publishers, however, insist on the shorter forms. Multiple typographies can be handled easily in current XML/XSLT based dictionary representations, namely, printed dictionaries and their screen-oriented versions come from the same XML source applying different XSL transformations. That's why multiple screen versions do not cause problems for the visualization of today's lexical resources.

As has been mentioned earlier, multiple dictionary look-up is another feature of intelligent dictionary systems. Visualization of entries coming from different sources need a special dynamic combination of search results to produce a virtual single entry. The dynamic structure of even a single dictionary entry plays an interesting role in these systems: users may or may not need some parts of the original entries (e.g. optional visualization of non-compulsory information). The original literal context of the running word in question can help the intelligent system to choose the actually not needed information from the dictionary entry. For example, there are many multi-word expressions listed in dictionary entries, and it is the actual context that helps to choose only those entries which play some role in the actual meaning of the word in question. Other contexts may choose other sub-entries from the original entry, so dynamic construction of a larger entry can be done very frequently in the intelligent dictionary systems with context-sensitive dictionary look-up.

Summarizing the above arguments, it can be claimed that today's dictionary structure is a sort of by-product of the Gutenberg-galaxy. The typical lexicographic abbreviations originate from typographic considerations where rules like "use fewer letters" or "save more paper" played a crucial role. In the development of new dictionary solutions, producers of electronic dictionaries play a similar role to the printing houses earlier. In case of traditional dictionaries, linguistic information needed for text comprehension was in the user's mind. Therefore, lexicographers tried to support users to find the needed information effectively. In case of intelligent computer dictionaries a dynamic comprehension module also "sees" what the user sees, therefore the computer is in a situation which was dedicated only for humans earlier. The starting point of the dictionary look-up in contemporary electronic systems is the actual text on the screen and the user triggers the needed dictionary process with some manipulation over this text (e.g. by clicking on the word to start dictionary search, or only leaving the mouse cursor over the actual word for a short while), and the look-up procedure starts with the actual word which is in the actual context. We have to make, however, an important economic consideration here: intelligent electronic dictionaries use language technology knowledge that is always bound to the source language in question, namely, stemming, spelling correction or parsing of the actual context are operations which are not language-independent. Intelligent dictionaries with specific language abilities are consequently bound to those markets where the actual source languages are widely used. In other words: if we have a general dictionary system, its market is the whole world separately from the languages of the dictionaries published with the help of them. In case of applying intelligent, language-specific modules, this market becomes smaller because of the language-dependent modules that guarantee intelligence.

4. Aspects of using electronic dictionaries

If people go to a bookshop, they are able to judge the quality of a paper dictionary with the help of many external features: number of pages (or at least, the thickness of the book), typographical solutions, letter size, etc. It is not too difficult to categorize a dictionary whether it is a reliable one or not. On the other hand, it is rather difficult to measure how up-to-date an electronic dictionary is. The exact size of an electronic dictionary is difficult to check, consequently, the biggest "declared" figures tend to "win" in the marketing competition. Marketing people are always able to "develop" a new way of enumeration which can show that their dictionary is the biggest on the market. Size, of course, is not the only feature which counts, but – again using the "automobile parallel"

– non-experts can be convinced by the speed of the model only. New films or musical productions people can get acquainted with via their reviews and criticisms, but dictionary criticism or particularly, electronic dictionary criticism is not a typical field, so users can only rely mainly on their personal experience.

It is a very interesting experiment how users choose electronic dictionaries. In case of paper dictionaries leafing through the book gives an impression whether it serves the purposes of the customer. The general judgment on the quality of an electronic dictionary is usually based on a simple lookup for a few words: if they are found, the dictionary is generally considered "good", if not, the dictionary is "bad". Generally, non-professional users – mostly non-professional internet users – don't consider the dictionary tools as important as professionals do, they are usually satisfied with a few hits which are provided by even the demo versions as well. Consequently, more and more users don't buy professional dictionaries (where the new look-up technologies can mostly be found) because their needs are already satisfied by lower level free dictionaries on the web. In the paper world, this dichotomy does not exist: users should pay some fee for even the lower level dictionaries. We have arrived to a critical issue here, namely, there is more and more free information on the internet, and this generates a temptation for many potential dictionary users: why to buy an electronic dictionary if an "almost" similar one is available for free. In the electronic world there are dictionaries for fee and dictionaries for free. The question is whether the brand name, the content or the applied services are enough to convince the non-professional end-users to pay for some dictionary content. What is interesting, it is not because of the eventual high price but because of the many freely available dictionaries on the web which also give acceptable results. So, if there are two candidate dictionaries – a professional one for a fee and a less reliable (but generally well-designed) internet dictionary – usually the general message of the web is applied, namely, "who cares whether something is not as professional as the other, but it is for free!"

In addition, end-users can easily see if something is not perfect in a paper dictionary, because the full version is in their hands even in the bookshop. In case of electronic dictionaries, you can meet the full version only if you have already bought it. Additionally, in the electronic world, you can meet special – in most cases: "non-official" – variants of well-known dictionaries which are not as easy to identify. For example, if dictionary entries are split up into pairs of source-target expressions, that is, entries without internal structure, then much less typography is required, consequently, identification of the original lexicographical source is not easy. What is more, in electronic dictionaries there is no "basic" order of entries, which is a crucial issue in comparing two paper dictionaries. Order of entries is again a feature which cannot be used for identifying the original source of an electronic wordlist because there can be various indices providing different ordering among the same entries. In some cases, special technical terms or occurrence of seldom used expressions can be clear signs of the origin of the dictionary. In case of general dictionaries there are not too many very specific entries, and it would be difficult to argue, for example, that *table*'s German equivalent is not *Tisch* in an English-German dictionary, or one of *horse*'s equivalent is not *Pferd*. The question is always the same: where is the border between common (bilingual) knowledge which is generally available for free and special lexicographical information that should be paid for?

5. "Truly electronic dictionaries" enriched with new types of information

As we have seen, dictionary content and/or reputation of a dictionary publisher may be crucial, but in the case of electronic dictionaries, technology is also be important. People generally don't have time enough for anything, and if the new technology helps to spare some seconds or minutes for them, they are getting interested. Users prefer less typing and they like if they don't need to open new applications which eventually partly cover the screen, mostly those parts where the text to be understood takes place. For example, if the mouse pointer is left over a word for more than one second indicates automatically that the user would like to have information about that word and its context, the hits to this query should be suddenly shown in a bubble on the screen. Users don't have much time for interaction, so the tool should rely on its own linguistic knowledge only: the actual context should be taken into consideration to identify all possible multi-word expressions in the context, even if word forms are inflected or the actual word order is different from the one of the lexical form of the expression. If no multi-word expressions are found, the tool displays a simple dictionary entry for the selected word (Figure 1). What is important is that the tool provides a list all possible translations found in all active dictionaries for the given language as source language.

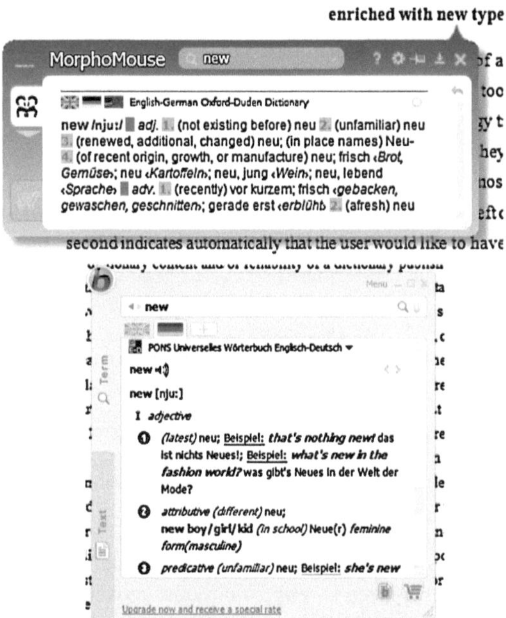

Figure 1: Look-up for a simple dictionary entry (MorphoMouse and Babylon)

The first attempt in the direction of new dictionaries was COMPASS (Feldweg/Breidt 1996). The system we try to illustrate the above features of intelligent dictionaries with is MorphoMouse, a technology that relies on the earlier MoBiMouse (Prószéky/Kis

2002). Atkins' "look-up mode" and "browsing mode" are supported: hits are shown either in a bubble-shaped pop-up window on the screen, or the same small bubble-like window which can be used traditionally via typing (Figure 2).

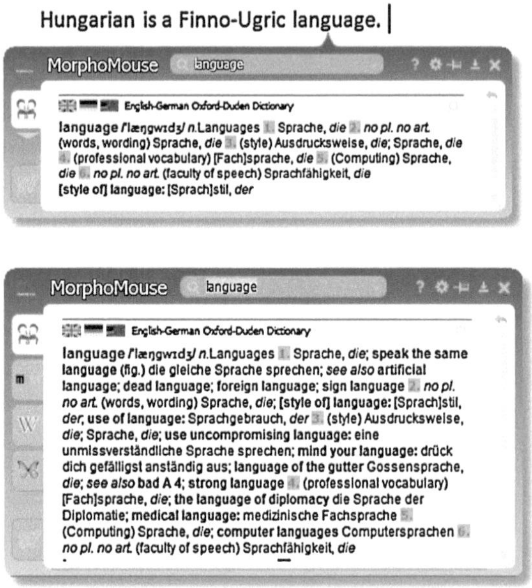

Figure 2: Look-up mode (partial entry) and browsing mode (full entry)

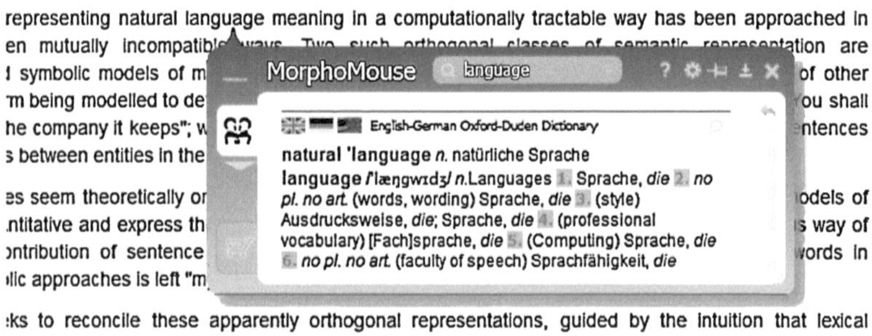

Figure 3: Contextual look-up

Instant dictionary look-up means that the mouse cursor is left over a word on the screen and dictionary look-up is triggered by either no mouse movement being identified in the next second or by the pressing of some special button (e.g. press Ctrl button twice). Look-up relies on the actual context: the potential stems of the actual word (under the cursor) are identified with the help of language technology modules: a language identifier, a morphological analyzer for the language in question and a sort of multi-word analysis is also done to check whether the actual entry and some surrounding words can form multi-word expressions or not (Figure 3).

Multi-entry look-up means that even in a normal dictionary there can be different head-words containing each word of the original input. Different multi-word entries can contain common parts, e.g. the dictionary entry of *ability* contains a sub-headword which contains *natural* and *for: she has a natural ability for teaching*. In the same dictionary we can find the entry of *natural* which also contains an expression with *for*, namely, *he was a natural for the job*. Both hits should be provided if the query consists of two words, *natural* and *for* (Figure 4).

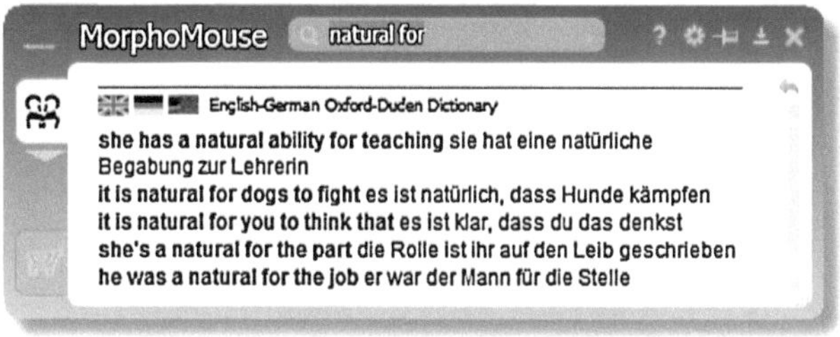

Figure 4: Parallel look-up for multi-word expressions in a single dictionary

Parallel multi-dictionary look-up is a procedure which goes through each open dictionary and the actual query is searched for all of them. Users are not generally interested in the details how to do this, or whether some dictionaries don't have equivalents for the actual input but some others do. The user would like to have as many hits as the available dictionaries are able to offer (Figure 5). Even multi-language look-up can help the user if he/she is able to use more than a single target language (Figure 6). Talking about true multilingual dictionaries Atkins says that in the past lack of space and commercial pressures made a true multilingual dictionary impossible (Atkins 1996) and continues: "If a multilingual dictionary is to be compiled, we have to devise an analysis technique common to all languages involved".

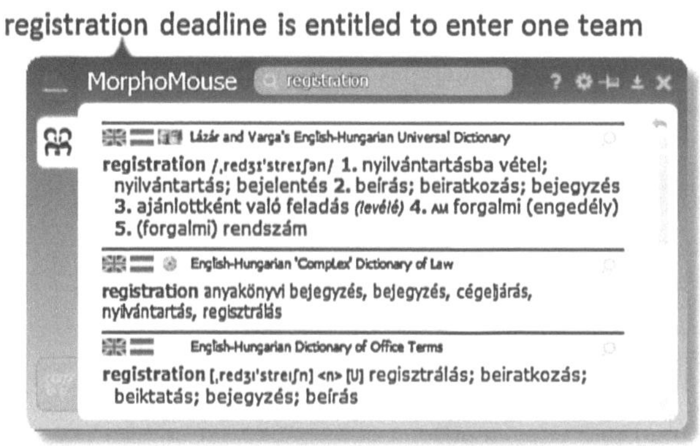

Figure 5: Combined parallel look-up in general and specific dictionaries

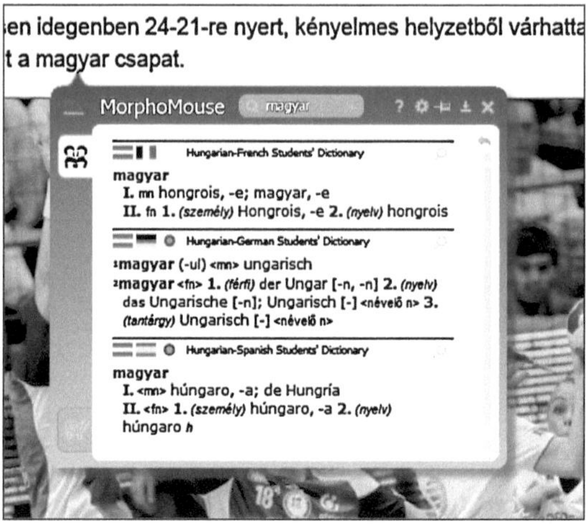

Figure 6: Multi-language look-up

Important combination of traditional dictionaries and other linguistic sources can be guaranteed by language technology solutions. Let's quote Atkins (1996) again: "research described in Atkins and Varantola shows that people often turn to a monolingual dictionary during a bilingual search. The ideal dictionary should offer monolingual functions (definitions, etymologies, usage notes) to the bilingual dictionary user". For example, a set of dictionary hits can be combined with hits from other, monolingual lexicographical sources or encyclopaedias: an example is shown from Wikipedia on Figure 7. "The ideal dictionary should allow the user to browse through genuine attested examples of the foreign expression in use in various types of texts" (Atkins 1996). Translation memories or just parallel corpora are available for today's electronic dictionaries: Figure 8 shows some hits (for the English verb *prefer*) in Hunglish, a web-based Hungarian-English bilingual corpus (Varga et al. 2005). Electronic dictionaries are frequently used in combination with machine translation applications, thus, not only the word and its local context are processed by linguistic technologies but the full sentence containing the word in question (Figure 9).

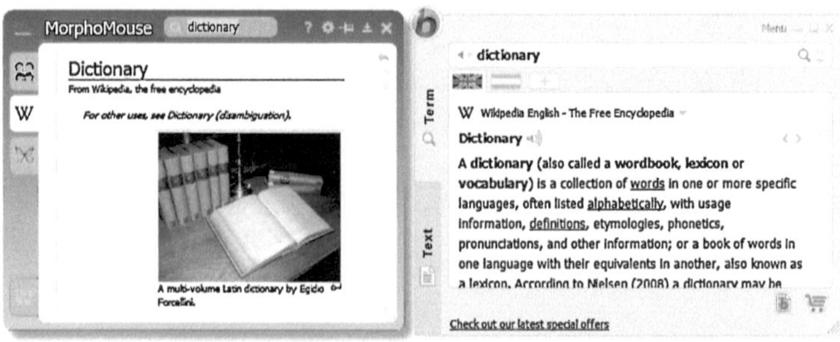

Figure 7: Combined instant look-up in other internet sources (Wikipedia)

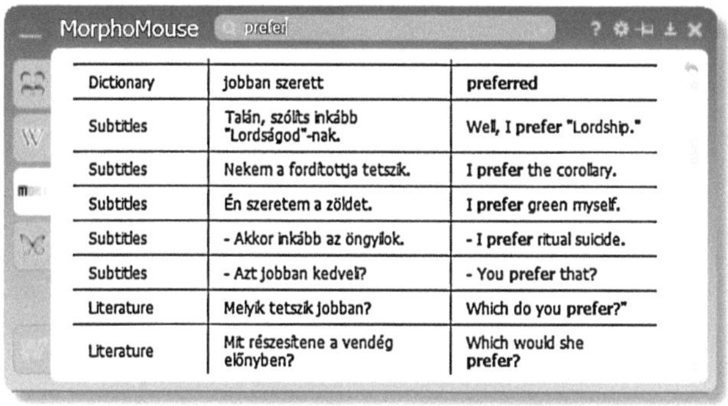

Figure 8: Parallel corpus as special dictionary

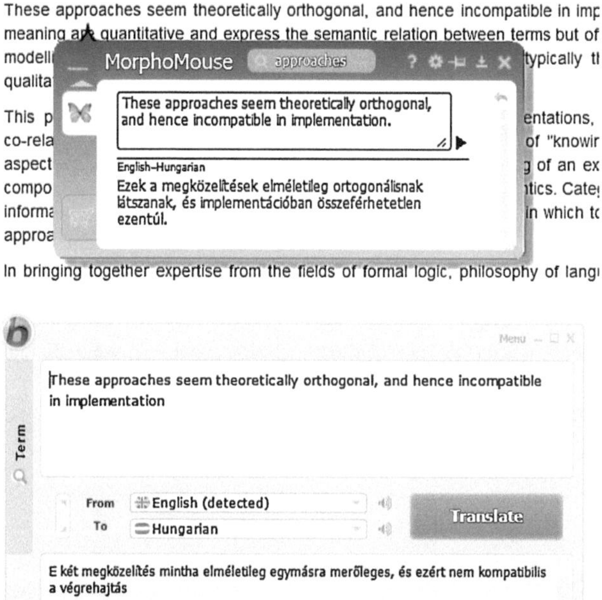

Figure 9: Combined instant look-up for sentence translation (MorphoMouse and Babylon)

6. Conclusion

Atkins (1996) says: "Many of the obstacles to the creation of tomorrow's improved bilingual dictionary have been removed in the past few decades by the advent of the computer (computer-assisted lexicography, rich electronic text corpora as sources of lexicographical evidence, computational searches of dictionaries, and so on)". She describes how new-age bilingual dictionaries must exploit the electronic medium. She lists a lot of claims which have become well-known since then, like "no space constraints", "flexible compiling liberated from alphabetical order", "alternative ways of presenting information", "rapid access to large amounts of lexicographical evidence in corpora" and many others. According to Atkins (1996) the electronic dictionaries of the mid-nineties were little more than reincarnation of print dictionaries. In our paper we have tried to show (via examples of publicly available tools) that around fifteen years later there are electronic dictionary systems which use technologies carrying out the plan sketched first by Sue Atkins. These new tools even use multi-dictionary look-up methods, language identification, stemming, linguistic treatment of multi-word expressions with the help of language technology solutions. Unfortunately, there are many features Atkins mentioned that no solutions have been made for since then. It's high time to read again about those challenging tasks of today's computational lexicography.

7. References

Atkins, B.T.S. (1996) Bilingual dictionaries – past, present and future. In: Gellerstam, M./ Järborg, J./Malmgren, S.-G./Norén, K./Rogström, L./Papmehl, C.R. (eds.): *Euralex '96 Proceedings*. Gothenburg: Gothenburg University, 515-590.

Corréard, M.-H. (ed.) (2002): *Lexicography and Natural Language Processing* (*a festschrift in honour of B.T.S. Atkins*). Grenoble: Euralex.

Feldweg, H./Breidt, E. (1996): COMPASS – an intelligent dictionary system for reading text in a foreign language. In: Kiefer, F./Kiss, G./ Pajzs, J. (eds.): *Papers in Computational Lexicography*. Budapest: Linguistics Institute, 53-62.

Prószéky, G./Kis, B. (2002): Context-sensitive dictionaries. In: Tseng, Shu-Chuan (ed.): *Proceedings of the 19th International Conference on Computational Linguistics*, Vol. II. Taipei: Howard International House, 1268-1272.

Segond, F./Aimelet, E./Lux, V./Jean, C. (2000): Dictionary-driven semantic look-up. In: *Computers and the Humanities* Vol. 34, No. 1/2, 193-197.

Varga, D./Németh, L./Halácsy, P./Kornai, A./Trón, V./Nagy, V. (2005): Parallel corpora for medium density languages. In: *Proceedings of the RANLP 2005*, 590-596.

Willy Martin

A Dutch recipe for the production of bilingual dictionaries

1. Introduction

In the announcement letter to this conference the following is stated:

> Nowadays people do not necessarily turn straight to a dictionary for information about words. They key their enquiry into a search engine, text a friend, or take any one of a number of other (chiefly online) routes to discover the information they want.
>
> With this in mind, the tenth EFNIL Conference will investigate the different ways in which people access lexical information – both in their own language and in other languages – and how governments, language institutions, publishers, and others go about the business of compiling and disseminating this lexical information in the first place.
>
> This theme cuts right to the heart of linguistic diversity of Europe. Each of our states has different ways of addressing the issues of language: some are more advanced along this road than others. Different peoples and different languages may need different solutions, but are there things we can learn from what our colleagues elsewhere in Europe are doing?

As you will have noticed, this passage ends with a question mark. So, in all honesty, I am not sure that you will but I really do hope that you can learn or unlearn from a project that was started in Flanders and the Netherlands in 1993, and that is finished by now, 20 years later, although, like a gardener's, a lexicographer's work never comes to an end. Therefore in this talk, I will not only deal with the past, but at the end also turn 'back to the future' as will become clear from the survey below:

1. Introduction
2. Government Policy and Dictionaries: the CLVV as a case in point
   - 2.1 Background
     - What, Why and How?
     - Tasks & Goals
   - 2.2 Specific Issues
     - Selection and Prioritization Criteria
     - Results
     - Infrastructure
3. Lessons and Remarks for the Future

2. Government policy and dictionaries: the CLVV as a case in point

2.1 Background

National governments often play a role in lexicographical matters as subsidizers of large, scientific, monolingual, so-called 'national' dictionaries, such as the *WNT* (Woordenboek der Nederlandsche Taal (Dictionary of the Dutch Language)) in the Netherlands and Flanders, the *Trésor de la Langue Française* in France or the *Deutsches Wörterbuch* in Germany. However, when it comes to bilingual dictionaries their role is much less obvious and much less known.

In 1993 the governments of the Netherlands and Flanders took a clear stand on that issue as the ministers of education of both countries decided to install an intergovernmental body of lexical experts in order to improve and stimulate the production of *bilingual dictionaries* and lexical databases with Dutch as a source or target language.

At its installation in March 1993 the CLVV (**C**ommissie voor **L**exicografische **V**ertaal **V**oorzieningen = Committee for Interlingual Lexicographical Resources) was given the following tasks:

1. establish Action Plans for the realization of a program of Dutch bilingual dictionaries,
2. define priorities based upon these APs,
3. evaluate project proposals, both on the level of contents and on that of management,
4. have technological projects carried out so to further lexicographical interlingual resources,
5. look for co-sponsoring and co-financing (partner countries, EU, government, trade, industry, ...),
6. supervise both quality and progress of the approved projects,
7. give advice on how to proceed,
8. give advice to those projects which were not prioritized or not subsidized.

Actually, these tasks were based on a report written previously in 1991 (see Martin/Theeuwes 1991), which drew up the state of the art with regard to bilingual dictionaries of Dutch and in which the following principles upon which to found a governmental subsidizing and intervention policy were recommended:

(1) Government should only intervene where the private market fails.
[In other words, one should be sure that the lacking dictionaries or lexical databases will not be published in a reasonable time by a private publisher unless there is a form of government support].

(2) Government support should only be given when the social merits are larger or at least equal to the social costs.
[Therefore, the intended dictionaries or lexical databases, should represent a real need, a.o. being expressed by the number of potential users. Next to that, other social merits dictionaries can bring along are positive external effects such as cultural identification, social integration, R&D activities, etc. These also should be taken into account].

The active policy of the Netherlands and Flanders in bilingual lexicographical matters has also been inspired by the fact that both countries considered bilingual dictionaries as important pieces of basic infrastructure, comparable to road infrastructure, offering people the possibility to come into contact with people from abroad, creating direct communicative connections between two linguistic communities. This fact is particularly important for so-called less-used languages which otherwise have to use an 'interlingua' such as English or another major language to come into contact with each other. If one wants to create equal possibilities for all citizens in a community, for instance in the EU, allowing them to take part in the information society, the use of a language should not be a hindrance, but a help.

Next to the fact that the CLVV had to formulate a program of *concrete lexicographical projects*, it also had to define the general policy lines for a *coherent, anticipatory* and *economically justified* policy. Coherence in this context implied abandoning the ad hoc, *first come, first served* subsidizing policy and replacing it by a systematic approach based an a plan, so, for the subsidizing bodies to know better what to do first and what to do later or not at all.

Furthermore, in order to anticipate needs and tackle them in an economic way, public funds, according to the CLVV, should be used to finance the development of *multifunctional and re-usable electronic lexical databases*. This point-of-view implied, among others, the following:

It should be possible to derive from the same database:

1. both graphical and electronic products,
2. several types of dictionaries,
3. the reverse part of it,
4. bidirectional dictionaries.

It should also be possible to link the languages involved in the original bilingual databases with other languages outside of it, so to yield new databases going beyond the languages of the original language pair (see below: the Hub-and-Spoke Model).

It goes without saying that this was a very ambitious programme. Given the limited budget (6.5 to 7 million euro) prioritization criteria were needed to make a selection of projects.

2.2 Specific issues

2.2.1 Selection and prioritization principles

Such as it is obvious that government should not intervene where the private market was successful, as is, for instance, the case for bilingual dictionaries such as Dutch-English, Dutch-French, Dutch-German and Dutch-Spanish, so too, in other cases the market was much less attractive and successful. Consequently, the CLVV has defined criteria with which to prioritize languages in order to come to an argued selection of languages.

In order to do so the *metaphor of dictionaries as connecting roads* has been further developed and made concrete by taking the *geographical context* into account. The area in which Dutch was spoken (the Netherlands and Flanders) was taken as the innermost of a series of ever growing *concentric circles*: the EU, Europe, the World. As the core or innermost circle itself showed already an internal, non-homogeneous structure (meaning that within that area already different languages were spoken), there should not only be roads from the inner towards the outer circles and vice versa, but also within the inner circle itself (see figure 1, also see Martin 2007).

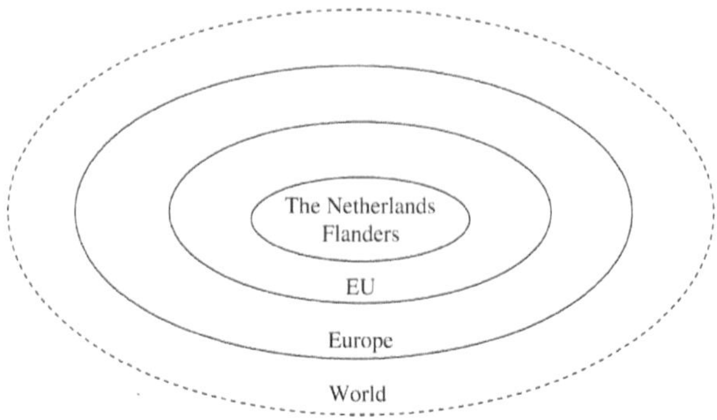

Figure 1: Language areas as concentric circles

As dictionaries were considered to be *connecting roads,* so languages were considered to represent *communities living in a certain area, wanting to come into contact with other communities.* The stronger the need for the contacts between the two communities, the greater the need for *roads* to make these contacts possible and easy. In order to measure the strength of this need, use was made of the following types of *indicators*:

Indicators for the need of bilingual dictionaries

1. Sociodemographic indicators
2. Economical indicators
3. Educational indicators
4. Cultural and Scientific indicators
5. Political indicators

To understand better what is meant with the respective *indicators* some examples are given for each of them in what follows.

1. The fact that, in countries such as the Netherlands and Flanders, not only the national language (Dutch) is spoken, but also languages of large groups of immigrants, such as Turks and Moroccans, is a strong argument in favour of a *connecting road* between these language communities.
2. Import and export trade serve, among others, as indicators for economical relationships between communities.
3. One could argue that the fact that one wants to learn the language of another community is a *derived* or *indirect* indicator, yet *educational* indicators are of importance to get an idea of the size of the need.
4. Some communities have a high cultural or scientific prestige or influence so that need arises to come into contact with them.
5. The fact that a political organization such as the EU not only grows in breadth (more countries), but also in depth (more domains that fall under its administration), makes it of extreme importance for countries and languages to find their way and define their position vis-à-vis the other.

Although the mentioned indicators only indirectly point at relationships and their strengths, yet they are of great help to select and prioritize between the otherwise quasi-unlimited mass of languages. Against this background, the concentric circles shown before have been *filled* as in figure 2:

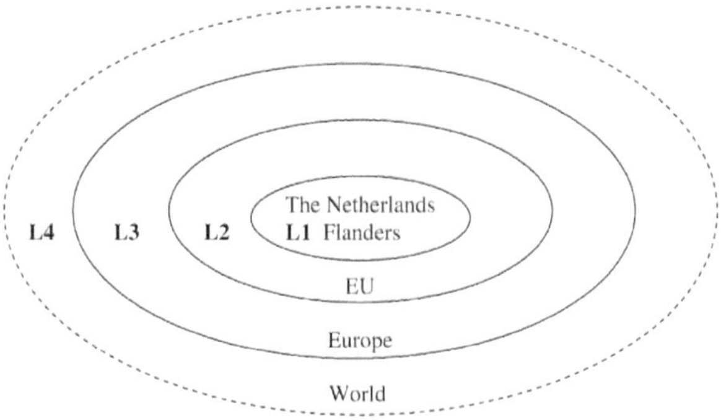

Fig.2: 'Prioritized' languages from a Dutch point-of-view
L1 = Arabic, Sranantongo, Turkish
L2 = (a) Danish, Finnish, Greek, Italian, Portuguese, Swedish (EU languages before 2004)
(b) Estonian, Hungarian, Polish, Czech (EU languages from 2004 onwards)
L3 = Norwegian, Russian, Rumanian
L4 = Indonesian, Korean

Notice that no circle has absolute priority, although certain indicators play a more prominent role in one circle compared to another (sociodemographic in the innermost, economical and political in the second and third, cultural, political and economical in the fourth).

2.2.2 Results

In the end 20 dictionary projects have been realized under the auspices or with the support of the CLVV, which itself resorts under the Dutch Language Union (Nederlandse Taalunie), the official institution for the Dutch Language. CLVV-paper dictionaries vary as to size and contents, the average one however contains 45,000 entries with a fairly rich microstructure and has about 800 to 1000 pages per volume. As a rule there is both a p- and an e-version. Table 1 gives a survey of the results with beginning and ending of editing phase and date of publication (+ publisher).

Project	Start-End	Publisher + Date
Dutch-Arabic v.v. Learners	1996-2000	Bulaaq, 2001
Dutch-Arabic v.v. Translation	1997-2002	Bulaaq, 2003
Dutch-Czech	1997	Leda, 1997
Dutch-Danish v.v.	1997-2001	Gyldendal, 2004

Project	Start-End	Publisher + Date
Dutch-Estonian	1997-2011	Pegasus, ?
Dutch-Finnish v.v.	2002-2007	Het Spectrum, 2012
Hungarian-Dutch	1995-2000	Akademiai, 2000
Dutch-Hungarian	1999-2002	Grimm, 2002
Dutch-Indonesian	1997-2002	KITLV, 2004
Dutch-Italian v.v.	1996-2001	Van Dale, 2001
Korean-Dutch	1999-2006	Hankuk University of Foreign Studies Press, 2007
Dutch-New Greek v.v.	1998-2007	Het Spectrum, 2008
Dutch-Norwegian	1998-2002	Boekwerk, 2007
Dutch-Polish v.v.	1996-2002	Pegasus, 2008
Dutch-Portuguese v.v.	1998-2002	Het Spectrum, 2004
Dutch-Rumanian	1997-2005	Pegasus, 2007
Russian-Dutch	1997-2002	Pegasus, 2002
Dutch-Sranantongo	2004	Het Spectrum, 2004
Dutch-Swedish v.v.	1995	Van Dale, 1996
Dutch-Turkish	1994-2007	Leiden University Press, 2012

Table 1: CLVV's bilingual dictionary projects

2.2.3 CLVV's approach to material and immaterial infrastructure

Financial resources were not fully used for the concrete dictionary projects as such, 20% of them being used for the development of *generic* tools and models with which to construct bilingual dictionaries in a cost-effective and yet high-quality way. In doing so, one could not only tackle *hic et nunc* needs but anticipate future ones as well. Moreover, dictionary projects not elected for financial support could apply for the use of the generic tools developed, such as OMBI and the RBN. In what follows the main characteristics of both these tools are mentioned. For more details on OMBI we refer the reader to the literature (Martin/Tamm 1996; Maks 2007).

OMBI: main characteristics

OMBI = editor for ***OM*** keerbare ***BI*** linguale Woordenboeken (editor or Dictionary Writing System for Reversible Bilingual Dictionaries).

OMBI is a device to guide, structure and correct input data according to a pre-defined grammar (= comparable to other editors).

OMBI was (in 1996), and still is, innovative in that it has a REVERSAL FUNCTION which reverses language pairs with GREAT PRECISION.

OMBI links at SEMANTIC LEVEL and specifies the LEXICAL RELATION (for instance: hyponym, hyperonym, synonym etc. plus their constraints) between semantic units.

E.g.: KAART = card (for games), card (piece of paper), ticket (for entrance), map (topographical) when reversed becomes: CARD (for games) = kaart, (piece of paper) = kaart; TICKET (for entrance) = kaart; MAP (topographical) = kaart [+ examples under the correct lexical unit].

Another piece of material infrastructure, namely the RBN, is briefly presented in what follows (for more details see van der Vliet 2007).

Material infrastructure: RBN

RBN = ***R***eferentie ***B***estand ***N***ederlands (= Reference Database of Dutch).

Meant as an exemplary lexical database for the production and understanding of Dutch (monolingual lexical database).

Multifunctional (not only being of use for monolingual lexicographical purposes, but for bilingual and NLP-purposes as well).

Corpus-based.

Size: 45,000 entries, very rich and explicit microstructure.

The CLVV considered the existence of a high-quality editor and of a good monolingual lexical database of Dutch as a *condition sine qua non* for the *accessibility* of Dutch in a multilingual context. The fact, for instance, that an 'own' database has been constructed offered various advantages as shown below:

1. the possibility to focus on relevant aspects not present in other resources (such as the systematic treatment of collocations, complementation, semantic typology of items etc.),
2. the possibility to compare and link the different projects,
3. the possibility to offer data to non-prioritized projects,
4. independence vis-à-vis other providers such as publishing houses (no monopoly position).

Examples of *immaterial* CLVV infrastructure are the *linking method* (not translating items from one language into another, but linking two monolingual resources at semantic level, for more details see Martin 2003), and the *hub-and-spoke model* which is a model to go *beyond bilinguals* and move from bilingual dictionary making to multilingual dictionary construction. Figures 3, 4 and 5 illustrate in a simplified way what is meant by this (also see Martin 2004).

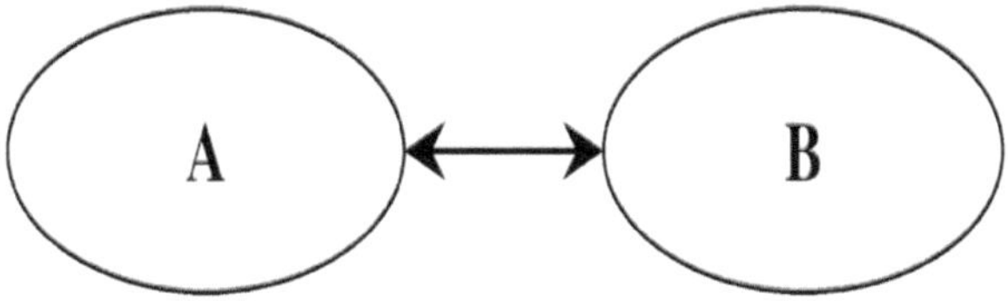

Fig. 3: The Hub-and-Spoke Model: linking two languages

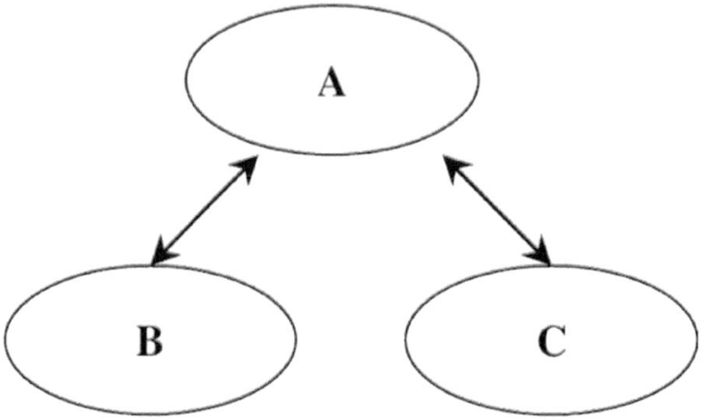

Fig. 4: The Hub-and-Spoke Model: linking two languages to one 'hub' language

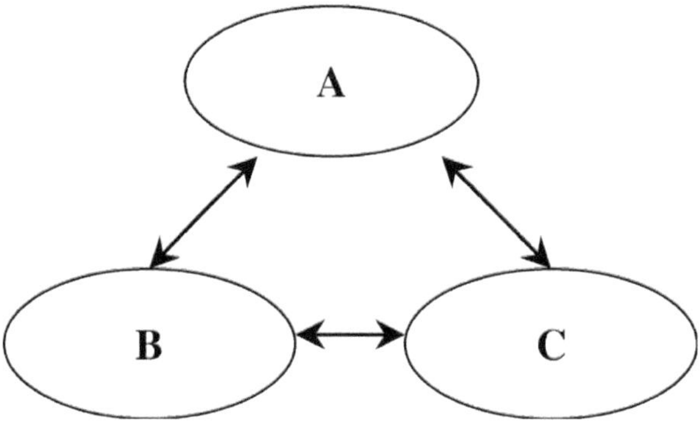

Fig. 5: The Hub-and-Spoke Model: Inferring links between two 'spoke' languages

3. Lessons and remarks for the future

In this last section I want to draw attention both to some strong points of the CLVV-project and to some of its weaknesses, and end with a couple of remarks on the changed and changing lexicographical scene.

3.1 Strong points

3.1.1 High productivity based on a well-founded plan

All in all in a period of less than twenty years, thirty bilingual volumes each containing 800 to 1000 pages have been finished. Without false modesty one can state that this is a result that even large language communities can envy.

This achievement certainly has contributed to strengthen the position of Dutch and its 'partner' languages not only at a linguistic, but also at a social, cultural, economical and political level. Moreover, the fact that most of the dictionaries published up till now are already sold out, requiring a second edition, proves that the dictionaries answered real users' needs, filling existing gaps for specific target groups.

3.1.2 Re-usable infrastructure

The CLVV has been active in the field of dictionary tool development and lexicographical infrastructure. Both OMBI and RBN can be regarded as advanced tools in this respect. Furthermore, the CLVV has considered dictionaries to be 'derived' products, underlying which were databases that should be reusable not only 'within' but also 'beyond' the Dutch context. This implies that, as a rule, the databases for Danish, Finnish, Portuguese etc. are reusable either alone or in combination with languages different from Dutch, thus opening perspectives for co-operation within a framework such as EFNIL. Another positive side effect of the choice for re-usable infrastructure is that for projects that are not selected for subsidizing, support still can be given in the form of infrastructure.

3.1.3 Metalexicographical impact

Next to the fact that the CLVV has been an active player on the lexicographical scene, it also has played a prominent metalexicographical role. In its projects the CLVV has tried to bring along its own, innovative view on the lexicon. Models such as the Hub-and-Spoke Model, functions such as reversing at semantic level (in tools such as OMBI) and the systematic organization of collocational data such as in the RBN, therefore are all grounded in the same concept of a relational, frame-based lexicon. Closely connected to this is the benchmarking function of the CLVV.

Because of the fact that the CLVV was quite successful on the lexicographical market – in fact no publisher in the Netherlands and Flanders was more active during the last decade – it served as a kind of benchmark in the field with a strong impact on quality assessment, standards and evaluation procedures in the Netherlands and Flanders.

3.2 Weak points

3.2.1 Time-management

Although the CLVV was quite successful in having its ambitious program carried out, it should have taken measures to come to a better time-management. As a rule projects needed more time than originally planned for. Bearing in mind that lexicographical projects are notorious in this respect and also taking into account the complexity of the task, the delay in most cases (two to three years) was still reasonable. Yet the CLVV could have done better if

- tools and infrastructure had shown less teething troubles (see further under 3.2.2);
- it had preferred, for certain projects, a 'slow' rather than a 'quick' start (see further under 3.2.3);
- publishers had been involved earlier in the project.

In most cases publishers were involved when the editing work was already finished with the result that often time got lost in coming to a final, both printed and electronic, version which fitted style, format and other desiderata of the publisher.

3.2.2 Infrastructural teething troubles

The fact that the CLVV had to develop its own infrastructure (RBN and OMBI) made its projects, though perhaps more innovative and challenging, also more vulnerable. The development from prototype to product (as, for instance, in the case of OMBI) took more time than expected and so, in the beginning, the teams did suffer from teething troubles of an infrastructure 'under construction'. Of course, things became better as time went by and the tools themselves profited from an intensive use but, with hindsight, it would have been better if the first projects could have disposed of less 'experimental' versions of both RBN and OMBI.

3.2.3 The know-how gap

The development of tools and data is one thing but perhaps as important as providing for infrastructure is providing for the necessary know-how to handle it. With hindsight, it would have been rewarding both for the teams and for the CLVV if the latter had provided for regular workshops in which people could have learned in a more systematic way how to make use of the infrastructure. The CLVV now provided for a help desk to solve infrastructural problems. This support certainly proved its value. However, next to that, a broader, more general kind of support in the form of workshops and/or master classes would have reached more people and enhanced expertise in a more systematic way.

3.3 The future

In what follows some remarks are given which should be taken into account when considering CLVV's heritage, its consolidation and follow-up.

1. The situation with regard to bilingual dictionaries for the Dutch speaking community anno 2012 is quite different from that anno 1993. The first priority now no longer is the *production* of bilingual dictionaries but their *consolidation* and *updating/outdating*. In other words, government, in co-operation with publishing houses, should see to it that the products delivered remain usable and up-to-date. A *wiki-environment* with online dictionaries as *freeware* could offer a solution here.
2. The follow-up and actualization just mentioned does not only regard the data but the *tools* and *infrastructure* as well. Tools not only need to be constructed, they also need to be *maintained.*
3. Government intervention does not stop once the aimed at products are delivered. Next to an action plan for the production, an *action plan for the consolidation, updating and follow-up of the 'deliverables' is now needed.*

   A new business plan should foresee and aim at the *integration/linking of the several resources developed* up till now in one all-encompassing database so that corrections/ updating can be done centrally instead of for each database separately.
4. The fact that within the community of linguists the conviction has grown that, contrary to what was believed by generative grammarians, language cannot be fully captured by rules, has strengthened the *position of corpora as instruments of lin-*

guistic description, next to grammars and dictionaries. Consequently, the question of the specific role and contents of each of these three components becomes more and more stringent.

5. There is not only the challenge for the lexicographer to find out what should be put in the dictionary and what should be left in corpus and grammar, he should also find out how to explore the huge mass of data he is confronted with, nowadays. Next to quantitative devices, *qualitative exploration devices* such as *frames* or any other *semantic corpus query system,* can offer a solution to this problem.
6. One of the most striking differences between lexicography now and lexicography some twenty years ago is the switch from p(aper)- to e(lectronic)- or internet dictionaries. Modern dictionaries should not be replicas of p-dictionaries but constructed in their own right, from which p-dictionaries can be derived, if needed, in this order and not the other way round (also see Fuentes-Olivera/Bergenholtz 2011).

4. References

Fuertes-Olivera, P./Bergenholtz, H. (eds.) (2011): *e-Lexicography. The Internet, digital initiatives and lexicography*. London/New York: Continuum.

Granger, S./Meunier, F. (eds.) (2008): *Phraseology. An interdisciplinary perspective.* Amsterdam/Philadelphia: John Benjamins.

Maks, I. (2007): OMBI: The Practice of Reversing Dictionaries. In: *International Journal of Lexicography* 20, 259-274.

Martin, W. (2003): Lexicography, lexicology, linking and the Hub-and-Spoke Model. In: Botha, W. (ed.): *Festschrift vir Dirk van Schalkwyk.* Stellenbosch: WAT, 268-285.

Martin, W. (2004): Simullda, the Hub-and-Spoke Model and Frames or How to make the best of three worlds? In: *International Journal of Lexicography* 17, 175-187.

Martin, W. (2007): Government policy and the planning and production of bilingual dictionaries. In: *International Journal of Lexicography* 20, 221-237.

Martin, W. (2008): A unified approach to semantic frames and collocational patterns. In: Granger, S./Meunier, F. (eds.): *Phraseology. An interdisciplinary perspective.* Amsterdam/Philadelphia: John Benjamins, 51-65.

Martin, W./Tamm, A. (1996): OMBI: an editor for constructing reversible lexical databases. In: M. Gellerstamm et al. (eds.): *Euralex 1996 Proceedings*. Göteborg: Göteborg University, 675-685.

Martin, W./Theeuwes, J. (1991): *Lexicografische Vertaalvoorzieningen in het Nederlandse Taalgebied.* Den Haag: Ministerie van OC&W.

van der Vliet, H. (2007): The Referentiebestand Nederlands as a multi-purpose lexical database. In: *International Journal of Lexicography* 20, 239-257.

c) Reports on different countries

Annette Klosa

Aktuelle Tendenzen in der deutschen Lexikographie der Gegenwart

Abstract

In this paper, some tendencies in contemporary German lexicography are described with an emphasis on Internet dictionaries. Several online dictionaries of German from publishing houses or published by academic institutions are introduced representing a wide range of possible presentations of lexicographic information on the Internet. The examples also illustrate how modern dictionaries profit from a corpus-based approach, how information on headwords can be presented in an innovative way and how the contact with the dictionary user can be established. Research into dictionary usage is also examined briefly. A short outlook on the possible future of German lexicography rounds off the survey given here.

Die deutsche Wörterbuchlandschaft hat sich während der vergangenen zwei Dekaden deutlich verändert: Während es in der Zeit vor den 90er Jahren des vorigen Jahrhunderts nur gedruckte Wörterbücher und später auch hierauf beruhende CD-ROM-Wörterbücher gab, werden seitdem mehr und mehr lexikographische Nachschlagewerke für das Deutsche im Internet angeboten, und zwar sowohl von akademischen Einrichtungen wie von Verlagen. Dabei konzentrieren sich akademische Einrichtungen (Akademien der Wissenschaften, Forschungsinstitute wie das Institut für Deutsche Sprache in Mannheim) auf spezifische, tendenziell monolinguale Wörterbuchprojekte, und die Verlage (Duden, Langenscheidt, Pons, Wahrig usw.) decken den Markt der allgemeinen Wörterbücher und Lernerwörterbücher im einsprachigen und zweisprachigen Sektor ab. Nur in seltenen Fällen arbeiten wissenschaftliche Einrichtungen und Verlage in Deutschland an der Erarbeitung von Wörterbüchern zusammen.

Vor diesem Hintergrund werden in diesem Beitrag verschiedene Wörterbuchprojekte am Institut für Deutsche Sprache (IDS) als Beispiele für Tendenzen in der akademischen Lexikographie des Deutschen vorgestellt. Zu diesen Tendenzen zählen Korpusgestütztheit, innovative Präsentation lexikographischer Angaben, Einbezug des Wörterbuchbenutzers und Wörterbuchbenutzungsforschung. Der Schwerpunkt wird dabei auf *elexiko* liegen, einem hypertextuellen Informationssystem bzw. Wörterbuch zur deutschen Gegenwartssprache, das sich noch im Aufbau befindet. *Elexiko* wird innerhalb des Wörterbuchportals OWID ("Online-Wortschatz-Informationssystem Deutsch") des IDS Mannheim publiziert. Daneben werden einige weitere lexikographische Projekte vorgestellt, z.B. der Berlin-Brandenburgischen Akademie der Wissenschaften. Auf diese Weise soll deutlich werden, wie deutschsprachige Wörterbuchprojekte den gegenwärtigen lexikographischen Herausforderungen begegnen.

1. Kurzer Überblick über deutschsprachige (Online-)Wörterbücher

Die sehr reiche lexikographische Tradition in Deutschland zeigt sich an der großen Zahl verschiedener Wörterbuchtypen für das Deutsche.[1] So gibt es Wörterbücher zu allen deutschen Dialekten in Deutschland, Österreich und der Schweiz und anderen deutschsprachigen Regionen, Wörterbücher zu allen historischen Varietäten des Deutschen oder Wörterbücher zu Spezialwortschätzen wie z.B. Neologismen oder Fremdwörter und vieles mehr. Fremdwörterbücher und Rechtschreibwörterbücher (hier insbesondere aus dem Duden-Verlag) nehmen dabei einen besonderen Rang ein, indem sie in der allgemeinen Öffentlichkeit sehr bekannt sind und viel konsultiert werden. Nach wie vor häufig benutzt wird auch das umfängliche historische "Deutsche Wörterbuch" von Jacob und Wilhelm Grimm, das bereits seit einiger Zeit online zur Verfügung steht.[2]

Deutsche Wörterbücher werden in gedruckter Form, als CD-ROM, im Internet, aber auch z.B. für die Nutzung in Smartphones publiziert. Zwar erscheinen weiterhin neue Printausgaben z.B. von Rechtschreib- und Lernerwörterbüchern oder zweisprachigen Wörterbüchern, doch sind die neuesten monolingualen, allgemeinsprachigen Wörterbücher des Deutschen Onlineangebote. Die letzten Auflagen der mehrbändigen allgemeinsprachigen deutschen Bedeutungswörterbücher im Druck stammen aus den 80er bzw. 90er Jahren des vorigen Jahrhunderts ("Wörterbuch der deutschen Gegenwartssprache" in 6 Bänden, letzte Auflage 1980-1982, und "Duden – Das große Wörterbuch der deutschen Sprache" in 10 Bänden, letzte Auflage 1999). Neueren Datums sind einige deutschsprachige gedruckte Lernerwörterbücher ("Hueber-Duden Wörterbuch Deutsch als Fremdsprache" 2007, "Langenscheidt Großwörterbuch Deutsch als Fremdsprache" 2010 und "PONS Großwörterbuch Deutsch als Fremdsprache" 2011).

Im Internet publizieren auch zwei Wörterbuchverlage Onlinewörterbücher, und zwar der PONS-Verlag unter der Webadresse www.pons.eu sowie der Dudenverlag unter www.duden.de. Bei PONS finden sich ein Rechtschreibwörterbuch und (neben einigen zweisprachigen Wörterbüchern mit Deutsch als einer der Sprachen) ein Lernerwörterbuch für Deutsch. Bei Duden online kann man in einem aus verschiedenen gedruckten Duden-Wörterbüchern zusammengestellten Angebot nachschlagen, das einen inhaltlichen Schwerpunkt auf Rechtschreibung, Bedeutungsangaben und Sinnrelationen (insbesondere Synonyme) legt.

An der Berlin-Brandenburgischen Akademie der Wissenschaften wird unter der Webadresse www.dwds.de eine retrodigitalisierte und inzwischen weiterentwickelte Version des "Wörterbuchs der deutschen Gegenwartssprache" angeboten.[3] Diese steht aber nicht

---

1 Vgl. zu deutschsprachigen Beispielen für die einzelnen Wörterbuchtypen Schlaefer (2009, 106ff.), zur Typologie der Wörterbücher vgl. auch Engelberg/Lemnitzer (2009, 24ff.). Einen Überblick über deutsche Wörterbücher in Geschichte und Gegenwart gibt außerdem Haß (2001).

2 Erreichbar unter der Webadresse www.woerterbuchnetz.de/DWB/ (Stand: 04.02.2013). Auf den Projektseiten des verantwortlichen Trierer Kompetenzzentrums für elektronische Erschließungs- und Publikationsverfahren in den Geisteswissenschaften finden sich zahlreiche Literaturhinweise zur Entstehung der digitalen Fassung des "Deutschen Wörterbuches" (vgl. http://kompetenzzentrum.uni-trier.de/de/publikationen/, Stand: 04.02.2013).

3 Zum Projekt DWDS vgl. Klein/Geyken (2010). Auf den Internetseiten des Projektes finden sich zahlreiche Literaturhinweise zur Erarbeitung der einzelnen Komponenten im DWDS (vgl. www.dwds.de/veroeffentlichungen/, Stand: 04.02.2013).

alleine, sondern wird ergänzt durch das digitalisierte "Etymologische Wörterbuch des Deutschen" in 3 Bänden (1989), den Zugriff auf die digitale Fassung des "Deutschen Wörterbuchs" von Jacob und Wilhelm Grimm, einen kollaborativ erarbeiteten Thesaurus ("OpenThesaurus"), Belege aus dem sogenannten DWDS-Kernkorpus und den sogenannten Wortprofilen (= Angaben zu Kollokationen). Das DWDS ("Digitales Wörterbuch der deutschen Sprache") ist damit weniger ein einzelnes Wörterbuch, sondern ein "Wortauskunftsystem zur deutschen Sprache in Geschichte und Gegenwart", in dem "über 410.000 lexikographisch geprüfte Einträge aus 5 Wörterbuchquellen", "1,8 Milliarden Korpusbelege aus 15 Korpora" und "statistische Wortprofile und Wortverlaufskurven" vereint sind (www.dwds.de, Stand: 04.02.2013).

Schließlich ist als monolinguales Onlinewörterbuch zur deutschen Standardsprache der Gegenwart das Wörterbuch *elexiko* (kurz für: elektronisches, lexikalisch-lexikologisches und korpusbasiertes Informationssystem) zu nennen.[4] Dieses Wörterbuch zum Gegenwartsdeutschen bildet einen Teil des Wörterbuchportals OWID[5] und verfügt über eine Wortliste mit zirka 300.000 Einträgen. Die *elexiko*-Wörterbuchartikel werden mithilfe der korpuslinguistischen und statistischen Methoden erarbeitet, die COSMAS II und die Kookkurrenzdatenbank CCDB bieten.[6] Dabei stützen sich die Projektmitarbeiter auf das regelmäßig aktualisierte *elexiko*-Korpus mit seinen rund 2,8 Milliarden Textwörtern aus deutschen, österreichischen sowie Schweizer Zeitungs- und Zeitschriftentexten. Bei der Konzipierung und für die Erarbeitung des Wörterbuches wurden und werden verschiedene linguistische, metalexikographische und korpuslinguistische Ideen und Methoden berücksichtigt und angewandt. Damit stellt sich *elexiko* als wissenschaftliches Wörterbuch dar.

Im Gegensatz zu vielen Printwörterbüchern wird *elexiko* nicht von A bis Z ausgebaut, sondern modular.[7] Kriterien zur Definition solcher Module können z.B. die Wortart, bestimmte Buchstabenstrecken, eine vergleichbare Frequenz, Zugehörigkeit zu Wortfeldern oder Wortfamilien sein. Derzeit werden die Stichwörter im Modul "Lexikon zum öffentlichen Sprachgebrauch", das aufgrund einer bestimmen Frequenz im *elexiko*-Korpus definiert wurde, in einer sehr umfangreichen Artikelstruktur mit komplexen Informationen versehen. Der so definierte Wortschatzausschnitt enthält die Wörter aus den zentralen politischen und gesellschaftlichen Diskursen, wie sie im *elexiko*-Korpus präsent sind. Hier wird der allgemein geläufige Wortschatz der öffentlichen Diskussion um politische und gesellschaftliche Themen sehr differenziert und sprachreflektierend dargestellt. Die einzelnen Artikel zu diesen Stichwörtern enthalten Angaben zur Bedeu-

---

[4] Zur ursprünglichen theoretischen Konzeption von *elexiko* vgl. generell Haß (2005a). Die praktische Umsetzung wird in Klosa (2011a) dargestellt. Einen kurzen Einblick in das Projekt bieten auch die Internetseiten unter www.owid.de/wb/elexiko/start.html (Stand: 04.02.2013). An diesen drei Stellen werden auch einzelne Aspekte wie die Stichwortliste oder das *elexiko*-Korpus näher behandelt.

[5] Details zur Konzeption und Entwicklung von OWID finden sich in Müller-Spitzer (2007), Engelberg/Klosa/Müller-Spitzer (2009) und Müller-Spitzer (2010) sowie auf den Internetseiten des Projekts unter www.owid.de (Stand: 04.02.2013).

[6] Näheres zu COSMAS II und zur CCDB (Belica 2001-2007) zeigen die jeweiligen Internetseiten der Projekte unter https://cosmas2.ids-mannheim.de/cosmas2-web/ bzw. http://corpora.ids-mannheim.de/ccdb/ (beide Stand: 04.02.2013).

[7] Einzelheiten zum modularen Ausbau und zum Modul "Lexikon zum öffentlichen Sprachgebrauch" finden sich in Klosa (2011b).

tung, Verwendung, Grammatik, Rechtschreibung und Wortbildung, außerdem gibt es zu einigen Lemmata gesprochensprachliche Belege, welche die Möglichkeit bieten, Aussprache und Betonung des Stichwortes im Satzzusammenhang zu hören, und Illustrationen, welche in einer oder mehreren Lesarten eines Stichwortes die Bedeutungserläuterung begleiten.

2. Einige Tendenzen in der (wissenschaftlichen) Lexikographie des Deutschen

2.1 Korpusgestütztheit

Dass immer mehr deutschsprachige Wörterbücher auf der Auswertung von umfangreichen, elektronischen Textkorpora beruhen, ist eine Entwicklung der letzten zehn bis fünfzehn Jahre.[8] In den Wörterbüchern hinterlässt dies verschiedene Spuren, z.B. mit der Integration neuartiger Angaben wie Angaben zur absoluten (vgl. Abbildung 1) oder relativen (vgl. Abbildung 2 und Abbildung 3) Frequenz des Stichwortes oder zur Entwicklung der Stichwortfrequenz über eine gewisse Zeitspanne hinweg (vgl. Abbildung 4).

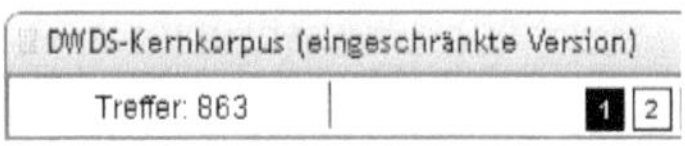

Abb. 1: Angabe der absoluten Häufigkeit zum Suchwort *Konferenz* in www.dwds.de (Stand: 04.02.2013)

Die Angabe zur absoluten Frequenz wie am Beispiel des DWDS-Kernkorpus ist dann möglich, wenn sich das Korpus nicht mehr verändert. Allerdings lässt sich so nur im Vergleich zu anderen Rechercheergebnissen im Wörterbuch bzw. im Korpus einschätzen, ob das ursprünglich gesuchte Stichwort relativ gesehen eher häufig oder eher weniger frequent ist. Solch eine Einschätzung ist dann möglich, wenn Stichwörter bestimmten Häufigkeitsklassen zugeordnet werden, sodass die Frequenzangaben relativ zueinander erfolgen. Im Duden-Angebot www.duden.de werden fünf Häufigkeitsklassen unterschieden; die in Abbildung 2 gezeigte Häufigkeitsklasse wird beispielsweise definiert als die Menge der Wörter, die "zu den 10.000 häufigsten Wörtern im Dudenkorpus mit Ausnahme der Top 1.000 gehören" (www.duden.de/hilfe/haeufigkeit, Stand: 04.02.2013).

Abb. 2: Angabe einer Häufigkeitsklasse zu *Konferenz* in www.duden.de (Stand: 04.02.2013)

Im Onlinewörterbuch *elexiko* werden insgesamt 13 Frequenzschichten unterschieden.[9] Neben der Zuordnung zu einer Frequenzschicht wird außerdem angegeben, in wie vielen verschiedenen Quellen und aus wie vielen verschiedenen Jahrgängen das Wort im

[8] Zu den Vor- und Nachteilen korpusgestützter Lexikographie vgl. einführend Klosa (2007).
[9] Vgl. genauer Klosa (2011c, 157ff.).

elexiko-Korpus belegt ist (Stand 2009), damit die Nutzer einen Eindruck davon bekommen können, wie verbreitet das Wort ist. Da sich das *elexiko*-Korpus auch weiterhin verändern wird, müssen diese Werte nach einer gewissen Zeit im Korpus überprüft und gegebenenfalls in den Wortartikeln aktualisiert werden.

Verteilung

Dieses Stichwort gehört im *elexiko*-Korpus der Frequenzschicht IX (10.001-50.000 mal belegt) an. Es ist in 17 verschiedenen Zeitungen oder Zeitschriften aus 23 Jahrgängen belegt.

Abb. 3: Angabe der Zugehörigkeit von *Konferenz* zu einer Frequenzschicht in www.elexiko.de (Stand: 04.02.2013)

Schließlich können Zeitverlaufsgraphiken illustrieren, "wie sich in den IDS-Textkorpora [...] das Aufkommen einer neuen Zeichenkette sowie ihr Gebrauch über die Jahre hinweg spiegelt" (www.ids-mannheim.de/kl/neoplots/anmerkungen.html, Stand: 04.02.2013). Besonders interessant ist dies natürlich für Neologismen, doch können auch bei schon länger im deutschen Wortschatz etablierten Lexemen solche Verläufe bei vergleichbarer Korpusgröße über die Zeit hinweg vor Augen führen, ob das Lexem im Gebrauch bestimmten Schwankungen unterworfen ist.

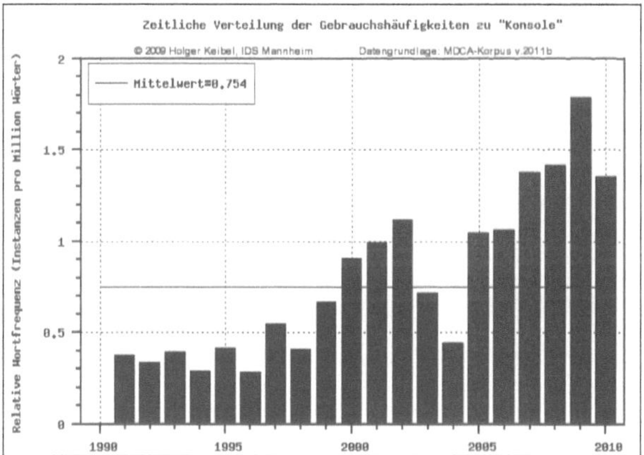

Abb. 4: Zeitverlaufsgraphik zum Stichwort *Konsole* im "Neologismenwörterbuch" in www.owid.de (Stand: 04.02.2013)

Dass elektronische Textkorpora die Basis für neuartige deutsche Wörterbücher sind, zeigt sich auch daran, dass aus ihnen entweder KWICs (= key word in context) oder ganze Belege in das Wörterbuch integriert werden. Im "Digitalen Wörterbuch der deutschen Sprache" (DWDS) ermöglichen KWIC-Zeilen den Zugriff auf alle Korpustreffer (vgl. Abbildung 5). Mithilfe dieser kleinen Textausschnitte mit dem Suchwort jeweils mittig angeordnet wird ein erster Eindruck von Bedeutung und Verwendung des gesuchten Wortes vermittelt. Klickt man in dieser Ansicht auf eine der Zeilen, kann man einen größeren Kontext und die entsprechenden bibliographischen Angaben anzeigen lassen.

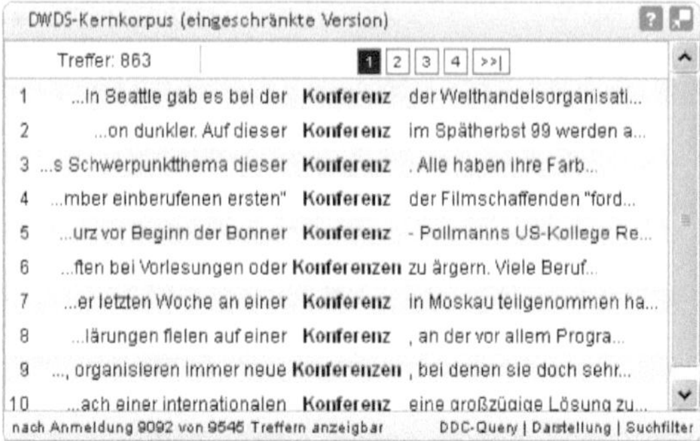

DWDS-Kernkorpus (eingeschränkte Version)

Treffer: 863 | 1 2 3 4 >>|

1	...In Seattle gab es bei der	**Konferenz**	der Welthandelsorganisati...
2	...on dunkler. Auf dieser	**Konferenz**	im Spätherbst 99 werden a...
3	...s Schwerpunktthema dieser	**Konferenz**	. Alle haben ihre Farb...
4	...mber einberufenen ersten"	**Konferenz**	der Filmschaffenden "ford...
5	...urz vor Beginn der Bonner	**Konferenz**	- Pollmanns US-Kollege Re...
6	...ften bei Vorlesungen oder	**Konferenzen**	zu ärgern. Viele Beruf...
7	...er letzten Woche an einer	**Konferenz**	in Moskau teilgenommen ha...
8	...lärungen fielen auf einer	**Konferenz**	, an der vor allem Progra...
9	..., organisieren immer neue	**Konferenzen**	, bei denen sie doch sehr...
10	...ach einer internationalen	**Konferenz**	eine großzügige Lösung zu...

nach Anmeldung 9092 von 9545 Treffern anzeigbar — DDC-Query | Darstellung | Suchfilter

Abb. 5: KWIC-Zeilen für das Suchwort *Konferenz* in www.dwds.de (Stand: 04.02.2013)

Andere Wörterbücher, wie z.B. *elexiko*, bieten in den Artikelansichten direkt längere Korpusbelege an. Dies stellt gegenüber der Belegungspraxis in traditionellen Belegwörterbüchern dann eine Neuerung dar, wenn solche Belege nicht durch Lexikographen, sondern mithilfe automatischer Verfahren ermittelt sind. In *elexiko* werden beispielsweise zu den noch nicht redaktionell bearbeiteten Stichwörtern drei Belege automatisch, wenn auch nicht nach rein statistischen Zufallskriterien aus dem Korpus ermittelt (vgl. die folgenden Belege zum Stichwort *Konferenz* in www.elexiko.de[10]).

Für die Rechtschreibung sind die Kultusminister der Bundesländer zuständig, für das "Amtsdeutsch", also die amtliche Schriftsprache, der Bundesinnenminister und die Innenminister der Länder. Diese beiden Gremien waren es auch, die den Experten den Auftrag zu Reformvorschlägen gegeben hatten, und diese beiden Gremien treffen auch die gültige Entscheidung für Deutschland. Peter Fränz von der Kultusministerkonferenz wundert sich über voreilige Verlage: "Die politische Ebene hat ja in Deutschland noch gar nicht entschieden. Nur die Fachbeamten haben sich auf der Wiener **Konferenz** geeinigt. Die politische Ebene muß erst zustimmen." (P95/SEP.31853 Die Presse, 14.09.1995, Ressort: Ausland/Seite Drei; Die Katastrofe wird vertagt)

Um sich Tipps von Experten zu holen, hatten die Organisatoren zum ersten Teil der Veranstaltung Vertreter zweier Top-Betriebe eingeladen, die ihre Strategien zum Erfolg aufzeigten: Erwin Horvath vom größten heimischen Milchverarbeiter "Berglandmilch" demonstrierte, wie mit Qualitätsmanagement der Weg zur Spitze erreicht wurde. Helmut Singer vom gerade an die Börse gehenden Mikroelektronik-Hersteller "Infineon" präsentierte die Leitprinzipien seiner Firmenphilosophie. "Da kann man sich als kleiner Betrieb einiges abschauen", waren viele Zuhörer überzeugt. Im zweiten Teil der **Konferenz** wurde einigen heimischen Jungunternehmen die Möglichkeit geboten, sich dem interessierten Fachpublikum vorzustellen. Ihr Auftritt fand ebenso großes Echo wie die Präsentation zweier wirtschaftspolitischer Maßnahmen, mit denen der oststeirischen Wirtschaft auf die Sprünge geholfen werden soll. (K00/MAR.18181 Kleine Zeitung, 05.03.2000, Ressort: Feldbach; Der Weg an die Spitze)

Steven Soderberghs Roman-Verfilmung "The Good German" ist bei der Berlinale nur zurückhaltend aufgenommen worden. Im tröpfelnden Beifall waren sogar einige Buh-Rufe zu hören. Der für seine formale Eigenwilligkeit bekannte Regisseur blickt zurück in das Berlin des Jahres 1945. Vor dem Hintergrund der Potsdamer **Konferenz** läuft ein Krimi um Nazi-Verbrecher und Nazi-

[10] Wortartikel *Konferenz*: www.owid.de/artikel/57426?module=ctx.all&pos=13 (Stand: 04.02.2013).

Jäger, Love-Story inklusive. In den Hauptrollen treten die Stars Cate Blanchett und George Clooney auf. (HMP07/FEB.01210 Hamburger Morgenpost, 11.02.2007, S. 17; Berlinale »The Good German« mit Clooney kam nicht so gut an)

Gegenüber gedruckten Wörterbüchern können in Onlinewörterbüchern, in denen der zur Verfügung stehende Platz kein Problem darstellt, die Menge an Textbelegen und die Länge der Belege anwachsen. In den im Wörterbuchportal OWID des Instituts für Deutsche Sprache vereinten Onlinewörterbüchern ist dies überall zu beobachten. Im "Sprichwörterbuch" enthält der Eintrag zu *Ende gut, alles gut*[11] beispielsweise insgesamt fünfzehn auch längere Textbelege, die zur Illustrierung der Bedeutungsangabe, der Gebrauchsbesonderheiten, der Formvarianten, der Illustrierung der typischen Verwendung im Text sowie der möglichen Ersetzung von Sprichwortkomponenten (vgl. die folgenden Belege) dienen:

[...] man wird [...] auch die Bundesbank nicht ganz von dem Vorwurf freihalten können, sie habe die abstimmung [...] zumindest nicht erleichtert. Finale **gut, alles gut**? gewiß, diesmal gab es nach einem verworrenen Zwischenakt noch einmal ein schönes Finale. wer garantiert aber, daß beim nächsten Mal nicht wieder ein unwürdiges Hin und Her abermals zum Spott reizt? (BZK/W59.01350 Die Welt, 20.11.1959, S. 9, Ressort: WIRTSCHAFT; Finale)

Peinlich, peinlich – [...] Kleider, Kreditkarten und Schlüssel – alles weg. Auch die Prostituierte [...] war plötzlich verschwunden. Die Türe hatte sie zugesperrt. Der Rechtsprofessor muss sich sehr nackt gefühlt haben [...] Er verschanzte sich auf dem Klo und alarmierte die Polizei. Befreiung **gut, alles gut**? Keineswegs. Es kam noch viel peinlicher. Die Prostitutierte wurde zwar [...] verurteilt, weil aber Gerichtsverfahren öffentlich sind, war der Name des Freiers bald Allgemeinwissen. Nicht nur Rechtsprofessor war er, sondern auch Anwalt, Mitglied der Bankenkommission und Ehemann einer [...] Politikerin. (E97/DEZ.31504 Zürcher Tagesanzeiger, 31.12.1997, S. 13, Ressort: Zürich und Region; Peinlich, peinlich – ein andere Rückblick (Serie))

Sponsor **gut, alles gut**? Bremens Unternehmer und die Kulturszene bewegen sich aufeinander zu: Der Flirt wird immer intensiver. "Die Unternehmen sind williger geworden." Manuela Rousseau, PR-Chefin der Beiersdorf AG, sieht Kultursponsoring auf dem Weg in eine verheißungsvolle Zukunft. (T01/MAI.25878 die tageszeitung, 31.05.2001, S. 29, Ressort: Kultur; Sponsor gut, alles gut?)

Ein Angabetyp, bei dem sich die Korpusgestütztheit in aktuellen Wörterbüchern des Deutschen deutlich zeigt, sind auch die Informationen zu Kollokationen. In Onlinewörterbüchern sind nicht nur teilweise deutlich mehr Kollokationen zu einem Stichwort in einer speziellen Lesart aufgeführt, als in gedruckten Wörterbüchern möglich ist, sondern für das Medium Internet werden auch neue Darstellungsmöglichkeiten erprobt (vgl. auch Abschnitt 2.2). In Printwörterbüchern stehen Kollokatoren zu einem Stichwort häufig durch Kommata getrennt hintereinander, eine Ordnung der Kollokatoren nach bestimmten inhaltlichen Kategorien ist nur bedingt erkennbar. In Onlinewörterbüchern werden die Kollokatoren z.B. in einer Wortwolke angezeigt. Bei www.duden.de kann man die Kollokatoren zusätzlich nach ihrer Wortart getrennt anzeigen lassen (vgl. Abbildung 6); diese Angaben werden maschinell auf der Basis statistischer Berechnungen erzeugt. Mit der Wortwolke soll "der Grad der Typizität zwischen dem (schwarzen) Stichwort und den (roten) Kontextwörtern [veranschaulicht werden]. Größer dargestellte Kontextwörter gehen dabei eine typischere Verbindung mit dem Stichwort ein als Wörter in kleinerer Schriftgröße." (www.duden.de/hilfe/typische-verbindungen, Stand: 04.02.2013).

[11] Wortartikel *Ende gut, alles gut*: www.owid.de/artikel/401702 (Stand: 04.02.2013).

Abb. 6: Adjektivische Kollokatoren zu *Konferenz* in www.duden.de (Stand: 04.02.2013)

Wesentlich differenziertere Darstellungs- und damit auch Rezeptionsmöglichkeiten der Kollokatoren bietet das "Digitale Wörterbuch der deutschen Sprache", indem die (automatisch ermittelten) Kollokatoren nach ihrer syntaktischen Funktion angezeigt werden können und die Menge der anzuzeigenden Kollokatoren individuell eingestellt werden kann (vgl. Abbildung 7). In dieser Präsentation kann man außerdem durch Klicken auf eines der Wörter in der Wortwolke die Textbelege öffnen, in denen das Stichwort mit dem ausgewählten Kollokator enthalten ist.

Abb. 7: Kollokatoren zu *Konferenz* im Wortprofil von www.dwds.de (Stand: 04.02.2013)

Während in diesen beiden Beispielen ausschließlich mithilfe statistischer Korpusmethoden ermittelte Kollokationen in Wörterbücher bzw. Wortinformationssysteme aufgenommen werden, werden diese Kollokationskandidaten im Wörterbuch *elexiko* redaktionell geprüft und in strukturierter Form in die Wortartikel aufgenommen.[12] So können die Wörterbuchbenutzer erfahren, mit welchen Wörtern die verschiedenen semantischen Rollen des Stichwortes in einer bestimmten Lesart realisiert werden. Alle Kollokatoren sind verteilt auf mehrere Sets aus Fragen und darauf antwortenden Wörtern aufgelistet, die zusammen ein Bild von der semantischen Umgebung des Stichwortes vermitteln. Bei-

[12] Vgl. Klosa/Storjohann (2011) sowie Haß (2005b).

spielsweise finden sich unter der Frage "Wie ist eine Krise?" im Stichwort *Krise* (Lesart 'kritische Situation')[13] die Adjektive *aktuell*, *akut*, *anhaltend*, *ernst*, *ernsthaft*, *existenzbedrohend* usw., unter der Frage "Was macht jemand oder etwas mit einer Krise?" solche Verben wie *abwenden*, *auslösen*, *beenden*, *durchleben*, *meistern* usw. und unter der Frage "Was gibt es in einer Krise?" solche Substantive wie *Anzeichen*, *Beginn*, *Höhepunkt*, *Lösung*, *Symptom* usw. Diese und weitere Frage-Antwort-Sets werden in *elexiko* in einer eigenen Wörterbuchrubrik "Kollokationen" untereinander aufgelistet (vgl. Abbildung 8).

Abb. 8: Kollokationen zu *Krise* (Lesart 'kritische Situation') in www.elexiko.de (Stand: 04.02.2013)

Weitere Angaben, bei denen sich eine korpusgestützte Erarbeitung eines Wörterbuches deutlich zeigt, sind etwa die Angaben zu typischen Konstruktionen, die auf Basis entsprechender Korpusauswertungen genauer, umfänglicher und unter Berücksichtigung variierender Elemente in Wortartikel eines Onlinewörterbuches integriert werden können.[14] Schließlich ist bei allen sprachlichen Phänomenen, die Varianz zeigen (z.B. Schreibung eines Stichwortes, Flexionsformen eines Stichwortes), bei korpusgestützter Erarbeitung nicht nur zu überprüfen, welche Schreibungen oder Wortformen tatsächlich vorkommen, sondern auch in welcher (absoluten und/oder relativen) Häufigkeit. Moderne Wörterbücher des Gegenwartsdeutschen können insofern eher einen deskriptiven als einen präskriptiven Ansatz verfolgen.[15]

[13] Wortartikel *Krise*: www.owid.de/artikel/211254/kritische%20Situation?module=elex_b (Stand: 04.02.2013).
[14] Zu den typischen Konstruktionen z.B. in *elexiko* vgl. Möhrs (2011).
[15] Als Beispiel hierfür kann z.B. die korpusgestützte Beschreibung von grammatischer Varianz in *elexiko* dienen, vgl. Klosa (2005, 281ff.).

2.2 Innovative Präsentation lexikographischer Angaben

Das Layout deutschsprachiger Printwörterbücher hat sich in den vergangenen 20 Jahren vor allem durch Einsatz einer zweiten Farbe (z.B. Druck der Stichwörter in Blau, Hervorhebung der durch die Orthographiereform geänderten Schreibweisen durch Rot[16]) und durch das Einbringen von Informationskästchen in die Wörterbuchspalten verändert. Insbesondere in Lernerwörterbüchern ist auch der Einsatz von Illustrationen zu beobachten.[17] Generell orientiert sich das Erscheinungsbild der deutschen Printwörterbücher aber nach wie vor an den Wörterbuchtraditionen (meist zweispaltiger Satz, starke Textkomprimierung, Einsatz verschiedener Satztypen zur Auszeichnung bestimmter Inhalte usw.). In elektronischen Wörterbüchern generell, insbesondere aber auch in Onlinewörterbüchern stehen dem viele neue Möglichkeiten der Präsentation der lexikographischen Angaben gegenüber.

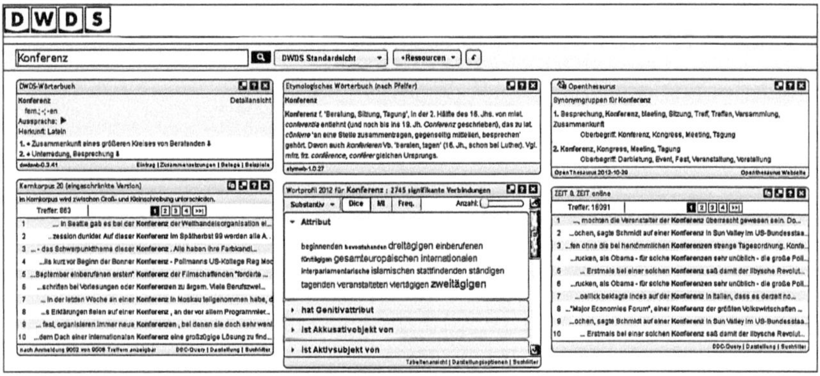

Abb. 9: Verteilung der lexikographischen Information auf Panels in www.dwds.de (Stand: 04.02.2013)

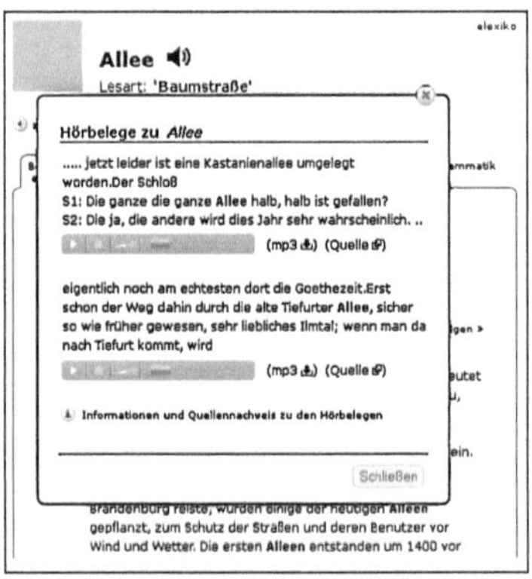

Abb. 10: Pop-up-Fenster mit Hörbelegen zum Stichwort *Allee* (Lesart 'Baumstraße') in www.elexiko.de (Stand: 04.02.2013)

---

16 Wie z.B. in "Hueber-Duden Wörterbuch Deutsch als Fremdsprache" bzw. in "Duden – Die deutsche Rechtschreibung".

17 Vgl. z.B. "Hueber-Duden Wörterbuch Deutsch als Fremdsprache".

Solche Wörterbücher erscheinen nicht nur zweifarbig, sondern durchgehend bunt,[18] und die lexikographische Information wird auf sogenannte Panels (vgl. Abbildung 9), auf Pop-up-Fenster (vgl. Abbildung 10) oder verschiedene Bildschirmansichten verteilt (vgl. die einzeln anklickbaren Wörterbuchrubriken in *elexiko* wie in Abbildung 8 für das Stichwort *Krise*, Lesart 'kritische Situation', gezeigt).

Häufig wird die lexikographische Information auch durch Überschriften gegliedert, sodass die Wörterbuchbenutzer leicht entscheiden können, wo die gesuchte Information zu finden ist (vgl. den Bildschirmausschnitt aus www.duden.de in Abbildung 11). Onlinewörterbücher nutzen außerdem, wie in Abschnitt 2.1 erwähnt, verschiedene Anordnungsmöglichkeiten für die lexikographischen Angaben, z.B. Listen und Wortgruppen (vgl. Abbildung 8) oder Wortwolken (vgl. Abbildung 6 und Abbildung 7).[19]

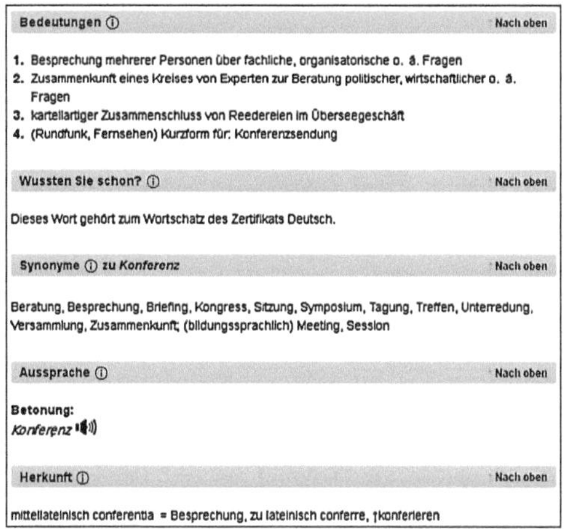
Bedeutungen ⓘ Nach oben

1. Besprechung mehrerer Personen über fachliche, organisatorische o. ä. Fragen
2. Zusammenkunft eines Kreises von Experten zur Beratung politischer, wirtschaftlicher o. ä. Fragen
3. kartellartiger Zusammenschluss von Reedereien im Überseegeschäft
4. (Rundfunk, Fernsehen) Kurzform für: Konferenzsendung

Wussten Sie schon? ⓘ Nach oben

Dieses Wort gehört zum Wortschatz des Zertifikats Deutsch.

Synonyme ⓘ **zu *Konferenz*** Nach oben

Beratung, Besprechung, Briefing, Kongress, Sitzung, Symposium, Tagung, Treffen, Unterredung, Versammlung, Zusammenkunft; (bildungssprachlich) Meeting, Session

Aussprache ⓘ Nach oben

Betonung:
Konferenz

Herkunft ⓘ Nach oben

mittellateinisch conferentia = Besprechung, zu lateinisch conferre, ↑konferieren

Abb. 11: Ausschnitt aus den lexikographischen Angaben zu *Konferenz* in www.duden.de (Stand: 04.02.2013)

Außerdem werden Hyperlinks eingesetzt, um zwischen Wörterbucheinträgen zu verweisen, aber auch, um auf andere Onlineangebote zu verlinken, z.B. auf andere Wörterbücher, Onlinegrammatiken oder Enzyklopädien. Nicht zuletzt ist auf einen Einsatz von multimedialen Elementen (Audiodateien, Illustrationen, Videos) hinzuweisen.[20] In *elexiko* lassen sich z.B. gesprochensprachliche Belege durch Klicken auf ein Lautsprechersymbol öffnen und anhören, die aus der "Datenbank Gesprochenes Deutsch" im "Archiv für Gesprochenes Deutsch"[21] des Instituts für Deutsche Sprache stammen. Diese Hörbelege bieten neben der abspielbaren Tondatei mit fünf Sekunden Kontext vor und fünf

[18] In den Abbildungen in diesem Beitrag kann die Farbigkeit aufgrund der technischen Bedingungen für den Druck nur in Schwarz-Weiß wiedergegeben werden.

[19] Zu einer Bewertung der verschiedenen Anordnungsmöglichkeiten durch potentielle Wörterbuchbenutzer vgl. die Ergebnisse einer Benutzungsstudie zu *elexiko* in Klosa/Koplenig/Töpel (2011, 22ff.).

[20] In OBELEX^dict, einer Online-Bibliographie zur elektronischen Lexikographie/Wörterbücher am IDS Mannheim, kann gezielt nach Internetwörterbüchern, die auditive Angaben, Videos und/oder Illustrationen enthalten, gesucht werden (unter www.owid.de/obelex/dict, Stand: 04.02.2013).

[21] Vgl. http://agd.ids-mannheim.de/datenbanken.shtml (Stand: 04.02.2013).

Sekunden Kontext nach dem Stichwort auch den gehörten Ausschnitt in Schriftform (vgl. Abbildung 10). Im Duden-Onlineangebot und im “Digitalen Wörterbuch der deutschen Sprache” wird dagegen eine normgerechte, isolierte Aussprache (seltener werden auch mehrere Aussprachevarianten) eines Stichwortes in einer Tondatei präsentiert. Illustrationen können beispielsweise begleitend zur Bedeutungserläuterung angezeigt werden und so die Wortbedeutung zu verdeutlichen helfen. In *elexiko* vermitteln in einigen Lesarten einzelner Stichwörter ein bis drei Fotos einen Eindruck davon, in welcher konkreten Form das mit dem Stichwort Bezeichnete vorliegen kann (vgl. Abbildung 12).

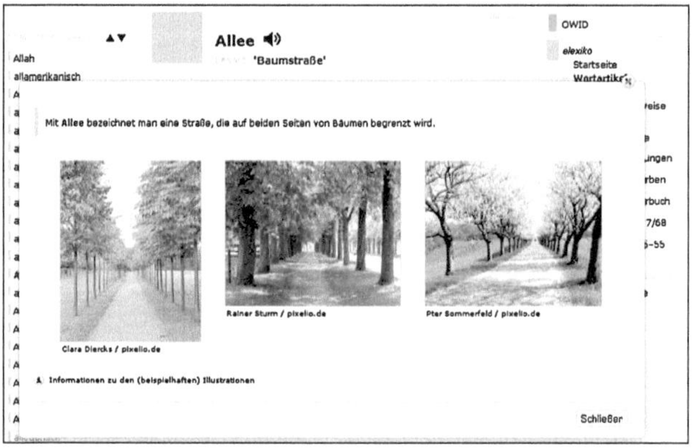

Abb. 12: Illustrationen zum Stichwort *Allee* (Lesart ‘Baumstraße’) in www.elexiko.de (Stand: 04.02.2013)

Beruht ein Onlinewörterbuch auf älteren Printwörterbüchern, kann sich die Darstellung auch noch an diesen orientieren. Am Beispiel des im “Digitalen Wörterbuch der deutschen Sprache” enthaltenen “Etymologischen Wörterbuchs des Deutschen” zeigt sich dies (vgl. den noch verdichteten, als Fließtext angeordneten Eintrag zu *Konferenz* unter “Etymologisches Wörterbuch” in Abbildung 13).

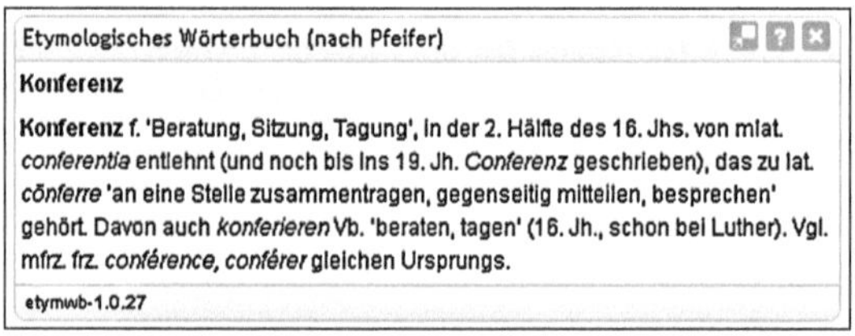
Etymologisches Wörterbuch (nach Pfeifer)

Konferenz

Konferenz f. 'Beratung, Sitzung, Tagung', in der 2. Hälfte des 16. Jhs. von mlat. *conferentia* entlehnt (und noch bis ins 19. Jh. *Conferenz* geschrieben), das zu lat. *cōnferre* 'an eine Stelle zusammentragen, gegenseitig mitteilen, besprechen' gehört. Davon auch *konferieren* Vb. 'beraten, tagen' (16. Jh., schon bei Luther). Vgl. mfrz. frz. *conférence, conférer* gleichen Ursprungs.

etymwb-1.0.27

Abb. 13: Eintrag zu *Konferenz* im Etymologischen Wörterbuch in www.dwds.de (Stand: 04.02.2013)

Zugleich verdeutlicht die Präsentation des für das Angebot unter www.dwds.de aufbereiteten “Wörterbuchs der deutschen Gegenwartssprache”, dass ein für den Druck stark komprimierter Wörterbuchtext für die elektronische Präsentation auch aufgelockert und somit optimiert werden kann (vgl. den mithilfe von Überschriften, klickbaren Elementen und umrahmten Textblöcken strukturieren Eintrag zu *Konferenz* unter “DWDS-Wörterbuch” in Abbildung 14).

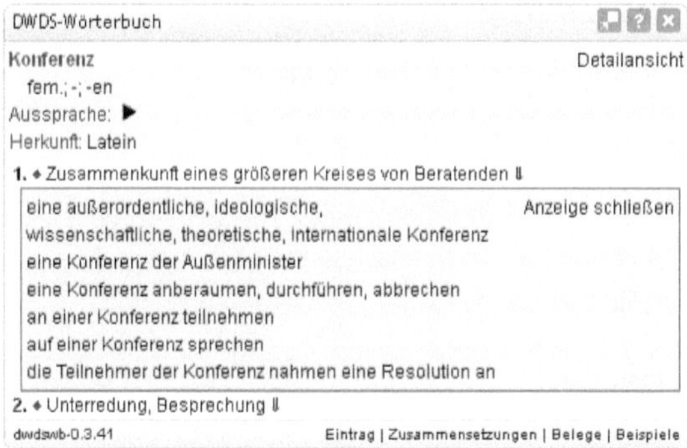

Abb. 14: Eintrag zu *Konferenz* im "DWDS-Wörterbuch" in www.dwds.de (Stand: 04.02.2013)

Generell ist festzuhalten, dass die gegenwartssprachlichen Onlinewörterbücher des Deutschen mit vielerlei Darstellungsmöglichkeiten operieren. Während sich manches bereits als Standard durchgesetzt zu haben scheint (z.B. ist in Onlinewörterbüchern häufig die Verwendung eines Lautsprechersymbols zu beobachten, das angeklickt werden muss, damit Tondateien abgehört werden können), sind bestimmte Visualisierungen oder Anordnungen (etwa Wortwolken, Listen) noch nicht auf bestimmte Angabebereiche festgelegt. Es bleibt abzuwarten, ob sich in der weiteren Entwicklung von Onlinewörterbüchern bestimmte Darstellungsformen durchsetzen werden.

2.3 Das Wörterbuch und seine Benutzer

Bei Onlinewörterbüchern des Gegenwartsdeutschen (und nicht nur hier) ist häufig die Tendenz festzustellen, in direkten und somit möglicherweise auch engeren Kontakt mit den Wörterbuchbenutzern zu treten, als dies bei gedruckten Wörterbüchern möglich war. So bietet z.B. die Seite www.duden.de ein Formular, in dem Nutzer ein Wort zur Aufnahme im Onlinewörterbuch vorschlagen können (vgl. Abbildung 15). In der Redaktion werden die Vorschläge gesammelt, gesichtet und dahingehend bewertet, ob sie zu berücksichtigen sind oder nicht. Alle Vorschlagende erhalten per E-Mail eine Rückmeldung dazu, ob ihr Vorschlag umgesetzt werden wird oder nicht (in diesem Fall mit einer Begründung).[22] Bei Wörterbuchverlagen kann dieses Angebot auch als Marketinginstrument verstanden werden, das der Nutzerbindung dient. Akademische Wörterbuchprojekte verzichten bislang eher auf solch eine Möglichkeit der Kontaktaufnahme, bieten aber an, an die Wörterbuchredaktion E-Mails zu senden, z.B. mit Formulierungen wie "Wenn Sie Fragen oder Anregungen haben, wenden Sie sich bitte an: elexiko@ids-mannheim.de" (www.owid.de/wb/elexiko/start.html).

[22] Mündliche Mitteilung von Karin Rautmann (Duden-Verlag Mannheim) im Rahmen eines Vortrags mit dem Titel "Duden online und seine Nutzer" im Symposium "Ihr Beitrag bitte! – Der Nutzerbeitrag im Wörterbuchprozess" beim GAL-Kongress "Wörter – Wissen – Wörterbücher" in Erlangen am 19.09.2012.

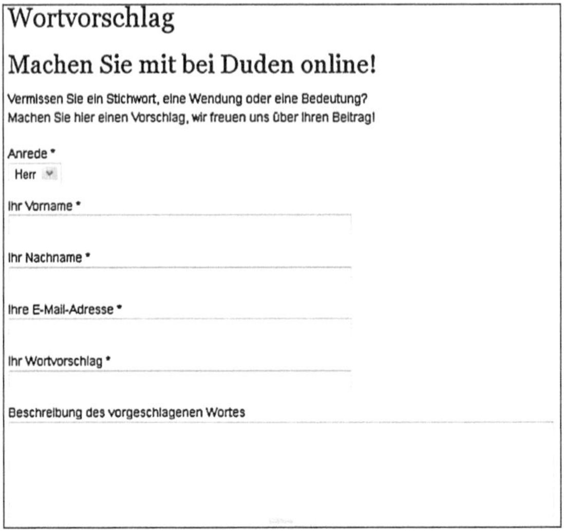

Abb. 15: Formular für Wortvorschläge in www.duden.de (Stand: 04.02.2013)

Eine andere Möglichkeit der Nutzerbindung an das Wörterbuch bieten Social Media wie Facebook und Twitter oder die Möglichkeit, Newsletter an registrierte Nutzer zu versenden. Der Pons-Wörterbuchverlag informiert auf seiner Facebook-Seite beispielsweise über Neuerscheinungen oder twittert entsprechende Meldungen. Aber auch akademische Projekte wie "Das Digitale Wörterbuch der deutschen Sprache" oder das am Trierer Kompetenzzentrum für elektronischen Erschließungs- und Publikationsverfahren in den Geisteswissenschaften/Center for Digital Humanities verantwortete Wörterbuchportal "Wörterbuchnetz" (www.woerterbuchnetz.de, Stand: 04.02.2013) senden Twittermeldungen. Der Dudenverlag informiert regelmäßig zu sprachlichen Themen mithilfe seines Newsletters (www.duden.de/newsletter, Stand: 04.02.2013) und des Duden-Podcast (www.duden.de/podcast, Stand: 04.02.2013). Sinnvoll können die genannten Möglichkeiten im Grunde allerdings nur dann eingesetzt werden, wenn die Bearbeitung der Nutzerrückmeldung (z.B. über Formulare oder E-Mails) in den lexikographischen Prozess eingeplant wird und wenn berücksichtigt wird, dass soziale Medien regelmäßig mit Meldungen bedient werden müssen, weil ansonsten keine Nutzerbindung erzielt werden kann.

Eine weitere Möglichkeit der Kontaktaufnahme mit Benutzern eines Wörterbuches besteht in der Durchführung von Wörterbuchbenutzungsforschung.[23] Während bei Wörterbuchverlagen entsprechende Studien eher zur Klärung der Marktsituation und der Eruierung der Käuferwünsche bezogen auf ein spezielles Wörterbuchprojekt dienen und

[23] Zu Wörterbuchbenutzungsforschung am Institut für Deutsche Sprache Mannheim vgl. die Internetseiten www.benutzungsforschung.de (Stand: 04.02.2013). Bibliographische Angaben zu Benutzungsforschung zu Internetwörterbüchern können in OBELEX^{meta}, der Online-Bibliographie zur elektronischen Lexikographie/Forschungsliteratur am IDS (www.owid.de/bibl/obelex/meta, Stand: 04.02.2013), abgerufen werden.

als Marketinginstrument einzuschätzen sind, haben sie im akademischen Kontext eine zweifache Funktion: Wörterbuchbenutzungsstudien können helfen, bestehende Wörterbücher zu verbessern oder noch in der Planungsphase befindliche Wörterbücher für die avisierte Nutzergruppen zu optimieren. Sie dienen aber auch einem metalexikographischen Zweck, indem die hierdurch gewonnenen Erkenntnisse zu einem besseren theoretischen Verständnis von Wörterbüchern und ihrer Benutzung dienen.

Als Beispiel für eine Wörterbuchbenutzungsstudie wird hier ein kleiner Ausschnitt aus den Ergebnissen einer Onlinefragebogenstudie zum Wörterbuch *elexiko*, die im Jahr 2011 mit 420 Probanden durchgeführt wurde, gezeigt.[24] Ein Ziel dieser Studie war, aufgrund der Ergebnisse die Benutzeroberfläche des Wörterbuches z.B. hinsichtlich der gewählten Terminologie und der Präsentation der lexikographischen Angaben optimieren zu können. Eine Frage in dieser Studie zielte darauf ab herauszufinden, ob Benutzer eines monolingualen Onlinewörterbuches wie *elexiko* bei Listen von Wörtern (z.B. von Kollokatoren oder von Wortbildungsprodukten, d.h., anderen Wörtern, die mit dem Stichwort gebildet sind) eine an der Frequenz orientierte Anordnung oder eine alphabetische Anordnung bevorzugen.

		bevorzugte Sortierung			
Testpersonen		**alphabetisch**	**frequenz-orientiert**	**keine Präferenz**	**Summe**
Gesamt		50,00%	36,62%	13,38%	100,00%
Studierende der Sprachwissenschaften	Ja	62,50%	32,50%	5,00%	100,00%
	Nein	45,10%	38,24%	16,67%	100,00%
Sprachwissenschaftler	Ja	38,00%	44,00%	18,00%	100,00%
	Nein	56,52%	32,61%	10,87%	100,00%

Abb. 16: Die bevorzugte Sortierung der Wortbildungsprodukte für www.elexiko.de

Das Ergebnis zu den Wortbildungsprodukten (vgl. Abbildung 16) zeigt, dass generell eine Tendenz zur alphabetischen Sortierung vorliegt, bei den sprachwissenschaftlich gebildeten Probanden aber eine Tendenz zur frequenzorientierten Sortierung. Aufgrund dieses Ergebnisses wurde für die Präsentation der Wortbildungsprodukte in *elexiko* entschieden, sowohl die alphabetische Sortierung (als Standardansicht) anzubieten als auch die Möglichkeit der frequenzorientierten Anzeige (vgl. Abbildung 17). Interessant ist solch ein Ergebnis auch, weil es deutlich zeigt, dass metalexikographische Forderungen nach einer Präsentation lexikographischer Daten in Onlinewörterbüchern, die sich an verschiedene Nutzerbedürfnisse bzw. Benutzungssituationen anpassen lässt,[25] durchaus berechtigt sind.

---

[24] Vgl. zu der hier vorgestellten Frage sowie den weiteren Ergebnissen der *elexiko*-Benutzungsstudien Klosa/Koplenig/Töpel (2011).

[25] Tarp (2012, 114) spricht in diesem Kontext z.B. von der “individualization of lexicographical e-tools”.

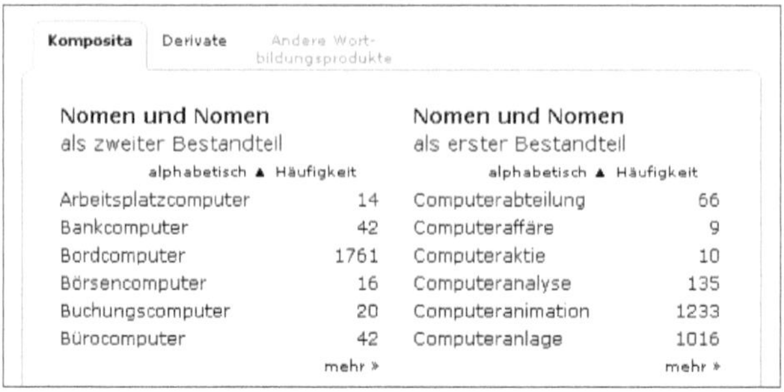

Komposita | Derivate | Andere Wortbildungsprodukte

Nomen und Nomen als zweiter Bestandteil		Nomen und Nomen als erster Bestandteil	
alphabetisch ▲ Häufigkeit		alphabetisch ▲ Häufigkeit	
Arbeitsplatzcomputer	14	Computerabteilung	66
Bankcomputer	42	Computeraffäre	9
Bordcomputer	1761	Computeraktie	10
Börsencomputer	16	Computeranalyse	135
Buchungscomputer	20	Computeranimation	1233
Bürocomputer	42	Computeranlage	1016
	mehr »		mehr »

Abb. 17: Sortierung der Wortbildungsprodukte (hier zum Stichwort *Computer*) in www.elexiko.de (Stand: 04.02.2013)

3. Ausblick

Die gegenwärtige deutschsprachige Wörterbuchlandschaft zeichnet sich (noch) durch große Vielfalt aus. Neben mehreren Wörterbuchverlagen gibt es eine große Zahl akademischer Wörterbuchprojekte und neben gedruckten Wörterbüchern werden zunehmend Wörterbücher im Internet publiziert, deren Design und Benutzbarkeit allerdings noch stark variieren. Der Kontakt mit den Wörterbuchbenutzern hat sich in den letzten Jahren insbesondere im Bereich der Onlinewörterbücher intensiviert, was sich auch daran zeigt, dass es inzwischen erfolgreiche halbkollaborative Internetwörterbücher (z.B. die zweisprachigen LEO-Wörterbücher, www.leo.org,[26] Stand: 04.02.2013) gibt, in denen Wörterbuchredaktion und Nutzer sinnvoll zusammenarbeiten. Ob dagegen völlig von Nutzern geschaffene Nachschlagewerke (z.B. das deutschsprachige Wiktionary, www.wiktionary.org[27]) eine Zukunft haben und von Fachleuten erarbeitete Wörterbücher ablösen werden, ist offen. Derzeit scheint es eher so, als seien die innovativen Entwicklungen im Wörterbuchsektor gerade nicht beim Wiktionary, das sich in großem Umfang bei den lexikographischen Angaben auf ältere Printwörterbücher stützt, zu erwarten. In der Zukunft werden zu solchen Fragen neue Wörterbuchbenutzungsstudien noch stärker an Bedeutung gewinnen. Ein anderes Themenfeld für die Wörterbuchbenutzungsforschung sind außerdem Design und Benutzbarkeit von Onlinewörterbüchern.

Es ist davon auszugehen, dass sich die Wörterbuchlandschaft in Deutschland, die sich durch das Aufkommen elektronischer Wörterbücher und insbesondere Internetwörterbücher in den vergangenen 20 Jahren bereits stark verändert hat, noch weiter wandeln wird. Auf der einen Seite sinken die Verkaufszahlen für Printwörterbücher kontinuierlich, auf der anderen Seite funktionieren Bezahlmodalitäten für deutschsprachige lexikographische Inhalte online offensichtlich (noch) nicht. Zugleich benutzen immer mehr Menschen in Nachschlagesituationen Internetsuchmaschinen wie Google, um orthographische Zweifel zu beseitigen oder Bedeutungserläuterungen zu finden. Es erscheint in diesem Kontext deshalb angeraten, dass die deutschsprachigen Wörterbuchverlage und die akademischen Wörterbuchprojekte sich gemeinsam darum bemühen, dass der

---

[26] Vgl. hierzu genauer Melchior (2012).

[27] Vgl. hierzu genauer Meyer/Gurevych (2012).

außerordentlich hohe lexikographische Standard für das Deutsche erhalten bleibt.[28] Lexikographische Netzwerke wie das vom IDS aus koordinierte und von der Deutschen Forschungsgemeinschaft geförderte "Wissenschaftliche Netzwerk Internetlexikografie" (www.internetlexikografie.de) sind in diesem Kontext wichtige Initiativen.

4. Literaturverzeichnis

4.1 Fachliteratur

Belica, C. (2001-2007): *Kookkurrenzdatenbank CCDB – V3.2. Eine korpuslinguistische Denk- und Experimentierplattform für die Erforschung und theoretische Begründung von systemisch-strukturellen Eigenschaften von Kohäsionsrelationen zwischen den Konstituenten des Sprachgebrauchs.* Mannheim: Institut für Deutsche Sprache.

Engelberg, S./Lemnitzer, L. (2009): *Lexikographie und Wörterbuchbenutzung.* 4., überarbeitete und erweiterte Auflage. Tübingen: Stauffenburg Verlag.

Engelberg, S./Klosa, A./Müller-Spitzer, C. (2009): *Challenges to Internet lexicography: The Internet dictionary portal at the Institute for German Language.* In: Kernerman Dictionary News (July 2009), 10-19.

Haß, U. (2001): *Deutsche Wörterbücher – Brennpunkt von Sprach- und Kulturgeschichte.* Berlin/New York: Walter de Gruyter.

Haß, U. (Hg.) (2005a): *Grundfragen der elektronischen Lexikographie. elexiko – das Online-Informationssystem zum deutschen Wortschatz.* (= Schriften des Instituts für Deutsche Sprache 12). Berlin/New York: de Gruyter.

Haß, U. (2005b): Semantische Umgebung und lexikalische Mitspieler. In: Haß, U. (Hg.): *Grundfragen der elektronischen Lexikographie. elexiko – das Online-Informationssystem zum deutschen Wortschatz.* (= Schriften des Instituts für Deutsche Sprache 12). Berlin/New York: de Gruyter, 227-234.

Haß, U./Schmitz, U. (2010): *Lexikographie im Internet 2010 – Einleitung.* In: Lexicographica 26, 1-17.

Klein, W./Geyken, A. (2010): *Das Digitale Wörterbuch der Deutschen Sprache* (*DWDS*). In: Lexicographica 26, 79-93.

Klosa, A. (2005): Grammatik. In: Haß, Ulrike (Hg.): *Grundfragen der elektronischen Lexikographie. elexiko – das Online-Informationssystem zum deutschen Wortschatz.* (= Schriften des Instituts für Deutsche Sprache 12). Berlin/New York: de Gruyter, 277-298.

Klosa, A. (2007): Korpusgestützte Lexikographie: besser, schneller, umfangreicher? In: Kallmeyer, W./Zifonun, G. (Hg.): *Sprachkorpora – Datenmengen und Erkenntnisfortschritt.* (= Jahrbuch des Instituts für Deutsche Sprache 2006). Berlin/New York: de Gruyter, 105-122.

Klosa, A. (Hg.) (2011a): *elexiko. Erfahrungsberichte aus der lexikographischen Praxis eines Internetwörterbuchs.* (= Studien zur Deutschen Sprache 55). Tübingen: Narr.

Klosa, A. (2011b): Einleitung. In: Klosa, A. (Hg.): *elexiko. Erfahrungsberichte aus der lexikographischen Praxis eines Internetwörterbuchs.* (= Studien zur Deutschen Sprache 55). Tübingen: Narr, 9-26.

[28] Eine "Offensive zugunsten der linguistisch-lexikografischen Qualität" fordern in diesem Kontext Haß/Schmitz (2010, 12ff.) ein.

Klosa, A. (2011c): Von Abbildung bis Wortelement: Weitere Ergänzungen und Änderungen in *elexiko*. In: Klosa, A. (Hg.): *elexiko. Erfahrungsberichte aus der lexikographischen Praxis eines Internetwörterbuchs*. (= Studien zur Deutschen Sprache 55). Tübingen: Narr, 157-172.

Klosa, A./Storjohann, P. (2011): Neue Überlegungen und Erfahrungen zu den lexikalischen Mitspielern. In: Klosa, A. (Hg.): *elexiko. Erfahrungsberichte aus der lexikographischen Praxis eines Internetwörterbuchs*. (= Studien zur Deutschen Sprache 55) Tübingen: Narr, 49-80.

Klosa, A./Koplenig, A./Töpel, A. (2011): *Benutzerwünsche und Meinungen zu einer optimierten Wörterbuchpräsentation – Ergebnisse einer Onlinebefragung zu elexiko*. (= OPAL – Online publizierte Arbeiten zur Linguistik 3/2011) Mannheim: Institut für Deutsche Sprache.

Melchior, L. (2012): *Halbkollaborativität und Online-Lexikographie. Ansätze und Überlegungen zu Wörterbuchredaktion und Wörterbuchforschung am Beispiel LEO Deutsch-Italienisch*. In: Lexicographica 28, 337-372.

Meyer, C./Gurevych, I. (2012): Wiktionary: A new rival for expert-built lexicons? Exploring the possibilities of collaborative lexicography. In: Granger, S./Paquot, M. (Hg.): *Electronic Lexicography*. Oxford: Oxford University Press, 259-292.

Möhrs, C. (2011): Die typischen Verwendungen in *elexiko*. In: Klosa, A. (Hg.): *elexiko. Erfahrungsberichte aus der lexikographischen Praxis eines Internetwörterbuchs*. (= Studien zur Deutschen Sprache 55). Tübingen: Narr, 81-98.

Müller-Spitzer, C. (2007): Das *elexiko*-Portal: Ein neuer Zugang zu lexikografischen Arbeiten am Institut für Deutsche Sprache. In: Rehm, G./Witt, A./Lemnitzer, L. (Hg.): *Datenstrukturen für linguistische Ressourcen und ihre Anwendungen. Proceedings of the Biennial GLDV Conference 2007 (April 11-13, 2007, Eberhard Karls Universität Tübingen)*. Tübingen: Narr, 179-188.

Müller-Spitzer, C. (2010): OWID – A dictionary net for corpus-based lexicography of contemporary German. In: Dykstra, A./Schoonheim, T. (Hg.): *Proceedings of the XIV Euralex International Congress. Leeuwarden, 6-10 July 2010*. Leeuwarden: Fryske Akademy, 445-452.

Schlaefer, M. (2009): *Lexikologie und Lexikographie. Eine Einführung am Beispiel deutscher Wörterbücher*. 2., durchgesehene Auflage. Berlin: Erich Schmidt Verlag.

Storrer, A. (2010): *Deutsche Internet-Wörterbücher: Ein Überblick*. In: Lexicographica 26, 155-164.

Tarp, S. (2012): From lexicographical p-works to e-tools. In: Granger, S./Paquot, M. (Hg.): *Electronic Lexicography*. Oxford: Oxford University Press, 107-118.

4.2 Internetquellen (alle Stand: 04.02.2013)

Archiv für Gesprochenes Deutsch (IDS Mannheim). Internet: http://agd.ids-mannheim.de/datenbanken.shtml.

Benutzungsforschung am IDS Mannheim. Internet: www.benutzungsforschung.de.

COSMAS II. Internet: https://cosmas2.ids-mannheim.de/cosmas2-web/.

Kookkurrenzdatenbank CCDB – V3.2. Internet: http://corpora.ids-mannheim.de/ccdb/.

OBELEX^{dict} – Online-Bibliografie zur elektronischen Lexikografie/Wörterbücher. Internet: www.owid.de/obelex/dict.

OBELEX^{meta} – Online-Bibliografie zur elektronischen Lexikografie/Forschungsliteratur. Internet: www.owid.de/bibl/obelex/meta.

5. Verzeichnis der Wörterbücher

5.1 Internetwörterbücher (alle Stand: 04.02.2013)

Digitales Wörterbuch der Deutschen Sprache. Internet: www.dwds.de.

Duden online. Internet: www.duden.de.

elexiko – Online-Wörterbuch zur deutschen Gegenwartssprache (2003ff.). In: *OWID – Online Wortschatz-Informationssystem Deutsch*. Hrsg. vom Institut für Deutsche Sprache, Mannheim. Internet: www.elexiko.de.

LEO Online-Wörterbücher. Internet: www.leo.org.

Neologismenwörterbuch (2005ff.). In: *OWID – Online Wortschatz-Informationssystem Deutsch*. Hrsg. vom Institut für Deutsche Sprache, Mannheim. Internet: www.owid.de/wb/neo/start.html.

OWID – Online-Wortschatz-Informationssystem Deutsch (2008ff.). Hrsg. vom Institut für Deutsche Sprache, Mannheim. Internet: www.owid.de.

pons.eu – Das Online-Wörterbuch. Internet: www.pons.eu.

Sprichwörterbuch (2010ff.). In: *OWID – Online Wortschatz-Informationssystem Deutsch*. Hrsg. vom Institut für Deutsche Sprache, Mannheim. Internet: www.owid.de/wb/sprw/start.html.

Wiktionary – Das freie Wörterbuch. Internet: http://de.wiktionary.org/wiki/Wiktionary:Hauptseite.

Wörterbuchnetz. Internet: www.woerterbuchnetz.de.

5.2 Gedruckte Wörterbücher

Deutsches Wörterbuch. Von Jacob und Wilhelm Grimm. 33 Bände. Leipzig/Stuttgart 1854-1971/1984, Nachdruck München 1984.

Duden – Das große Wörterbuch der deutschen Sprache. Hrsg. vom Wissenschaftlicher Rat der Dudenredaktion. 10 Bände. 3. Auflage. Mannheim 1999.

Duden – Die deutsche Rechtschreibung. Hrsg. vom Wissenschaftlicher Rat der Dudenredaktion. 25. Auflage. Mannheim 2009.

Hueber-Duden Wörterbuch Deutsch als Fremdsprache. Hrsg. von Kathrin Kunkel-Razum, Ursula Kraif, Andreas Tomaszewski. Ismaning/Mannheim 2007.

Langenscheidt Großwörterbuch Deutsch als Fremdsprache. Hrsg. von Dieter Götz, Günther Haensch, Langenscheidt-Redaktion. Neuauflage. München 2010.

PONS Großwörterbuch Deutsch als Fremdsprache. Hrsg. von Werner Wolski. Stuttgart 2011.

Wörterbuch der deutschen Gegenwartssprache. Hrsg. von Ruth Klappenbach und Wolfgang Steinitz. 6 Bände. Letzte Auflage. Berlin 1980-1982.

John Simpson

Mediums of access to the *Oxford English Dictionary*

The *Oxford English Dictionary* (*OED*) was not the first of the great national historical dictionaries edited in the nineteenth century, but it has been one of the most successful. This paper examines how the contents of the dictionary can be manipulated computationally to offer the user new modes of access for investigating the language. These methods are of course relevant not only to dictionaries of the English language, and similar techniques are being followed by lexicographical scholars and computational linguists throughout the world.[1]

1. The basics

A dictionary needs a tight editorial policy (covering the selection of entries, its defining and etymological methodology, etc.) and a formally established structure in which the lexical information is held.

The following illustration shows a typical single-sense *OED* entry for a borrowed word, in this case the word *puttony* (a kind of basket used in the wine trade) from Hungarian. A short examination of the entry reveals the marriage of content and structure. We need to understand the structure of the content before we can appreciate what is feasible computationally.

The **headword form** *puttony* shows us the dictionary spelling of the word, based on an analysis of the evidence of the word's usage available to the editors.

This is followed immediately by the **pronunciation**, offering a standardized British and American English variety. This isn't 'absolute' information, but is a guide to how the word is or might typically be pronounced in both regions. After this, there is **inflectional** information on ways in which (in this case) the plural form may be written. For a term which is still recognized as a foreign word, it is not surprising that both the Hungarian plural and a standardized English plural form is provided.

The **etymology** is more extensive, and is one of the features of any entry that presents additional hooks for computational analysis. In this case we see that the English word comes from modern Hungarian (we use the same spelling form in English), and that the Hungarian word derives from the regional German *Butten* recorded in Austria and Bavaria. Several additional notes supplement the detailed information of the word's form and pronunciation. The etymology is significant in reminding us of the historical links between Hungarian and German. A word would not pass from the southern German dialects into Hungarian without some reason, and of course geographical propinquity and common industrial and trade interests provide possible reasons.

[1] *OED Online* images are copyright to Oxford University Press and are reprinted by permission of the Secretary to the Delegates of Oxford University Press.

The **definition** is generally regarded as the heart of a dictionary entry, though in a national dictionary such as the *OED* it has to fight for this billing alongside several other major information sections. Here, we see that the definition immediately remarks that the sense is known principally in Hungary (so that readers are not misled into thinking it may have more widespread currency). The basket is defined concisely and appropriately, and its function is then briefly described. A secondary definition is added, arising from the documentary evidence of the quotation paragraph. This definition is not for a form of basket but a measure (a basketful) of dried grapes used in the manufacture of the wine Tokay.

puttony, *n.*

Text size: A A

View as: Outline | Full entry

Quotations: Show all | Hide all

Pronunciation: Brit. /ˈpuːtɒn(jə)/ , U.S. /ˈputan(jə)/

Inflections: Plural *puttonyos, puttonos, puttonys, puttonyok.*

Etymology: < Hungarian *puttony* basket of wood or wickerwork, open at the top and becoming narrower and elongated towards the bottom, to be carried on the shoulder, now chiefly denoting a basket for gathering grapes < German regional (Austria, Bavaria) *Butten* , regional variant of *Bütte* basket (in southern Germany, Austria, and Switzerland also in unmutated form *Butte*): see BIT *n.*[3]

The form *puttonyos* reflects the Hungarian adjective *puttonyos* 'holding as much as goes into one puttony' (in e.g. *öt puttonyos tokaji aszú* five-basket Tokay Aszú; < *puttony* + *-os*, suffix forming adjectives), rather than the Hungarian plural form (which is *puttonyok*, whence the occasional English plural *puttonyok*), but was reapprehended in English as a plural form, apparently due to its final *-s*.

O.E.D. Suppl. (1982) gives the non-naturalized pronunciation (pu·ton^y) / putoɲ/ , which reflects the Hungarian pronunciation (in Hungarian, *ny* is the conventional spelling of the palatalized nasal /ɲ/).

(Show Less)

In Hungary: a basket usually made of wooden staves or wickerwork and designed to be carried on the back, used to transfer grapes from the vineyard to the wine press. Hence: a measure of dried overripe grapes equivalent to the contents of such a container, added to the fermentation cask in making Tokay, the number of measures added determining the richness of the wine.

Thesaurus »
Categories »

1940 H. J. GROSSMAN *Guide to Wines, Spirits & Beers* viii. 99 The grapes are gathered in wooden vessels known as *puttonyos*, holding about 25 quarts.

1959 W. JAMES *Word-bk. Wine* 190 Pickers carry a small container called a puttony, into which they put selected overripe berries..; the number of full puttonyos mixed with the ripe but not overripe grapes in the fermentation cask determines the richness of the wine, the range being from one to five (and occasionally six) puttonyos.

1967 A. LICHINE *Encycl. Wines & Spirits* 426/2 The collar label on every bottle of Tokaji Aszu will state: 3 Puttonos, 4 Puttonos, etc.—the export agency simplifies the spelling by removing the 'y'.

1972 *Guardian* 26 Jan. 9/5 In theory there can be a Tokay of 6 puttonyos; but in practice only the five turns up.

1989 *Daily Tel.* 16 Sept. (Colour Suppl.) 66/3 Tokay Aszu—The more puttonys, the longer it can live.

2005 *Wine Internat.* Jan. 54/1 For this tasting we concentrated on sweet Aszú wines ranging from 4 to 6 puttonyos as well as the modern late-harvest styles.

(Hide quotations)

Fig. 1: The *OED Online* entry for *puttony* n.
"puttony, n." *OED Online*. December 2012. Oxford University Press. 2 January 2013
www.oed.com/view/Entry/155284?rskey=SKKWxt&result=22&isAdvanced=true

Finally, the entry structure is completed by the paragraph of **illustrative quotations**. These document the occurrence and use of the word (or each sense of a word) in English, from the earliest appearance up to the date of editing (or of the term's obsolescence).

In the case of *puttony* we can see that it is at present first recorded in English in 1940, in the context of wine-making and wine-drinking, and it continues in this use into the 21st century, moving out of the highly specialized register of wine guides to the slightly less ethereal wine pages of the newspapers.

In multi-sense entries definition and quotation sections are repeated to accommodate each sense.

From this short explanation of a rather minor entry in the register of the English language it is possible to suggest the wealth of information classified in many of the much larger entries. With competent computational retrieval and display tools it should be possible to generate significant information about the language.

But this is not the only aim of the online dictionary. Historical dictionaries tell us not simply about words, but about the people who use them and the times and places in which they are used. If we question the dictionary properly, then we may be surprised at the amount of social and cultural data we can extract and analyse. Having said that, we should also bear in mind that the current software does not necessarily enable us to discover everything we would like to know from the data, and that future technological developments are likely to improve the quality of the information we can uncover from the dictionary's entries.

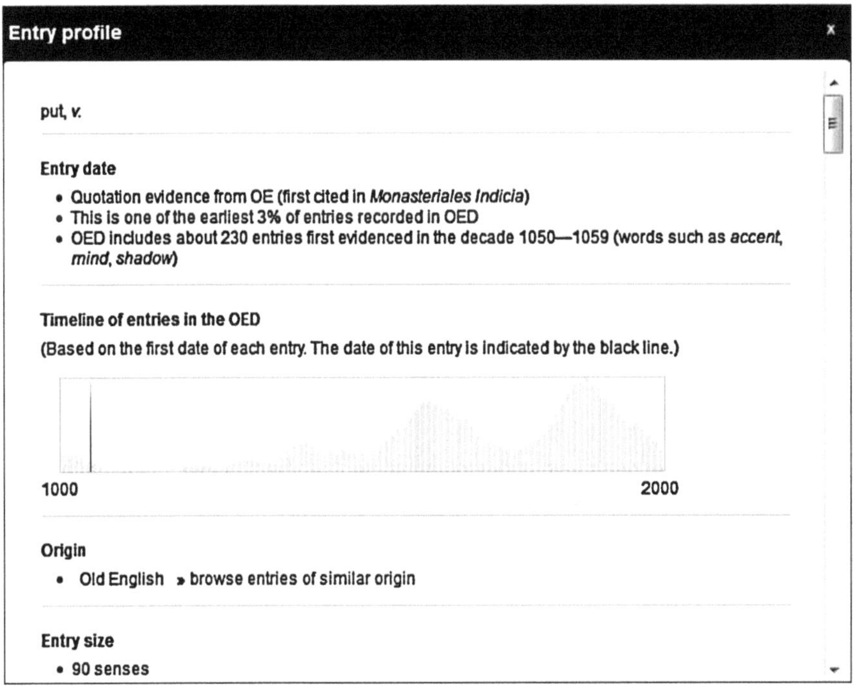

Fig. 2: Entry "profile" for *put* (*OED Online*)

1.1 An entry "profile"

Dictionaries can seem dry and unwieldy. One of the advantages of having access to a big dictionary online is that you can often choose "views" of the data with which you feel comfortable. Near to *puttony* we have the enormous entry for the verb *put* – one of the biggest entries in the whole of the *OED*. For every entry in the online *OED* there exists an entry "profile" generated from the data within the entry. If any feature of the entry changes when the database is regularly updated, then these changes will also be applied to the "profile".

The entry "profile" for *put* (see Fig. 2) is quite extensive. It starts with some general information about the word: it dates from the Old English period, and is (according to the *OED*) one of the oldest 3% of words recorded in English. The *OED* also gives you access to other words first recorded in the same decade (1050-1059), such as *accent*, *mind*, and *shadow*. The word's position as one of the oldest words in the language is plotted on a timeline (the dark needle at the left).

Not shown here, the "profile" continues with a further digest of information: a visual representation of the emergence of new senses of *put* over time; lists of words referred to and referring to *put*; etc. By using computational means, we can select and display information which the reader requires before launching head first into a substantial entry.

1.2 Filtering results

One of today's computational idioms is the "filter". This process of interrogation involves iteratively creating subsets of subsets until you arrive at the level you require.

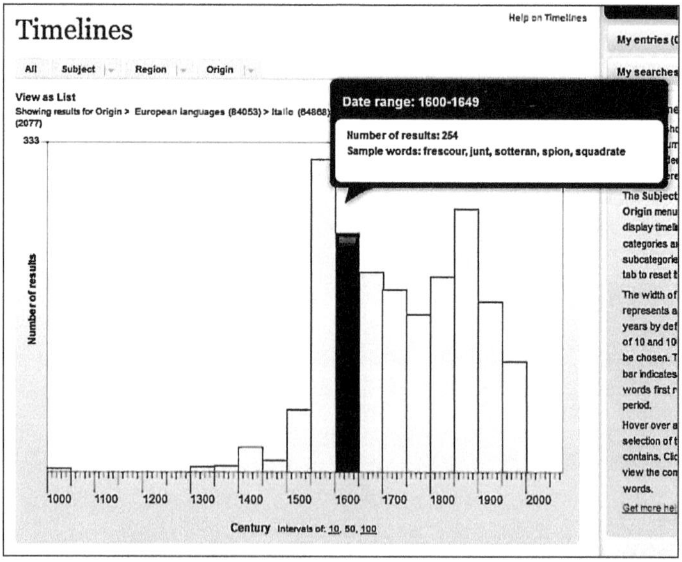

Fig. 3: Graph showing *OED* entries from Italian, arranged on a timeline based on their earliest reference in English

This means of access has been applied to numerous areas of the *OED Online*. We can take languages as an example. It is now possible to ask the database to report back on each of the entries which derive immediately from, say, Italian. Formerly this search would have included any entry which mentions the word "Italian" anywhere within the etymology text of an entry. But more recently the tagging of etymologies has been strengthened so that the software is able to disregard chance references to "Italian" and locate only those entries deriving directly from the language.

The results are revealing. Disregarding outliers (which are often problematic), the graph shows that although a number of Italian words entered English in the fifteenth and early sixteenth century, the first substantial influx occurred in the late sixteenth century. We can plot this against our real-world knowledge of when the influence of the European Renaissance started to have a substantial effect in Britain, and when we might expect the vocabulary of the Renaissance to begin to emerge in English texts.

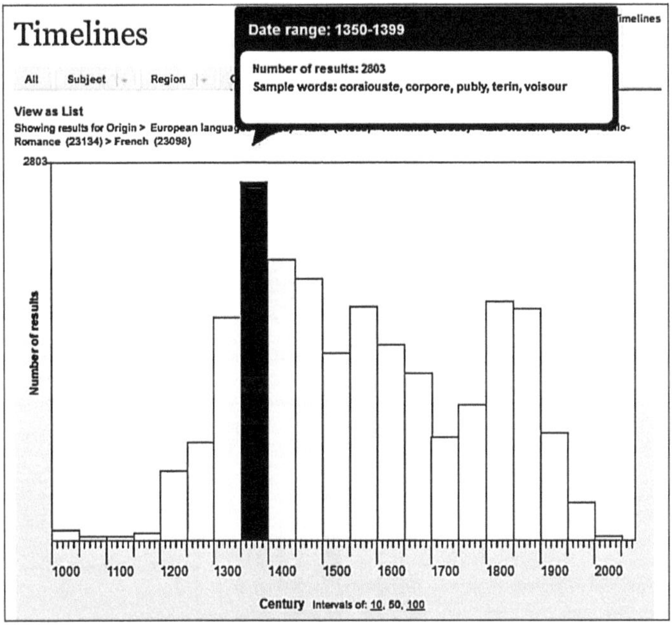

Fig. 4: Graph showing *OED* entries from French, arranged on a timeline based on their earliest reference in English

Note also that if the cursor is allowed to float over any of the columns of the graph, then a small box appears listing some of the Italian words which entered English in this time period (the span of which can be altered). A full click on any column will take the reader to a traditional-style word-list of all of the words from Italian which are recorded by the dictionary as entering English at this time. The possibilities for this sort of display in schools, for example, are easy to see. Students could be asked to compare the sorts of words which entered English from Italian (or any other language) in, say, the late sixteenth century and the late nineteenth century. What do the different types of words illustrated in these two time periods tell us about the relationship between Britain (or the English-speaking world) and Italy then? What types of new vocabulary are characteristic of each period? And so on.

A wider picture can then be obtained by comparing the picture for Italian words with that of French words which entered English, as documented by the *OED*. The picture is, as you might expect, slightly different from the Italian picture. The shape of the graph is different, with an earlier peak for French in the late fourteenth century, documenting a different type of relationship between the two languages and the two countries. This is also hinted at by the bare numbers: although there are 2,077 Italian words recorded as the basis of English words, the number of French words is far higher, at 23,098. And the types of words introduced from Italian differ in kind from their French counterparts. Altogether, an analysis and comparison of each graph allows us insights into the relationship between the languages over time.

We might also note that a stronger picture would emerge if we had comparable information on Italian loans to and from French (and vice versa), to complete the triangle of languages. We can hope that in future more information may become available about the relationship between other languages.

The issue of filtering does not stop here. One can, for example, take the English words from French and request a timeline graph restricted simply to scientific (or political, or colloquial) vocabulary. Here is the graph for scientific terms:

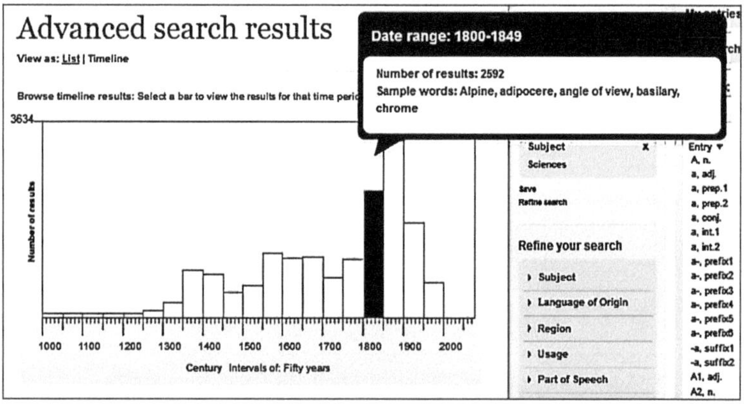

Fig. 5: Graph showing *OED* entries from French which are also categorized as scientific, arranged on a timeline based on their earliest reference in English

Here the peak has shifted to the late nineteenth century, but with a solid series of results from the late fourteenth showing a continuing involvement by the English in scientific words deriving from French.

The concept of filtering is not, as we have seen, restricted to language words. The filter can operate on any of the defined subject/discipline categories covered by the dictionary, on geographical spread, on register (slang, colloquial usage, etc.), and on a number of other criteria. Overall, it forms a very powerful tool for accessing the historical data locked in the *OED*.

1.3 Taking trips outside the *OED*

Looking inside the *OED* is rewarding work. Nowadays the focus of interest is not only the individual word but, through advances in computational lexicography, the language as a whole. We can at last find out information about linguistic trends, if we ask the right questions.

But there is also a world outside the dictionary. The more external resources that the dictionary can link to, the stronger it becomes. In 2009 Oxford University Press published a *Historical Thesaurus of the OED*, which was the result of a long research programme at the University of Glasgow. The dominant idea behind the thesaurus was to produce a reference tool which allowed the user to search by theme rather than by word. It might enable one, for example, to search for all of the legal terminology covered by the *OED*.

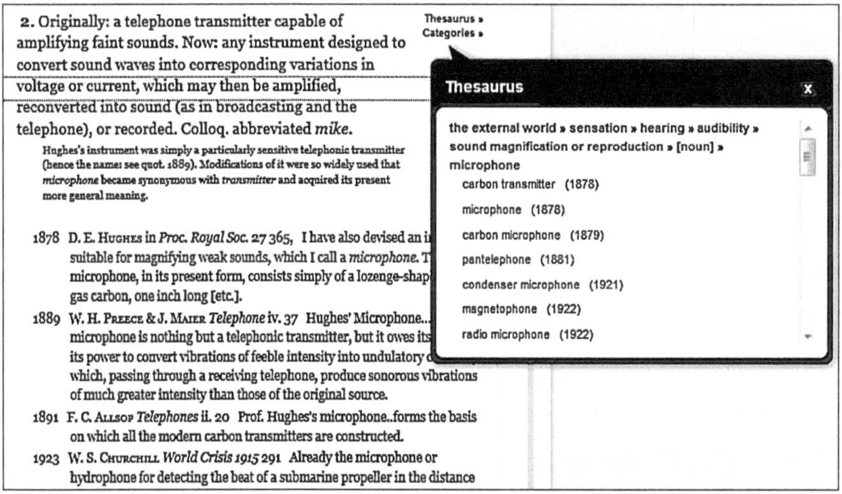

Fig. 6: Links from the *OED*'s entry for *microphone* to a chronological list of synonyms or near-synonyms classified by the *Historical Thesaurus of the OED*

The project sought to achieve this not by the simplistic route of searching for all entries and senses explicitly labelled "Law" (which would have missed many legal terms which have not been explicitly labelled for one reason or another) but by adopting a more systematic approach. The procedure was to write out almost all of the meanings of words in the *OED* on to index cards, along with their date of first use. These cards were then ordered thematically. The result is that the book allows us to find all words in the *OED* relating, for example, to motor transport.

One of the searches described above already uses this thesaurus, which has now been "plugged into" the *OED* computationally. We found all words of French origin in the dictionary, and then filtered that down to all scientific words of French origin. In order to isolate the 'scientific' words, the software used the thesaurus linkages.

These links can be seen at many entries throughout the dictionary. The illustration shows the *OED*'s entry for *microphone* with links displayed as targets elsewhere in the dictionary. The *Historical Thesaurus* is able to show that at much the same time as the word *microphone* was coined (1878), English-speakers were using several other terms for the same concept (in this case *carbon transmitter*, *carbon microphone*, and *pantelephone*). With the power of hindsight we can say how pleased we are that the right word won out!

The online site also allows readers access to the framework of the thesaurus, and then – in the process of following up a lead or suggestion – back to the entry in the dictionary itself.

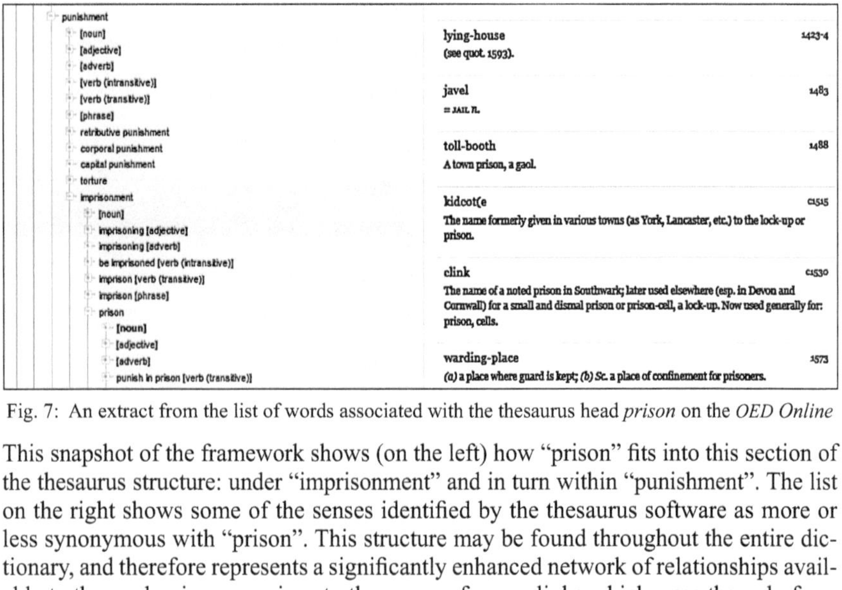

Fig. 7: An extract from the list of words associated with the thesaurus head *prison* on the *OED Online*

This snapshot of the framework shows (on the left) how "prison" fits into this section of the thesaurus structure: under "imprisonment" and in turn within "punishment". The list on the right shows some of the senses identified by the thesaurus software as more or less synonymous with "prison". This structure may be found throughout the entire dictionary, and therefore represents a significantly enhanced network of relationships available to the reader, in comparison to the cross-reference links which were the only form of linkage available previously.

It is now also possible to link outwards from an entry in the *OED* to equivalent entries in other dictionaries. This feature requires the user to have a subscription to the target text if one is necessary. So if the reader would like to find additional detailed information on a word current in the Middle English period, he or she would visit the relevant link in the central panel of the *OED*'s entry, and click through to the equivalent entry in the *Middle English Dictionary*. The same linking functionality is available with the *Dictionary of Old English* (in progress in Toronto), from where it is also possible to link back into the *OED*. An extract from the *OED*'s entry for *god* shows the links currently available outside the dictionary to other reference texts:

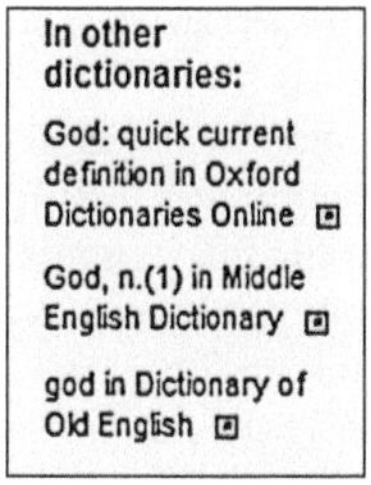

Fig. 8: Link from *OED* entry to other reference sources

It would be a relatively simple matter to engineer links to other texts: to other major on-line dictionaries, to the texts of sources cited as quotations in the dictionary, and to other data which might be useful to the reader when investigating a particular word or trend in language.

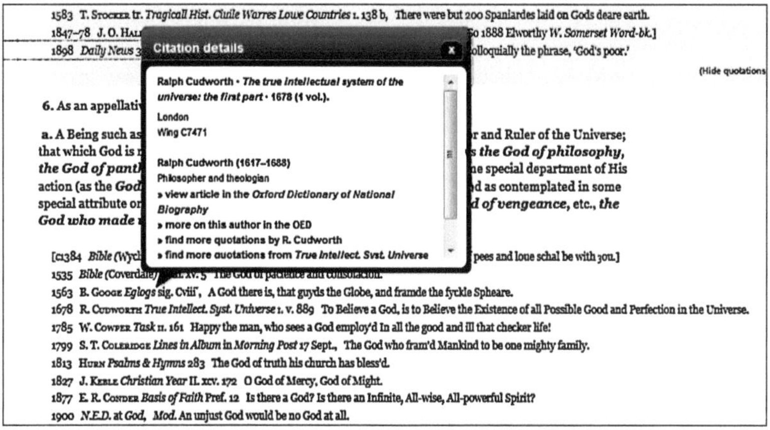

Fig. 9: Additional information on authors and works is available through a clickable link in the short title

We can end this brief survey of lexicographical functionality by looking at another area which has received extensive computational assistance, for the benefit of the reader.

There are now over three million illustrative quotations in the *OED*, cited normally by date of publication, author, work-title, and other bibliographical apparatus. Traditionally much of this information has been abbreviated, to save space in the print dictionary. Space is certainly still an issue; the modern lexicographer needs to present data in a concise and elegant manner to the reader, and not to use the amount of memory space available to allow the content to become loose. But there are other ways to expand this shortened data.

At present most bibliographical short titles in the text of dictionary entries have hyperlinks. If we look at the quotation dated 1678 at sense 6a of GOD n., we see it is from "R. Cudworth", and in particular his "True Intell. Syst. Universe". If we click on the short-title a small box appears on the screen with additional information about the author and text. We learn that the author is Ralph Cudworth (1617-1688), and that his book is called "The True Intellectual System of the Universe", published in one volume in 1678. Brief notes indicate that Cudworth was a philosopher and theologian, and we are invited to click another link to read his full biography in the *Oxford Dictionary of National Biography*. Further links allow you to access a specific page for Cudworth (also accessible through the "Sources" link of Top 1,000 authors and works cited in the dictionary) and to read that Cudworth is the 337th most frequently quoted source in the *OED*, with a total of 1,280 quotations in all. We also see that he is currently registered by the *OED* as the first recorded source for 197 words and 191 senses and compounds. It is also possible to click through to the quotations themselves. The reader should note that these numbers (and their accompanying data) may change at each three-monthly update of the *OED Online* database.

As a final comment we might note that the 1,141 quotations from Cudworth's *True Intellectual System* (89% of all Cudworth quotations in the *OED*) are by a long way the largest block of quotations taken from a single Cudworth work. We might then want to consider what this means: whether Cudworth is a particularly significant writer in terms of the language he uses, or whether his work was read by one of the dictionary's more dogged readers, or whether there are some other factors involved.

2. Accessing the dictionary in the future

So far we have been looking at new ways of accessing data within the dictionary and linking to external sources. We can now take a step back and examine broader issues relating to access in the future.

2.1 Access on new devices

When the *OED* was first released in machine-readable form in the early 1990s it was on the new medium of CD-ROM. This instantly brought a new tier of users to the dictionary and provided a means of advanced access to the data of a kind that simply wasn't possible previously. In the mid 1990s we experimented with options for establishing a searchable web site for the *OED* – in the early days of web-searchable databases – and finally went live with this in the year 2000.

Since then the readership – or usership – of the dictionary has broadened considerably, and we are thinking about how best to provide information for these new constituencies without prejudicing the quality of the content.

These are early days. The *OED* can of course be accessed on tablet computers, and it reads well on, for example, an iPad. The structure of the dictionary translates well to electronic devices. At present a mobile version of the *OED* is not available, and it is uncertain whether it would be satisfactory to try to represent the full content of the dictionary on a small mobile screen. If this proves not to be an option, then there is the possibility to presenting reduced "views" of the data in this format, with the full picture only available on larger devices.

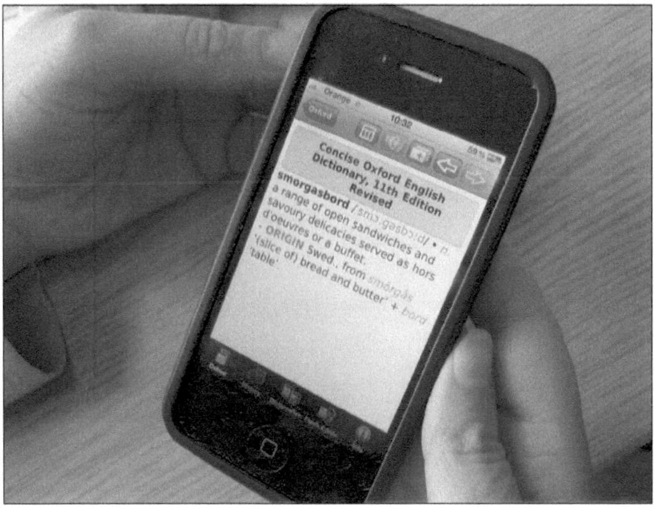

Fig. 10: The *Concise Oxford* accessible on a smartphone

But how would one go about selecting the best way to reduce the data? This is a problem that anyone working in this environment is encountering, and at present the answer is not clear as regards the *OED*. Maybe we shouldn't try to solve the problem for this generation of mobile devices, but await new technological developments which may be more satisfactory for complex language data. The present generation works well with smaller dictionaries, such as the *Concise Oxford* (see illustration).

2.2 Crowd-sourcing

Another of the ways in which the relationship between the dictionary and its readers is changing is through the medium of crowd-sourcing, or opening up an issue to as many people as possible through the Internet in order to increase the likelihood of finding a successful solution. But crowd-sourcing is not new to the *OED*. Long before the term "crowd-sourcing" was invented, the *OED* was appealing to English speakers throughout the world to contribute to the compilation of the dictionary, especially by providing the editors with additional evidence of language use from historical texts.

This procedure has proved extremely successful over the years, and the *OED* has benefited immeasurably for the assistance of the general public. The new media allow us to extend this idea, and for several years now science-fiction aficionados have had their own wiki through which they can publish their lexical findings and be sure that these are considered for the rolling revision of the dictionary.

At the *OED*'s sci-fi web site (www.jessesword.com/sf/) there are pages for each of the *OED*'s science-fiction terms, along with an explanation of what new material would be helpful. There are also pages for terms not yet in the dictionary but for which readers might like to contribute information.

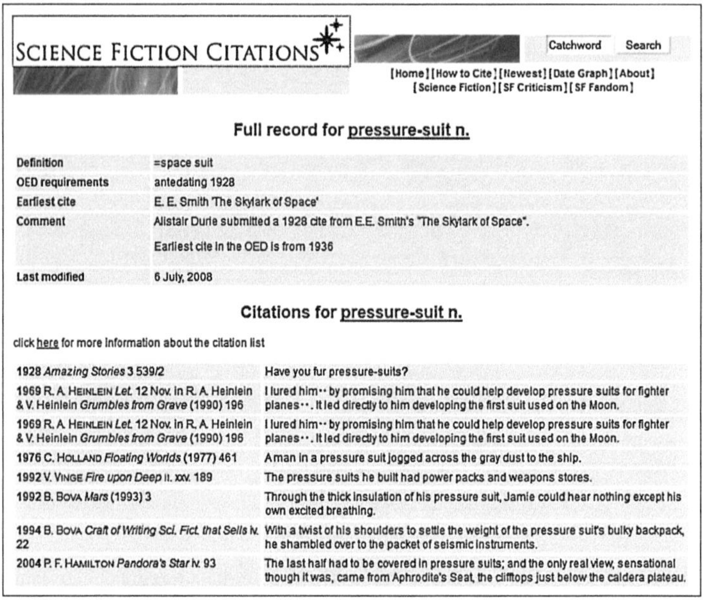

SCIENCE FICTION CITATIONS

Catchword Search

[Home] [How to Cite] [Newest] [Date Graph] [About]
[Science Fiction] [SF Criticism] [SF Fandom]

Full record for pressure-suit n.

Definition	=space suit
OED requirements	antedating 1928
Earliest cite	E. E. Smith 'The Skylark of Space'
Comment	Alistair Durie submitted a 1928 cite from E.E. Smith's "The Skylark of Space". Earliest cite in the OED is from 1936
Last modified	6 July, 2008

Citations for pressure-suit n.

click here for more information about the citation list

1928 *Amazing Stories* 3 539/2	Have you fur pressure-suits?
1969 R. A. HEINLEIN *Let.* 12 Nov. in R. A. Heinlein & V. Heinlein *Grumbles from Grave* (1990) 196	I lured him·· by promising him that he could help develop pressure suits for fighter planes··. It led directly to him developing the first suit used on the Moon.
1969 R. A. HEINLEIN *Let.* 12 Nov. in R. A. Heinlein & V. Heinlein *Grumbles from Grave* (1990) 196	I lured him·· by promising him that he could help develop pressure suits for fighter planes··. It led directly to him developing the first suit used on the Moon.
1976 C. HOLLAND *Floating Worlds* (1977) 461	A man in a pressure suit jogged across the gray dust to the ship.
1992 V. VINGE *Fire upon Deep* II. xxv. 189	The pressure suits he built had power packs and weapons stores.
1992 B. BOVA *Mars* (1993) 3	Through the thick insulation of his pressure suit, Jamie could hear nothing except his own excited breathing.
1994 B. BOVA *Craft of Writing Sci. Fict. that Sells* iv. 22	With a twist of his shoulders to settle the weight of the pressure suit's bulky backpack, he shambled over to the packet of seismic instruments.
2004 P. F. HAMILTON *Pandora's Star* iv. 93	The last half had to be covered in pressure suits; and the only real view, sensational though it was, came from Aphrodite's Seat, the clifftops just below the caldera plateau.

Fig. 11: Evidence for the expression *pressure suit* collected for the *OED*'s science-fiction wiki site

We can take as an example the expression *pressure suit* (defined by the *OED* as "an all-body garment that can be made airtight and inflated to protect the wearer against low ambient pressure (as in high-altitude flight)"). The previous printed version of the *OED* (1989) offered an earliest use for the term from *Flight* magazine in 1936. Readers have contributed numerous further examples of the expression, the earliest of which from 1928.

In future it would be possible to extent the concept of dedicated (and controlled) subject-specific wikis to other areas of language for which there is an active community of users eager to contribute to the *OED*, or simply to publish their findings for others to see.

The earliest appeals to the public from the *OED* in the late 1850s requested volunteers to read through specific texts extracting data that would be useful to a dictionary intended to describe the English language throughout the world and over many centuries. But soon these appeals turned into lists of desiderata, printed and circulated in the hope that members of the public would know just that piece of information that the editors required.

More recently, appeals have also been made through other media, the most extensive being the BBC2 television series *Balderdash & Piffle*, aired in 2006 and 2007. In this series a set of words was issued as a challenge to the public, who were asked to provide printed or other verifiable earlier evidence for the existence of the terms. The show was very successful, with many of the appeals (such as *ploughman's lunch*, *something for the weekend*, and *made-up* (= "happy, pleased")) proving successful. In 2012 a new on-going Appeal was launched. After starting with a handful of active appeals, new requests are regularly added (*blue-arsed fly*, *party animal*, *blues and twos*, etc.) and findings are fed back to the editor for incorporation in the dictionary.

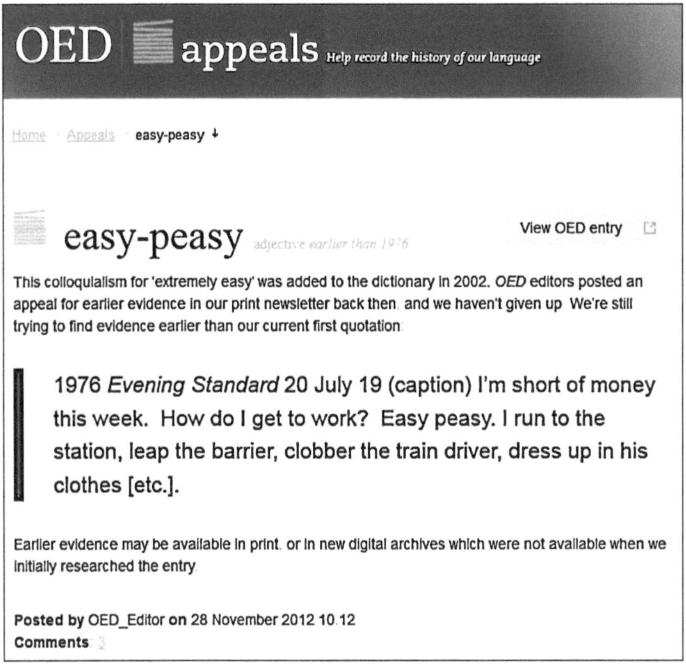

Fig. 12: An online appeal launched by the *OED* in November 2012

In the light of the success of both these models, it is possible to imagine in future that the dictionary will operate some form of wiki-based system for collecting information from the public about any English word or meaning, while at the same time running directed appeals for specific words for which editors actively need more data.

This is turn ties in with another idea which is in general circulation in the reference community, and that is the publication of so-called "stub" entries, as in Wikipedia. Publishers and editors are aware that the expectations of readers have changed over the years with their growing familiarity with information obtained from the Internet. Whereas previously the assumption was that published information should be fully researched and edited before it was released, there is now an expectation that although finalized, authoritative text is required it may also be acceptable to show unfinished work, as long as it is properly identified. Readers would therefore be able to see which new words, for example, might be edited in the near future (and for which they may be able to provide additional information), or they may even be offered the chance to provide a new or improved definition for a term (as they would expect to do in any case on projects such as the *Urban Dictionary*).

This is not to signal a free-for-all in publishing. Information would need to be flagged with regard to its level of authority, and all work would still be moving towards the fully finalized entry. But readers would perhaps benefit from seeing how work is progressing, and they could also contribute to moving the entry on to the next stage.

At present the *OED Online* is provided on the basis of a subscription model. In the UK and New Zealand most public libraries offer access free to their readers through separate agreements with Oxford University Press. But the expectation of many on the Internet now is that content should be provided free of charge to the end user. This appears to offer content providers little scope for directly recouping costs – which can be substantial.

Different providers are examining different ways to overcome this obstacle. At the two extremes we find funded bodies (often national language bodies or universities) posting content without charge to the user. At the other extreme, substantial changes are levied which often result in even large universities and other substantial organizations being unable to afford important resources.

There are any number of options within these two alternatives. Charges can be levied on individual searches or by results; shorter- or longer-term subscriptions can be offered; the resources can be separated into 'premium' content, for which charges are incurred, and regular content, which may be searched free, perhaps alongside paid advertisements.

There are major issues involving user satisfaction here. Whilst the user may appreciate being able to run basic searches on an important resource, he or she may become increasingly frustrated at being prevented from drilling down into results without further payment drip-feed. But others will only ever need to look at one type of information (perhaps definitions in the case of dictionaries), and so a publisher might be unwilling to satisfy 100% of the needs of this class of user without any charge whatsoever.

The *OED* is still considering all of these options, as are many other data providers. We would expect to emerge from this debate with new plans, but at present it is uncertain what these would be.

3. Conclusion

The *OED Online* is a major resource for the documentation and study of the English language. As a result of its most recent functional update it offers a broad range of search strategies (often based around the notion of filtering down from previous results). It also offers much additional discursive information on the dictionary and the language, and digests of material analysed from the main dictionary database. Over the years we can expect to see the diversity of this functionality and information extended.

Many of the issues addressed and being addressed by the *OED* are common to other national historical dictionaries and, indeed, to any organization offering material on the Internet. As well as enhancing the dictionary content by regular quarterly updates we can expect further software development to expand the ways in which data can be accessed or displayed on the site. Furthermore, we might reasonably expect further links to other historical dictionary sites outside the English-speaking world, and to other types of sites (holding modern or historical text, encyclopaedic or other reference information, images, etc.).

As well as this, data providers need to examine more closely the options for making proprietary data available over the Internet, whether this is by fully open access, free access to restricted segments (however generated), premium charges for specialist data, or by some other mechanism. This is not the sort of issue which has only one answer, and we can expect to see different answers testing the water. Perhaps the final outcome will be influenced by the fact that although we are data providers, at heart and at bottom we are all users ourselves.

Pádraig Ó Mianáin

The New English-Irish Dictionary

1. The project

The New English-Irish Dictionary (NEID) is the first major English-Irish Dictionary since 1959, when de Bhaldraithe's *English-Irish Dictionary* was published. The NEID is being produced and funded by Foras na Gaeilge, the cross-border body with responsibility for the promotion of the Irish language throughout the island of Ireland, with a project budget of €6m. The project started in 2000 and is scheduled to be completed at the end of 2015. The project is divided into three major phases:

Phase 1: Planning and design (began 2000, completed 2007). As the field of large-scale bilingual lexicography in Ireland had been dormant for such a long period, the project relied heavily on outside expertise in the initial stages. The planning and design phase was carried out by Lexicography Masterclass and delivered key elements such as a headword list, a draft style guide and, most importantly, the English and Irish corpora which would underpin the entire project.

Phase 2: Compilation, Writing and Editing (began 2008, to be completed 2015). This phase concerns the production of the final text of the dictionary, and was further divided into three subphases:

> **2A: The English-language content** (began 2008, completed 2011). Lexicography Masterclass also supplied the English-language database on which the source language content of the dictionary is based. This is a lexicographical database of c. 60k headwords and 150k sense units derived from a systematic analysis of the project's 1.7 billion word English corpus. Each entry contains a detailed description of headwords in terms of senses, phrases, collocations, grammar, usage, register etc, with over 640,000 examples taken from the corpus as evidence. The final product, *Database of Analysed Texts of English* (the DANTE database) is a 16 million word, target-language neutral, lexicographical database a demo version of which can be accessed online at www.webdante.com. This is a unique resource for lexicographers working on monolingual or bilingual English dictionaries, linguists, researchers and teachers.
>
> **2B: The Irish-language content** (began 2009, completed 2012). In the translation phase, Irish-language equivalents were provided for the English-language material. Apart from terminology, the Irish-language material was initially translated without recourse to existing reference sources, in order to ensure currency and originality in the translations. Also, the most frequent 1000 words in English were each translated by three translators, one from each of the main dialects. The translation team was recruited and managed directly by Foras na Gaeilge and was comprised of three full-time and a large number of part-time translators. In this phase nearly 4 million words in Irish were added to the English database to produce a 20-million-word bilingual corpus.

2C: Editing the final entries (began 2011, ongoing). In this phase the editing team first select the final English-language content for each entry and subsequently the equivalent Irish-language content. The editing team of three full-time editors and a number of part-time editors was directly recruited and managed by Foras na Gaeilge.

Phase 3: Publication (began 2011, ongoing). In this phase the final entries are prepared for publication, first online and ultimately in book form. The online and mobile versions of the dictionary, containing a third of the eventual content, were launched in January 2013 at www.focloir.ie and will be followed by an app version. The full dictionary will be online by the end of 2014 with a printed version to follow in 2015. NEID will eventually contain some 100,000 sense units (c. 40,000 headwords) and will be available in both electronic and book formats.

2. Practical challenges

The project to produce a modern bilingual English-Irish dictionary faced a number of significant practical challenges. Some of these challenges may be common to other minority languages, while others stemmed from the specific situation of Irish-language lexicography and in particular the difficulties arising from the shortage of available personnel with the appropriate skills and experience necessary for such a large-scale project at editorial and managerial level.

- **The absence of adequate electronic corpora of Irish**. Modern lexicography is largely corpus-based and relies heavily on the ability of computers to analyse huge digital corpora. Unfortunately such corpora did not exist in the Irish language, and although the project produced a new 30 million word Irish-language corpus, it falls far short in terms of size, content and representativeness when compared to the norm in other projects internationally, as exemplified in the 1.7 billion word corpus of English produced specifically for the NEID during Phase 1 of the project.
- **Qualified, experienced staff**. Finding qualified and/or experienced translators and editors has been a major obstacle throughout the course of the project. From a purely lexicographical point of view, there is a critical shortage of people who have the lexicographical expertise and the necessary knowledge of the Irish language; as mentioned previously, the last major English-Irish dictionary was published in the 1950s and the last Irish-English dictionary in the 1970s. Even from a translation point of view, while there are many qualified and skilled translators working in a professional capacity, the concentration on currency in both source and target languages of the current project required competency in registers not normally central to academic or professional activities and which are beyond the scope of what professional translators deal with on a daily basis.
- **An innovative approach to dictionary compilation.** The approach followed in the NEID project is groundbreaking in that the final content of the dictionary is entirely derived from a unique lexicographical database. A more traditional, straightforward approach would have been to start with a substantial English-language dictionary framework from a recent bilingual dictionary by a major international company, then

have a team of translators 'fill the blanks', so to speak, to provide the target language content; this model would also have required a much smaller editorial team. Working from the lexicographical database, however, required all translators and editors to exercise a higher level of judgement throughout, highlighting even more the lack of experienced staff available to the project. In the long term, however, the approach adopted should have major advantages for any future projects.

- **Technical challenges**. The technical/electronic working environment of modern lexicography posed a significant challenge, both at the organisational level dealing with various databases hosted externally and at individual level where a lot of training was required to enable the staff, most of whom were working remotely, to use the systems as efficiently as possible and as quickly as possible.
- **Management of staff and processes**. The varied nature of the project and the overlapping of the various phases and sub-phases required careful organisation and management, particularly as a lot of the processes in the translation and editing stages were being developed from scratch. There were a number of recruitment drives due to turnover of part-time personnel and to meet project deadlines, and there was also a significant amount of coordination involved with staff from other departments within Foras na Gaeilge who were seconded on a temporary basis in the period leading up to the launch.
- **Training and upskilling of staff**. The shortage of experienced people at all levels in the project required a significant and continuous programme of training and monitoring as the processes for each phase of the project were being implemented. Unfortunately, much of this training effort was expended on part-time staff who may not be available to work on future projects.

3. Linguistic challenges

The project also faced a number of challanges arising from the particular situation of the Irish language.

- **Lexical gaps as a minority language**. Bearing in mind that the last major English-Irish dictionary was in 1959, the emphasis in NEID on contemporary English, as in all modern bilingual dictionaries, meant that a large proportion of the Irish-language translations could not be sourced from existing sources and thus had to be produced first-hand. Also, as with many minority languages, many words and phrases that become current in the major language would often remain untranslated among native Irish speakers, and such material is often difficult to translate in a natural register that would not offend a native speaker's ear.
- **Official Standard(s) or Dialects**. There are three major dialects of modern Irish and many subdialects within them as well as dialects emerging outside the traditional Gaeltacht (Irish-speaking) areas. None of these dialects is universally accepted as standard, and although there has been an Official Standard of grammar and orthography since 1957, which is an attempt at a compromise between the dialects, it has never been fully accepted among the native speaker population. Given the nature of the translations required to capture the essence of the living language, there is at times a

tension and a divergence between dialect and Official Standard. Also there have been two separate revisions of the Official Standard since the writing phase of NEID started. The Revised Official Standard was published as recently as August 2012 without any involvement of senior project staff

- **'Book-Irish' or 'Real Irish'**. As with any language where the standard norm is not accepted by the majority of its speakers, the prescriptive versus descriptive question is particularly pertinent to NEID. There is a constant debate within the language community over the validity of current language as it is generally spoken by native speakers, especially where high-level or 'more correct' usage is being replaced by common and simpler forms, or where the influence of the English language is being reflected more and more in day-to-day usage of Irish.

4. The aim of NEID

Ultimately the NEID project aims to produce a practical resource that will cater for a range of users from the native or highly proficient Irish-speaker to learners both within and without the education system. The increasingly democratic nature of modern dictionaries, where currency of language dictates coverage, is reflected in NEID in both the English-language content, as evidenced in the corpus analysis, and the Irish-language content, where priority is given to natural or ordinary expression over the more formal register that would have been the norm in previous Irish dictionaries. In summary, the stated aims of the NEID project are to provide:

- an accessible guide to self-expression in correct and contemporary Irish for learners; and
- an authoritative guide to current and best practice in the Irish language for native or fluent speakers.

5. Further information

Further information regarding the NEID project can be found at the following websites:

The New English-Irish Dictionary: www.focloir.ie

The Database of Analysed Text of English: www.webdante.com

Foras na Gaeilge: www.gaeilge.ie

Anna Dąbrowska / Walery Pisarek

National Corpus of Polish and *Great Dictionary of Polish*. Two leading projects of present-day Polish lexicography

Streszczenie

Tekst poświęcony jest krótkiemu przedstawieniu narodowego korpusu języka polskiego (NKJP) i powstającemu w oparciu o NKJP wielkiemu słownikowi języka polskiego. W pierwszej części wymienione są instytucje współtworzące korpus i narzędzia stworzone do jego obsługi. Omówiona została struktura korpusu, jego zrównoważoność i reprezentatywność, anotacja składniowa, informacja morfo-syntaktyczna oraz anotacja semantyczna. Dodatkowo wspomniane są – wynikające z informacji podawanych w NKJP – słowa dnia. Krótko wymienia się też inne możliwości wykorzystania NKJP.

Część druga artykułu poświęcona jest *Wielkiemu słownikowi języka polskiego* (WSJP) – jednemu z wielkich projektów dotyczących języka polskiego na początku XXI wieku. Nowością w leksykografii polskiej jest to, że powstaje on jedynie w wersji elektronicznej. Konsekwencją tego jest zakładane jego stałe uzupełnianie i modyfikowanie, praktycznie bez końca. WSJP ma w założeniu charakter współczesny i deskryptywny. W tekście wymienia się 19 elementów tworzących hasło słownikowe (m.in. czas pojawienia się danego wyrazu, jego pochodzenie, definicję semantyczną, kwalifikatory, składnię, kolokacje, cytaty, informacje normatywne).

1. National Corpus of Polish

National corpora of various languages have been built since the 1960s (British, American, Chinese Mandarin, Dutch, Czech, Croatian, Russian, Slovak, Slovenian etc.). In Poland, several groups of linguists, computer scientists and lexicographers have been working on corpora of the Polish language since the 1990s. They work in the following institutions:

- IPI PAN: *Institute of Computer Science, Polish Academy of Sciences* (http://nlp.ipipan.waw.pl);
- IJP PAN: *Kraków Institute of Polish Language Polish Academy of Sciences* (http://ijp-pan.krakow.pl);
- PELCRA: *Polish and English Language Corpora for Research and Application, University of Łódź* (http://pelcra.pl) (since 1995);
- *Polish Scientific Publishers* PWN.

Between the years 2001-2004 they created a 250 million word corpus. The researchers involved in the creating of the corpus participate in some European corpus linguistics projects: CLARIN (*Common Language Resources and Technology Infrastructure*, www.clarin.eu), CESAR (*Central and South-East European Resources*, www.meta-net.eu/projects/cesar/) and ATLAS.

After a few years of working separately, the Consortium *National Corpus of Polish* was set up in 2006. Its participant institutions were those mentioned above and their representatives are:

- Adam Przepiórkowski – Institute of Computer Science, Polish Academy of Sciences;
- Rafał Górski – Institute of Polish Language, Polish Academy of Sciences;

- Barbara Lewandowska-Tomaszczyk – University of Łódź;
- Marek Łaziński – University of Warsaw;
- Mirosław Bańko – Polish Scientific Publishers PWN.

Since 2011 NKJP with its largest corpus of Polish has been available free of charge (nkjp.pl) and has become a basis for scientific research and among other things, for the *Great Dictionary of Polish* being currently worked on by a team led by Piotr Żmigrodzki (www.wsjp.pl).

1.1 The usefulness of NKJP in research

1.1.1 Lexicographic and lexicological works

Lexicographers were the first to notice the substantial usefulness of corpus data, allowing them to go far beyond the somewhat inconvenient collections of paper index cards. However, not all linguists were convinced of the usefulness of these corpora – the strong influence of generativism (psychological, introspective, anti-empirical) restrained the use of corpora of various languages built in the 1990s. Lexicographers roused themselves first. The first dictionary in the world based on corpus data was published in 1987: *The Collins Cobuild English Language Dictionary*. It was also shown that the corpus was very useful for the creation of so-called *learner's dictionaries*. Moreover, due to corpora it is possible to use so-called descriptive normativism (based on tradition and corpus data). In Poland, the first dictionary using corpus data to a large extent was *Inny słownik języka polskiego* (*Another dictionary of Polish*) by M. Bańko (2000). *Słownik dobrego stylu* (*The Dictionary of good style*) (2006), i.e. a dictionary of collocations is fully based on the corpus. Currently the *Great Dictionary of Polish* is being worked on as well as other smaller lexicographic works are being created.

1.1.2 Linguistic research

Corpus related linguistics can be characterized by three approaches in research: *corpus illustrated* (corpus – informer), *corpus based* (verification of an earlier formulated hypothesis) and *corpus driver* (taxonomic construction of grammar on the basis of empirical data from the corpus). In corpus related linguistics, looking for tendencies is more frequent that looking for rules.

The corpus brings, first of all, statistical data. It additionally examines mutual relations between grammar and vocabulary, pragmatics, stylistics etc. It also examines competing grammatical forms (e.g. *pisarzy – pisarzów*[1]). Corpus data can also be used for the purpose of examining collocations (see: *Dictionary of good* style by M. Bańko) or the stylistic diversity of a language.

1.1.3 Corpus in translations

Translators may verify the forms they choose in a corpus. This is necessary both in the translator's work and in didactics when future translators are trained.

It is common nowadays to use Internet browsers in translations and to compare language equivalents in multilingual Wikipedia entries.

---

1 'Writers'; two forms differing from each other by an ending.

1.2 Profile of NKJP

NKJP can be described as representative and balanced. It is assumed that a representative corpus should reflect the language "in its entire variety" (NKJP 2012, 29), thus each type of a text should have its (at least small) contribution to the corpus. Sometimes decisions of this type must be arbitrary (e.g. 7% of Internet texts). Representativeness refers to the reality beyond the corpus. In the subcorpus of spoken texts representativeness refers to the authors of these texts (speakers), whereas the component of writers reflects reception of written Polish (structure of readership in Polish).

Balance means that none of text types covers more than half of the corpus (NKJP 2011, 30).

Table 1 presents the model structure of the corpus.

Type of the text	% contribution to the corpus
Political commentaries and short press releases	50.0%
Belles-lettres	16.0%
Non-fiction	5.5%
Informative and handbook type	5.5%
Scientific and didactic type	2.0%
Other written texts	3.0%
Books other than fiction non-classified	1.0%
Transcripts of conversations, media-based spoken and quasi-spoken – together	10.0%
Internet texts – static and dynamic together	7.0%

Table 1: Model structure of the corpus (source: NKJP 2012, 33)

The chronological selection of texts prefers those created after 1945; an exception was made in relation to literary texts – some of these originate from the beginning of the 20th century.

80% of texts appeared after 1990, 15% were produced in a period 1945-1990, and only 5% appeared before 1945. They are overwhelmingly contemporary texts.

1.2.1 Structure of the corpus

Currently NKJP numbers 1.5 billion words and is not stylistically balanced; however, it has been tagged and made grammatically unambiguous. There is a so-called 1M – one million, manually marked-up (tagged) subcorpus, which remains a very important part of the corpus. It is a basis for programmes servicing the whole corpus. It contains only texts coming from the period after 1945.

Additionally the following can be distinguished:

100M demo – comprising one hundred million words,
300M – balanced corpus covering three hundred million segments (250 million words).

Table 2 presents categories of texts as parts of 1M (proportions shown guarantee its balance).

Category	% contribution to the corpus
Daily newspapers Other periodicals and journals Political commentary books	25.5% 23.5% 1.0%
Belles-lettres	16.0%
Non-fiction	5.5%
Informative and handbook type	5.5%
Scientific and didactic type	2.0%
Internet-related interactive (blogs, forums, Usenet) Internet-related non-interactive (static websites, Wikipedia)	3.5% 3.5%
Quasi-spoken (minutes of Parliament sessions) Media-related spoken Conversational spoken	2.5% 2.5% 5.0%
Other written texts	3.0%
Books other than fiction non-classified	1.0%

Table 2: Categories of texts (source: NKJP 2012, 53)

1.2.2 Mark-up levels for the corpus

a) Segmentation of the text into sentences and words

The inflection classes distinguished in NKJP are slightly different than traditional ones (new classes appeared such as e.g. *burkinostkas, kubliks* or *foreign objects*). Burkinostkas are uninflected forms whose distribution is limited to precisely defined tokens (*omacku, trochu, naprzeciwka* in *po omacku, po trochu, z naprzeciwka*),[2] but with the exception of parts of proper names; Kubliks are an incoherent class of uninflected lexemes. They are mainly tokens modifying various classes including nouns (*nawet, głównie, prawdopodobnie, nie, -ż, również*[3] (adverbs with no comparison forms); foreign objects are foreign tokens which do not directly interact with tokens of the Polish language (*errare*). Thus lemmatization does not agree with the parts of speech appearing in grammars (additionally *kubliks*, *burkinostkas* and *foreign objects* appear).

2 In translation: 'blindfold', 'little by little, from across'.
3 In translation: 'even', 'mainly', 'probably', likewise/also/too'.

b) Morpho-syntactic information

It is necessary to follow strict mark-up procedures for annotation processes (each paragraph is annotated by 2 linguists and verified by a super-annotator, as a result of which a final version is approved).

The NKJP tagset is morpho-syntactic in its nature. As compared with the IPI PAN tagset it contains new solutions being developed from earlier ones. The morpho-syntactic annotation undertaken by the Morfeusz (morphological analyser) involved weak dehomonymisation; strong dehomonymisation was undertaken by an annotator. Each token had to be made unambiguous by an annotator, which was not always easy. On the basis of manual annotation of the 1M corpus, a PANTERA (= *Polskiej Akademii Nauk Tager Ekstrahujący Reguły Automatycznie*) tool was developed and trained, with which the morpho-syntactic description of the full corpus was made unambiguous. The Brill algorithm with a small tagset designed for the English language was adopted for this purpose; however, it had to be modified to serve an inflected language such as Polish. Similar procedures have previously been adopted in relation to Czech: tagging was divided into three stages. During the first, the tagger decides on a grammatical class of a given token and on values of chosen grammatical categories (here: case and person). Next it establishes other categories. The distinction of cases, especially Nominative, Accusative and Genitive (syncretism) as well as distinction of certain masculine genders (mainly in relation to pronouns and prepositions) are the issues which cause the biggest problems.

For example – the gender of a noun was established in this way on the basis of diagnostic contexts:

Widzę jednego[4] ______ z tych, których lubię.	m1
Widzę jednego ______ z tych, które lubię.	m2
Widzę jeden _______ .	m3
Widzę jedno _______ .	n
Widzę jedną _______ .	f

c) Semantic annotation

Semantic Word Sense Disambiguation – WSD (http://nlp.ipipan.waw.pl/Anotatornia) was undertaken in order to use automatic disambiguation. Vocabulary of senses means labels for ambiguous words. These are different to those in existing dictionaries, in which they are too detailed. While creating the dictionary of senses, 106 lexemes were chosen (out of the IPI PAN basic word list) – mainly nouns and verbs. Not more than 6 coarse senses were assigned to each lexeme. The frequency of appearance in relation to the use of a given word in a given sense was important here. In the created dictionary one word has 2.85 senses on average. The system automatically decides which of the meanings appeared in a given context. For example:

Zamek$_2$ w drzwiach trzeba było wymienić.	'a lock in a door'
Okazały zamek$_1$ stał na wzgórzu.	'a castle'

[4] 'I see one ..., of those I like' (in various genders).

There are more than 34 thousand appearances of ambiguous words in the 1M subcorpus. Experiments have been conducted to test these methods – 315 tests have been conducted for each ambiguous word, which gives us 22,790 verified methods. A fragment of a table with statistical data is presented in table 3.

Word	**Number of appearances**	**Number of senses**	**Distribution of senses**	**MFS**
action (akcja)	369	2	257/112	0,696
near (blisko)	279	2	196/83	0,703
take (brać)	299	7	142/98/30/17/6/4/2	0,475
Go (chodzić)	675	4	401/270/3/1	0,594
body (ciało)	256	3	238/17/1	0,930
member (członek)	368	3	363/3/2	0,986
Feel (czuć)	354	2	352/2	0,994

Table 3: Statistics for manually marked-up appearances of ambiguous words (source: NKJP 2012, 221)

d) Syntactic annotation

This addresses the problem of the distinction of syntactic words and syntactic groups. Syntactic words contain analytical forms (tense, mode, comparison, discontinuous conjunctions) as well as multiword units, e.g. *do czysta* 'clean' is an adverb at the level of syntactic words and an adverb group at the level of syntactic groups.

In syntactic groups a syntactic centre and a semantic centre are distinguished. The majority of groups consist of one (39%) or two (31%) semantic words.

Element	**Number**
token	1,068,035
sentence	72,944
syntactic word	993,684
syntactic group	305,806

Table 4: Number of elements for the syntactically annotated corpus (source: NKJP 2012, 126)

e) Annotation of proper names

There are names of people, places, institutions and temporal periods.

The annotation of units connected with Europe and the European Union was extremely complicated due to the metonymous nature of use of lexemes *Europe* and *European*, as they hardly ever referred to the continent and most frequently they referred to inhabitants of Europe as a continent or as an organisation (the *European Union* as a block of countries or as an institution). So *Europe is* treated as a geographic or geopolitical name or as a name of an organisation, e.g.

> Odnalazłem przylądek św. Wincentego – miejsce, gdzie kończy się Europa [geogName]
> Europa i Ameryka miały inne sprawy na głowie [orgName]
> Europa powinna popierać ideę, iż wydatki na edukację [...] powinny osiągnąć w ciągu następnych 10 lat przeciętnie 10% [orgName]

For NKJP data, two Internet browsers are available: PELCRA and Poliqarp. PELCRA is available at http://pelcra.ia.uni.lodz.pl. Poliqarp at http://nkjp.pl/poliqarp/help/pl.html. The PELCRA Internet browser is based on the syntax of corpus related inquiries.

As automatic mark-up of the whole corpus is subject to mistakes, work is being done in order to minimise their appearance. This is done under the European project CESAR/META-NET (www.meta-net.eu/projects/cesar).

f) Words of the day

Words of the day are one of subprojects for NKJP. They are words whose frequency of occurrence is clearly variable in time. They come from four daily newspapers: *Dziennik. Gazeta Prawna, Gazeta Wyborcza, Polska. The Times* and *Rzeczpospolita*. Every morning words from the previous day are published (the sport section is ignored). Words of the day are selected on the basis of the comparison of their absolute and relevant frequency in a given day and in the whole preceding year. This may be a hint as to which of them should be noted in dictionaries or language handbooks. The whole idea of selecting words is taken from the website *Wörter des Tages* of University of Leipzig.

Słowa dnia

Data: << 2012-10-16 >> Odśwież

# Słowo	Kluczowość	Komentarz	Przykłady	Trendy	Prenumeruj
1. Anglia	69:2	tu w znaczeniu 'kadra piłkarzy nożnych Anglii' (w związku z informacjami sportowymi)			
2. mecz	115:40	tu głównie w połączeniach typu: odwołać mecz, organizatorzy meczu (w związku z informacjami sportowymi)			
3. ulewa	12:1	tu w połączeniu typu: potężna ulewa przeszła nad Warszawą (w związku z informacjami krajowymi)			
4. stadion	56:13	tu między innymi w połączeniu: murawa Stadionu Narodowego (w związku z informacjami sportowymi)			
5. protokołować	6:1	tu w połączeniu typu: nagrywać, a nie protokołować (w związku z informacjami krajowymi)			
6. nadwyżka	11:1	tu w połączeniu typu: nadwyżka w handlu (w związku z informacjami ekonomicznymi)			
7. senacki	12:1	tu w połączeniu typu: senacka komisja (w związku z informacjami krajowymi)			

Tematy dnia z 2012-10-16

Fig. 1: Words of the day

In other words, this means monitoring the relative popularity of given words. Reflection of political and social realities can be observed by the appearance of certain words highly ranked on a list of words for a given day. In the future, it is planned to look for "key key words" from the key words.

Analogically, words of the month and words of the year have lately been chosen; e.g. *prezydencja* ('presidency'), *kryzys* ('crisis'), *katastrofa* ('catastrophe') and *krzyż* ('cross') have been recognized for the words of 2011.

2. WSJP or Great Dictionary of Polish[5]

Taking into account its status, the amount of financial support granted from the state budget and the number of researchers and universities engaged in its development, 'Wielki słownik języka polskiego PAN' or the 'Polish Academy of Sciences – Great Dictionary of Polish' (the abbreviation of the Polish title is WSJP) deserves to be taken as the second leading project in the Polish linguistics – or rather the linguistics of Polish – of the initial decades of XXI century.

'Wielki słownik języka polskiego PAN' or WSJP is the fifth in the history of Polish linguistics attempt to collect and describe the inventory of the entire Polish vocabulary being contemporarily in use after the following:[6]

1. 'Słownik języka polskiego' (Dictionary of Polish) with ca. 80,000 entries in six volumes, edited by Samuel B. Linde and published in Warsaw 1807-1814, known as the Linde Dictionary;
2. 'Słownik języka polskiego' (Dictionary of Polish) with ca. 280,000 entries in seven volumes, edited by Jan Karłowicz, Antoni Kryński and Władysław Niedźwiecki, published in Warsaw in 1900-1927; known as the Warsaw Dictionary;[7]
3. 'Słownik języka polskiego' (Dictionary of Polish) with ca. 125,000 entries in eleven volumes, edited by Witold Doroszewski, published in Warsaw 1958-1969, known as the Doroszewski Dictionary;[8]

---

5 This presentation of the WSJP is based mainly on the article by Piotr Żmigrodzki (see Żmigrodzki 2011).

6 For more information about the latest history of Polish lexicography, see Żmigrodzk (2009).

7 The Warsaw Dictionary, as the Linde Dictionary, should, in the intention of their editors, comprise the whole stock of Polish words since XVth till the end of XVIIIth century (Linde Dictionary) up to the end of XIXth century (Warsaw dictionary).

8 The 11-volume Doroszewski Dictionary, according to the intention of its editor and publisher, covered the Polish vocabulary from 1750 to 1950. "Although its approximately 125,000 entries amount to less than a half of the SW [Warsaw Dictionary] entries, the description in SJPD [Doroszewski Dictionary] is much richer, including in particular authentic examples of word usage. Separate sections in the entry word description were devoted to phraseologisms and proverbs. Inflexion tables and a system of reference markers provided detailed information on inflexion. The dictionary played a major role in the Polish lexicography of the second half of the 20th century, becoming the source of material (and the theoretical basis) for many smaller popular dictionaries, especially the 3-volume PWN Dictionary of Polish ['Słownik języka polskiego PWN', called "the Szymczak Dictionary" – SJPSz], which sold in two million copies between 1978 and 2004, and the Little Dictionary of Polish

4. 'Praktyczny słownik współczesnej polszczyzny' (Practical Dictionary of Contemporary Polish) with ca. 133,000 entries in 50 volumes, edited by Halina Zgółkowa and published in Poznań in 1994-2005, known as the Zgółkowa dictionary.

But it is also in many ways a dictionary different to all its predecessors. What distinguishes it from them?

Firstly, it was meant, according to the founding resolution, as "a concerted endeavour of Polish humanists, and especially the whole linguistic branch of Polish studies", and really the WSJP is "a kind of a **linguistic joint venture**": its editorial team (not counting former or present temporary collaborators) included linguists from the universities of Cracow, Warsaw, Katowice, Toruń, and Olsztyn as well from the Institute of Polish Language of the Polish Academy of Sciences which serves as the leading unit of the whole project.

Secondly, it is developed in an **electronic** version and will be (and partly already is) available online for free. According to the editor, "there will be no printed version of the whole dictionary; in the future, however, the WSJP database may serve as a source for derived dictionaries, which could be published in the printed form" (Żmigrodzki 2011, 10);

Thirdly, the development of the WSJP is conceived as a **permanent** process. Its editor declared: "the dictionary is to be further developed after 2012, and due to the open nature of the project, the work should continue without end" (Żmigrodzki 2011, 11).

Fourthly, the WSJP is **based on two corpora** of Polish texts since 1945: the National Corpus of Polish ['Narodowy Korpus Języka Polskiego', NKJP] and supported by an auxiliary corpus created at the PAS IPL specifically to serve the needs of the emerging dictionary. This comprises texts which for various reasons were not (and are not going to be) included in the NKJP. Polish Internet sites constitute a third source.

Fifthly, the editor and authors seek to give to the WSJP an **academic** character, aiming "to employ wherever possible the achievements of Polish 20th-century linguistics, especially in the field of semantic, inflexional and syntactic description of lexical units, at the same time keeping in mind that the description must be accessible to a very broad group of Polish language users" (Żmigrodzki 2011, 10).

['Mały słownik języka polskiego', MSJP], first published 1968 and re-issued a number of times, in its original form, as well as in various modified versions. Even the 2003 Universal Dictionary of Polish ['Uniwersalny słownik języka polskiego'] directly draws from the tradition of SJPD and the lexicographical framework developed by Witold Doroszewski. Since the late 1970s, however, the SJPD framework had been criticized by lexicographers of the younger generation. In mid-1980s efforts were made to create a new great dictionary of Polish but due to a number of unfortunate circumstances and also because of the political changes in Poland, this attempt was unsuccessful. After the breakthrough of 1989, it seemed that the emergence of private publishing houses would prompt new lexicographical works. Indeed, there appeared many popular dictionaries (e.g. the Dictionary of Contemporary Polish, edited by Bogusław Dunaj ['Słownik współczesnego języka polskiego' – SJPDun], yet the need for a comprehensive academic lexicographical description of the Polish language remained unfulfilled." (Żmigrodzki 2011, 8-9).

Moreover, the WSJP is presented as "in principle synchronic"[9] and "in principle descriptive".[10]

The editors and authors of the WSJP see its specific value in quality and quantity of information on individual words. The full structure of the entry consists of the following nineteen fields:

1. **Headform**. For nouns, the headword form is the nominative singular (or plural, in the case of plurale tantum), for adjectives and numerals, the nominative singular masculine and for verbs, the infinitive form.
2. **Entry sub-type**. This is a technical field, i.e. it is not visible to the dictionary user; for "regular" entries, the sub-type is related to the lexical category of a given item (noun, verb, adjective, etc.), for "discontinuous" ones – with the structure (clause, verb phrase, noun phrase). The choice of the sub-type determines which forms will be added to other fields to be filled in (e.g. Syntax, Inflexion, Collocations).
3. **Variants**. Information included in this field refers to different phenomena, depending on entry type. For "regular" entries, phonetic-orthographic variants are noted here, that is such cases where a change in spelling is accompanied by a change in pronunciation, e.g. *pośpieszny* and *pospieszny*.
4. **Chronology**. Initially, the editors of the dictionary were planning to include here the exact year of the first appearance of a given headword in Polish texts, yet this plan proved unfeasible. Thus, information on chronology is reduced to information about the appearance of a particular word (or rather its graphic form) in an older dictionary of Polish. This compromise has been criticized by some Polish researchers, but the editors believe that even this kind of information on chronology may be of some help to the dictionary user and it is possible to complete the chronology data in the future.
5. **Origin**. So far this field offers etymological information only on lexemes of foreign origin. Further work on etymological information on all lexemes is planned for the future.
6. **Semantic description**. According to the editors of WSJP, the average user of the dictionary is looking most often for semantic information. Therefore, they treat it with due attention. "Thanks to the fact – the editor explains – that the entries are not created in the alphabetical order but according to a thematic classification, the work on semantic description is made easier in that the authors can start by identifying the problems and strategies of defining lexemes which belong to a given semantic field. Apart from the definition, in the case of headwords with more than one meaning there is one more component in the semantic description field, namely the guide-

[9] It covers first of all the Polish vocabulary of the XXI century "although the year 1945 was accepted as the beginning of the time span covered, due to the nature of the sources, to which we shall return later on, the overwhelming majority of the material will belong to the last decades of the 20th and the beginning of the 21st century" (Żmigrodzki 2011, 10).

[10] "The authors are not going to eliminate from description any lexicographical facts deemed incorrect or – for whatever reasons – unworthy of being noted in a dictionary, as long as these facts are well attested in the sources. The authors will only point out the normative unacceptability of a given fact [...] and mark the stylistic qualification of sub-standard units." (Żmigrodzki 2011, 10).

word (or, as we call it, the semantic identifier). Guidewords are single words or short phrases indicating the meaning of the lexeme explained in the particular sub-entry." (Żmigrodzki (2011, 18).

7. **Labels**. The WSJP employs a system of labels developed on the basis of a critical analysis of the choice and use of labels in other Polish dictionaries. The labels are given before the semantic definition.
8. **Thematic classification**. "The WSJP is – according to its editor – the first general dictionary of Polish which makes use of a thematic classification of the vocabulary. We employ a three-tier classification scheme (about 80 categories altogether). [...] In our classification, every separate meaning of a headword is of course categorized independently." (Żmigrodzki (2011, 19).
9. **Semantic relations**. The sub-entries can include lexical units exhibiting the relations of synonymy, antonymy, hyperonymy or incompatibility to the headword. However the WSJP should not be treated as a practical dictionary of synonyms.
10. **Inflexion**. The WSJP is the first general dictionary of Polish to provide direct and exhaustive information about inflexion. Full inflexion paradigms are given for all inflected lexemes, as well as the indication of gender, aspect of verbs, comparison, etc.
11. **Syntax**. The valence of the units is indicated; this information is made available to the user in the shape of symbolic syntactic schema. These might be accompanied – if need be – by a note that a given unit takes an unusual syntactic sequence or that there apply rules of semantic selection (that is the meaning of words determines their ability to form a sequence with a given lexical unit).
12. **Collocations**. Collocations, here understood as statistically frequent combinations of the headword with other lexemes, form the main bulk of the WSJP exemplification material.
13. **Quotations**. A small number (max. five per one headword meaning) of authentic quotations are included. Both quotations and collocations are taken mainly from the NKJP, some also come from other sources previously mentioned in the present paper.
14. **Abbreviations**. The WSJP also notes frequently used abbreviations of a given lexeme, e.g. *dr* from *doktor* [doctor], *zob.* from *zobacz* [see, as in "see above/below", etc.]. These abbreviations are also described in separate entries.
15. **Normative information**. Although the WSJP is a descriptive dictionary it notes in this field that a given form or usage of the headword deviates from the linguistic norm as contained in the latest edition of the 'PWN Wielki słownik poprawnej polszczyzny' (Great Normative Dictionary of Polish). This opinion is not verified or commented by the editors of the WSJP.
16. **Notes on usage**. This field includes any additional information on the headform word that could not be entered in any of the previous fields. For example: that the given word is sometimes confused with another one.
17. **Derivatives** – this field is completed for "proper name" entries only, in the description of the names of towns and states. The sub-fields include: the name of the male inhabitant, the name of the female inhabitant and the derivative adjective.

18. **Expansion**. This field is devoted to information only on entry-types 'abbreviations' (e.g. nr = numer [number], prof. = profesor [professor]) and 'acronyms' (e.g. PIT, for 'Personal Income Tax'.
19. **Lexemes**. This field is used for the entry-type "morphemes" and contains several examples of words in which the headword morpheme is found.

As was said, the full structure of the entry consists of nineteen fields (elements of description). However, the structure of particular entries and the range of information included, depend on the type of the described lexical units. The WSJP distinguishes seven types of entries:

regular (single words);
discontinuous (idioms, proverbs, winged words);
abbreviations;
acronyms;
proper names;
functional lexemes;
morphemes.

The last three (of the nineteen) fields are opened only for some types of entries and in particular: the field Derivatives is opened only for proper names; the field Expansion is opened only for abbreviations and acronyms and the field Lexemes is opened only for morphemes.

The WSJP is – to use the term coined by its editor Piotr Żmigrodzki (2008) – a primarily online dictionary, which means that it has been developed to be presented on the computer screen. As a result, the basic entry view that presents itself to the user is a structured "tab view".

The work to be completed by the end of 2012 is just the beginning of the whole program. The number of entries should be further expanded until practically all lexical units of 21st-century Polish language are described. Due to the electronic form of the work – a form open by its nature – the development of the WSJP can continue without end. On the one hand, new entries can be always added, and on the other hand, the existing descriptions can be extended, new fields included and entries improved.

3. References

NKJP (2012): *Narodowy Korpus Języka Polskiego*. Red. Adam Przepiórkowski, Mirosław Bańko, Rafał L. Górski, Barbara Lewandowska-Tomaszczyk, w przygotowaniu, kwiecień 2012.

Żmigrodzki, P. (2008): *Słowo – słownik – rzeczywistość. Z zagadnień leksykografii i metaleksykografii*. [Word – Dictionary – Realisty. Problems of Lexicography and Metalexicography]. Kraków: Lewis.

Żmigrodzki, P. (2009): *Wprowadzenie do leksykografii polskiej*. [Introduction to the Polish Lexicography]. Third expanded edition. Katowice: Wydawnictwo Uniwersytetu Śląskiego.

Żmigrodzki, P. (2011): Polish Academy of Sciences Great Dictionary of Polish. History, presence, prospects. In: *Studies in Polish Linguistics* 2011/6, 7-26.

Cecilia Robustelli

Il *Vocabolario dell'Accademia della Crusca* e i primi grandi vocabolari delle lingue europee[1]

Abstract

The *Vocabolario degli Accademici della Crusca* was published in 1612 as the result of three decades of work by the members of the Accademia della Crusca (learned men, laywers, poets, and artists). Founded in 1582 as an association of friends, mostly noble and well-off Florentine men interested in amicable cultural discussions, soon after the entry of Leonardo Salviati the Accademia's aim changed completely: all its activities became devoted to the preservation of the Florentine vernacular modelled on the authors of the Trecento and to the description of it as "the" language for literature. In the pursuit of this end, the *Vocabolario* constituted an essential instrument. It was not planned as an historical dictionary, in the sense of one that provides evidence of the development of the Italian language, but as a dictionary in which Italian writers could find only those words which were "permitted" according to the Cruscan model of language, shaped by Bembo's theories as developed and modified by Leonardo Salviati. Four additional editions followed the *princeps* (1623; 1691; 1729-1738; 1863-1923), all of which can now be read on the web and also searched as a database. Each edition has an lengthy preface stating the most controversial principles of the lexicographic work which has been under discussion during the long years of preparation: the selection of authors to be included, the possible inclusion of foreign or obsolete words, the choice of examples taken from non-literary texts, especially from the technical languages,and so on. The fifth and last edition was interrupted at the word *ozono* as the project was cancelled by the Government. In the Fifties the Accademia planned a new dictionary, explicitly based on "historical principles". Between 1983 and 1985 the lexicographic work for the dictionary was taken up by a research unit of the Italian National Research Council, then called *Opera del Vocabolario Italiano* (OVI). The *Tesoro della Lingua Italiana* (TLIO), covering the period from the first Italian texts up to 1375, constitutes the first chronological section of the complete historical dictionary of Italian (the ultimate goal of the OVI Institute).

The dictionary became a benchmark in the early years of European lexicography and served as a model for the first dictionaries of other European national languages: the first French, Portuguese, Spanish, English and German dictionaries all explicitly refer to the *Vocabolario*, even if they were based on different

[1] Questo articolo intende offrire una panoramica molto generale delle edizioni del *Vocabolario degli Accademici della Crusca* e dei suoi rapporti con i primi grandi vocabolari delle lingue europee. La bibliografia sul *Vocabolario* è ormai molto ampia: mi limito quindi a rimandare, per gli studi più recenti, ai saggi contenuti nei seguenti volumi: *La Crusca nella tradizione letteraria e linguistica italiana,* Atti del congresso internazionale per il IV centenario dell'Accademia della Crusca (Firenze, 29 settembre-2 ottobre 1983), Firenze, Accademia della Crusca, 1985; *The Fairest Flower: the Emergence of Linguistic National Consciousness in Renaissance Europe*, Proceedings of the International Conference of the Center for Medieval and Renaissance Studies, University of California (Los Angeles, 11-12 December 1983), Firenze, Accademia della Crusca, 1985; *Una lingua, una civiltà. Il Vocabolario*, Accademia della Crusca, Varese, Era Edizioni, 2008; *Il Vocabolario degli Accademici della Crusca (1612) e la storia della lessicografia italiana*, Atti del X Convegno internazionale dell'Associazione per la Storia della Lingua Italiana (Padova-Venezia, 29 novembre-1 dicembre 2012), a cura di Ivano Paccagnella e Lorenzo Tomasin, Firenze, Franco Cesati Editore, 2013. Si veda anche Pietro G. Beltrami and Simone Fornara, 'Italian historical Dictionaries: from the Accademia della Crusca to the Web', *International Journal of Lexicography*, 17/4, pp. 357-384. Sulla lessicografia italiana a partire dai primi lessici medievali si veda Claudio Marazzini, *L'ordine delle parole*, Bologna, il Mulino, 2009, in particolare per le vicende del *Vocabolario* i capitoli III-VIII. Il sito dell'Accademia della Crusca (www.accademiadellacrusca.it) permette di consultare il suo ricco patrimonio archivistico e bibliografico, comprese le cinque edizioni del Vocabolario, l'archivio generale, il Fondo dei Citati.

principles and criteria. Perusal of the prefaces of their first editions, such as the French *Dictionnaire de l'Académie* (1694), the *Vocabulário Portuguez e Latino* (1712-1728), the *Diccionario de la lengua castellana* (1726), the *Dictionary of the English language* (1752), the *Deutsches Wörterbuch* (1852-1961), gives the reader a clear picture of their relationship, and at times of their debt, to the *Vocabolario*.

1. La nascita del *Vocabolario* e la sua prima edizione: 1612

Il *Vocabolario degli Accademici della Crusca* rappresenta il frutto più significativo dell'attività filologica e lessicografica che ha animato l'Accademia della Crusca a partire dalla sua fondazione, avvenuta nel 1582 a Firenze per iniziativa di un gruppo di amici: Giovanni Battista Deti, Anton Francesco Grazzini, Bernardo Canigiani, Bernardo Zanchini, Bastiano de' Rossi. L'ingresso nell'Accademia, pochi mesi dopo, di Leonardo Salviati, ne determinò e delimitò gli interessi, da allora vòlti decisamente allo studio della lingua. A questo si dedicheranno negli anni successivi anche i nuovi accademici, non necessariamente linguisti o filologi ma ecclesiastici, filosofi, letterati in una prima fase, poi anche medici, naturalisti, speziali e artisti, scienziati. Il progetto di un *Vocabolario degli Accademici della Crusca,* che vedrà la luce nel 1612 a Venezia presso Giovanni Alberti, si delinea già nei primi anni di attività dell'Accademia e avrà come promotori, autori e finanziatori (ché l'impresa non godrà di finanziamenti pubblici ma rimarrà privata) gli stessi accademici. Il lavoro si dimostrò colossale fin dalle lunghe sedute preparatorie in cui furono decisi la sua impostazione metodologica e i criteri relativi alla selezione dei testi destinati allo spoglio, alla redazione delle singole voci, alla scelta delle citazioni.[2] Il risultato fu di tale portata da imprimere una svolta nelle lessicografia nazionale e anche in quella europea, dove la conoscenza e la diffusione del *Vocabolario* fu probabilmente favorita dalla presenza, già nel primo periodo di attività dell'Accademia, di soci stranieri.[3] Anche per questo si può sostenere che il *Vocabolario degli Accademici della Crusca* rappresenta il primo grande vocabolario di una lingua europea e che costituisce come vedremo più avanti, un modello per i dizionari delle altre lingue.

Nella prefazione alla prima impressione del 1612, in un unico volume di 1092 pagine, Bastiano de' Rossi dichiara che il materiale lessicale lemmatizzato e le citazioni d'autore che lo accompagnano sono tratti da un corpus di testi scelti in base a un modello linguistico di tipo arcaizzante, corrispondente al fiorentino del Trecento proposto da Pietro Bembo, il canonizzatore cinquecentesco della lingua letteraria:

> Nel compilare il presente Vocabolario (col parere dell'Illustrissimo Cardinal Bembo, de' Deputati alla correzion del Boccaccio dell'anno 1573 e ultimamente del Cavalier Lionardo Salviati) abbiamo stimato necessario di ricorrere all'autorità di quegli scrittori, che vissero, quando questo idioma principalmente fiorì, che fu da' tempi di Dante, o ver poco prima, sino ad alcuni anni, dopo la morte del Boccaccio. Il qual tempo, raccolto in una somma di tutto un secolo, potremo dir, che

---

[2] Sul materiale relativo alla preparazione della prima edizione del Vocabolario si veda Severina Parodi (a cura di), *Gli atti del primo Vocabolario*, Firenze, Sansoni, 1974, poi ristampato con aggiunta di indici (Firenze, Accademia della Crusca, 1983).

[3] Tra i primi soci stranieri si ricordano lo spagnolo Francesco Ximenes, dal 1651; il danese Niels Steensen dal 1668; il francese *Jean-François-Paul de Gondi* dal 1670; l'inglese John Price dal 1651; l'olandese Nicolaas Heinsius dal 1652; i tedeschi Marco Welser, corrispondente di Galileo dal 1613 e, ancora prima, Lodovico d'Anhalt, "L'Acceso", dal 1600. Sui soci stranieri nell'Accademia si veda Alfredo Reumont, *Dei soci esteri dell'Accademia della Crusca*, Firenze, coi tipi della Galileiana, 1855, e la sezione "Gli Accademici" contenuta nell'Archivio Digitale dell'Accademia della Crusca.

> sia dall'anno del Signore 1300 al 1400 poco più, o poco meno [...] assicuratici prima, che, se non tutti, almeno la maggior parte di essi, o fossero scrittor Fiorentini o avessero adoprato nelle scritture loro, vocaboli e maniere di parlare di questa Patria.

E precisa che *Vocabolario* oltre che sulle opere contenute in questo vero e proprio "nucleo" si basava anche su "volgarizzamenti, e traslatamenti d'opere altrui, tratti parte dal Latino, e parte dal Provenzale", su opere di scrittori non toscani, come Ariosto, e su testi non letterari. Traspaiono da queste aperture gli interventi di Varchi e di Salviati, che ampliò il ristretto canone bembiano fino ad accettare anche voci non fiorentine e voci tecnico-scientifiche seppure – queste seconde – in numero e con definizioni molto ridotte.[4] Solo l'attestazione delle voci in testi toscani antichi, tuttavia, garantiva il loro prestigio letterario, cosicché per aumentarne il numero lo scavo filologico si allargò alla tradizione manoscritta, decisione che non mancò di suscitare perplessità fra gli stessi accademici.

Rispetto alla lessicografia cinquecentesca precedente la grafia adottata e i criteri di organizzazione delle voci, come dichiarato nella prefazione, presentano novità. Per esempio il nesso *–ct-* viene sostituito da *–tt-*, la *h* etimologica viene abolita (eccetto che in *huomo* e nei suoi derivati), ecc. Le locuzioni avverbiali sono citate sotto la parola "principale" messa a lemma:

> Gli avverbi composti di più parole son dichiarati, il più delle volte, nel discorso della parola più principale, come A modo sotto la voce modo: A martello sotto la voce martello: e all'ordine dell'Abbiccì sarà tratto fuori A modo vedi modo, A martello, vedi martello, ec.

Si segnalano entrambe le possibilità d'uso dei termini impiegati anche con valore metaforico: "De' nomi, e de' verbi s'è le più volte dichiarato nel primo luogo il senso più proprio, e dipoi il traslato, o men proprio, per metafora, o per similitudine, ec.".

L'accoglienza dell'opera da parte degli intellettuali del tempo non fu scevra da critiche che si appuntavano soprattutto sulla scelta del modello di lingua arcaizzante proposto dal *Vocabolario* e sull'esclusione di molti scrittori del Cinquecento, Tasso su tutti. Mi limito qui a ricordare Paolo Beni che con *L'Anticrusca ovvero il paragone dell'italiana lingua: nel qual si mostra chiaramente che l'antica sia inculta e rozza: e la moderna regolata e gentile*, pubblicata nello stesso anno della prima edizione del *Vocabolario*, innescò una furiosa polemica linguistica dai pericolosi risvolti politici (vi furono coinvolti Cosimo II de' Medici e il senato di Venezia). Altre reazioni giunsero dai letterati di Siena, la città toscana in cui era stata istituita nel 1589 la cattedra di lingua toscana e che più di ogni altra insidiava a Firenze il primato linguistico.[5]

2. La seconda edizione: 1623

L'attività lessicografica degli accademici produsse la seconda edizione del *Vocabolario* nel 1623, ancora in un volume e ancora stampata a Venezia, ma presso Jacopo Sarzina. Nella prefazione lo si dichiara "riveduto, e ampliato, con aggiunta di molte voci degli autor del buon secolo" tratte non solo dalle opere dei più famosi "i quali sono Dante, Boccaccio, Petrarca, Giovan Villani, e simili" ma anche di autori "forestieri" (cioè non

---

[4] Valeria Della Valle, 'La lessicografia', in: *Storia della lingua italiana*, a cura di Luca Serianni e Pietro Trifone, I, 1993, 29-91.

[5] Per le reazioni al *Vocabolario* rimando a quanto dichiarato alla n. 1.

fiorentini), da volgarizzamenti, da manoscritti, purché "giudicate da noi belle, significanti e dell'uso nostro". Sembra riecheggiare qui l'affermazione di Giambullari nelle sue *Regole della lingua fiorentina* III, 115 "è adunque l'uso il vero maestro; lo uso, dico, di que' tanti che parlano, o scrivono", e invero questa convinzione sembra condivisa dagli autori di questa seconda edizione se proprio l'esser "voci dell'Uso" motiva l'inserimento di molte voci tratte anche da autori moderni, seppure quelli "tenuti da noi per migliori". I criteri di fondo che guidano la redazione di questa seconda edizione ricalcano in sostanza quelli della prima anche se in essa sono presenti alcune modifiche significative, per esempio riguardo alla definizione di voci scientifiche che testimoniano l'intervento di Galileo, accademico della Crusca dal 1605.[6] Non si placano quindi le critiche che formulano, con opere dettagliatissime e puntute fin dal titolo, gli avversari. Tra queste risaltano due opere accomunate dal non costituire una trattazione ordinata bensì una serie di singole osservazioni polemiche: *Incognito da Modana contro ad alcune voci del Vocabolario della Crusca*, che raccoglie una serie di postille di Alessandro Tassoni (sotto il cui nome furono pubblicate nel 1698 anche le *Annotazioni sopra il Vocabolario degli Accademici della Crusca* di Giulio Ottonelli), e *Il torto e il diritto del Non si può* di Daniello Bartoli (1655) che respinge con fulminante ironia il principio di autorità contenuto nelle condanne pronunciate dai grammatici.

3. La terza edizione: 1691

La terza edizione del *Vocabolario*, iniziata verso la metà del Seicento, ebbe una lunga fase preparatoria che si innesta in un periodo di grande attività lessicografica di respiro europeo. Escono a Parigi i primi vocabolari etimologici di due grandi lingue europee, il francese e l'italiano, a opera di Gilles Ménage: le *Origines de la langue française* nel 1650 e, tra il 1666 e il 1669, le *Origini della lingua italiana*, in cui confluì anche molto materiale preparato da Francesco Redi e da Carlo Dati per un vocabolario etimologico progettato dall'Accademia della Crusca e mai realizzato.[7] Nel 1691 viene pubblicato in Germania *Der Teutschen Sprache Stammbaum und Fortwachs oder Teutscher Sprachschatz*, il primo dizionario tedesco moderno, a opera del poeta e filologo Kaspar Stieler. Nello stesso anno esce finalmente, e per la prima volta a Firenze, presso la Stamperia dell'Accademia della Crusca, la terza edizione del *Vocabolario* "nuovamente corretto e copiosamente accresciuto". Questa edizione, articolata in tre volumi, è davvero innovativa rispetto alle precedenti e a essa guarderanno le grandi imprese lessicografiche europee. Infatti l'attenzione all'uso moderno, sostenuto dai suoi principali collaboratori, Buommattei e Dati, e insieme lo sforzo di mantenere un equilibrio con le posizioni più tradizionali e conservatrici, fanno sì che le novità non siano poche:[8] si amplia l'apertura a scrittori di area diversa da quella toscana – entra finalmente Tasso che nonostante la fama non era stato incluso nelle prime due edizioni – e ai "moderni"; cresce il numero

---

[6] La questione è affrontata da Paola Manni nel suo saggio '*Galileo accademico della Crusca*', in: *La Crusca nella tradizione letteraria e linguistica italiana*, cit., 119-136.

[7] Da ricordare anche le *Origenes linguae italicae* (1676) di Ottavio Ferrari, in latino, dedicato all'etimologia delle voci del dialetto milanese e del dialetto veneto.

[8] Si veda a questo proposito il saggio di Maurizio Vitale 'La III edizione del Vocabolario della Crusca. Tradizione e innovazione nella cultura linguistica fiorentina secentesca' nel suo volume *L'oro nella lingua. Contributi per una storia del tradizionalismo e del purismo italiano*, Milano-Napoli, Ricciardi, 1986, 273-333.

delle voci tratte dal lessico tecnico-scientifico (anche se Galileo era stato già inserito fra gli autori citati nella seconda edizione) grazie anche alla presenza nel comitato di redazione di uomini di scienza come Redi e Magalotti; vengono contrassegnate le Voci Antiche "non perché i Moderni, in scrivendo l'adoperino, ma perchè in leggendo gli Antichi gli intendano". Una revisione dei criteri di lemmatizzazione porta all'eliminazione dei rinvii a voci più importanti, sostituiti con nuove definizioni, e all'inserimento di voci anche senza la citazione d'autore.

4. Il *Vocabolario* e le grandi imprese lessicografiche europee tra Seicento e Settecento

Tutte le grandi imprese lessicografiche europee dichiarano, più o meno esplicitamente, che il *Vocabolario degli Accademici della Crusca* – di cui nella prima metà del Settecento uscirà la quarta impressione (v. oltre) – rappresenta ormai il modello con cui misurarsi.[9] L'Accademia della Crusca del resto favorisce la conoscenza del *Vocabolario* e i contatti scientifici con le altre istituzioni attraverso una crescente apertura all'Europa, testimoniata fin dai suoi primi anni di attività, come ho già ricordato in 1., dalla cooptazione di molti soci stranieri, alcuni dei quali sono anche membri di illustri accademie nei loro paesi. La lessicografia tedesca riconosce in Lodovico di Anhalt, fondatore nel XVII secolo della *Fruchtbringende Gesellschaft* modellata sull'Accademia della Crusca, uno dei suoi primi esponenti:

> Lodovico di Anhalt non solo contribuì a far viepiù gustare in Germania i pregi della poesia italiana, fra le cui opere con maggior plauso venne accolto il poema dell'Ariosto e più quello del Tasso, ma si diede a fondare, sulle norme della Crusca in cui egli sedé uno dei primi membri stranieri, quella Società chiamata Fruttifera, la quale bene meritò della lingua e letteratura alemanna.[10]

Lo scopo dei grandi lessicografi che tra Sette e Ottocento tenteranno di realizzare un grande dizionario della lingua tedesca sarà definitivamente raggiunto solo con il grande *Deutsches Wörterbuch* dei fratelli Grimm, in sedici volumi (iniziato nel 1852 e completato nel 1961), per il quale il *Vocabolario* fungerà da vero e proprio modello:

> Wenn die Herausgeber bei Leben und Gesundheit erhalten werden, so gedenken sie das gesammte Werk in sechs oder sieben starken, enggedruckten Bänden Kennern und Freunden der deutschen Sprache vorzulegen und es zugleich so einzurichten, dass es auch von Ausländern gebraucht werden könne, ungefähr in Art und Weise des *Vocabulario* [sic] *della Crusca*, dessen Muster hier überhaupt mehr vorgeschwebt hat, als der Plan und die Anordnung der übrigen bedeutenden Wörterbucher.[11]

---

9 Anche Antonio Mascis, autore del Vocabolaro Toscano e Turchesco pubblicato a Firenze nel 1677, aveva tenuto conto del *Vocabolario* 2to enrich his work with common Italian words" (Petek Kurtböke, '17th-century Italian-Turkish Dictionaries', in: *Proceedings of 6th Euralex International Congress on Lexicography,* a cura di Willy Martin, Willem Meijs, Margreet Morland, Elsemiek ten Pas, Piet van Sterkenburg & Piek Vossen, Amsterdam, The Netherlands, 1994, 540 (v. www.euralex.org/elx_proceedings/Euralex1994/60_Euralex_Petek%20Kurtboke%20-%2017th-century%20Italian-Turkish%20Dictionaries.pdf).

10 Alfredo Reumont, *Descrizione di Firenze nel 1598 del principe Lodovico d'Anhalt, nell'Accademia della Crusca* "L'Acceso", Firenze, coi tipi di M. Cellini & C., 1859, 5.

11 La citazione è tratta dall'annuncio dell'opera attribuito a Jacob Grimm, v. Walter Boehlich, 'Ein Pyrrhussieg der Germanistik. Die Vollendung des 'Deutsches Wörterbuchs der Brüder Grimm', *Der Monat* 13, 154, 1961, 38-55 (citazione a 39). Per il rapporto tra il Vocabolario e la lessicografia tedesca si veda Harro Stammerjohann, 'The Vocabolario and the German Lexicographie', in: *The Fairest Flower,* cit. 68-69.

4.1

Nel 1694, tre anni dopo la terza impressione del *Vocabolario* della Crusca, esce il *Dictionnaire de l'Académie française,* primo frutto dell'istituzione fondata nel 1635 della quale molti membri sono anche accademici della Crusca. La contiguità cronologica fra le due opere, la funzione di "autorità" in campo linguistico che entrambe assumeranno nei rispettivi paesi, l'omogeneità di origine e progettazione (entrambe sono il risultato del lavoro di un'accademia), indurrebbero a presupporre una vicinanza anche dei criteri di selezione dei testi e di organizzazione del materiale lessicografico, che invece non sussiste. Si leggano a questo proposito le parole di Giovanni Nencioni pronunciate in occasione del Convegno per il terzo centenario del *Dictionnaire*:[12]

> Les deux Académies se sont rencontrées au carrefour de la lexicographie linguistique, l'aînée projetant et composant un dictionnaire de la langue des auteurs depuis la treizième jusqu'au seizième siècle, c'est-à-dire un dictionnaire historique et philologique qui montrait les règles grammaticales et les tournures stylistiques dans les exemples des écrivains; la cadette projetant et composant un dictionnaire tout à fait nouveau et original, adéquat à la situation linguistique et politique moderne de la France du Grand Siècle, c'est-à-dire un dictionnaire de la langue nationale vivante, parlée dans les conversations des personnes cultivées et à la cour du Roi Soleil, et écrite par les poètes et les prosateurs classiques du même siècle. Les deux méthodes étaient, l'une at l'autre, légitimes, et donnèrent naissance à deux chefs-d'œuvre lexicographiques.

Dalla prefazione alla prima edizione emerge chiaramente che il *Dictionnaire* si distacca dal *Vocabolario* per quanto riguarda la lemmatizzazione, prevedendo la disposizione per famiglie di parole anziché quella in ordine alfabetico (introdotta a partire dalla seconda edizione)[13]

> Comme la Langue Françoise a des mots Primitifs, & des mots Derivez & Composez, on a jugé qu'il seroit agreable & instructif de disposer le Dictionnaire par Racines, c'est à dire de ranger tous les mots Derivez & Composez aprés les mots Primitifs dont ils descendent, soit que ces Primitifs soient d'origine purement Françoise, soit qu'ils viennent du Latin ou de quelqu'autre Langue

E che il materiale lessicale non deve includere termini arcaici né provenire dai linguaggi specialistici di tipo tecnico-scientifico, ma deve essere tratto – differenza, questa, davvero fondamentale rispetto al *Vocabolario* – dalla lingua contemporanea:

> C'est dans cet estat où la Langue Françoise se trouve aujourd'huy qu'a esté composé ce Dictionnaire; & pour la representer dans ce mesme estat, l'Académie a jugé qu'elle ne devoit pas y mettre les vieux mots qui sont entierement hors d'usage, ni les termes des Arts & des Sciences qui entrent rarement dans le Discours; Elle s'est retranchée à la Langue commune, telle qu'elle est dans le commerce ordinaire des honnestes gens, & telle que les Orateurs & les Poëtes l'employent.

L'unica caratteristica considerata comune al *Vocabolario* e al *Dictionnaire* dai redattori della prima impressione di questo sembra proprio il costituire, per entrambi, il punto di arrivo di una lunga gestazione, dovuta alla complessità del lavoro e alla partecipazione all'opera di un gran numero di accademici, e il frutto di un lavoro d'équipe:

---

[12] Messaggio di saluto di Giovanni Nencioni in: *Le Dictionnaire de l'Académie française et la lexicographie institutionnelle*, Actes du Colloque International, 17.18 et 19 november 1994, publiés par Bernard Quemada, Paris, Honoré Champion, 1998, 17. Il primo progetto di *Dictionnaire*, redatto da Jean Chapelain (membro dell'Académie Française, dell'Académie des Inscriptions e, dal 1654, anche dell'Accademia della Crusca) e poi non realizzato, prendeva a modello il *Vocabolario*, cfr. Claudio Marazzini, *L'ordine delle parole*, cit., 136

[13] Per il testo e un commento alle prefazioni delle edizioni del *Dictionnaire* si veda *Les Préfaces du Dictionnaire de l'Academie française*, 1694-1992, a cura di B. Quemada, Paris, H. Champion, 1997.

> [...] la maniere de travailler des Compagnies en general & de l'Académie en particulier, où tous ceux qui la composent disent successivement leur avis sur chaque mot & ou la diversité des opinions apporte necessairement de grands retardemens. La celebre Académie de Florence connuë sous le nom della Crusca en est une preuve convaincante. Elle a employé quarante ans à composer le Dictionnaire dont elle a enrichi la Langue Italienne & plus encore à l'augmenter & à le perfectionner, ce qui l'a mis en Estat de servir de regle pour toutes les difficultez de cette Langue. Et c'est en cela que la lenteur du travail d'une Compagnie est avantageusement recompensée par l'authorité de ses Décisions.

4.2

Nel 1713 era stata istituita la *Real Academia Española* con il proposito di "fijar las voces y vocablos de la lengua castellana en su mayor propiedad, elegancia y pureza", e nel 1726 esce la prima edizione del *Diccionario de la lengua castellana, en que se explica el verdadero sentido de las voces, su naturaleza y caledad, con las phrases o modos de hablar, los proverbios o refranes, y otras cosa convenientes al uso de la lengua.* Nella prefazione viene dichiarata esplicitamente l'adozione, come modello per la costruzione dell'opera, del *Vocabolario* della Crusca:

> 3. Como basa y fundamento de este Diccionario, se han puesto los Autóres que ha parecido à la Académia han tratado la Léngua Española con la mayor propriedcd y elegáncia [...]. 4. Para la formación de este Diccionario se han tenido presentes los de la Lénguas extrangéras, y especialmente el Vocabulario de la Crusca, cuya última edición, que fué la tercera, se hizo el año de 1691.

Anche il *Vocabulário Portuguez e Latino* di Rafael Bluteau, uscito fra il 1712 e il 1728, basato sui testi dei migliori scrittori, come è dichiarato nel frontespizio ("autorizado com exemplos dos melhores escritores portuguezes, e latinos"[14]) guarda al *Vocabolario.* Bluteau ne conosce la terza edizione, dal momento che nella dedica *Ao leitor estrangero* fa riferimento a una edizione in tre volumi:

> Outo volumes deste tamanho de vozes Portuguezas, quando os Academicos da Crusca em tres toda a lingoa Italiana, & a Academia Real de França em quatro volumes encerrou a fecundidade, & facundia da lingoa Franceza?

e più avanti

> No tocante aos vocabolarios da Crusca, & de Academia Real de França naõ fazem tantos volumes, como este, porque faõ monoglottos, quero dizer, de hum só idioma; hum he Francèz, outro he Italiano; mas este Vocabulario he bilingue, Portuguèz, & Latino, [...].

[14] Si vedano le osservazioni di João Paulo Silvestre, 'A recepção do Vocabolario della Crusca e do Dictionnaire de l'Académie na lexicografia portuguesa: o Vocabulario de Rafael Bluteau', Atti del XII Congresso Internazionale di Lessicografia, a cura di Elisa Corino, Carla Marello, Cristina Onesti (Torino, 6-9 settembre 2006), I, Alessandria, Edizioni dell'Orso, 2006, 97-102: "A língua portuguesa conhece no início do século XVIII o primeiro dicionário monumental, no seguimento da publicação da terceira edição do Vocabolario della Crusca (1691), do Dictionnaire de l'Académie Françoise (1694) e quando se preparava o Diccionario de la lengua castellana (1726-1739). Cerca de 1690, Rafael Bluteau inicia a redacção do Vocabulario Portuguez e Latino (1712-1728) tentando reproduzir em Portugal os métodos de trabalho, os objectivos e as funções que geralmente se associam aos primeiros dicionários dos vernáculos europeus, nomeadamente a constituição de sessões académicas". Sulla lessicografia lusitana dell'epoca Monica Lupetti, 'Tra Cardoso e Bluteau: la lessicografia portoghese del Seicento', *Quaderni del CIRSIL* 4, 2005, 65-77, www.lingue.unibo.it /cirsil.

4.3

A Dictionary of the English Language di Samuel Johnson, che sarebbe uscito nel 1752, rappresenta il punto di arrivo della lessicografia inglese che aveva mosso i primi passi due secoli prima con il *Latin-English Dictionary* dell'umanista Thomas Elyot nel 1538. L'opera era destinata, nelle intenzioni dell'autore a un pubblico ampio. Presenta molti punti di contatto con il *Vocabolario* della Crusca: l'impostazione fondamentalmente puristica, l'ostracismo verso i forestierismi particolarmente marcato per i prestiti "di lusso", e soprattutto il criterio di fondarsi sull'autorità di testi scritti del passato. Le ragioni di questa scelta sono però diverse rispetto a quelle che avevano guidato i redattori del *Vocabolario*. Nella lunga prefazione Johnson la motiva non con la superiorità della lingua antica quanto con il pessimo stato della lingua contemporanea, dovuta a incertezze grafiche e a mancanza di regole certe, che egli riconduce alla varietà di pronunce esistenti nel paese.[15] Il corpus prescelto non comprenderà né autori contemporanei,[16] con rarissime eccezioni, né di un passato troppo remoto,[17] ma solo quelli vissuti tra l'età elisabettiana e quella della Restaurazione.[18] In due passi compaiono riferimenti espliciti al *Vocabolario*[19]. Nel primo dopo aver giustificato la mancanza, nel suo *Dictionary*,

---

15 "When I took the first survey of my undertaking, I found our speech copious without order, and energetick without rules: wherever I turned my view, there was perplexity to be disentangled, and confusion to be regulated; choice was to be made out of boundless variety, without any established principle of selection; adulterations were to be detected, without a settled test of purity; and modes of expression, to be rejected or received, without the suffrages of any writers of classical reputation or acknowledged authority. Having therefore no assistance but from general grammar, I applied myself to the perusal of our writers [...]."

16 "My purpose was to admit no testimony of living authours, that I might not be misled by partiality, and that none of my contemporaries might have reason to complain; nor have I departed from this resolution, but when some performance of uncommon excellence excited my veneration, when my memory supplied me, from late books, with an example that was wanting, or when my heart, in the tenderness of friendship, solicited admission for a favourite name."

17 "But as every language has a time of rudeness antecedent to perfection, as well as of false refinement and declension, I have been cautious lest my zeal for antiquity might drive me into times too remote, and croud my book with words now no longer understood."

18 "I have studiously endeavoured to collect examples and authorities from the writers before the restoration, whose works I regard as *the wells of English undefiled*, as the pure sources of genuine diction. [...] I have fixed *Sidney's* work for the boundary, beyond which I make few excursions. From the authours which rose in the time of *Elizabeth*, a speech might be formed adequate to all the purposes of use and elegance. If the language of theology were extracted from *Hooker* and the translation of the Bible; the terms of natural knowledge from *Bacon*; the phrases of policy, war, and navigation from *Raleigh*; the dialect of poetry and fiction from *Spenser* and *Sidney*; and the diction of common life from *Shakespeare*, few ideas would be lost to mankind, for want of *English* words, in which they might be expressed."

19 Il *Vocabolario* era evidentemente molto noto fuori dai confini italiani anche ai non specialisti, come documenta una lettera di Lord Chesterfield pubblicata su *The World* del 28 novembre 1754 in cui nomina la *crusca* "MANY people have imagined that so extensive a work would have been best performed by a number of persons, who should have taken their several departments, of examining, sifting, winnowing (I borrow this image from the Italian *crusca*) purifying, and finally fixing our language, by incorporating their respective funds into one joint stock)" e più avanti fa riferimento a un dizionario della lingua fiorentina: "The celebrated dictionaries of the Florentine and French academies owe their present size and perfection to very small beginnings. Some private gentlemen at Florence, and some at Paris, had met at each others houses to talk over and consider their respective languages; upon which they published some short essays, which essays were the embrio's of those

di termini tecnici relativi a arti e mestieri col fatto che conoscerli era impossibile perché essi non risultavano documentati da testi scritti ma erano affidati solo alla comunicazione orale:

> it was unavoidable: I could not visit caverns to learn the miner's language, nor take a voyage to perfect my skill in the dialect of navigation [...] to gain the names of wares, tools and operations, of which no mention is found in books

sostiene che la loro presenza nel *Vocabolario* sarebbe stata permessa da una serie di testi stati scritti appositamente ('professedly") per documentarli:

> To furnish the academicians *della Crusca* with words of this kind, a series of comedies called *la Fiera*, or *the Fair*, was professedly written by *Buonaroti*; but I had no such assistant, and therefore was content to want what they must have wanted likewise, had they not luckily been so supplied.

Il secondo riferimento, che non contiene il nome dell'Accademia della Crusca ma è ugualmente inequivocabile, compare nella parte finale della prefazione. Johnson, secondo un *topos* comune, giustifica i suoi eventuali errori e li attribuisce all'aver intrapreso e concluso da solo un lavoro che in altri casi si è rivelato imperfetto anche se condotto da schiere di studiosi come a era avvenuto, appunto, per gli "*Italian* academicians":

> I have only failed in an attempt which no human powers have hitherto completed. If the lexicons of ancient tongues, now immutably fixed, and comprised in a few volumes, be yet, after the toil of successive ages, inadequate and delusive; if the aggregated knowledge, and co-operating diligence of the *Italian* academicians, did not secure them from the censure of *Beni*; if the embodied criticks of *France*, when fifty years had been spent upon their work, were obligated to change its oeconomy, and give their second edition another form, I may surely be contented without the praise of perfection, which, if I could obtain, in this gloom of solitude, what would it avail me?

5. La quarta edizione: 1729-1738

Probabilmente Johnson aveva avuto modo di vedere la quarta edizione del *Vocabolario*, uscita in sei volumi tra il 1729 e il 1738 a Firenze presso lo stampatore Domenico Maria Manni. I criteri organizzativi delle voci sembrano ormai sostanzialmente consolidati nonostante alcuni ritocchi, annunciati nella prefazione, come la lemmatizzazione separata degli omonimi quando, rispetto al loro significato, "sono molto tra loro diversi". Qualche segnale di arroccamento su posizioni conservatrici rispetto alle aperture della terza edizione si nota invece nello spoglio delle opere, che si allarga a testi di autori fiorentini (Benvenuto Cellini) anche moderni (Anton Maria Salvini) mentre vengono espunte opere di scrittori forestieri (il grammatico Marcantonio Mambelli detto "'il Cinonio") e di tipo tecnico (come il *Vocabolario toscano dell'arte del disegno* di Filippo Baldinucci). Particolarmente significativa la chiusura nei confronti del linguaggio della scienza, parallela a quella attuata nella prima edizione del *Dictionnaire de l'Académie française*.[20]

perfect productions, that now do so much honour to the two nations." (http://johnsonsdictionaryonline.com/?page_id=3246).

[20] Per il linguaggio tecnico e scientifico la lessicografia italiana e europea dimostra però già da tempo vivo interesse, come provano il *Dictionnaire Universel* di Antoine Furetière (1690), il *Dictionnaire des arts et des sciences* (1694), l'*Universal Dictionary of Arts and Sciences* di Ephraim Chambers (1728).

L'ancoraggio a posizioni conservatrici e ai "Classici Autori di lingua" viene mitigato da (moderate) aperture all'uso, a proverbi, a neologismi, a forestierismi.

Copie pirata, compendi e edizioni con aggiunte del *Vocabolario* potrebbero far pensare a un suo ruolo da protagonista nella lessicografia del tempo, ma il parallelo fiorire di opere lessicografiche di altro carattere, come i lessici e i primi dizionari dialettali (anche se questi fanno sovente rispettoso riferimento al *Vocabolario* con l'affiancare ai singoli dialettismi i corrispondenti toscani) mostra che le esigenze lessicografiche e più ampiamente linguistiche – diremmo quasi "comunicative" – di questo periodo travalicano i limiti ormai angusti del *Vocabolario*.[21]

6. La chiusura dell'Accademia (1783) e la quinta edizione del *Vocabolario*: 1863-1923

Dopo un periodo di chiusura dell'Accademia, decretata dal granduca di Toscana Pietro Leopoldo nel 1783, e il suo accorpamento insieme a quella degli Apatisti nell'Accademia fiorentina, in ragione della sua ormai mancata rispondenza alle necessità culturali dell'epoca, nel 1811 se ne ha il ripristino. L'impresa del *Vocabolario* torna in discussione e si progetta una nuova edizione di cui tra il 1843 e il 1852 vengono pubblicati i primi sette fascicoli, nel 1863 il primo volume. Ma la lessicografia italiana è ormai cambiata e se il modello proposto dalla Crusca gode ancora di qualche approvazione molti sono i dizionari e vocabolari che se ne distaccano e acquistano un prestigio proprio. L'esempio più eclatante è rappresentato dal grande *Dizionario universale critico enciclopedico della lingua italiana* di Francesco Alberti di Villanuova, pubblicato tra il 1797 e il 1805, che includeva i forestierismi e moltissime voci del vocabolario tecnico escluse dal *Vocabolario,* di cui verrà a costituire un vero e proprio modello alternativo e, dobbiamo dire, vincente, vista l'ampia diffusione. La pubblicazione, contemporanea al primo volume della quinta impressione del *Vocabolario*, del *Dizionario della lingua italiana* di Tommaseo, caratterizzato dall'equilibrio tra lingua letteraria, lingua dell'uso e linguaggi tecnico-scientifici, scalzerà definitivamente il *Vocabolario* dalla sua posizione di dominio del panorama lessicografico italiano, né la pubblicazione di altri dieci volumi sarà sufficiente a permettergli di riconquistarla.

7. L'impresa del *Vocabolario* dal Novecento a oggi: il progetto per la costruzione di un vocabolario storico e il *Tesoro della lingua italiana delle origini*

Nel 1923, in pieno periodo fascista, l'impresa viene interrotta dal ministro dell'istruzione del tempo, Giovanni Gentile, e il *Vocabolario* si interrompe alla voce *ozono*. L'attività dell'Accademia si concentra sulla filologia e sebbene negli anni successivi siano pubblicati lessici e abbozzati progetti di nuovi dizionari il progetto di un *Vocabolario* verrà rimesso in discussione solo nel dopoguerra.[22]

---

[21] Rimando alle osservazioni nel capitolo di Tina Matarrese 'Lessicografia e grammatiche', in: *Il Settecento*, il Mulino, Bologna, 1993, 165-183.

[22] Si veda Claudio Marazzini, *L'ordine delle parole*, cit., 383-388. Escono, fra le altre opere, in questo periodo l'*Enciclopedia Italiana*, il *Lessico Universale Italiano* e il *Vocabolario*, tutte realizzate dall'Istituto della Enciclopedia Italiana, di matrice fascista.

Nel 1961 la pubblicazione del *Grande dizionario della lingua italiana* di Salvatore Battaglia, cui subentrò nel 1971 Giorgio Bàrberi Squarotti, in XXI volumi l'ultimo dei quali uscito nel 2002, riempì il vuoto che si era creato con la soppressione del *Vocabolario*. Si trattava di un vero e proprio vocabolario storico, nato con lo scopo di rivedere e aggiornare il dizionario di Tommaseo, che oggi comprende lemmi e citazioni tratti dalla letteratura, ma anche da testi non letterari, del Novecento fino all'età contemporanea.

Nel 1964 l'Accademia della Crusca riprende il progetto di fare un vocabolario, questa volta con criteri del tutto diversi rispetto alla serie precedente: sarebbe dovuto essere un grande vocabolario storico,[23] anzi, il *Vocabolario Storico della Lingua Italiana* (VSLI), costruito alla luce delle grandi imprese lessicografiche europee e dei progressi della tecnologia informatica. La mancanza di finanziamenti adeguati suggerì però di procedere per tappe. Nel 1973 fu progettata la prima sezione, dalle origini al 1375, anno della morte di Boccaccio. Nel 1985 la struttura dell'Accademia dedicata al vocabolario è diventata il Centro di Studi Opera del Vocabolario Italiano, oggi Istituto del Consiglio Nazionale delle Ricerche, diretto dal 1992 da Pietro Beltrami. Attualmente la prima sezione del vocabolario, in avanzato stato di realizzazione e nota come *Tesoro della Lingua Italiana delle Origini* (TLIO), è completamente digitalizzata[24] ed è affiancata da una banca dati consultabile separatamente. Il TLIO è "redatto di prima mano, cioè studiando direttamente i testi e non prendendo parole, definizioni ed esempi dai vocabolari esistenti, se non in casi limitati che vengono sempre segnalati. Per fare ciò si serve della grande banca dati dell'italiano antico che l'OVI ha elaborato a questo scopo".[25]

Le cinque edizioni del *Vocabolario* della Crusca sono ora in rete,[26] corredate dalla riproduzione fotografica del testo e dalla sua trascrizione informatica, e consultabili liberamente da tutti coloro che intendono studiarne contenuto, proposte e criteri.

---

[23] Sulla questione, oltre a Claudio Marazzini, *L'ordine delle parole*, op.cit., 394-409, si veda Giovanni Nencioni, *Saggi di lingua antica&moderna*, Torino, Rosemberg&Sellier, 1989, 365-372. Per una discussione della nozione di "vocabolario storico" rimando a Pietro G. Beltrami, 'Past and Present of Italian Historical Dictionaries', in: *Quo vadis lexicography?*, 6th Working Meeting of German Language Academy Dictionaries (Berlin 2-5 September 2009), http://dwb.bbaw.de/tagung09/indexengl.html.

[24] Sul TLIO si vedano, tra gli altri, Pietro G. Beltrami, 'Il Tesoro della Lingua Italiana delle Origini (TLIO)', in: *Italia linguistica anno Mille, Italia linguistica anno Duemila*, Atti del XXXIV Congresso SLI (Firenze, 19-21 ottobre 2000) a cura di Nicoletta Maraschio e Teresa Poggi Salani, Roma, Bulzoni 2003, 605-608; Pietro G. Beltrami e Andrea Boccellari, 'Banche dati e dizionari on-line. *Il Tesoro della Lingua Italiana delle Origini* e la banca dati dell'italiano antico dell'Opera del Vocabolario Italiano', in: *Nuovi media e lessicografia storica*, Atti del colloquio in occasione del settantesimo compleanno di Max Pfister (Saarbrücken, 21-22 aprile 2002), a cura di Wolfgang Schweickard, Tübingen, Niemeyer, 2006, 3-14; Pietro G. Beltrami, 'La lessicografia italiana a Firenze e l'Opera del Vocabolario Italiano', in: *Firenze e la lingua italiana fra nazione ed Europa*, Atti del Convegno di studi (Firenze, 27-28 maggio 2004) a cura di Nicoletta Maraschio, Firenze, Firenze University Press, 2007, 181-188; Id. 'La nuova lessicografia dell'italiano antico. Il *Tesoro della Lingua Italiana delle Origini*', *Bollettino dell'Atlante Lessicale degli Antichi Volgari Italiani*, I, 2008, 33-52; Id., 'The Lexicography of Early Italian: its Evolution and Recent Advances', in: *Perspectives on Lexicography in Italy and Europe*, a cura di Silvia Bruti, Roberta Cella and Marina Foschi Albert, Newcastle upon Tyne, Cambridge Scholars Publishing, 2009, 27-53.

[25] www.ovi.cnr.it/index.php?page=il-vocabolario.

[26] Per le caratteristiche tecniche della digitalizzazione delle cinque edizioni si veda Massimo Fanfani, Marco Biffi, 'La lessicografia della Crusca in rete', in: Atti del XII Congresso Internazionale di Lessicografia, cit. 409-416, accessibile all'indirizzo www.euralex.org/elx_proceedings/Euralex2006/.

Guðrún Kvaran

Modern Icelandic lexicography

1. Introduction

Iceland is a small country of around 320,000 inhabitants. Nonetheless there is a vibrant book publishing industry and the general public buys a substantial number of books, both domestic and translated works. On account of how few people speak the language, extensive education in foreign languages is needed. The first foreign language taught in schools is English, the second language is Danish, owing to the fact that Iceland was part of the Danish state until 1944. Iceland is a member of the Nordic Council, which is a geo-political, inter-parliamentary forum for co-operation between the Nordic countries. The council places great emphasis on a mutual and internal understanding of Nordic, especially Scandinavian, languages, and Danish continues to be taught in Icelandic elementary and high schools. Other foreign languages taught in the upper levels of elementary schools and in high schools are primarily French, German and Spanish.

Language teaching and the use of foreign languages entails a need for dictionaries, with the country's language both as a target and source language. For a long time efforts were made to meet this need, but in the last decade little work has been done in this field and most of the available books are in serious need of extensive revision. Lexicography is time consuming and expensive work, and publishing companies show little interest. To the best of my knowledge no new or revised dictionary is in process in Iceland. However, several things are now happening towards improving the situation.

The University of Iceland had for sixty years an institute for lexicography, Orðabók Háskólans (The University Dictionary). This has now been merged with four other institutions in the field of Icelandic studies under the name the Árni Magnússon Institute for Icelandic Studies (www.arnastofnun.is). Originally the Institute for lexicography worked solely on a historical dictionary, work that was started in 1943. I will very briefly say something about this dictionary, but the main emphasis of this lecture will be on some novel developments, and in particular on a web-based dictionary called ISLEX. In addition, three projects of the department of lexicography of the Árni Magnússon Institute will be introduced, that are intended (in part) to strengthen and support dictionary making. Finally I will introduce an online website called "Snara". Dictionaries and some other reference works have been made publicly accessible there.

2. Historical dictionary of the Icelandic language

In the Nordic countries interest in historical dictionaries arose early. The reason why work was started on a historical dictionary in Iceland was simply that among the projects which the Arni Magnusson Institute in Copenhagen had embarked on and provided funds for in 1939, was the compiling of a historical dictionary of the ancient Icelandic language from the oldest known texts up to the middle of the 16th century. This date was based on the first printing of a book in Icelandic in 1540, a translation of the New Testament.

In 1943 the governing council of the University of Iceland agreed to begin a work on an Icelandic historical dictionary, ranging from 1540 and up to this present day, i.e., to continue where the Copenhagen dictionary project ended. By the millennium, most of the collection of slips, about two and a half million, with examples culled from printed books and manuscripts ranging over four centuries, had been made accessible on the Internet through the home page of the Institute and further under "Ritmálsafn Orðabókar Háskólans". Work is underway to make a collection from the colloquial language, around 300,000 slips, accessible in the same way. Since the funding for the institute comes from the state treasury the access must be free and open to all.

With increased technology by the end of the last century, interest in making the collection of examples easier enjoyed support, and the institute has now accumulated a fairly good corpus of chosen texts for searching, with about 80 million running words. The corpus is open to the general public for searching and grows at a steady rate. It has been indexed by content for those who are looking for something in a special field, but the entire text in the corpus can also be searched. The access is through the home page of the Institute under the link "Gagnasöfn" (corpuses) and further under "Íslenskt textasafn" (Icelandic collection of texts). In addition the institute has, in collaboration with others, made a tagged Icelandic corpus, of which I will say more later on.

Due to lack of funding the historical project has hardly moved forward in the last decade, with more emphasis being placed on projects that were eligible for grants or more suitable for collaborations with others. Among other things, one concern was to strengthen the Institute in the field of dictionary making in general and making it better suited to take part in collaborative efforts. As a state funded institute it cannot, however, engage in direct competition with private publishers serving the general market.

3. The ISLEX-project

Although the work on the historical dictionary has been on hiatus, experience shows that the slip-collections, the corpus and several side projects are extremely useful for all kinds of work on Icelandic dictionaries. This is brought out, for example, by a collaboration that started in 2006 and reached an important milestone in 2011. This project, spearheaded by the department of lexicography, is an Icelandic-Scandinavian multilingual dictionary, usually called ISLEX. The headwords are Icelandic and the translations are into five languages: Danish, Swedish, Norwegian (both bokmål and nynorsk) and Faroese. The dictionary describes modern Icelandic. It is of a medium-size with about 50,000 lemmas. In addition it has a large number of collocations, phrases and idioms and many examples of use intended both for Icelandic and foreign users.

Icelandic is a language with a complicated inflectional system, and therefore it is very useful for foreign users to have a link to a database of inflections (nouns, adjectives, verbs) which I will come to later in this paper. ISLEX was opened to the general public on the "Day of the Icelandic language" on November 16th 2011, but the Faeroese part will only be ready in 2014, as the work on this part started later. Work on Finnish will commence at the beginning of the year 2013 with Nordic and domestic grants. How these two projects will fare is entirely dependent on grants, but it is increasingly difficult to procure funds for salaries, without which no translators can be hired.

ISLEX is now, at the end of 2012, the result of the collaboration of five Nordic countries. It will combine six Nordic languages and will therefore be an important contribution to the understanding between these nations – which are all closely related culturally and historically but speak different languages. The sixth language, Finnish, is a welcome addition, as Finnish is one of the Nordic languages even if it is of a different language family. The ISLEX-project has enhanced the relations between the participating universities and institutes and has received generous grants from Nordic funds. The dictionary is open to the public on the web, free of charge.

The ISLEX-partners are six Nordic institutes:

- Iceland: Stofnun Árna Magnússonar í íslenskum fræðum, Reykjavík.
- Denmark: Det Danske Sprog- og Litteraturselskab (DSL), Copenhagen.
- Norway: The University of Bergen.
- Sweden: Institutionen för svenska språket, Göteborg.
- Faroe Islands: Fróðskaparsetur Føroya, Tórshavn
- Finland: The University of Helsinki.

Each institute is a special unit team who takes care of the translations into their respective languages. They are also responsible for the financing of their part of the project. The project is mainly funded by the government of each participating country. Otherwise it would never have become reality, but substantial grants, mostly Nordic but also some domestic, have also been awarded for specific aspects of the project and collaborative effort, such as yearly consultation meetings.

ISLEX was designed from the beginning for the web and has never been intended as a printed book. It is operated and maintained in a central database, located in Reykjavík, but the editorial work was done simultaneously in the five countries as will be the fact with Faroese and Finish until the work has been completed. Many features of the web have been used, such as pictures, sounds, and hyperlinks, plus a range of search functions, etc. The database also functions as a communication tool.

From the start the recordings of the pronunciation of the headwords was on the list of desired features. Recently a grant was acquired for this work and recording of the lemmas and a great deal of the collocations will be finished at the end of 2012. The goal is also to record the phrases too.

The translations are in different stages of completion: the Swedish and Danish are nearly finished; and the Norwegian translations of the lemmas and a part of the collocations will be finished at the end of 2012. As the Faroese first joined the project in February 2011 they have still much work to do.

For those who are interested in looking something up, ISLEX can be accessed in four ways (a choice of different user profiles according to the metalanguage of the web page):

- Icelandic: www.islex.is,
- Danish: www.islex.dk,
- Norwegian: www.islex.no,
- Swedish: www.islex.se.

The dictionary is also available on mobile phones (iPhone, Nokia windows and Android).

There can be no doubt that the project would not have progressed as well as it did if the basic lexicographical data of the Institute in Reykjavík had not been available. The slip-collection on the Internet and the text corpus were extensively used for clarification and searching for examples and collocations, phrases and idioms.

The outcome of the ISLEX-project has been extensively used ever since it was launched, both in Iceland and in the Nordic countries. Originally the main emphasis was towards translators, but now the dictionary is in equal terms directed at children, teenagers and students in the Nordic countries with a view towards increasing their understanding of Nordic languages. Users can submit questions and comments, and the administrators of the project try to answer them and react to suggestions for improvements as far as possible. Currently means for continuing the project are being sought as a project like ISLEX will soon be outdated if nothing can be done to add new words, phrases and collocations and correct translations and misspellings.

After the formal presenting of ISLEX in 2011 interest has sprung up regarding collaborating on more dictionaries. In the summer 2012 the ambassadors of France and Germany to Iceland visited the department of lexicography of the Árni Magnússon institute to discuss the first ideas about collaborations on an Icelandic-German and Icelandic-French dictionary and talks are also underway about an Icelandic-Polish dictionary. A significant number of Poles have immigrated to Iceland in the last decades.

4. The Database of Modern Icelandic Inflection

As I mentioned before, Icelandic is a morphologically rich language with a complex inflectional system. It has up to 16 inflectional forms of a noun, 120 of an adjective, and 107 of a verb, not including variants. The endings that mark grammatical categories can, in some instances, have a number of variants, and stem changes are common, both in vowels and consonants. As an example I will show the word *köttur* 'cat' in all cases, plural and singular, with and without a suffixed article.

Case	Singular	With suffixed article	Plural	With suffixed article
Nom.	köttur	kötturinn	kettir	kettirnir
Acc.	kött	köttinn	ketti	kettina
Dat.	ketti	kettinum	köttum	köttunum
Gen.	kattar	kattarins	katta	kattanna

The database contains about 270,000 paradigms from Modern Icelandic, with over 5.8 million inflectional forms. It is accessible through the institute's home page and further under "Beyging orða" (the inflection of words). The database was created as a multipurpose resource, for use in language technology, lexicography, and as an online resource for the general public. It is e.g. much used by teachers and pupils as well as university students. This information is taken from an article by Kristín Bjarnadóttir, the editor of the database (2012). The article is available online (see the references section).

Traditional Icelandic dictionaries provide limited information on inflection. The tradition is to give only certain inflectional forms as indicators of inflectional class, such as the genitive singular and nominative plural for nouns, either by showing the endings or, in the case of vowel change, by showing the whole inflectional form. Information on the inflection in other word classes is also fragmentary. The description of verbs is usually confined to the principal parts, i.e. three or four inflectional forms, depending on inflectional class, four for the so called strong verbs and three for weak verbs. The inflection of adjectives is very often omitted altogether, although it is not easily predictable from the base forms. This information is enough for most Icelanders, but certainly not all, and they are insufficient for foreign users. It is for this reason that at the start of the ISLEX-project it was decided not to list traditional inflectional forms, but instead put in a link to the *Database of Modern Icelandic Inflection*. This has proven to be a very good and popular decision.

5. The Tagged Icelandic Corpus

Although the institute has collected a reasonably extensive corpus to facilitate searching for examples for dictionary making and every type of language studies, as mentioned above, it has the drawback that it is not tagged and each word form must be searched for separately. Therefore it was decided to establish a different kind of collection in collaboration with the University of Iceland and the Reykjavík University. This is called *The Tagged Icelandic Corpus* and consists of about 25 million tokens of contemporary Icelandic texts collected from varied sources during the years 2006-2010. The corpus is intended for use in Language Technology projects, for linguistic research and for lexicography. The corpus is available for search through a web interface and has already proved to be useful. The permission for the use of texts in the corpus has been secured from all copyright holders. To get all the permits required much work, but the effort was worth while. The researchers can now obtain the texts and use them for their projects (Helgadóttir et al. 2012).

6. The Icelandic Word Net

The third project I would like to mention is the *Icelandic Wordnet* (Íslenskt orðanet). It is best described with the words of Jón Hilmar Jónsson, research professor at the Department of Lexicography, who has developed it with the assistance of Þórdís Úlfarsdóttir.

> It is an ongoing lexicographic project which aims to analyse and describe the Icelandic vocabulary and its internal semantic relations on the basis of syntactic and morphological relations in word combinations and compounds. Disambiguation and lemmatisation of multi-word lexical units plays a central role in the construction of the wordnet. The multi-word lemmas are grammatically tagged, which enables grammatical sorting and an interaction between semantic and grammatical features. The wordnet combines the functions of a synonym and a concept dictionary. (Jónsson 2012, 64)

The product of the analysis is open and accessible as an online dictionary.

7. Icelandic dictionaries on the Web

As I mentioned earlier the publishing companies have at present no dictionary projects ongoing, neither mono- nor bilingual dictionaries, and this has been the case for several years. One of the largest publishing companies in the country has taken the route of setting up a collection of previously published dictionaries in one place, in cooperation with computer specialists and other publishers. This project is called *Snara*, and subscriptions are at a low fee of roughly 3 EUR per month. It now contains seventeen dictionaries, for example an English-Icelandic and Icelandic-English, Danish-Icelandic and Icelandic-Danish, along with seven other handbooks. According to information from the administrators of the collection, all Icelandic universities – seven in all – and two foreign ones, are subscribers and students and staff can make use of the collection free of charge. The same goes for all high schools in Iceland and a great number of elementary schools and communities. The collection is thus used extensively in language learning and foreign communication. It helps to meet a serious need but many of the books are growing old and urgently in need of revision.

8. Conclusion

I consider it unlikely that major printed dictionaries will be published in Iceland in the future. I also do not consider it likely that a publisher would embark on a new dictionary project without cooperating with the Árni Magnússon Institute. The models I envisage are electronic dictionaries made in collaboration between the Institute and local and foreign partners. A great mass of data is already at hand at the institute, and additions are constantly being made that greatly facilitate the work on new editions of bilingual dictionaries.

9. References

Jónsson, J.H. (2012): Að fanga orðaforðann [To catch the vocabulary]. In: *Orð og tunga* 14, 39-65.

Bjarnadóttir, K. (2012): The Database of Modern Icelandic Inflection. In: *LREC 2012 Proceedings: Proceedings of "Language Technology for Normalization of Less-Resourced Languages", SaLTMiL 8 – AfLaT 2012.* Internet: www.lrec-conf.org/proceedings/lrec2012/index.html: Workshops, SaLTMil-AfLaT.

Helgadóttir, S./Svavarsdóttir, Á./Rögnvaldsson, E./Bjarnadóttir, K./Loftsson, H. (2012): The Tagged Icelandic Corpus (MÍM). In: *LREC 2012 Proceedings: Proceedings of "Language Technology for Normalization of Less-Resourced Languages", SaLTMiL 8 – AfLaT 2012.* Internet: www.lrec-conf.org/proceedings/lrec2012/index.html: Workshops, SaLTMil-AfLaT.

10. Online addresses

Icelandic Text Corpus: www.arnastofnun.is/page/gagnasofn_textasafn.

Icelandic Word Net: www.ordanet.is.

Kristín Bjarnadóttir: www.lexis.hi.is/kristinb/kristinb.html#rit.

Online dictionaries: www.snara.is.

Ritmálssafn Orðabókar Háskólans: http://lexis.hi.is/cgi-bin/ritmal/leitord.cgi.

The Árni Magnússon Institute of Icelandic Studies: www.arnastofnun.is.

Christian Mattsson

The Swedish Lexin Project – dictionaries in 22 minority languages

Lexin is a series of dictionaries in 22 minority languages, especially targeted at immigrants. This article is a presentation of the Lexin project with focus on the dictionaries published on the Internet.[1] A more theoretical account of Lexin is given by Gellerstam (1999), and a critical review by Loenheim (2012).

1. Lexin and the Swedish Language Act

Let's start by looking at a passage of the Swedish Language Act (2009:600) which was adopted in 2009. The purpose of this act is to specify the position and use of Swedish and other languages in Sweden. The act is also intended to protect the Swedish language and language diversity in Sweden, and the individual's access to language:

> All residents of Sweden are to be given the opportunity to learn, develop and use Swedish. In addition, persons belonging to a national minority are to be given the opportunity to learn, develop and use the minority language [...] Persons whose mother tongue is not one of the languages specified[2] [...] are to be given the opportunity to develop and use their mother tongue.

This is exactly what Lexin sets out to do: to help people to develop not only their Swedish language skill, but also to develop their skills in their own native language. So when the first Lexin dictionaries were published in the early 1980s you could say that the lexicographers were very much ahead of their time, of rather ahead of legislation. Making dictionaries for minorities is quite in line with the Swedish Language Act.

2. Dictionaries in 22 languages

The Lexin project has grown continually since the beginnings about 30 years ago, and today we have dictionaries in 22 minority languages. These are *Albanian*, *Amahric*, *Arabic*, *Assyrian*, *Azerbaijani*, *Bosnian*, *Croatian*, *Finnish*, *Greek*, *Macedonian*, *North Kurdish* (*Kurmanji*), *Pashto*, *Persian*, *Romani*, *Rumanian*, *Russian*, *Serbian*, *Somali*, *South Kurdish* (*Sorani*), *Spanish*, *Tigrinja* and *Vietnamese*.

Sweden used to be more or less monolingual but this is no longer the case: today we have about 200 minority languages in Sweden. In fact, it is not easy to keep track of all languages spoken in Sweden. Unfortunately, we don't have any official statistics to tell us how many speakers there are of a certain language. When you come to Sweden as an immigrant you are not asked what language you speak, just your citizenship. In consequence, it can sometimes be difficult to know what languages need a dictionary the most.

---

[1] http://www.lexinlexikon.se.

[2] I.e. not Finnish, Meänkieli, Romany, Sami and Yiddish.

Of these estimated 200 minority languages Lexin includes only 22. This might seem a fairly limited selection, but we believe that these 22 languages meet the needs of the vast majority of immigrants in Sweden. In addition, some languages, e.g. Russian and Arabic, can often be used as a second language by people who don't have access to a Lexin dictionary in their own native language.

The majority of the Lexin dictionaries have some 28,000 entries including idioms and examples of language in use. Some have less, but we hope to extend these in the future. Most of the dictionaries are now available on the Internet. However, some of the older dictionaries are only available in print. Our website has proved to be a great success, and in 2012 we registered more than 170 million searches, which equals more than 5 searches every second. This is a 25 per cent increase since 2011.

3. From a monolingual into a bilingual dictionary

Lexin is basically a Swedish monolingual dictionary which has been translated into 22 different minority languages. The printed dictionaries all go *from* Swedish into a foreign language, so there are only Swedish-Arabic, Swedish-Albanian dictionaries etc., not in the other direction. However, on the Internet you can look up a word in the target language as well. But what is shown is the Swedish entry where the translation in the target language occurs. This is true *only* if this word is included as a translation of a Swedish word. In consequence, there are no culture specific words of the target language included, simply because they don't appear as translations of a Swedish word. But this rarely seems to be a problem for the users, since we have had very few complaints.

The reason for not making genuinely bidirectional dictionaries is mainly financial. One could also argue that it is more important for the users to be able to decode Swedish, and to understand a Swedish word, rather than to find out how a word in your own language is translated into Swedish. So in this respect the dictionaries online are more useful than the ones in print. In addition, access to our Internet site is free, of course, whereas you have to pay for the printed dictionaries.

4. Selection of entries

In addition to the 28,000 or so most frequent words and phrases, which can be said to make up the basic vocabulary of the Swedish language, Lexin also lists a number of words that describe the Swedish system, i.e. the workings of the Swedish society, concepts which have to do with the health care system, pensions, sick leave, laws and regulations, organizations, political parties etc. As a newcomer to Sweden you are not only confronted with a strange and difficult new language, you are also immersed in a whole new society and culture, which can be more or less incomprehensible at first. So these words are essential in a dictionary for new citizens, but seldom found in other dictionaries.

5. The dictionary entries

The dictionaries contain a wealth of information. Let's look at the entry *hand* (which is the same word in both Swedish and English) in the Albanian dictionary:

- **hand** [han:d] LYSSNA subst.
(hand, handen, händer)
yttersta delen av en människas arm
dorë
BILD SVENSKA / BILD ALBANSKA

Exempel:

- tvätta händerna – pastroj duart, laj duart
- sy för hand – qep me dorë
- gå hand i hand – eci dorë për dorë

Uttryck:

- ta hand om ("vårda o dyl") – kujdesem për diçka (dikë)
- efter hand ("fortlöpande") – shkallë-shkallë, gradualisht
- på egen hand ("själv") – vetë, në mënyrë të pavarur
- i första hand ("viktigast, främst") – pikësëpari, së pari, para së gjithash
- ha till hands ("ha klart till användning") – kam gati, kam në dorë, zotëroj

Sammansättningar:

- hand|bagage – bagazh dore

Figure 1: The entry "hand" in the Swedish-Albanian dictionary

The information categories include the following: Pronunciation in given both in writing and as recorded sound files. Part of speech is indicated throughout, as well as inflexion.

A feature unique to Lexin is that the present tense, not the infinitive form, is used as the entry form for verbs. The reason is pedagogical: in Swedish it is easier to infer the other forms of a verb if you look at the verb in present tense, rather than the infinitive form.

When it comes to the semantic part we are somewhat unorthodox, in that we present not only the translation in the majority language, but also the definition of the Swedish word. So here it is obvious that Lexin is both monolingual and bilingual at the same time. This doubled information can be very useful, since many Lexin languages are culturally more or less different from Swedish, indeed many are non-European. This means that some words or concepts have no exact match in the target language. So the user can get help from the translation, which can be more or less approximate at times, as well as from the more exact definition.

Another feature that is particularly useful for learners is that all words are clickable. This means that the user can click on any word in a translation or in a definition that she or he doesn't understand and be directed to the entry where this word is explained or translated.

The Lexin dictionaries also contain plenty of examples of usage, the contexts in which the word is typically used, both semantically and syntactically. Here the user is guided e.g. on the use of prepositions. Lexin also lists many idioms and expressions, very much appreciated by the users, since this is often one of the most demanding parts of the language for a foreigner speaker.

Many entries also include a section of compounds, which is a very common feature in Swedish. In fact, compounds can be difficult to find in a dictionary if you don't even know if the word *is* a compound or written in two words. So when you look up e.g. the word *hand*, you can see all other entries where the word *hand* occurs, both as part of a compound and as a single word. Many entries also have syntactical information, which is intended mainly for more advances users. So we don't expect all users to make use of all the details in the dictionary. Indeed, the users can be anything from almost illiterate to people with a Ph.D.

6. Illustrations and videos

However, Lexin is not all about words. Some of the most basic concepts are perhaps better explained by a picture. And so we have included some 1,800 illustrations, mainly of nouns, which all have been grouped together thematically. For instance the Swedish word *snö* (snow) is included in the theme called weather, together with *rain, hail, storm* etc.

When it comes to verbs a picture may seem somewhat static. Here we have attached over 100 short videos which illustrate all sorts of basic human activity, e.g. *yawn, laugh, cry, run, cut* and *sleep*. Both the pictures and the videos are particularly useful as a starting point for those with very little training in their own language. In fact, there are many immigrants who can neither read nor write in their own language when they arrive in Sweden. And of course children too appreciate this.

7. Sharing experiences – encouraging further development

We believe that Lexin dictionaries have made integration easier for all those who come to Sweden from all over the world, and now make up more than 10 per cent of our population. And Lexin has proved to be a useful model for dictionary making not only in Sweden. The other Scandinavian countries too have been inspired by Lexin, above all Norway, where Lexin started in the mid 90s. To date dictionaries in 15 minority languages have been produced, many of which have been adapted from the Swedish data base. This was made possible by an agreement giving Norway free access to use our dictionaries to make their own. Of course the adaption from Swedish to Norwegian was greatly facilitated by the fact that these two languages are very closely related. Actually it was possible to recycle or reuse about 80 per cent of the original Swedish bilingual dictionaries. South Africa too has shown interest in Lexin lately. This country has eleven official languages and there are tentative plans for a monolingual English dictionary which will then be translated into all eleven languages, using Lexin as a model.

We are very happy to share our experiences, but also our data bases. With the growing demand for free language tools and linguistic infrastructure we have decided to make all our dictionaries available under the Creative commons license (BY). This means that anyone can reuse our data to create other dictionaries or applications, teaching aids etc.

We also allow commercial use as long as the origin of the dictionary data is indicated. In this way we can contribute to a better linguistic infrastructure, by making quality dictionaries available for anyone to develop. We believe that this is a good way to promote the Swedish language.

8. References

Creative Commons licenses: http://creativecommons.org.

Gellerstam, M. (1999): Lexin – lexikon för invandrare. In: *LexicoNordica* 6, 3-18.

Lexin online: http://www.lexinlexikon.se.

Lexin online (Norwegian website): http://decentius.hit.uib.no/lexin.html.

Loenheim, L. (2012): Lexins svenska lexikon. In: *LexicoNordica* 19, 295-316.

Swedish Language Act: http://www.government.se/sb/d/8317/a/138133.

Margit Langemets

"To think outside the paper": The case of Estonia

Abstract

This article intends to give an overview of the lexicographic scene in Estonia from the perspective of modern lexicography, i.e. e-lexicography. We have been developing our in-house Dictionary Writing System EELex for some time already. However, the modern lexicography expects more: the multifunctionality of the database, special needs of the specific user, etc. I will briefly characterise some of the lexical resources of Estonian, tools for lexicographers, as well as some theoretical matters together with the issues of language technology, e.g. the concept-based method vs. word-based method (Tavast 2008) for compiling dictionaries. I will sum up with an overview of typical properties of online Estonian dictonaries.

1. The background

Strategic planning of the development of the Estonian language began in 1998 when the Ministry of Education was assigned the task of drawing up a development strategy of the Estonian language. In 2000 the Estonian Committee for the organization of the European Year Languages (later the Estonian Language Council) was set up. In 2004 the first Development Strategy of the Estonian Language 2004-2010 was adopted by the Government. Since 2011 we have been living an age of the new strategic plan, The Development Plan of the Estonian Language 2011-2017 (henceforth, The Plan 2011). All the activities foreseen by The Plan (2011) are expected to be funded from the budgets of the state and local governments, universities and research institutions, national programmes, etc.

This article is written from the perspective of the Institute of the Estonian Language[1] (Tallinn, henceforth the Institute), thus the expression of 'the case of Estonia' in its title reflects foremost the lexicographic work practiced at the Institute, not Estonia as a whole. However, it might be justified for at least some reasons.

Firstly, the Institute is one of the many establishments and institutions, which have significant positions from the perspective of use and development of The Plan (2011). It is an important participant in language management, the study of Estonian and language resources, as well as language-technological applications. Secondly, the Institute is the owner and developer of several lexical resources – in the current state of language technology support, characterised as "cautiously optimistic" in the META-NET White Paper Series (Liin et al. 2012, 35). Since 2012 the Institute has been a member of the Center of Estonian Language Resources (CELR),[2] together with the University of Tartu and the Tallinn University of Technology. Thirdly, the Institute was the organiser of the third biennial conference of electronic lexicography in the 21st century eLex 2013,[3] Tallinn,

---

1 Institute of the Estonian Language (http://portaal.eki.ee/, last visited: 28.01.2013).

2 The Center of Estonian Language Resources (http://keeleressursid.ee/ressursid_eki.html, last visited: 28.01.2013).

3 eLex 2013 (http://eki.ee/elex2013/, last visited: 28.01.2013).

together with Trojina Institute for Applied Slovene Studies, as well as a participant in previous eLex conferences.[4] And last but not least, the Institute is widely acknowledged in Estonia to compile and edit dictionaries essential for the national culture.

2. Tasks for modern lexicography

The overall and very general task for lexicography, also mentioned in The Plan (2011), is to provide society with language resources (dictionaries, manuals, and databases) and guidance (incl. advice and courses). The other very general claim is that resources should be trustworthy and efficient, i.e. the content should be very carefully designed and fulfilled, as well as the mechanisms for reaching it should be fast and comfortable, preferably all in one.

The conferences on electronic lexicography and other forums have discussed the differences between paper and electronic dictionaries, as well as comparisons of their advantages and disadvantages for quite a long time already. However, the focus nowadays has moved to find different ways of how to exploit the rich potential of electronic medium in order to respond (quickly) to the needs of the new types of users, as well as to the needs of modern lexicographers. The slogan of eLex 2013 has been worded as "to think outside the paper", i.e. one has to forget about conventional approaches and be innovative, to conceptualize the dictionary with an electronic format in mind. This is not at all an easy task for lexicographers to get used to working in new environments, in different dictionary systems, rather thinking systematically following the rules of the advanced database than simply writing down a next dictionary article in line with all information one can remember. For users it is definitely much easier: they just formulate their queries, the simpler the better – in any device, in any place – and expect quick, correct and easily understood answers. The system builder, together with lexicographers, has to perform like a fortune teller to guess all possible needs of a user, when speaking of dictionaries.

Fuertes-Oliveira/Bergenholtz (2011) have proposed broadening lexicographic theory to other reference sources, considering lexicography as an integral part of information science with the aim of 'solving the problems' of the user, developing access to different (extralexicographical) data and different data presentation possibilities (e- and p-lex; pupil, semi-expert, or expert, etc.). They introduce the notion of dynamic SmartDictionaries or 'true lexicography', however, they do not focus on the content of the lexicographic system, i.e. gathering, analysing, processing, etc. of the data, expecting somehow that all the necessary content is already there. They even have expressed hostility towards linguistics and the role of linguistic theory in presenting lexicographical data (Fuertes-Oliveira/Bergenholtz 2011, 20-29).

Estonia is still at the stage of e-dictionaries and their pros and cons, not of dynamic SmartDictionaries or 'true lexicography', quoting Fuertes-Olivera/Bergenholtz (2011).

[4] eLex 2009 was held in Louvain-la-Neuve, Belgium, and eLex 2011 in Bled, Slovenia.

3. Dictionary Writing System EELex

We have been developing our web-based Dictionary Writing System EELex[5] since 2005 and by now nearly 50 dictionaries, incl. 7 terminological ones, have been compiled and edited using the system.

One of the earlier public applications was the Estonian-X dictionary database, which was compiled to provide a core for the new bilingual dictionaries to be produced by the system (Langemets et al. 2010). The database contains only source language (Estonian) data: headword, grammatical information, definitions, usage examples, etc. The data of the target language – translation equivalents with the rest of the necessary information – will be supplied by the user compiling the new dictionary. The system presents a preliminary standard form of the entry, open for the lexicographer who can modify, if necessary, both the content and form of the entry.

One of the newest functions of EELex is generating dictionaries of a particular type by selecting individual elements from the source dictionary database(s) (Kallas/Langemets 2012). It is possible to generate specialized dictionaries by reorganizing the preview (and layout) of the existing dictionary articles, or generating a brand new dictionary database. The latter is still in need of improvement, together with the function of importing data from several databases into one target database. The existing dictionary articles might be reorganized using the article preview generator function or the customization function of the XML query. Both options display the content of the dictionary for a user (i.e. lexicographer) in a new, individualised way (Kallas/Langemets 2012).

There are still many features needed, e.g. a lemmatiser to identify all the base forms of the constituents of (a) the multiword expressions (MWE) (for linking MWE-s to several headwords), or (b) the definitions in the learner's dictionary (for checking the controlled vocabulary). Automatic linking of sense references has yet to be improved. The overall user-friendliness is almost lacking, especially compared to commercial DWS-s,[6] neither do we have very nice tutorials.

4. Lexical resources: databases and dictionaries

The META-NET White Paper declares the situation with regard to lexical resources as "reasonably good for Estonian since substantial resources have been built in recent decades" (Liin et al. 2012, 35). However, on a five-point scale the Speech and Text Resources for Estonian were evaluated as last but one ("Fragmentary support"), together with Danish, Finnish, Slovene, etc., a step behind German, Dutch, Hungarian, etc. ("Moderate support"), whereas the best and only one in this category, English, was scored as "Good support" (yet not "Excellent") (Liin et al. 2012, 64). My personal opinion on this matter is that regarding the dictonaries and lexical databases – not dealt with special care in the White Paper – the situation is much better: "reasonably good" as stated in the above overview. "Fragmentary" would be fairer when evaluating access modes to online dictionaries (see below).

5 EELex (http://eelex.eki.ee/, last visited: 28.01.2013).

6 See T-Lex (http://tshwanedje.com/tshwanelex/), Léacslann (Dublin) (http://lxln.prettydata.eu/), iLEX, the integrated XML system (www.emp.dk/ilexweb/) (all last visited: 28.01.2013).

As mentioned earlier, there are nearly 50 dictionaries of different types (monolingual and bilingual, general and learners' dictionaries, etc.) in our Dictionary Writing System EELex. The standard XML mark-up and flexible functions should make EELex a huge multi-purpose lexicographic repository consisting of different databases. In the following, I will mention only some of them.

(1) The Estonian-X dictionary database was developed in different sizes: 80,000 headwords for a voluminous dictionary (on the basis of an Estonian-Russian dictionary, 1997-2009), 40,000 for a medium-sized dictionary, 15,000 for a small, and later on, 5,000 for a basic dictionary. Also, according to the type of dictionary required, three standards of morphological description have been developed to facilitate the presentation of Estonian morphology (Langemets et al. 2010). The full morphological description (all basic inflectional forms, the inflectional type number, part of speech) is presented brackets < > (see Figure 1); |.....| marks the place for translation equivalent and |----| the place for the translation of the definition, if necessary.

kuld <k'uld kulla k'ulda k'ulda, k'ulda[de k'ulda[sid_&_k'uld/i **22** ***S***>
1 (*teatud väärismetall* 'a yellow precious metal') |----|
♦ ***puhas kuld*** |.....|; ***kullast ehted*** |.....|
2 (*värvuselt ja läikelt kulla sarnane* 'colour resembling gold') |----|
♦ ***päikesekuld*** |.....|; ***sügiskuld*** |.....|; ***kased puistavad juba kulda*** |.....|
3 (*midagi väärtuslikku ja head* 'sth highly respected') |----|
♦ ***tema nõuanded on kulda väärt*** |.....|

Figure 1: The preliminary dictionary entry for *kuld* ('gold') (Langemets et al. 2010)

(2) Dictionary of Word Families (Vare 2012) serves as a Word Formation database of Estonian. The compounding and derivation are the main productive devices for forming new lexical items. The design of the database is based on the word families method, which consists of the organization of words on the basis of common stem morphemes and word formation relations (Viks et al. 2010). As an agglutinative-fusional language, Estonian is characterised by a rich word formation system in which different word formation kinds, types and means combine in complex ways, and stems are subject to different types of change. It is headed by the simplex word (the head of the family) that represents the common stem. Inside the word family, words (family members) are arranged semasiologically, according to word formation. The words are organized in an integrated hierarchical network on the basis of a stepwise immediate constituent analysis, which permits to visualise the internal structure of complex words by simultaneously showing their base word and their immediate constituents (Figure 2).

SPORT 'sport'
sport=**lane** ('sport=NOUN SUFFIX, sportsman, athlete')
sport|**las=lik** ('sportsman=ADJECTIVAL SUFFIX, sportsmanly')
sport|**las|likk=us** ('sportsmanly=NOUN SUFFIX, sportsmanship')

Figure 2: An excerpt of the word family *sport* 'sport' (Viks et al. 2010)

The majority of Estonian vocabulary consists of derivations and compounds: the database contains about 9,000 lexical entries, i.e. word families, with a total of about 120,000 lexical items, and 600 simplex words with no attested derivations or compounds (Vare

2012). The database was compiled manually following a fixed schema of the Dictionary Writing System.

The Word Formation database will be probably most used for research (available on the Web since January, 2014), as well as for language learning and language technology, e.g. to create the independent word formation module as part of the rule-based morphology of Estonian, which already covers the fully regular word formation.

(3) The Explanatory Dictionary of Estonian (EKSS 2009, 2nd edition, 6 volumes, 150,000 headwords). In the 1960s, the compilation of the first comprehensive dictionary of Estonian was started – roughly 300-200 years later than those of French, English, or German, and 100 years later than in the Nordic countries – and the first fascicle appeared in 1988. Thinking of the Finno-Ugric languages one may say that the publication of a comprehensive explanatory dictionary is highly coincident with statehood, and also with population (ca 1 million for Estonia) (Langemets 2008). Of the eight Finno-Ugric languages that are state languages (Hungarian, Finnish, Estonian, Komi, Udmurt, Mari, Erzyan and Moksha), only three have a comprehensive dictionary: first the Finns and Hungarians (1950s-1960s),[7] and next the Estonians (EKSS 1988-2007; 2nd, revised edition EKSS 2009). The EKSS contains about 150,000 words. It is a typical first explanatory dictionary: it abounds in literary examples (ca 50,000) and usage examples devised by lexicographers, the entries are long as many polysemous words (especially verbs) have been subjected to a really thorough meaning differentiation. The dictionary took 50 years to prepare. We were extremely lucky in having the opportunity to produce the dictionary in an electronic form from the very beginning. EKSS has been on the Web since 2010,[8] and on META-SHARE since 2012.

The next higher 'lexicographic storey' is under construction, representing an one-volume desktop version of the explanatory Estonian dictionary (ca 100,000 words, to appear in 2018), following the example of several European languages. The focus lies on 'more theoretical' lexicosemantic description and usage examples are considerably fewer than in EKSS, while etymological information has been added. Most of the usage examples come from a text corpus, from which they are extracted by the Sketch Engine software (Kilgarriff et al. 2004) and special Estonian Sketch grammar (Kallas 2013). The prospective user is an educated adult native Estonian (Langemets et al. 2010).

Estonian monolingual lexicography of the 20th century is represented by two main kinds of dictionary: a descriptive explanatory dictionary (EKSS) and a prescriptive dictionary of Standard Estonian or the language planning dictionary (ÕS).

(4) The Dictionary of Standard Estonian ÕS 2006 (ÕS 2006). The first language planning dictionary (20,000 headwords), published in revolutionary times, was a contemporary of the Estonian state born in 1918. Now, the new explanatory, one-volume Dictionary of Estonian (to appear in 2018) celebrates the centennium of the Republic of Estonia as well as the line of monolingual lexicography of Estonian.

---

[7] The Finnish *Nykysuomen sanakirja* (1951-1961), the Hungarian *A magyar nyelv értelmező szótára* (1959-1962).

[8] EKSS 2009: www.eki.ee/dict/ekss/ (last visited: 28.01.2013).

In 1989 the Law on Language declared Estonian the sole official language of Estonia. According to a Government regulation of 2006, the literary norm should be based on the most recent dictionary of Standard Estonian (then ÕS 2006) issued by the Institute of the Estonian Language – an interesting fact, probably not common to many languages. The new edition of the revised Dictionary of the Standard Estonian (ÕS 2013) is to appear in 2013, thus being the 'updated' official norm of the standard language. ÕS 2006 has been on the Web since 2010,[9] and on META-SHARE since 2012, as well as being usable via mobile phone application.

(5) The Basic Estonian Dictionary (to appear in 2014). Beside the two above-mentioned mainstreams, the Basic Estonian Dictionary (4,500 headwords) is under compilation (Jürviste et al. 2011). It is a comprehensive print and online dictionary of contemporary Estonian compiled for learners of Estonian as a second or foreign language (A2, B1 proficiency level). In order to support the development of lexical and grammatical competence, the dictionary aims to present explicitly the syntagmatic relations of Estonian content words: substantives, adjectives, adverbs and verbs (Kallas 2013). The Basic Estonian Dictionary is another dictionary compiled using the Sketch Engine software (Estonian Sketch grammar) for extracting relevant syntagmatic collocations. The learners' dictionary will be on the Web from 2015, a year after being published in print. The web version will be prepared in cooperation with Speech Technology, being one of the applications of Speech Synthesis of Estonian.

5. Tools for lexicography

(1) Morphological analysis and synthesis. Estonian dictionaries have a long tradition of presenting morphological information, as Estonian is characterised by a great number of inflected forms and extensive variation of morphological units. The morphology modules have been successfully used in lexicography for generating the grammar component in dictionary entries (Viks 2000, 2008). The system is semi-automatic, utilising a rule-based module. The module generates the inflectional type, part-of-speech, inflected forms, morphonological marking (degree of quantity, morpheme boundaries, etc.) and morphological references for inflected forms considerably different from headwords (e.g. *peo* SgGEN → *pihk* 'palm').

(2) Syntax and semantics. Syntactic parsers with a broad coverage of Estonian have been developed only using one rule-based grammatical formalism. Semantic tools and resources are scored low in the White Paper and syntactically and semantically annotated corpora are small in size (Liin et al. 2012, 59). It is true that we lack basic tools in semantics.

We have so far manually assigned semantic class tags (ARTEFACT, HUMAN, etc.) when editing the explanatory one-volume dictionary of Estonian (to appear in 2018, see above) for the purpose of linguistics research (patterns of systematic polysemy, e.g. ACTIVITY-ARTEFACT, MATERIAL/SUBSTANCE-ARTEFACT, etc.) (Langemets 2010). In the future we hope to link a semantic inventory/dictionary to concordance lines (cf. super senses, Word Sketch).

9 ÕS 2006: www.eki.ee/dict/qs/ (last visited: 28.01.2013).

(3) Estonian Reference Corpus and Corpus Query tools. Since 2010 the Sketch Engine for Estonian (Kallas 2013) has been used at the Institute of the Estonian Language to compile two monolingual dictionaries: the explanatory one-volume dictionary of Estonian and the Basic Estonian Dictionary (see above). The Sketch Engine for Estonian uses the Estonian Reference Corpus[10] of 250 million tokens as input. The corpus had previously been annotated morphologically, lemmatised, partially disambiguated, and annotated by clause by the private company Filosoft LLC. Syntagmatic relations of content words are described in the Grammar for Estonian (Kallas 2013) as lexico-grammatical constructions (ca. 85 rules or grammatical relations) defined by means of morphosyntactic categories (phrase type, part of speech, inflectional categories). Figure 3 shows the Word Sketch for the noun *diskussioon* 'discussion'. We also use the Good Examples option in the Sketch Engine software, though it is not fully automatical yet. In the future we expect to detect novel senses (by the means of the Sketch Engine), as well as to find good examples of a word sense.

diskussioon () EstonianRC freq = 5934 (23.8 per million)

Adj_modifier	2206	3.9	subject_of	400	1.6	object_of	216	3.0	omastav_modifies	821	1.2
avalik	240	7.05	käima	57	4.37	alustama	33	4.65	objekt	93	6.2
poliitiline	110	5.83	tekkima	36	4.36	tekitama	23	4.47	teema	71	4.51
elav	87	6.86	toimuma	33	3.77	algatama	18	5.08	tulemus	46	2.91
tõsine	77	6.21	jätkuma	32	5.62	jätkama	14	4.09	küsimus	29	1.36
pikk	72	5.13	algama	26	4.31	pidama	12	0.61	tekitamine	20	5.82
äge	66	8.15	kestma	17	4.37	ärgitama	11	8.45	algatamine	20	5.6
sisuline	49	7.31	järgnema	13	5.29	avama	8	3.11	algus	12	0.73
ühiskondlik	44	6.9	minema	11	1.03	laskuma	6	6.9	arendamine	10	2.8
terav	35	6.63	puhkema	10	5.82	korraldama	6	2.37	tase	10	1.31
käiv	32	7.3	näitama	8	1.6	vallandama	5	5.64	alune	9	0.19

N_PP	117		saav_modifier	172	1.9	alalütlev_modifier	137	1.6	seesütlev_modifier	115	1.2
N_PP_üle	77	25.0	objekt	57	5.51	teema	91	4.88	ajakirjandus	11	2.52
N_PP_ümber	13	20.7	tekitamine	12	5.17	tulemus	11	0.85	komisjon	8	0.18
N_PP_käigus	8	11.1	alune	10	0.35	taust	4	1.71	ühiskond	7	1.3

predicate_Adj	21	1.4	participle_modifier	292	3.2	ja/või	166	1.0
elav	3	2.13	toimuma	55	4.51	arutelu	21	4.04
kahepoolne	2	4.23	puhkema	28	7.33	ettekanne	14	3.95
mõttetu	2	3.8	kestma	20	4.61	seminar	10	4.4
loomulik	2	2.6	tekkima	16	3.19	dialoog	7	4.34
vajalik	2	0.21	avama	13	3.81	loeng	6	3.99

Figure 3: Word Sketch of the noun *diskussioon* 'discussion' in the Estonian Reference Corpus (Kallas 2013, 121)

6. What is the best model for compiling bilingual dictionaries?

Arvi Tavast (2008) has been arguing for an onomasiological model for compiling better, i.e. more systematic and consistent dictonaries for some time already. He has called his view *instrumentalist* (opposed to *linguacentric*) to be summarised in the statement that "language is just a tool" (Tavast 2008, 11, cf. Fuertes-Olivera/Bergenholtz 2011). Tavast

[10] Estonian Reference Corpus: www.cl.ut.ee/korpused/segakorpus/ (last visited: 28.01.2013).

argues that an instrumental view results in better decisions, both in terminography as well as general (bilingual) lexicography. Since 2012 the Institute of the Estonian Language has been participating in the EU project for *Development of the Estonian-Latvian and Latvian-Estonian dictionary* (2012-2015), together with the Latvian Language Agency.

The role of the Institute (as the leading participant) was to adapt the Dictionary Writing System EELex for producing two dictionaries (Estonian-Latvian and Latvian-Estonian). We decided to compile these dictionaries in a totally new way – in a *technically onomasiological*, i.e. in a *concept-based* database. It has been proved by Tavast (2008, 64) that this is the second best method (after systematic terminology work, unfortunately impossible in many cases) to prevent numerous internal inconsistencies unavoidable when compiling otherwise semasiologically, i.e. in a word-based database. The System is supplied with a mechanism for the conversion the concept-based database into a traditional word-based dictionary. Thus, the two versions of the bilingual dictionaries (Estonian-Latvian, as well as Latvian-Estonian) will be created fully automatically from the same database.This is slightly reminiscent of the Dutch system OMBI using *semantic links* in the 1990-ies for creating bilingual dictionaries from the multifunctional and reusable electronic lexical databases (Martin/Tamm 1996; Martin 2007).

The root data element of the concept-based database is a concept (meaning/sense description), not a term (word). The terms (source words and target words) are associated with the concept (meaning) as well as with definiton (in both languages, if needed) and context. Both languages have the same status, i.e. during the conversion into the (paper) dictionary format, both of them may be selected as a source language. Basically everything is related to the concept, e.g. synonyms are together in one concept – or they are not synonyms at all (within the precise definition of the dictionary) (Tavast 2008, 58 and 66-67).

E.g. the concept with the definition 'eye doctor/ophthalmologist' may contain the terms *silmaarst*, *okulist*, *oftalmoloog*, *oftalmologs*, *acu ārsts*. The mechanism for converting defines how the data is presented to the user depends on editors' decisions. One might choose between different options: (a) to show all the source words as equal in every article, (b) to show source words as separate headwords, together with the same definition and same target words, or (c) to assign one source word the role of a primary term which is connected to others via references (vt 'see') (Figure 4). A database can be converted into the (Estonian-Latvian or vice versa) dictionary in a fully automatic manner.

(a) Estonian-Latvian:
silmaarst (okulist, oftalmoloog) – acu ārsts, oftalmologs
okulist (silmaarst, oftalmoloog) – acu ārsts, oftalmologs
oftalmoloog (silmaarst, okulist) – acu ārsts, oftalmologs

(b) Estonian-Latvian:
silmaarst ('eye doctor/ophthalmologist') – acu ārsts, oftalmologs
okulist ('eye doctor/ophthalmologist') – acu ārsts, oftalmologs
oftalmoloog ('eye doctor/ophthalmologist') – acu ārsts, oftalmologs

(c) Estonian-Latvian:
silmaarst (okulist, oftalmoloog) – acu ārsts, oftalmologs
okulist – vt silmaarst
oftalmoloog – vt silmaarst

Figure 4: Converting of the concept-based database into the word-based dictionary

Tavast (2008, 16) has alleged that, unfortunately, people do not distinguish between words and their meanings, or terms and concepts. One should achieve a small, but crucial change in thinking to get used to working with such a database. Neither non-experts nor lexicographers feel it an easy task.

The onomasiological database for compiling bilingual dictionaries is a free software TERMEKI[11] offered by the Institute.

7. To sum up: online dictionaries of Estonian

Finally, I will give a short overview of typical properties of online dictionaries of Estonian, following criteria and oppositions described in Lew (2011).

The overall policy for the Institute of the Estonian Language, supported by The Plan (2011) and Ministry of Education and Research, has been to offer all our dictionaries free of charge when published. Or, to be precise, one year after publishing in print. There are different types of dictionaries: general and specialised, monolingual and bilingual, descriptive and prescriptive, etc. We have not set up any open, user compiled dictionaries. The feedback from users is sent by mail to the lexicographers via the web page.

Like most traditional dictionaries they exist standalone, however, they are gathered more or less on the single web page.[12] There have been some attempts to create Dictionary portals,[13] but they do not seem very user-friendly so far.

Regarding the access to content the dictionaries are mostly presented like paper dictionaries in an electronic form, fulfilling the goal of searchableness, but nothing more. Usually all the content is displayed: no 'Show Less'/'Show More' options or other customisation by users are available. The step-wise access with content displayed partially is used only for searching an extremely sophisticated database of Word Formation – the Dictionary of Word Families (Vare 2012) – where the user gets the remaining parts of the hierarchical entry by clicking the '+' icons.[14]

Multimedia is yet to come in the future: illustrations and audio recordings will be available when the learners' dictionary – Basic Estonian Dictionary (to appear in 2014) – will be published online.

And last but not least, p-lex or e-lex? The answer is: definitely e-lex, but so far mostly p-dictionaries on the web. We are still largely constrained by the paper model, thus having rathe a lot to achieve to come 'to think outside the paper'.

---

[11] TERMEKI: http://term.eki.ee/ (last visited: 28.01.2013).

[12] Lexical resources of the Institute of the Estonian Language: http://portaal.eki.ee/keelekogud.html (last visited: 28.01.2013).

[13] Keeleveeb: www.keeleveeb.ee/ (last visited: 28.01.2013).

[14] The Database of Word Families will be publicly available since January 2014.

8. References

EKSS 1988-2007 = Karelson, R./Kullus (Põlma), V./Raiet, E./Tiits, M./Valdre, T./Veskis, L. (eds.) (1988-2007): *Eesti kirjakeele seletussõnaraamat 1988-2007* (vihikud 1-26). Eesti Keele Instituut. [The Explanatory Dictionary of Standard Estonian. 26 fascicles.] Tallinn: Eesti Keele Sihtasutus.

EKSS 2009 = Langemets, M./Tiits, M./ Valdre, T./Veskis, L./Viks, Ü./Voll, P. (eds.) (2009): *Eesti keele seletav sõnaraamat I-VI*. ("Eesti kirjakeele seletussõnaraamatu" 2., täiendatud ja parandatud trükk). Eesti Keele Instituut. [The Explanatory Dictionary of Estonian, 2nd, improved edition.] Tallinn: Eesti Keele Sihtasutus.

Fuertes-Olivera, P./Bergenholtz, H. (eds.) (2011): *e-Lexicography: The Internet, digital initiatives and lexicography*. London: Continuum.

Jürviste, M./Kallas, J./Langemets, M./Tuulik, M./Viks, Ü. (2011): Extending the functions of the EELex dictionary writing system using the example of the Basic Estonian Dictionary. In: *Electronic Lexicography in the 21st Century: New Applications for New Users: Proceedings of eLex 2011, 10-12 November 2011, Bled, Slovenia*. Ljubljana: Trojina, Institute for Applied Slovenian Studies, 106-112.

Kallas, J. (2013): *Eesti keele sisusõnade süntagmaatilised suhted korpus- ja õppeleksikograafias*. Tallinna Ülikool, Doktoritöö. [The Syntagmatic Relationships of Estonian Content Words in Corpus and Pedagogical Lexicography.] Tallinn: Tallinna Ülikooli Kirjastus.

Kallas, J./Langemets, M. (2012): Automatic generation of specialized dictionaries using the Dictionary Writing System EELex. In: Tavast, A./Muischnek, K./Koit, M. (eds.): *Human Language Technologies – The Baltic perspective*. (= Frontiers in Artificial Intelligence and Applications 247). Amsterdam: IOS Press, 103-110.

Kilgarriff, A./Rychly, P./Smrž, P./Tugwell, D. (2004): The Sketch Engine. In: Williams, G./ Vessier, S. (eds.): *Euralex 2004. Proceedings of the Eleventh Euralex International Congress*. Lorient: Universite de Bretagne-Sud, 105-116.

Langemets, M. (2010): *Nimisõna süstemaatiline polüseemia eesti keeles ja selle esitus eesti keelevaras*. Eesti Keele Instituut. [Systematic polysemy of nouns and its lexicographic treatment in Estonian.] Tallinn: Eesti Keele Sihtasutus.

Langemets, M./Loopmann, A./Viks, Ü. (2010): Dictionary management system for bilingual dictionaries. In: Granger, S./Paquot, M. (eds.): *eLexicography in the 21st century: new challenges, new applications. Proceedings of eLex 2009*. (= Cahiers du CENTAL 7). Louvain-la-Neuve: Presses universitaires de Louvain, 425-430.

Langemets, M./Tiits, M./Valdre, T./Voll, P. (2010): *In spe*: üheköiteline eesti keele sõnaraamat. In: *Keel ja Kirjandus* 11, 793-810.

Lew, R. (2011): Online dictionaries of English. In: Fuertes-Olivera, P./Bergenholtz, H. (eds.): *e-Lexicography: The Internet, digital initiatives and lexicography*. London: Continuum, 230-250.

Liin, K./Muischnek, K./Müürisep, K./Vider, K. (2012): *The Estonian language in the Digital Age/Eesti keel digiajastul*. Edited by Georg Rehm and Hans Uszkoreit. (= White Paper Series). Berlin: Springer.

Martin, W. (2007): Government policy and the planning and production of bilingual dictionaries: the "Dutch" approach as a case in point. In: *International Journal of Lexicography* 20.3, 221-238.

Martin, W./Tamm, A. (1996): OMBI: an editor for Constructing Reversible Lexical Databases. In: Gellerstam, M., et al. (eds.): *Euralex '96. Proceedings I-II*. Göteborg: Göteborg University, Department of Swedish, 675-685.

ÕS 2006 = Erelt, T. (ed.) (2006): *Eesti õigekeelsussõnaraamat ÕS 2006*. Eesti Keele Instituut. [The Dictionary of Standard Estonian ÕS 2006]. Tallinn: Eesti Keele Sihtasutus.

Tavast, A. (2008): *The translator is human too: A case for instrumentalism in multilingual specialised communication*. Tartu Ülikool. PhD dissertation. Tartu: Tartu University Press.

The Plan 2011 = *The Development Plan of the Estonian Language 2011-2017*. Tallinn: Eesti Keele Sihtasutus.

Vare, S. (2012): *Eesti keele sõnapered I-II*. Eesti Keele Instituut. [The Dictionary of Estonian Word Families 1-2.] Tallinn: Eesti Keele Sihtasutus. [Index on the Internet: http://portaal.eki.ee/dict/spi/ (last visited: 28.01.2013)].

Viks, Ü. (2000): Tools for the generation of morphological entries in dictionaries. In: *Proceedings of the Second International Conference on Language Resources and Evaluation. Athens, Greece, 31 May-2 June 2000*, 383-388.

Viks, Ü. (2008): Eesti-X-keele sõnastik ja grammatika. In: *Eesti Rakenduslingvistika Ühingu aastaraamat* 4, 247-261.

Viks, Ü./Vare, S./Sahkai, H. (2010): The Database of Estonian Word Families: a Language Technology Resource. In: *Human Language Technologies. The Baltic Perspective: Proceedings of the Fourth International Conference, Baltic HLT 2010*. Amsterdam: IOS Press, 169-176.

Jolanta Zabarskaitė

Lithuanian lexicography in the 21st century: quo vadis?

1. A few facts about the Lithuanian lexicography

The Lithuanian lexicographical tradition dates back to the 16th century. Authored by Konstantinas Sirvydas, a professor at Vilnius University, the first dictionary was published circa the year 1620. It was a trilingual Polish–Lithuanian–Latin dictionary entitled *Dictionarium Trium Linguarum* (Pakalka 1997).

As far as Lithuanian philology is concerned, the voluminous thesaurus called *The Dictionary of the Lithuanian Language* (further LKŽ) is of particular relevance; back in 1930, a national Dictionary Desk was set up to compile the dictionary. This desk has eventually evolved into the Institute of the Lithuanian Language, which operates Lithuania's only Centre of Lexicography. The Centre of Lexicography specialises in theoretical aspects of lexicology and lexicography, the lexicon and semantics of Lithuanian, monolingual and multilingual lexicography, electronic lexicography and bilingual dictionaries of lesser used languages. The Centre of Lexicography also deals with the prospects of future dictionaries and has established three new pillars (see Zabarskaitė 2009, 135-147).

2. The first pillar: a new live for classical lexicographic resources

The biggest work in Lithuanian linguistics of the 20th century is *The Dictionary of the Lithuanian Language* (LKŽ I-XX/1941-2002). The final 20th volume of this was released in 2002, completing the work of several generations of linguists. The Dictionary serves as a source of national identity and linguistic investigation of the development of written and spoken Lithuanian and targets the world community working in the humanities and society at large. The scope of the Dictionary is ca. 22,000 pages, 0.5 million lexicographic entries, and 11 million words. It gives access to archaic, dialectal and contemporary layers of the lexicon of Lithuanian. Illustrations of word meanings have been taken from various sources covering the period from 1547 to 2001: research and religious texts, fiction, folklore and dialects recorded in the last century, starting from 1902. The Dictionary is based on a card index consisting of 4.5 million items collected from almost 1,000 lexicographic sources (both hand-written and printed); dialectal words have been recorded in more than 500 Lithuanian settlements (more: Kažukauskaitė 2002, 29-33; Klaviņš 2002; Топоров 2004, 408-415; Забарскайте/Нактинене/Шяпятите 2005, 340-355; Zabarskaitė/Naktinienė 2007, 32-34).

IT specialists together with lexicographers had to face the issues of the sophisticated Dictionary structure (more: Zabarskaitė/Naktinienė 2004, 187-190; Zabarskaitė 2007, 261-272), the variety of characters and symbols, and other problems (for information on the technical solutions for creation of electronic version further refer to Zinkevičius 2004, 170-173; Zinkevičius 2007, 349-355).

Researches and doctoral students all over the world use the academic edition of *The Dictionary of the Lithuanian Language* (LKŽ) on the website www.lkz.lt. Yet rapidly evolving digital technology requires new solutions for the application and distribution of LKŽ (as well as other dictionaries) (see Zabarskaitė/Naktinienė 2010, 780-787).

2.1 Solution no. 1: multi-platform

The technological environment for dictionary applications (and desktop applications in general) has however changed quite a lot in the recent years. While just some time ago, one could get away with a Windows-only dictionary application sold as a CD, nowadays linguists, software developers and managers have to consider the colourful and diverse range of devices that their users hold in their hands. As there is no more a single winner in the operating system or mobile device market, publishers of dictionary applications must "hit" them all: Windows, Mac OS X, Linux based computers, iPhone mobile phones, iPod touch multimedia players, iPad tablets, Android mobile phones, Android tablets, etc. Currently, LKŽ supports three platforms: Windows, Mac OS X and Linux. Dictionary applications for iPhone, iPod, iPad and Android platforms are at the development stage.

2.2 Solution no. 2: software delivery

The approach to software delivery in Compact Discs (CDs) is highly outdated. The CD did not prove its reliability in household environments as it is prone to scratches. Also, newer laptops do not even have a CD-ROM that would be able to read the CD with the dictionary application. The LKŽ application is delivered to the users using two new methods:

- USB flash drives. While the USB flash drive adds some additional cost to the final price of the product (compared to a CD), it has increased longevity and almost all desktop PCs (both new and old) have a USB port. Delivering the software product on a USB flash drive is useful for those clients who like to have a "material thing" (a physical installation medium) with their purchase (as opposed to software deliveries over the Internet, where users do not get a physical installation medium).
- Delivery over the Internet. Nowadays, not all users can (or want to) go and buy a physical installation medium with the dictionary application. In the case of our dictionary, LKŽ, the product is in high demand among the Lithuanian diaspora in various countries (the US, the UK, and Australia, to name a few), and it would be both easier and cheaper if the dictionary users from foreign countries could avoid ordering physical media with the dictionary, and be able to buy and download the dictionary directly, in a matter of minutes, instead. Thus, we argue that a modern dictionary application must have a strategy on how it could be purchased and delivered over the Internet to the end-user.

2.3 Solution no. 3: advanced tools

Even in the age of automatic machine translation one of the main tools for the day-to-day human translator remains the monolingual and the bilingual dictionary application.

The dictionary application is a highly important and useful tool for the amateur translator too, who just wants to find out how to say "pancakes and coffee, please" in French. Additionally, the monolingual and bilingual dictionaries can be used as applications for various languages and have a considerable demand in the general user market (more Zabarskaitė/Naktinienė/Valiukas 2013).

Software available for the Lithuanian language is limited in its functionality. Advanced tools, such as treebanks, WordNet, and so on, are yet to be developed for the Lithuanian language, or are still in the pipeline (Vaišnienė/Zabarskaitė 2012). Even though machine translation tools have been developed recently, it is only just now that the first steps are being taken to design the most advanced of resources – the so-called general applications. Obviously, texts that have a structure as complicated as LKŽ has can be used for the purposes of developing this kind of research. And so, dictionaries outlive their authors.

Conclusion: classical dictionaries should be adapted to latest technology.

3. The second pillar: innovative technology and dictionaries

The 21st century is the century of digital technology and Internet. In contrast to printed dictionaries, online dictionaries and thesauruses offer a complete range of possibilities to use sound and video materials. The array of available tools is practically endless: from images, historical pictures and photographs of works of art to videos, movie clips and animation. All of this not only helps learn a language, but also broadens the understanding of language and culture. If such tools were used to create multilingual dictionaries, or even dictionaries that cover several languages, such multimedia dictionaries could reflect two cultures or more and carry out a two-way function of helping learn a language better and opening the door to a culture a little bit wider. A multimedia Lithuanian-English dialectal dictionary (Lietuvių tarmės 2000-2011) has been developed in Lithuania:

> The Lithuanian language, still rich in dialects, is interesting for linguistic studies world-wide as one of the most ancient Indo-European languages, and therefore it must be safeguarded and made accessible for scientific research everywhere. The first attempt in this direction was made by creating the Multimedia Dictionary of Lithuanian Dialects. This interactive CD-ROM demonstrates multimedia dictionary possibilities: a reader can see a picture of an object, to listen to pronunciation of a word in different dialects and to see how it is written in the Lithuanian language. Therefore it can be used without any previous knowledge of a language. (Telksnys/Kligienė 2001, 57-65)

This dictionary won the gold medal at the world EXPO 2000 in Hanover, Germany for utilising multimedia in lexicography and for the dissemination of ethnic culture.

Dictionaries are more than just a tool to learn and use a language. Every dictionary is a cultural text, one that reflects the unique character and values of the culture it represents.

Another very important thing is that multimedia is indispensable when sign language dictionaries are prepared.

Conclusion: In future, lexicography will most probably use an increasing amount of multimedia options both when it comes to designing new dictionaries, and adapting classical dictionaries to the digital media.

4. The third pillar: lexicographical infrastructures

It is becoming apparent that corpuses, dictionaries, catalogues, digests, and databases have to be integrated to create uniform infrastructures that would allow performing searches against a variety of parameters and combine different linguistic resources through common searches. The most important search unit within such infrastructures is a word. Hence, the future in lexicography belongs not to isolated dictionaries, but also to various infrastructures of dictionaries and other infrastructures of linguistic resources, which should cover both classical and modern dictionaries. Currently, Lithuania is implementing a programme called "The Lithuanian Language in Information Society". The framework of this programme will include the digitalization of many Lithuanian language resources, improvement or development of language technologies or solutions (such as tools for machine translation, syntactic/semantic analysis, etc.) for the Lithuanian language. The Lexicography Centre of the Institute of the Lithuanian Language coordinates the implementation of "Developing and Providing Access to IRT Solutions and Content Geared Towards Preservation of the Lithuanian Language in Public Space", a project within the aforementioned programme. This project will see the development of a Lithuanian language information system, which will provide the public with free access to digital Lithuanian thesauruses and dictionaries covering the languages of our closest neighbours: Lithuanian-Latvian-Lithuanian, German-Lithuanian and Lithuanian-Polish-Lithuanian bilingual dictionaries. The system will come with many functions that will allow its users to easily and conveniently find both translations of words they are after, and synonyms and antonyms for those words, among other things. In future, this infrastructure will be augmented with other lexicographical resources for one or several languages, it will be integrated into international alliances like META-NET, etc. In future, we will be able to see more clouds of multi-lingual linguistic resources, dictionaries among them, which will most likely be joined together to make a digital sky. That would greatly facilitate communication on the European level and would promote the dispersion of its cultural diversity.

The Lithuanian digital resource infrastructure facilitates the learning and teaching of language(s), as well as linguistic field-work. However, with a plethora of different infrastructures in place, the matter of training to use them in a creative way gains a certain degree of relevance. Lithuania is currently playing host to seminars for teachers, aiming to introduce them to the latest digital resources and the possibilities to use them.

Conclusion: Lexicographical infrastructures and infrastructures of other linguistic resources are a much better tool that helps satisfy the needs of different users and enhance the possibilities to utilise various dictionary data.

5. References

Kažukauskaitė, O. (2002): Le grand dictionnaire d'une petite nation, une histoire de cent ans. In: *Cahiers lituaniens* 3, 29-33.

Kļaviņš, P. (2002): Lietuvju valodas vārdnica (I-XX sējums). In: *Brīvā Latvija* (Rīga), 27 jūlijs-2 augusts.

Lietuvių kalbos žodynas (I-XX/1941-2002): elektroninis variantas / Naktinienė, Gertrūda et al., Vilnius: Lietuvių kalbos institutas, 2005, 2008. Internet: www.lkz.lt. [The dictionary of the Lithuanian language (Vol. 1-20/1941-2002): electronic release [online], 2005, renewed version, 2008.]

Lietuvių tarmės 1-3 (2000-2011): elektroninis išteklius /Lithuanian dialects: electronic release. Vilnius: Lietuvių kalbos institutas. Internet: www.mch.mii.lt/tarmes/Tarmes/.

Pakalka, K. (ed.) (1997): *Senasis Konstantino Sirvydo Žodynas*. Vilnius: Mokslo ir enciklopedijų leidybos institutas. [The old dictionary of Konstantinas Sirvydas. Facsimile and comments.]

Telksnys, L./Kligiene, N. (2001): Facing challenges of new media on the crossroads of East-West and past-future (Lithuanian case study). In: *Cultural Heritage and Technologies in the Third Millennium*. Milan: Politecnico di Milano, 57-65.

Vaišnienė, D./Zabarskaitė, J. (2012): *The Lithuanian language in the Digital Age/Lietuvių kalba skaitmeniniame amžiuje*. (= White Paper Series/Baltųjų knygų serija). Berlin: Springer.

Zabarskaitė, J. (2007): Prameny a databáze Institutu pro litevský jazyk. In: *Europeica – Slavica – Baltica*. (= Publikace Slovanské Knihovny 56). Praha: Národní knihovna České republiky, Slovanská knihovna, 261-272.

Zabarskaitė, J. (2009): The Institute of the Lithuanian Language and Centres of Baltic Studies. In: *The Baltic languages and the Nordic countries*. Vilnius: Lietuvių kalbos institutas, 135-147.

Zabarskaitė, J./Naktinienė, G. (2004): On the linguistic databases of the Institute of the Lithuanian language. In: *Human Language Technologies: the Baltic perspective: the first Baltic conference*. Riga, 187-190.

Zabarskaitė, J./Naktinienė, G. (2007): Слоўнікі ў інтэрнэце: дыялог мовазнаўцы і носьбіта мовы. In: *Слово и словарь. Vocabulum et Vocabularium*, Гродно: ГрГУ, 32-34.

Zabarskaitė, J./Naktinienė, G. (2010): The dictionary of Lithuanian (LKŽ) and its Future in Databases and Electronic Version. In: *Proceedings of XVI Euralex International Congress*. Ljouwert: Fryske Akademy – Afuk, 780-787.

Zabarskaitė, J./Naktinienė, G./Valiukas, L. (2013): Contemporary dictionary application: tips and tricks of getting it right. In: *TRALOGY II: futures in technologies for translation*. Paris. Internet: www.tralogy.eu.

Zinkevičius, V. (2004): Creating the electronic version of the dictionary of Lithuanian. In: *Human Language Technologies: the Baltic perspective: the first Baltic conference*. Riga, 170-173.

Zinkevičius, V. (2007): The digitization of the dictionary of the Lithuanian language. In: *The Third Baltic Conference on Human Language Technologies*. Kaunas, 349-355.

Забарскайте, Й./Нактинене, Г./Шяпятите, Р. (2005): Современность и перспективы большово "Словаря литовского языка". In: *Исторический путь литовской письменности*. Вильнюс: Институт литовского языка, 340-355.

Топоров, В.Н. (2004): К выходу в свет большого "Словаря литовского языка". In: *Балто–славянские исследования* XVI. Москва, 408-415.

d) Reports on special projects

Uwe Mohr

Poliglotti4.eu – ein Projekt der EU *Civil Society Platform on Multilingualism*

> "Die Sprachenvielfalt stellt für Europa eine Herausforderung dar, es handelt sich allerdings unserer Ansicht nach um eine lohnende Herausforderung."
> (Amin Maaloof, Intellektuellengruppe für den interkulturellen Dialog)

> "Translation is the language of Europe."
> (Umberto Eco)

> "Wer fremde Sprachen nicht kennt , weiß nichts von seiner eigenen."
> (Johann Wolfgang von Goethe)

Abstract

The promotion of multilingualism has always been one of the key objectives of the European Commission. The importance of multilingualism is also expressed in the European Commission's ET 2020 Strategy (co-operation in the fields of education and training). The promotion of lifelong learning and mobility as well as the concentration on skills to realise one's potential in a modern European society imply the promotion of foreign language training and learning. Based on several published orientation documents and directives, the European Commission has introduced two methods of dialogue and theme definition: The "open method of coordination" with the governments of the member states and the "structured dialogue" that led to the establishment of two platforms: The Business Platform on Multilingualism and the Civil Society Platform on Multilingualism. The Civil Society Platform brings together a very diverse group of 29 major European organisations from the fields of education, translation, culture, media and social integration that all share the common goal of promoting multilingualism in Europe and in their respective fields of expertise. Following a request from the European Commission, in 2011 the Civil Society Platform published "Policy Guidelines and Recommendations" in the fields of education, translation, language policy and social integration. The Platform has been re-launched and will continue working over the next two years. Based on the findings and deliberations of the Civil Society Platform, nine of its member organisations have formed a consortium to conduct the Poliglotti4.eu project. This project has resulted in the creation of an On-line Observatory, reporting on best practice in language policy and language learning. The observatory provides policymakers, language teachers and learners as well as civil society organisations with a powerful toolkit for benchmarking and enhancing their activities, in non-formal and informal education and learning sectors. The project is co-funded through the European Commission's Lifelong Learning Programme (LLP). This project will, hopefully, contribute to maintain the engagement of EFNIL in the activities of the Platform and to enhance the co-operation with EUNIC.

1. Kontext

Mehrsprachigkeit ist ein erklärtes Ziel der Europäischen Kommission und wird als solche gefördert, wann immer dies möglich ist. Entsprechend haben die Staats- und Regierungschefs der Europäischen Union 2002 in Barcelona das Ziel formuliert, dass jeder EU-Bürger seine Muttersprache plus zwei Fremdsprachen sprechen können soll. 2007 wurde die Mehrsprachigkeit als eigenes Ressort der Europäischen Kommission ausgegliedert. Kommissar für Mehrsprachigkeit war von Januar 2007 bis Februar 2010 der Rumäne Leonard Orban, der sich in besonderem Maße für Mehrsprachigkeit einsetzte.

Das Ressort wurde mit Aufnahme der Arbeit der Kommission Barroso II im Februar 2010 wieder in das Bildungsressort (Directorate-General "Education and Training") zurückverlegt, es gibt seitdem keine eigenständige Multilingualism Unit und keinen eigenständigen Kommissar für Mehrsprachigkeit mehr.

Dennoch unternimmt die Europäische Kommission viele Aktivitäten im Bereich Mehrsprachigkeit (Konferenzen, Durchführung und Förderung von Projekten u.v.m.). Ihr Engagement drückt sich auch in dem 2009 verabschiedeten "Strategischen Rahmen für die europäische Zusammenarbeit auf dem Gebiet der allgemeinen und beruflichen Bildung" (ET 2020) aus. Ziele dieser Zusammenarbeit sind unter anderem die Verwirklichung von Lebenslangem Lernen und Mobilität, Verbesserung der Qualität und Effizienz von Bildung sowie die Förderung von Innovation und Kreativität.

EFNIL ist einer der wichtigsten Akteure im Europäischen Mehrsprachigkeitsdiskurs und aufgrund des Renommees seiner Mitgliedsverbände, der zahlreichen Projekte im Bereich der Europäischen Mehrsprachigkeit und seiner Mitgliedschaft in der EU Civil Society Platform on Multilingualism ein prädestinierter Partner für EUNIC, das Goethe-Institut und die Europäische Mehrsprachigkeitsplattform. Deshalb freue ich mich, dass mir diese Konferenz die Gelegenheit gibt, den Mitglieder von EFNIL über ein zentrales Projekt der Civil Society Platform zu berichten. Dies wird, so hoffe ich, auch dazu beitragen, die verschiedenen Aktivitäten von EFNIL und EUNIC miteinander in Verbindung zu bringen.

2. Vorgaben und Grundsatzpapiere der Europäischen Kommission

Am 18. September 2008 nahm die Europäische Kommission die Mitteilung "Mehrsprachigkeit: Trumpfkarte Europas, aber auch gemeinsame Verpflichtung" an, in der die Sprachen in Zusammenhang mit sozialem Zusammenhalt und Wohlstand gebracht werden. In der Mitteilung werden die EU-Mitgliedstaaten und die anderen EU-Institutionen aufgerufen, ihre Anstrengungen zu koordinieren und gemeinsam die Bürger zum Erlernen von Sprachen zu ermuntern und sie dabei zu unterstützen.

Nachdem der Rat der Europäischen Union die Erläuterungen der Europäischen Kommission zu ihrer Mitteilung angehört und einen Gedankenaustausch durchgeführt hatte, nahm der Rat am 21. November 2008 eine Entschließung zu einer europäischen Strategie für Mehrsprachigkeit an.

Am 12. Mai 2009 legte der Rat der Bildungsminister der EU seine Schlussfolgerungen zu einem strategischen Rahmen für die europäische Zusammenarbeit auf dem Gebiet der allgemeinen und beruflichen Bildung vor. Darin wird festgelegt, dass neue Kompetenzen für neue Beschäftigungen entwickelt, neue Technologien, Innovation, Kreativität und Schlüsselkompetenzen (Computer, Lesen, Naturwissenschaften, Mathematik) gefördert werden sollen, mit Hauptaugenmerk auf frühzeitige Schul- und Ausbildungsabgänger, Zuwanderer und Lernende mit besonderen Bedürfnissen.

3. ET 2020 – vier strategische Ziele

"Allgemeine und berufliche Bildung 2020" (ET 2020) ist ein neuer strategischer Rahmen für die europäische Zusammenarbeit auf dem Gebiet der allgemeinen und beruflichen Bildung und verfolgt vier strategische Ziele.

1. Die Verwirklichung von lebenslangem Lernen und Mobilität;
2. Die Verbesserung von Qualität und Effizienz der allgemeinen und beruflichen Bildung;
3. Die Förderung von Gerechtigkeit, sozialem Zusammenhalt und aktivem Bürgersinn;
4. Die Förderung von Innovation und Kreativität – einschließlich Unternehmergeist – auf allen Ebenen allgemeiner und beruflicher Bildung.

4. Indikatoren und europäische Durchschnittsbezugswerte („benchmarks“) bis 2020

Bis 2020 sollen 15% der Erwachsenen am lebenslangem Lernen teilnehmen und der Anteil der 15-jährigen mit schlechten Leistungen in den Bereichen Lesen, Mathematik und Naturwissenschaften unter 15% liegen. Weiterhin wird angestrebt, dass mindestens 40% der 30-34-jährigen einen Hochschulabschluss besitzen und der Anteil frühzeitiger Schul- und Ausbildungsabgänger bis 2020 weniger als 10% beträgt. Schließlich sollen mindestens 95% der Kinder im Alter zwischen vier Jahren und dem gesetzlichen Einschulungsalter in den Genuss einer Vorschulbildung kommen. Bei all diesen Zielen sollen die Bereiche Mobilität, Beschäftigungsfähigkeit und Fremdsprachenerwerb (Muttersprache plus 2 Fremdsprachen) besondere Beachtung finden.

5. Zwei Prozesse der Themenfindung und Politikbeeinflussung

Die Europäische Kommission hat zwei Mechanismen ins Leben gerufen, die sich gegenseitig ergänzen und befruchten sollen, außerdem ist ein Dialog der beiden untereinander vorgesehen.

Der erste der beiden Mechanismen ist die "Offene Koordinierungsmethode mit den Mitgliedsstaaten". Hierfür wurden zwei Gruppen mit Regierungsvertretern aller Mitgliedsstaaten zum Thema "Early Language Learning" und "Language and Business" gebildet.

Der zweite Mechanismus ist der "Strukturierte Dialog mit den Vertretern der Zivilgesellschaft" durch Civil Society Platforms. Derer gibt es ebenfalls zwei, einmal die "Business Platform for Multilingualism" mit Vertretern aus Industrie, Arbeitgeberverbänden, Gewerkschaften und anderen Lobbyverbänden und zum anderen die "Civil Society Platform on Multilingualism", die sich aus Vertretern der Bereiche Kultur, (literarische) Übersetzung, Theater, Medien, Schriftsteller, lebenslanges Lernen, frühkindliches Lernen, Integrationsprogramme für Migranten und sozial Benachteiligte, Austausch- und Bildungseinrichtungen zusammensetzt.

6. EU Civil Society Platform on Multilingualism (CSPM)

Die CSPM wurde von der Europäischen Kommission im Oktober 2009 für den strukturierten Dialog mit der Zivilgesellschaft ins Leben gerufen. Das Ziel der Plattform ist es, Mehrsprachigkeit in Europa in den Bereichen Kultur, Medien und nichtstaatlicher Bildung zu fördern.

6.1 Themen und Projekte der Plattform 2010-2012

Die Themen, mit denen sich die Plattform auseinandersetzt, werden zu einem Großteil von den Bereichen bestimmt, mit denen sich die Mitgliedsorganisationen der Plattform hauptsächlich beschäftigen. Neben den bereits genannten Bereichen sollten hier noch Erwachsenenbildung, Untertitelung, Terminologie, Sozialarbeit, Zertifizierung und Sprachunterricht genannt werden. Dabei legt die Plattform Wert auf den Aspekt der Zivilgesellschaft, denn ihre Mitglieder entstammen dem nichtstaatlichen Bereich außerhalb des offiziellen Bildungssystems.

Weiterhin hat die Plattform unter dem Vorsitz von Uwe Mohr (EUNIC in Brussels; Goethe-Institut Brüssel) vier Arbeitsgruppen zu den Themen Übersetzung und Terminologie, Bildung, Sprachenvielfalt und soziale Einbeziehung sowie Sprachpolitik gegründet. Die Gruppen arbeiten an Themen wie der Mehrsprachigkeit in Online-Communities (Facebook, andere soziale Netzwerke), der Motivation für Mehrsprachigkeit und ihrer Rolle in der Kommunikation, Lobbyarbeit für Sprachenvielfalt und Mehrsprachigkeit, Edutainment, der Untertitelung anstatt der Synchronisierung von Filmen und einem Multilingual Label (ein Qualitätssiegel für Gemeinden, Verwaltungen, Organisationen, Unternehmen oder Touristenattraktionen).

6.2 Politische Empfehlungen der CSPM

Nachdem die CSPM bemängelt hat, dass die europäische Sprachenpolitik immer noch lückenhaft sei und Vorhaben und deren Umsetzung im Bereich Mehrsprachigkeit oft weit auseinander liegen, hat die Plattform Forschungen in allen Bereichen der Zivilgesellschaft zum Thema durchgeführt und die Ergebnisse in einem Bericht und in politischen Empfehlungen zusammengefasst. Der Bericht erschien im Juni 2011 und seine Empfehlungen richten sich vor allem an die Europäische Kommission, die Mitgliedsstaaten und regionale Behörden.

Die CSPM fordert, dass mehrsprachige Bildung in der EU die Regel werden sollte, denn Englisch ist zwar ein Muss, aber nicht genug. Mehrsprachige Bildung bedeutet, dass jeder EU-Bürger seine Muttersprache plus zwei Fremdsprachen beherrschen sollte, um den eigenen Horizont zu erweitern, neue Menschen zu treffen und neue Dinge zu erfahren. Dabei sollte mit dem Sprachenlernen bereits im frühen Alter spielerisch begonnen werden, Kinder müssen Fremdsprachen als etwas Angenehmes erfahren. Denn Sprachenlernen darf nicht als "stumpfsinnige und schwierige Grammatikübung" wahrgenommen werden, sondern als nützlich und als Chance. Diesem Ziel kann man in einem späteren Stadium der Schullaufbahn (ab Sekundarstufe I) unter anderem durch die großflächige Einführung von integriertem Fremdsprachenlernen und Sachunterricht (CLIL) ein Stück näher kommen. Es müssen aber auch informelle Lernmöglichkeiten außerhalb des Klassenraums geschaffen und entwickelt werden (Untertitelung von Filmen anstelle von Synchronisation, mehrsprachige Spiele, mehrsprachige Lernmittel, Online-Hilfen). Auch benachteiligte Gruppen, Migranten, sozial Ausgeschlossene, Schulabbrecher etc. müssen in Fremdsprachen unterrichtet und beim Lernen besser unterstützt werden, um ihre Integration und den sozialen Zusammenhalt zu fördern.

Aber auch öffentliche Einrichtungen und Behörden müssen an ihren Sprachkenntnissen arbeiten und diese verbessern. Sie sollten eine Sprachpolitik entwickeln, um Mehrsprachigkeit zu fördern und Nichtmuttersprachlern zu helfen, sich im alltäglichen Leben und/oder Ausnahmesituationen wie bei der Polizei, bei Anmeldeverfahren, in öffentlichen Verkehrsmitteln, Krankenhäusern, usw. zurechtzufinden. Um öffentliche Dienste zu verbessern, muss der Austausch von Ideen und Best Practice angeregt und unterstützt werden, damit diese auch in anderen Bereichen und Regionen Europas Anwendung finden können.

Da Fremdsprachen ein fundamentaler Bestandteil moderner Bildung sind, sollten darüber hinaus fundierte Studiengänge, insbesondere im Bereich Sprachvermittlung und Übersetzung, eingeführt und gefördert werden sowie Mobilitätschancen besonders für junge Menschen entwickelt werden. Wir müssen junge Menschen dazu ermuntern, ins Ausland zu reisen, um Fremdsprachen zu lernen. Es ist aber auch notwendig, Schülern und Studenten eine Reihe verschiedener Fremdsprachen anzubieten, also auch die von Einwanderern gesprochenen, um die in unserer Gesellschaft bereits vorhandenen Sprachkenntnisse zu nutzen.

Die CSPM steht Politikern gerne beratend und mit zuverlässigen Informationen zur Seite, da sie einen wichtigen Beitrag zur Förderung der Mehrsprachigkeit in öffentlichen Einrichtungen und in der Bildung leisten kann und muss.

Die Plattform betont in ihren Empfehlungen außerdem, dass Übersetzung nicht als zweitbeste Lösung nach Mehrsprachigkeit betrachtet werden darf. Mit Hilfe von Übersetzungen können linguistische und kulturelle Grenzen überwunden und so einem breiteren Publikum der Zugang zum gemeinsamen europäischen Literaturerbe eröffnet werden. Daher ist es nur konsequent, dass die Plattform von der Politik fordert, die Arbeitsbedingungen für Übersetzer zu verbessern und das Bewusstsein von Politikern, Pädagogen und Eltern im Hinblick auf Mehrsprachigkeit zu schärfen.

Schließlich wird Europa dazu aufgefordert, eine Sprachpolitik zu entwickeln, die den Sprachgebrauch beobachtet und die Gleichberechtigung der europäischen Sprachen sicherstellt. Abschließend empfiehlt die CSPM, eine dauerhafte Plattform zur Sicherung des Dialogs zwischen der politischen Ebene und der Zivilgesellschaft sicherzustellen, da die Organisationen der Zivilgesellschaft die perfekte Plattform sind, um Mehrsprachigkeit zu fördern. Ihre Netzwerke müssen daher verbessert und auf europäischer Ebene miteinander vernetzt werden.

7. Poliglotti4.eu

Das Ziel des Projekts Poliglotti4.eu ist die Förderung der Mehrsprachigkeit in Europa. Das Projekt ist die sichtbare Konsequenz der Beratungen der CSPM, die sich dazu entschieden hat, ein Online Language Observatory zu schaffen. Das Observatory wird über Best Practice in Sprachpolitik und Sprachenlernen berichten und wird vom Bildungsprogramm für lebenslanges Lernen (LLP) der Europäischen Kommission finanziert.

7.1 Partner

Die Projektpartner sind allesamt Mitglieder der Civil Society Platform on Multilingualism. Die neun Konsortiumsmitglieder sind:

- Goethe-Institut Brüssel,
- Fundación Academia Europea de Yuste,
- The Danish Cultural Institute,
- European Theatre Convention,
- British Council,
- European Association for the Education of Adults,
- ALTE (Association of Language Testers in Europe),
- EUNIC in Brussels und
- Mercator (European Research Centre on Multilingualism and Language Learning).

7.2 Für wen?

Das Projekt richtet sich an Politiker auf europäischer, nationaler, regionaler und lokaler Ebene, die Zivilgesellschaft, soziale und gemeinnützige Einrichtungen, Lernende und Lehrende.

7.3 Ziele

Im Rahmen des EU-Mehrsprachigkeitsprojekts Poliglotti4.eu werden Daten über Mehrsprachigkeit gesammelt und ausgewertet und ein Katalog mit Mehrsprachigkeitswerkzeugen ausgearbeitet. Weiterhin soll das Interesse der Öffentlichkeit auf das Thema Mehrsprachigkeit und ihre Bedeutung für Europa gelenkt werden. Das Projekt bietet Politikern aber auch Hilfe bei der Entwicklung und Umsetzung einer Mehrsprachigkeitspolitik an, beispielsweise durch die Bereitstellung von zuverlässigen Informationen und Beratung. Schließlich sollen auch Beispiele von Best Practice durch das Projekt über die Netzwerke von zuständigen Politikern verbreitet werden, damit diese auch in anderen Gegenden Europas Anwendung finden und die Mehrsprachigkeit so gefördert werden kann.

7.4 Output

Das mehrsprachige Online Language Observatory soll als Diskussionsplattform für Lernende, Lehrende, die Zivilgesellschaft, soziale und gemeinnützige Einrichtungen sowie für Politiker dienen, damit diese sich über Mehrsprachigkeit austauschen können. Die auf dem Observatory vorgestellten Best Practice Beispiele und verlässlichen Informationen zum Thema sind eine weitere Anregung für Politiker, bessere Bedingungen für Mehrsprachigkeit zu schaffen.

Weitere Ergebnisse des Language Observatory sind ein Katalog mit Mehrsprachigkeitswerkzeugen, eine Datenbank mit Nachrichten, Dokumenten und Events zum Thema Mehrsprachigkeit und die Präsentation von Fördermöglichkeiten an der Basis. Schließlich erklärt das Observatory die Bedeutung und Wichtigkeit der Mehrsprachigkeit für Europa.

7.5 Nachhaltigkeit

Durch EUNIC in Brussels wird garantiert, dass das Language Observatory auch fünf Jahre nach Projektende noch online ist und gepflegt wird. Weiterhin bleiben die Botschafter für Mehrsprachigkeit sowie die Mitglieder der Civil Society Plattform in der Sache engagiert, wozu auch gehört, dass ihre Fachkenntnisse den entsprechenden Zielgruppen weiterhin zur Verfügung stehen. Abschließend werden durch das Projekt die Netzwerke europaweit arbeitender Experten für Mehrsprachigkeit gestärkt und die Mehrsprachigkeit damit nachhaltig gefördert.

8. Warum ist Mehrsprachigkeit so wichtig?

Fremdsprachen formen unser Denken, sie verbessern unser Verständnis der globalen Gesellschaft und eines mehrsprachigen/multikulturellen Europas. Jede neue Fremdsprache öffnet uns die Tür zu einer neuen Kultur und einer anderen Sichtweise auf die Welt, sie helfen uns, toleranter zu werden, Kultur- und Sprachenvielfalt zu verstehen und uns in der globalisierten Welt besser zurechtzufinden. Dabei wird jeder, der mehr als eine Fremdsprache gelernt hat, festgestellt haben, dass das Erlernen einer neuen Sprache umso einfacher wird, je mehr andere Sprachen man bereits spricht. Aus diesen Gründen müssen Fremdsprachen immer einen Platz in unserem Leben haben, zu jeder Zeit in jeder Lebenssituation, nicht nur in der Schule, nicht nur im Bereich der staatlichen Bildung, sondern auch bei nichtstaatlicher Bildung und in informellen Situationen. Dies ist nur zu erreichen, wenn der Fremdsprachenunterricht in alle Ausbildungs- und Lernsituationen in allen Gesellschaftsschichten integriert wird und informelle Lernmöglichkeiten außerhalb des Klassenraums gefördert werden. So kann das Lernen von Fremdsprachen ein lebenslanger Lernprozess werden. Europäische Programme können zur Finanzierung von vielversprechenden Mehrsprachigkeitsprojekten beitragen und Akteure in ganz Europa miteinander verbinden, wodurch die Mehrsprachigkeit nachhaltig gefördert wird.

Fremdsprachen und Mehrsprachigkeit haben aber auch eine große wirtschaftliche Bedeutung, da sie wichtig sind, um Geschäfte zu machen. Immer mehr Unternehmen werden sich bewusst, dass beispielsweise das Führen von Verhandlungen in einer Drittsprache zu Verwirrung und im schlimmsten Fall zu Verlusten führen kann. Somit leisten Fremdsprachen auch einen Beitrag zur Wettbewerbsfähigkeit Europas. Aus diesen Gründen sind Mitarbeiter mit Fremdsprachenkenntnissen auf dem europäischen und weltweiten Arbeitsmarkt sehr gefragt und bekommen bessere Arbeitsplätze.

Georg Rehm / Hans Uszkoreit

An Extended Summary of the META-NET Strategic Research Agenda for Multilingual Europe 2020

Abstract

Recognising Europe's exceptional demand and opportunities for multilingual language technologies, 60 leading research centres in 34 European countries joined forces in META-NET, a European Network of Excellence. Working together with numerous additional organisations and experts from a variety of fields, META-NET has developed a Strategic Research Agenda (SRA) for multilingual Europe – the complex planning and discussion process took more than two years to complete. While the complete SRA has been published elsewhere (Rehm/Uszkoreit 2013), this heavily condensed version provides an extended summary as an alternative mode of access and to enable interested parties to familiarise themselves with its key concepts in an efficient way.

1. Introduction

The multilingual setup of our European society imposes grand societal challenges on political, economic and social integration and inclusion, especially in the creation of the single digital market and unified information space targeted by the Digital Agenda (EC 2010). As many as 21 European languages are at risk of digital extinction (Rehm/ Uszkoreit 2012). They could become victims of the digital age as they are under-represented online and under-resourced with respect to language technologies. Huge market opportunities remain untapped because of language barriers. If no action is taken, many European citizens will find that speaking their mother tongue leaves them at a social and economic disadvantage.

Language technology is the missing piece of the puzzle that will bring us closer to a single digital market (see Figure 1). It is the key enabler and solution to boosting future growth in Europe and strengthening our competitiveness. The key question is: Will Europe wholeheartedly decide to participate in this fast growing market?

Although we use computers to write, phones to chat and the web to search for knowledge, IT does not yet have access to the meaning, purpose and sentiment behind our trillions of written and spoken words. Technology will bridge the rift separating IT and the human mind using sophisticated technologies for language understanding. Today's computers cannot understand texts and questions well enough to provide translations, summaries or reliable answers, but in less than ten years such services will be offered for many languages. Technological mastery of human language will enable a host of innovative IT products and services in commerce, administration, government, education, health care, entertainment, tourism and other sectors.

Recognising Europe's exceptional demand and opportunities, 60 leading research centres in 34 European countries joined forces in META-NET (www.meta-net.eu), a European Network of Excellence dedicated to the technological foundations of a multilingual, inclusive, innovative and reflective European society and partially supported through several EC-funded projects. META-NET assembled the Multilingual Europe Technology Alliance (META) with more than 650 organisations and experts representing multiple stakeholders. Working together with numerous additional organisations and experts from a variety of fields, META/META-NET has developed a Strategic Research Agenda (SRA; Rehm/Uszkoreit 2013). Our recommendations for Multilingual Europe 2020, as specified in the SRA, are based on a thorough planning process involving more than one thousand experts.

Figure 1: Language Technology unlocks the Single Digital Market

We predict, in line with many other forecasts, that the next generation of IT will be able to handle human language, knowledge and emotion in competent and meaningful ways. These new competencies will enable an endless stream of novel services that will improve communication and understanding. Many services will help people learn about and understand things such as world history, technology, nature and the economy. Others will help us to better understand each other across language and knowledge boundaries. They will also drive many other services including programmes for commerce, localisation, and personal assistance.

Our ultimate goal is monolingual, crosslingual and multilingual technology support for all languages spoken by a significant population in Europe. To achieve this, we recommend focusing on three priority research topics connected to innovative application scenarios that will provide European R&D in this field with the ability to compete with other markets and subsequently achieve benefits for European society and citizens as well as an array of opportunities for our economy and future growth. We are confident that upcoming EU funding programmes, specifically Horizon 2020 (EC 2012b) and Connecting Europe Facility (EC 2011a), combined with national and regional funding, can provide the necessary resources for accomplishing our joint vision.

A recent policy brief (Veugelers 2012) proposes that Europe specialises in new ICT sectors as a means for post-crisis recovery. The European problem lies less in the generation of new ideas than in their successful commercialisation. The study identifies major obstacles: the lack of a single digital market, and the absence of ICT clusters and powerful platform providers. It suggests that the EU policy framework could overcome these barriers and leverage the growth potential of new ICT markets by extending research and infrastructure funding to pre-commercial projects, in particular those involving the creation of ICT clusters and platforms. This is exactly the goal we are trying to achieve. Our recommendations envisage five lines of action for large-scale research and innovation. First, there are three priority research themes: Translingual Cloud, Social Intelligence and e-Participation and Socially Aware Interactive Assistants. The other two themes focus upon Core technologies and resources for Europe's languages and a European service platform for language technologies.

The objective of the priority research themes is to turn our joint vision into reality and allow Europe to benefit from a technological revolution that will overcome barriers of understanding between people of different languages, people and technology, and people and the digitised knowledge of mankind.

2. Multilingual Europe: Facts and opportunities

During the last 60 years, Europe has become a distinct political and economic structure. Culturally and linguistically it is rich and diverse. However, everyday communication between Europe's citizens, enterprises and politicians is inevitably confronted with language barriers. They are an invisible and increasingly problematic threat to economic growth (Economist 2012). The EU's institutions spend about one billion Euros per year on translation and interpretation to maintain their policy of multilingualism (EC 2012c) and the overall European market for translation, interpretation, software localisation and website globalisation was estimated at 5.7 billion Euros in 2008.

The only – unacceptable and rather un-European – alternative to a multilingual Europe would be to allow a single language to take a predominant position and replace all other languages in transnational communication. Another way to overcome language barriers is to learn foreign languages. Given the 23 official EU languages plus 60 or more other languages spoken in Europe (EC 2012a), language learning alone cannot solve the problem. Without technological support, our linguistic diversity will be an insurmountable obstacle for the entire continent. Only about half of the 500 million people who live in the EU speak English! There is no such thing as a lingua franca shared by the vast majority of the population.

Less than 10% of the EU's population are willing or able to use online services in English which is why multilingual technologies are badly needed to support and to move the EU online market from more than 20 language-specific sub-markets to one unified single digital market with more than 500 million users and consumers. The current situation with "many fragmented markets" is considered one of the main obstacles that seriously undermine Europe's efforts to exploit ICT fully (EC 2010).

Language technology is a key enabler for sustainable, cost-effective and socially beneficial solutions to overcome language barriers. It will offer European stakeholders tremendous advantages, not only within the European market, but also in trade relations with non-European countries, especially emerging economies.

In the late 1970s the EU realised the relevance of language technology as a driver of European unity and began funding its first research projects, such as EUROTRA. After a longer period of sparse funding (Lazzari 2006; Joscelyne/Lockwood 2003), the European Commission set up a department dedicated to language technology and machine translation a few years ago. Selective funding efforts have led to a number of valuable results. For example, the EC's translation services now use Moses, which has been mainly developed in European research projects. However, these never led to a concerted European effort through which the EU and its member states systematically pursue the common goal of providing technology support for all European languages.

Europe now has a well-developed research base. Through initiatives such as CLARIN and META-NET the community is well connected and engaged in a long term agenda that aims gradually to strengthen language technology's role. What is missing in Europe is awareness, political determination and political will that would take us to a leading position in this technology area through a concerted funding effort. This major dedicated push needs to include the political determination to modify and to adopt a shared, EU-wide language policy that foresees an important role for language technologies.

Europe's more than 80 languages are one of its richest and most important cultural assets, and a vital part of its unique social model (EC 2008, 2012a). While languages such as English and Spanish are likely to thrive in the emerging digital marketplace, many European languages could become marginal in a networked society. This would weaken Europe's global standing, and run counter to the goal of ensuring equal participation for every European citizen regardless of language. A recent UNESCO report on multilingualism states that languages are an essential medium for the enjoyment of fundamental rights, such as political expression, education and participation in society (UNESCO 2007, 2008, 2011b; Vannini/Le Crosnier 2012).

Many Europeans find it difficult to interact with online services and participate in the digital economy. According to a recent study, only 57% of internet users in Europe purchase goods and services in languages that are not their native language. 55% of users read content in a foreign language while only 35% use another language to write e-mails or post comments on the web (EC 2011c). A few years ago, English might have been the lingua franca of the web but the situation has now drastically changed. The amount of online content in other European as well as Asian and Middle Eastern languages has exploded (Ford/Batson 2011). Already today, more than 55% of web-based content is not in English.

The European market for translation, interpretation and localisation was estimated to be 5.7 billion Euros in 2008. The subtitling and dubbing sector was at 633 million Euros, language teaching at 1.6 billion Euros. The overall value of the European language industry was estimated at 8.4 billion Euros and expected to grow by 10% per year, i.e., resulting in ca. 16.5 billion Euros in 2015 (EC 2009b, 2011b). Yet, this existing capacity is not enough to satisfy current and future needs, e.g., with regard to translation (DePalma/Kelly 2009). Already today, Google Translate translates the same volume per day that all human translators on the planet translate in one year (Och 2012).

Despite recent improvements, the quality, usability and integration of machine translation into other online services is far from what is needed. If we rely on existing technologies, automated translation and the ability to process a variety of content in a variety of languages will be impossible. The same applies to information services, document services, media industries, digital archives and language teaching. The most compelling solution for ensuring the breadth and depth of language usage in tomorrow's Europe is to use appropriate technology. Still, the quality and usability of current technologies is far from what is needed. Especially the smaller European languages suffer severely from under-representation in the digital realm.

Drawing on the insights gained so far, today's hybrid language technology mixing deep processing with statistical methods could be able to bridge the gap between all European languages and beyond. In the end, high-quality language technology will be a must for all of Europe's languages for supporting the political and economic unity through cultural diversity. The three priority research themes are mainly aimed at Horizon 2020 (EC 2012b). The more infrastructural aspects, platform design and implementation and concrete language technology services are aimed at CEF (EC 2011a). An integral component of our strategic plans are the member states and associated countries: it is of utmost importance to set up, under the umbrella of the SRA, a coordinated initiative both on the national (member states, regions, associated countries) and international level (EC/EU), including research centres as well as small, medium and large enterprises who work on or with language technologies.

3. How can Language Technology help?

We believe that *Language Technology made in Europe for Europe* will significantly contribute to future European cross-border and cross-language communication, economic growth and social stability while establishing for Europe a worldwide, leading position in technology innovation, securing Europe's future as a world-wide trader and exporter of goods, services and information. There are many societal changes and challenges as well as economic and technological trends that confirm the urgent need to include sophisticated language technology in our European ICT infrastructure. Among these changes and challenges are language barriers (EC 2009a), an ageing population, people with disabilities, immigration and integration, personal information services and customer care, operation and cooperation on a global scale, preservation of cultural heritage, linguistic diversity (WSIS 2003; UNESCO 2011a), social media and e-participation as well as market awareness and customer acceptance.

Multilingualism has become the global norm rather than the exception (Vannini/Le Crosnier 2012). Future applications that embed information and communication technology require sophisticated language technologies. Fully speech-enabled autonomous robots could help in disaster areas by rescuing travellers trapped in vehicles or by giving first aid. Language technology can significantly contribute towards improving social inclusion and can help us provide answers to urgent social challenges while creating genuine business opportunities. Language technology can now automate the very processes of translation, content production, and knowledge management for all European languages. It can also empower intuitive language/speech-based interfaces for household electronics, machinery, vehicles, computers and robots.

4. Language Technology 2012: Current state

Answering the question on the current state of a whole R&D field is both difficult and complex. For language technology, even though partial answers exist in terms of business figures, scientific challenges and results from educational studies, nobody has collected these indicators and provided comparable reports for a substantial number of European languages yet. In order to arrive at a comprehensive answer, META-NET prepared the White Paper Series "Europe's Languages in the Digital Age" (Rehm/Uszkoreit 2012) that describes the current state of language technology support for 30 European languages (including all 23 official EU languages). This immense undertaking was in preparation from mid 2010 and was published in the Summer of 2012. More than 200 experts participated to the 30 volumes as co-authors and contributors.

The differences in technology support between the various languages and areas are dramatic and alarming. In all of the four areas we examined (machine translation, speech processing, text analytics, language resources), English is ahead of the other languages but even support for English is far from being perfect. While there are good quality software and resources available for a few larger languages and application areas, others, usually smaller or very small languages, have substantial gaps. Many languages lack even basic technologies for text analytics and essential language resources. Others have basic resources but the implementation of semantic methods is still far away. Currently no language, not even English, has the technological support it deserves. Also, the number of badly supported and under-resourced languages is unacceptable if we do not want to give up the principles of solidarity and subsidiarity in Europe.

The META-NET White Paper Series is fully available online at www.meta-net.eu/whitepapers. On this website we also present the press release "At least 21 European Languages in Danger of Digital Extinction" which was circulated on the occasion of the European Day of Languages 2012 (Sept. 26), and also its impact around the world. The echo generated by our press release shows that Europe is very passionate and concerned about its languages and that it is also very interested in the idea of establishing a solid language technology base for overcoming language barriers.

5. Language Technology 2020: The META-NET technology vision

We believe that in the next IT revolution computers will master our languages. Just as they already understand measurements and formats for dates and times, the operating systems of tomorrow will know human languages. They may not reach the linguistic performance of educated people and they will not yet know enough about the world to understand everything, but they will be much more useful than they are today and will further enhance our work and life.

The broad area of **communication among people** will see a dramatically increased use of sophisticated LT. By the year 2020, with sufficient research effort on high-quality automatic translation and robust accurate speech recognition, reliable dialogue translation for face-to-face conversation and telecommunication will be possible for at least hundreds of languages, across multiple subject fields and text types, both spoken and written. Authoring software will check for appropriate style according to genre and purpose and help evaluate comprehensibility. It will flag potential errors, suggest corrections, and use authoring memories to suggest completions of started sentences or even whole paragraphs. By 2020 tele-meetings will be the norm for professional meetings. LT will be able to record, transcribe, and summarise them. Brainstorming will be facilitated by semantic lookup and structured display of relevant data, proposals, pictures, and maps. Business email will be embedded in semantic process models to automate standardised communication. Even before 2020, email communication will be semantically analysed, checked for sentiment indicators, and summarised in reports. Semantic integration into work processes, threading, and response management will be applied across channels, as will machine translation and analytics.

Human language will become the primary medium for **communication between people and technology**. Today's voice-control interfaces to smartphones and search engines are just the modest start of overcoming the communication barrier between humankind and the non-human part of the world. Only a few years ago the idea of talking to a car to access key functions would have seemed absurd, yet it is now commonplace. Recently the concept of a personal digital assistant has increased in popularity. We will soon see much more sophisticated virtual personalities with expressive voices, faces, and gestures. They will become an interface to any information provided online. The metaphor of a personal assistant is powerful and extremely useful, since such an assistant can be made sensitive to the user's preferences, habits, moods, and goals. By the year 2020 we could have a highly personalised, socially aware and interactive virtual assistant. Having been trained on the user's behaviour and communication space, it will proactively offer advice and it will be able to speak in the language and dialect of the user but also digest information in other natural and artificial languages and formats. The assistant will translate or interpret without the user even needing to request it. By 2020 there will be a competitive landscape of intelligent interfaces to all kinds of objects and services employing human language and other modes for effective communication.

In the context of the Semantic Web, Linked Open Data and the general semantification of the web as well as knowledge acquisition and ontology population, LT can perform many tasks in the **processing of knowledge and information**. It can sort, categorise, catalogue, and filter content and it can deliver the data for data mining in texts. LT can connect web documents with meaningful hyperlinks and it can produce summaries of larger text collections. Opinion mining and sentiment analysis can find out what people think about products, personalities, or problems and analyse their feelings about such topics. In the next few years we will see considerable advances for all these techniques. For large parts of research and application development, language processing and knowledge processing will merge. The predicted and planned use of language and knowledge technologies for social intelligence applications will involve text and speech analytics, translation, summarisation, opinion mining, sentiment analysis, and several other technologies. In 2020, LT will enable forms of knowledge evolution, transmission and exploitation that speed up scientific, social, and cultural development. The effects for other knowledge-intensive application areas such as business intelligence, scientific knowledge discovery, and multimedia production will be immense.

The wide range of novel or improved applications in our shared vision represent only a fragment of the countless opportunities for LT to change our work and everyday life. Language-proficient technology will enable or enhance applications wherever language is present. It will change the production, management, and use of patents, legal contracts, medical reports, recipes, technical descriptions, and scientific texts, and it will permit many new voice applications such as automatic services for the submission of complaints and suggestions, for accepting orders, and for counselling in customer-care, e-government, education, community services, etc.

6. Language Technology 2020: The META-NET Priority Research Themes

In ten years or less, basic language proficiency is going to be an integral component of any advanced IT. It will be available to any user interface, service and application. Additional language skills for semantic search, knowledge discovery, human-technology communication, text analytics, language checking, e-learning, translation and other applications will employ and extend the basic proficiency. The shared basic language competence will ensure consistency and interoperability among services. Many adaptations and extensions will be derived and improved through sample data and interaction with people by powerful machine learning techniques.

In the envisaged big push toward realising this vision by massive research and innovation, the technology community is faced with three enormous challenges:

1. *Richness and diversity*. A serious challenge is the sheer number of languages, some closely related, others distantly apart. Within a language, technology has to deal with dialects, sociolects, registers, jargons, genres and slangs.
2. *Depth and meaning*. Understanding language is a complex process. Human language is not only the key to knowledge and thought, it also cannot be interpreted without shared knowledge and active inference. Computational language proficiency needs semantic technologies.
3. *Multimodality and grounding*. Human language is embedded in our daily activities. It is combined with other modes and media of communication. It is affected by beliefs, desires, intentions and emotions and it affects all of these. Successful interactive language technology requires models of embodied and adaptive human interaction with people, technology and other parts of the world.

It is fortunate for research and economy that the only way to effectively tackle the three challenges involves submitting the evolving technology continuously to the growing demands and practical stress tests of real world applications. Only a continuous stream of technological innovation can provide the economic pull forces and the evolutionary environments for the realisation of the grand vision.

We propose five major action lines of research and innovation:

- **Three Priority Research Themes** along with application scenarios to drive research and innovation. These will demonstrate novel technologies in show-case solutions with high economic and societal impact. They will open up numerous new business opportunities for European language-technology and -service providers.
  1. **Translingual Cloud**: generic and specialised federated cloud services for instantaneous reliable spoken and written translation among all European and major non-European languages.
  2. **Social Intelligence and e-Participation**: understanding and dialogue within and across communities of citizens, customers, clients and consumers to enable e-participation and more effective processes for preparing, selecting and evaluating collective decisions.
  3. **Socially Aware Interactive Assistants** that learn and adapt and that provide proactive and interactive support tailored to specific situations, locations and goals of the user through verbal and non-verbal multimodal communication.
- The other two themes focus upon base technologies and a service platform:
  4. **Core technologies and resources for Europe's languages**: a steadily evolving system of shared, collectively maintained interoperable core technologies and resources for the languages of Europe and selected other languages. These will ensure that our languages will be sufficiently supported and represented in the next generations of IT.
  5. A **European service platform for language technologies** for supporting research and innovation by testing and showcasing research results, integrating various services, even including professional human services, will allow SME providers to offer component and end-user services, and share and utilise tools, components and data resources.

These priority themes have been designed with the aim of turning our vision into reality and to letting Europe benefit from a technological revolution that will overcome barriers of understanding between people of different languages, between people and technology and between people and the knowledge of mankind. The themes connect societal needs with LT applications.

6.1 Priority Theme 1: Translingual cloud

The goal is a multilingual European society, in which all citizens can use any service, access all knowledge, enjoy all media and control any technology in their mother tongues. This will be a world in which written and spoken communication is not hindered anymore by language barriers and in which even specialised high-quality translation will be affordable. The citizen, the professional, the organisation, or the software application in need of cross-lingual communication will use a single access point for channelling text or speech through a gateway that will instantly return the translations into the requested languages in the required quality and desired format. Behind this access point will be a network of generic and special-purpose services combining automatic translation or interpretation, language checking, post-editing, as well as human creativity and quality assurance.

One key component of this service (see Figure 2) is a use and provision platform for providers of computer-supported top-quality human translation, multilingual text authoring and quality assurance by experts. Other important components are trusted service centres as certified service providers fulfilling highest standards for privacy, confidentiality and security of source data and translations and quality upscale models embedded into services permitting instant quality upgrades if the results of the requested service levels do not yet fulfil the quality requirements.

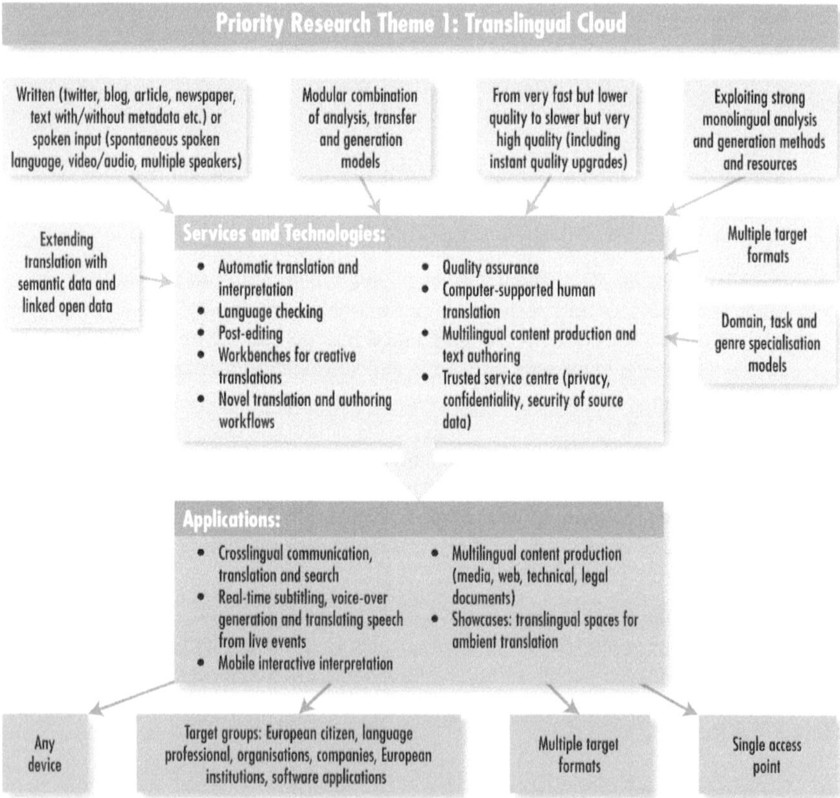

Figure 2: Priority Research Theme 1: Translingual Cloud

6.2 Priority Theme 2: Social intelligence and e-participation

The central goal behind the second theme is to use information technology and the digital content of the web for improving effectiveness and efficiency of decision-making in business and society (see Figure 3). Social intelligence builds on improved text analytics methodologies but goes far beyond the analysis. One goal is the analysis of large volumes of social media, comments, blogs, forum postings etc. of citizens, customers, consumers and other stakeholder communities. Part of the analysis is directed to the status, opinions and acceptance associated with the individual information units. As the formation of collective opinions and attitudes is highly dynamic, new developments need to be detected and trends analysed. Emotions play an important part in individual actions such as voting, buying, supporting, donating and in collective opinion formation, the analysis of sentiment is a crucial component of social intelligence.

Social intelligence can also support collective deliberation processes. Today any collective discussion processes involving large numbers of participants are bound to become intransparent and incomprehensible rather fast. By recording, grouping, aggregating and counting opinion statements, pros and cons, supporting evidence, sentiments and new questions and issues, the discussion can be summarised and focussed. Decision processes can be structured, monitored, documented and visualised, so that joining, following and benefitting from them becomes much easier. The efficiency and impact of such processes can thus be greatly enhanced.

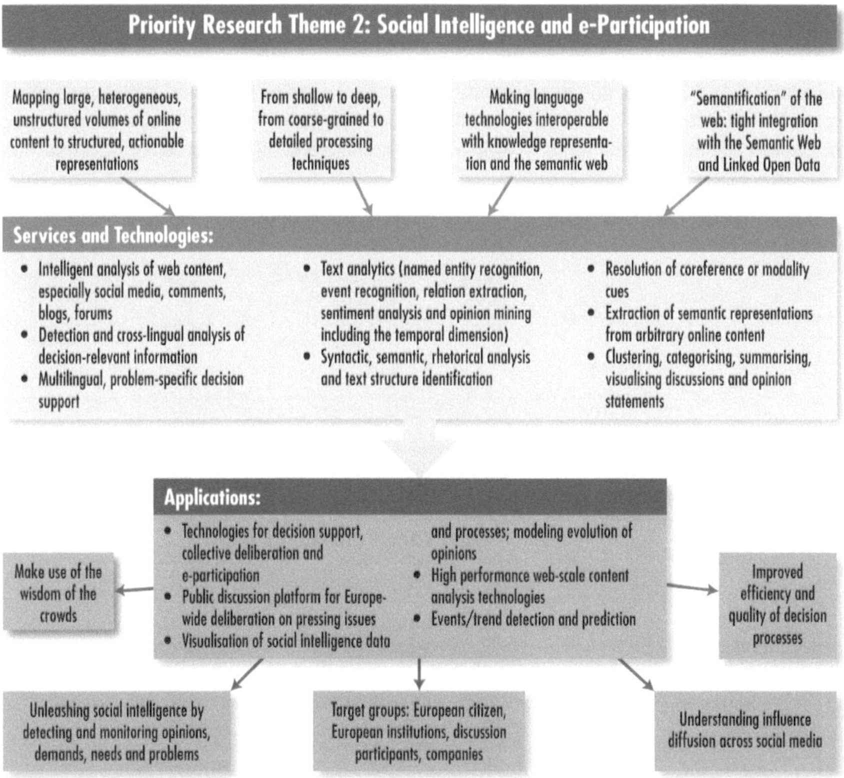

Figure 3: Priority Research Theme 2: Social intelligence and e-participation

A key enabler will be technologies that can map large, heterogeneous, and, to a large extent, unstructured volumes of online content to actionable representations that support decision making and analytics tasks. Such mappings can range from the relatively shallow to the relatively deep, encompassing coarse-grained topic classification at the document or paragraph level or the identification of named entities, as well as in-depth syntactic, semantic and rhetorical analysis at the level of individual sentences and beyond or the resolution of co-reference or modality cues within and across sentences. Technologies such as, e.g., information extraction, data mining, automatic linking and summarisation have to be made interoperable with knowledge representation and semantic web methods. Drawing expertise from related areas such as knowledge management, information sciences, or social sciences is a prerequisite to meet the challenge of modelling social intelligence (Genereux/Hamon 2012).

6.3 Priority Theme 3: Socially aware interactive assistants

Socially aware interactive assistants are conversational agents (see Figure 4). Their socially-aware behaviour is a result of combining analysis methods for speech, non-verbal and semantic signals. They support people interacting with their environment, including human-computer, human-agent/robot, and computermediated human-human interaction. The assistants must be able to act in various environments, both indoor, outdoor and virtual environments, and also be able to communicate, exchange information and understand other agents' intentions. They must be able to adapt to the user's needs and environment and have the capacity to learn incrementally from all interactions and other sources of information.

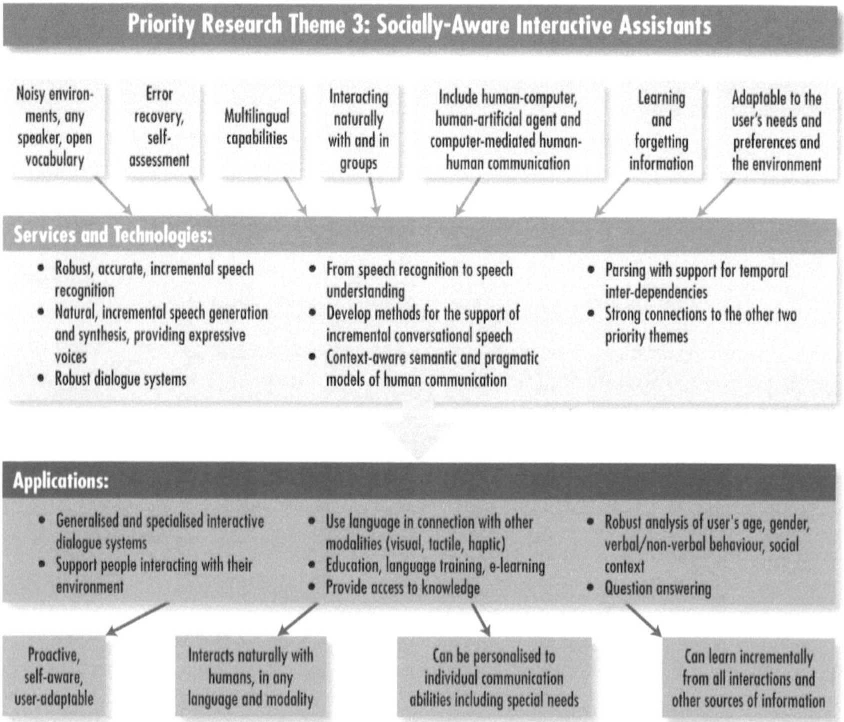

Figure 4: Priority Research Theme 3: Socially aware interactive assistants

The ideal socially aware multilingual assistant can interact naturally with humans, in any language and modality. It can adapt and be personalised to individual communication abilities, including special needs (for the visual, hearing, or motor impaired), affections, or language proficiencies. It can recognise and generate speech incrementally and fluently. It is able to assess its performance and recover from errors. It can learn, personalise itself and forget. It can assist in language training and education, and provide synthetic multimedia information analytics.

In addition to significantly improving core speech and language technologies, the development of socially aware interactive assistants requires several research breakthroughs. With regard to speech recognition, accuracy and robustness have to be improved. Methods for self-assessment, self-adaptation, personalisation, error-recovery, learning and forgetting information, and also for moving from recognition to understanding have to be developed. Concerning speech synthesis, voices have to be made more natural and expressive, control parameters have to be included for linguistic meaning, speaking style, emotion etc. They also have to be equipped with methods for incremental conversational speech, including filled pauses and hesitations.

6.4 Core language resources and technologies

The three priority research themes share a large and heterogeneous group of core technologies for language analysis and production that provide development support through basic modules and datasets. To this group belong tools and technologies such as, among others, tokenisers, part-of-speech taggers, syntactic parsers, tools for building language models, information retrieval tools, machine learning toolkits, speech recognition and speech synthesis engines, and integrated architectures. Many of these tools depend on specific datasets (i.e., language resources), for example, very large collections of linguistically annotated documents (monolingual or multilingual, aligned corpora), treebanks, grammars, lexicons, thesauri, terminologies, dictionaries, ontologies and language models. Both tools and resources can be rather general or highly task- or domain-specific. Tools can be language-independent. Datasets are, by definition, language-specific. There are also several types of resources, such as error-annotated corpora for machine translation or spoken dialogue corpora, that are specific to one or more of the three priority themes.

A key component of this research agenda is to collect, develop and make available core technologies and resources through a shared infrastructure so that the research and technology development carried out in all themes can make use of them. Over time, this approach will improve the core technologies, as the specific research will have certain requirements on the software, extending their feature sets, performance, accuracy etc. through dynamic push-pull effects. Conceptualising these technologies as a set of shared core technologies will have positive effects on their sustainability and interoperability. Also, many European languages other than English are heavily under-resourced (Rehm/Uszkoreit 2012).

The European academic and industrial technology community is fully aware of the need for sharing resources such as language data, language descriptions, tools and core technology components as a basis for the successful development and implementation of the priority themes. Initiatives such as FLaReNet (Calzolari et al. 2011) and CLARIN have prepared the ground for a culture of sharing, META-NET's open resource exchange infrastructure, META-SHARE, is providing the technological platform as well as legal and organisational schemes. All language resources and basic technologies will be created under the core technologies umbrella.

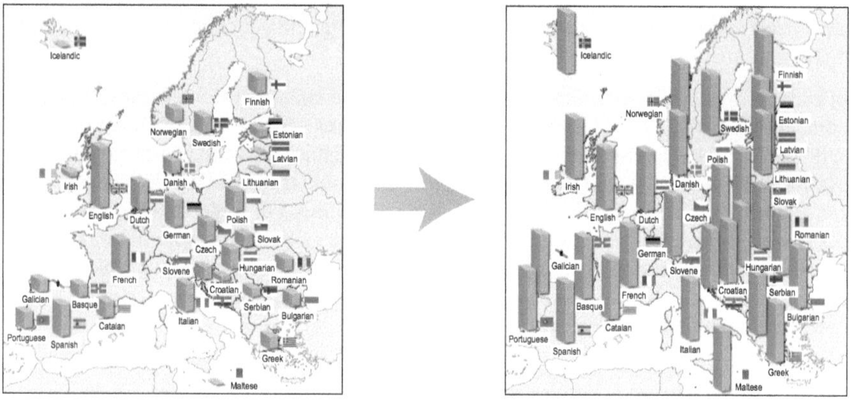

2013 **2020**

Figure 5: Towards appropriate and adequate coverage of language resources and technologies for Europe

6.5 A European service platform for Language Technologies

We recommend the design and implementation of an ambitious large-scale platform as a central motor for research and innovation in the next phase of IT evolution and as a ubiquitous resource for the multilingual European society. The platform will be used for testing, show casing, proof-of-concept demonstration, avant-garde adoption, experimental and operational service composition, and fast and economical service delivery to enterprises and end-users (see Figure 6). The creation of a cloud platform for a wide range of services dealing with human language, knowledge and emotion will not only benefit the individual and corporate users of these technologies but also the providers. Large-scale ICT infrastructures and innovation clusters such as this one are foreseen in the Digital Agenda for Europe (EC 2010, 24).

A top layer consists of **language processing** such as text filters, tokenisation, spell, grammar and style checking, hyphenation, lemmatising and parsing. At a deeper level, services will be offered that realise some degree and form of **language understanding** including entity and event extraction, opinion mining and translation. Both basic language processing and understanding will be used by services that support **human communication** or realise human-machine interaction. Part of this layer are question answering and dialogue systems as well as email response applications. Another component will bring in services for processing and storing **knowledge** gained by and used for understanding and communication. This part will include repositories of linked data and ontologies. These in turn permit a certain range of rational capabilities often attributed to a notion of intelligence. The goal is not to model the entire human intelligence but rather to realise selected forms of **inference** that are needed for utilising and extending knowledge, for understanding and for successful communication. These forms of inference permit better decision support, pro-active planning and autonomous adaptation. A final part of services will be dedicated to **human emotion**. Since people are largely guided by their emotions and strongly affected by the emotions of others, truly user-centred IT need facilities for detecting and interpreting emotion and even for expressing emotional states in communication.

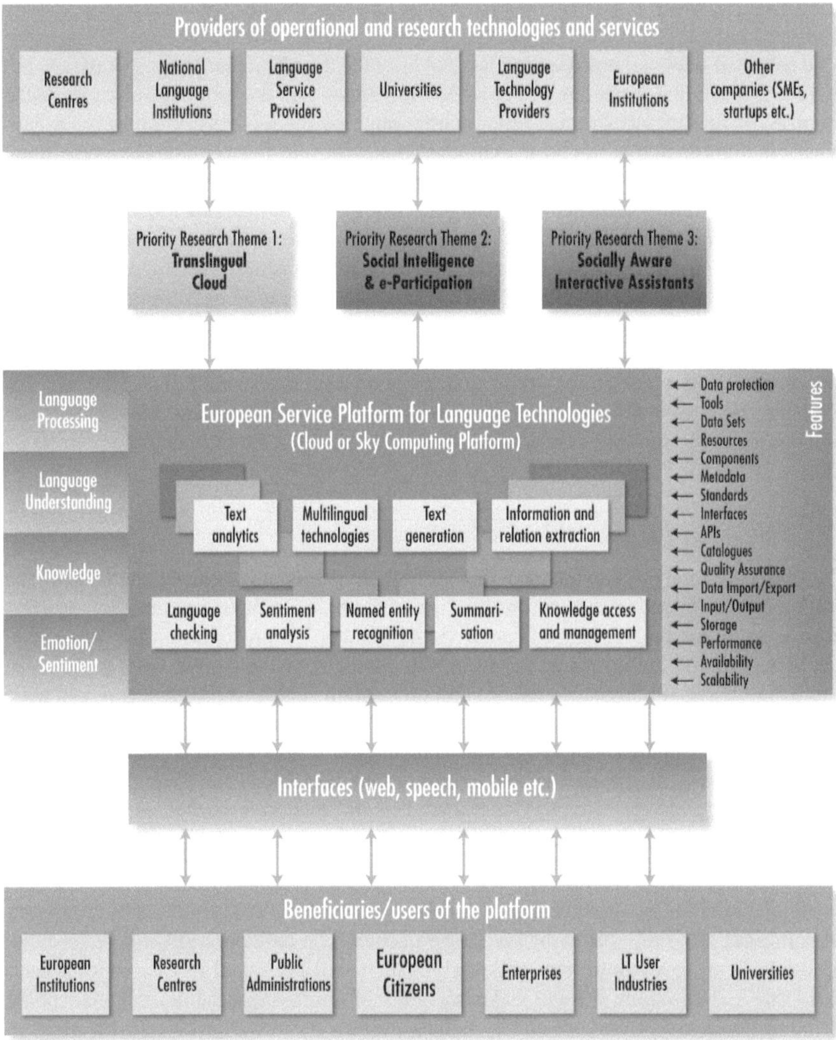

Figure 6: European service platform for Language Technologies

All three priority areas will be able to contribute to and at the same time draw immense benefits from this platform. There are strong reasons for aiming at a single service platform for the three areas and for the different types of technologies. They share many basic components and they need to be combined for many valuable applications, including the selected showcase solutions of the three areas.

6.6 Languages to be supported

The SRA has a much broader scope in terms of languages to be supported than our study "Europe's Languages in the Digital Age" (Rehm/Uszkoreit 2012). The set of languages to be reflected with technologies include not only the 23 official languages of the EU but also recognised and unrecognised regional languages and the languages of associated countries or non-member states. Equally important are the minority and immigrant languages that are in active use by a significant population in Europe (for Germany, these are, among others, Turkish and Russian; for the UK, these include Bengali, Urdu/Hindi and Punjabi). An important set of languages outside our continent are those of important political and trade partners such as, for example, Chinese, Japanese, Korean, Russian, and Thai. META-NET already has good working relationships with several of the respective official bodies, especially EFNIL (European Federation of National Institutions for Language), NPLD (Network to Promote Linguistic Diversity), and also the Maaya World Network for Linguistic Diversity. The concrete composition of languages to be supported by this agenda's research programme up until the year 2020 and beyond, depends on the composition of participating countries and regions and also on the specific nature of the funding instruments used and combined for realising the ambitious plan.

6.7 Structure and principles of research organisation

The three proposed priority research themes overlap in technologies and challenges. The overlap reflects the coherence and maturation of the field. At the same time, the resulting division of labour and sharing of resources and results is a precondition for the realisation of this highly ambitious programme. The themes need to benefit from progress in core technologies of language analysis and production such as morphological, syntactic and semantic parsing and generation. But each of the three areas will concentrate on one central area of language technology: the Translingual Cloud will focus on cross-lingual technologies such as translation and interpretation; the Social Intelligence strand will take care of knowledge discovery, text analytics and related technologies; the research dedicated to Interactive Assistants will take on technologies such as speech and multimodal interfaces.

The final model for the organisation of collaboration will have to be guided by a thoughtful combination of the following basic approaches. The collaboration will be interdisciplinary, flexible, evolutionary and analytical. It will be staged in two major phases (2015-2017, 2018-2020). We will make heavy use of improving systems by bootstrapping earlier systems and prototypes and by collaborating very closely with relevant areas of service and technology industries.

7. Towards a shared European programme

In the Strategic Research Agenda META-NET recommends setting up a large, multi-year programme on language technologies to build the technological foundations for a truly multilingual Europe. The research strands and associated sets of applications we suggest to build in the next ten years are of utmost importance for Europe. Through these technologies we will be able to overcome language barriers in spoken and written communication, we will be able to carry out country- and language-border-crossing debates and we will enable new forms and means of communication. We are confident that the impact of our technologies will be so immense that they will be able to help establishing a sense of a European identity in the majority of European citizens. The research plan described in the SRA will generate a countless number of opportunities, it will significantly participate to Europe's future growth and will secure Europe's position in many global markets.

Due to the scope and duration of the suggested action, our preferred option is to set up a shared programme between the European Commission and the Member States as well as Associated Countries. First steps along those lines have been taken at META-NET's META-FORUM 2012 conference in Brussels, Belgium, on June 21, 2012, when representatives of several European funding agencies (Bulgaria, Czech Republic, France, Hungary, The Netherlands, Slovenia) who participated in a panel discussion on this topic, unanimously expressed the urgent need for setting up such a shared programme (META-NET 2012a).

The programme will include a carefully planned governance structure. Here, first steps have also been taken: META-NET has an Executive Board with currently 12 members, the operations of the network and its bodies are specified in its Statutes (META-NET 2012b). Furthermore, a legal person for META-NET was established. This legal person, META-TRUST AISBL, is an international non-profit organisation under Belgian law (META-NET 2012c). These proven and established structures can be used as starting points for the governance structure of a future programme.

8. Acknowledgements

This paper is an extended summary of the *META-NET Strategic Research Agenda for Multilingual Europe 2020* (Rehm/Uszkoreit 2013). The work presented in this article would not have been possible without the dedication and commitment of our colleagues Aljoscha Burchardt, Kathrin Eichler, Tina Klüwer, Arle Lommel and Felix Sasaki (all DFKI), the 60 member organisations of the META-NET network of excellence, the ca. 70 members of the Vision Groups, the ca. 30 members of the META Technology Council, the more than 200 authors of and contributors to the META-NET Language White Paper Series (Rehm/Uszkoreit 2012) and the ca. 200 representatives from industry and research who contributed to the META-NET SRA.

META-NET is co-funded by the 7th Framework Programme of the European Commission through the following grant agreements: T4ME Net (no. 249 119), CESAR (no. 271 022), METANET4U (no. 270 893) and META-NORD (no. 270 899).

More information is available at www.meta-net.eu and via office@meta-net.eu.

References

Calzolari, N./Bel, N./Choukri, K./Mariani, J./Monachini, M./Odijk, J./Piperidis, S./Quochi, V./ Soria, C. (2011): *Language resources for the future – the future of language resources*. Internet: www.flarenet.eu/sites/default/files/FLaReNet_Book.pdf.

DePalma, D.A./Kelly, N. (2009): *The business case for machine translation. How organizations justify and adopt automated translation.* Common sense advisory. Internet: www.commonsenseadvisory.com.

EC (2008): *Multilingualism: an asset for Europe and a shared commitment*. European Commission. Internet: http://ec.europa.eu/languages/pdf/comm2008_en.pdf.

EC (2009a): *Report on cross-border e-commerce in the EU*. European Commission. Internet: http://ec.europa. eu/consumers/strategy/docs/com_staff_wp2009_en.pdf.

EC (2009b): *Size of the language industry in the EU*. Directorate-General for Translation of the European Commission. Internet: http://ec.europa.eu/dgs/translation/publications/studies.

EC (2010): *A digital agenda for Europe*. European Commission. Internet: http://ec.europa.eu/information_ society/digital-agenda/publications/.

EC (2011a): *Connecting Europe Facility: Commission adopts plan for 50 billion Euros boost to European networks*. European Commission. Internet: http://europa.eu/rapid/pressReleases Action.do?reference=IP/11/1200.

EC (2011b): *Languages mean business*. European Commission. Internet: http://ec.europa.eu/languages/languages-mean-business/.

EC (2011c): *User language preferences online*. Directorate-General Information Society & Media of the European Commission. Internet: http://ec.europa.eu/public_opinion/flash/fl_313_en.pdf.

EC (2012a): *Europeans and their languages*. European Commission. (= Special Eurobarometer 386/77.1). Internet: http://ec.europa.eu/languages/languages-of-europe/eurobarometer-survey_en.htm.

EC (2012b): *Horizon 2020: The Framework Programme for Research and Innovation*. European Commission. Internet: http://ec.europa.eu/research/horizon2020/.

EC (2012c): *Languages*. European Commission. Internet: http://ec.europa.eu/languages/.

Economist (2012) = The Economist Intelligence Unit The (2012): *Competing across borders. How cultural and communication barriers affect business*. Internet: www.managementthinking.eiu.com/competing-across-borders.html.

Ford, D./Batson, J. (2011): *Languages of the World* (*Wide Web*). Internet: http://googleresearch.blogspot.com/2011/07/languages-of-world-wide-web.html.

Genereux, M./Hamon, T. (eds.) (2012): *Workshop on Language Technology for Decision Support at the Fourth Swedish Language Technology Conference*. Internet: http://permalink.gmane.org/gmane.science.linguistics.corpora/15911.

Joscelyne, A./Lockwood, R. (2003): *The EUROMAP Study. Benchmarking HLT progress in Europe*. Internet: http://cst.dk/dandokcenter/FINAL_Euromap_rapport.pdf.

Lazzari, G. (2006): *Human Language Technologies for Europe*. Internet: http://cordis.europa.eu/documents/documentlibrary/90834371EN6.pdf.

META-NET (2012a): *META-FORUM 2012: A strategy for multilingual Europe. Panel discussion "Plans for LT Research and Innovation in Member States and Regions"*. [Videos available at www.meta-net.eu/events/meta-forum-2012/programme].

META-NET (2012b): *META-NET Statutes. Version 1.1.* Internet: www.meta-net.eu/META-NET-Statutes.pdf.

META-NET (2012c): *META-TRUST AISBL (Association internationale sans but lucratif)*. Internet: www.meta-trust.eu.

Och, F. (2012): *Breaking down the language barrier – six years in*. Internet: http://googleblog.blogspot.de/2012/04/breaking-down-language-barriersix-years.html.

Rehm, G./Uszkoreit, H. (eds.) (2012): *META-NET White Paper Series: Europe's Languages in the Digital Age*. Heidelberg/New York/Dordrecht/London: Springer. Internet: www.meta-net.eu/whitepapers. [31 volumes on 30 European languages].

Rehm, G./Uszkoreit, H. (eds.) (2013): *The META-NET Strategic Research Agenda for Multilingual Europe*. Heidelberg/New York/Dordrecht/London: Springer. Internet: www.meta-net.eu/sra.

UNESCO (2007): *Intersectoral mid-term strategy on languages and multilingualism*. Internet: http://unesdoc.unesco.org/images/0015/001503/150335e.pdf.

UNESCO (2008): *UNESCO Information for All Programme: International Conference Linguistic and Cultural Diversity in Cyberspace: Final Document. Lena Resolution*. Internet: http://portal.unesco.org/ci/en/files/27519/12218169309lena_resolution_en.pdf/lena_resolution_en.pdf.

UNESCO (2011a): UNESCO *Information for All Programme (AFP)*. Internet: www.unesco.org/new/en/communication-and-information/intergovernmental-programmes/information-for-all-programme-ifap/.

UNESCO (2011b): *UNESCO Information for All Programme: Second International Conference Linguistic and Cultural Diversity in Cyberspace: Final Document. Yakutsk Call for Action*. Internet: www.maayajo.org/IMG/pdf/Call_for_action_Yakutsk_EN-2.pdf.

Vannini, L./Le Crosnier, H. (eds.) (2012): *Net.Lang – Towards the multilingual cyberspace. The Maaya World Network for Linguistic Diversity*. Paris: C&F éditions. Internet: http://net-lang.net.

Veugelers, R. (2012): *New ICT sectors: Platforms for European growth?* (= Bruegel Policy Contribution 2012/14). Brussels: Bruegel. Internet: www.bruegel.org/publications/.

WSIS (2003): *World Summit on the Information Society: Declaration of Principles – Building the Information Society: a global challenge in the new Millennium*. Internet: www.itu.int/wsis/docs/geneva/official/dop.html.

e) The Budapest Resolution

The Budapest Resolution on the Lexical Challenges in Multilingual Europe

(in 22 European languages)

The declaration presented here in 22 European languages takes into account all of EFNIL members' views and attitudes to the important issues put forth and synthesizes the different positions of those who continued the discussion with the Executive Committee after the 10th EFNIL conference in Budapest 2012, during which the first draft of this Declaration was discussed.

bg	български	hr	hrvatski jezik	no – Bokmål	Norsk (Bokmål)
cs	čeština	ga	Gaeilge	no – Nynorsk	Norsk (Nynorsk)
da	dansk	is	íslensk	pl	polski
de	Deutsch	it	italiano	pt	português
el	ελληνικά	lv	latviešu valoda	sk	slovenčina
et	eesti keel	le	Lëtzebuergesch	sl	slovenščina
en	English	hu	magyar		
fr	français	nl	Nederlands		

bg

БУДАПЕЩЕНСКА РЕЗОЛЮЦИЯ ЗА ПРЕДИЗВИКАТЕЛСТВАТА ПРЕД ЛЕКСИКОГРАФИЯТА В МНОГОЕЗИЧНА ЕВРОПА

1. *Европейската федерация на националните институции за език* призовава към създаване на общоевропейска многоезикова инфраструктура като основна предпоставка за Европа, в която гражданите наистина общуват на много езици.

2. Разработването на модерна висококачествена лексикографска инфраструктура, състояща се от надеждни (паралелни) корпуси, едноезикови, двуезикови и многоезикови речници и лексикални ресурси, тезауруси, терминологични бази от данни, лексикално-семантични мрежи и съотносими езикови инструменти е *conditio sine qua non* за изучаването и използването на (чужди) езици от европейските граждани, за писмения и устния превод, както и за развитието на езиковите технологии в служба на компютърните системи и устройства, опериращи с естествен език.

3. Необходими са базови лексикални ресурси и качествени езикови корпуси за всички официални езици на ЕС; те трябва да включват двуезикови корпуси и програми за обработка за двойките езици, които не са достатъчно обезпечени в сравнение с езиците, които са обект на търговски ориентираната езикова индустрия.

4. Очаква се ЕС да играе активна роля в развитието на инфраструктурата, която обединява официалните езици на страните членки, като се има предвид, че многоезичността надхвърля по обхват която и да било отделна езикова зона или държава.

5. На това основание *Европейската федерация на националните институции за език* настоява правителствата на страните членки, както и Евпропейската комисия и други структури на ЕС, имащи отношение към езиковите въпроси:
   а) да съдействат за развитието и достъпността на двуезикови речници, съотносими програмни продукти и онлайн услуги за всички двойки езици, за които е налице такава нужда в съответните езикови общности, независимо от търговските аргументи относно разработването и маркетинга на подобни продукти;
   б) да стимулират иновационни технологии и методи, които използват новите начини за събиране и изграждане на езикови ресурс и да подкрепят съответните мрежи от експерти и общите проекти между езиковите институции на различните държави членки на ЕС;

в) да насърчават партньорството между обществени и/или обществени и частни организации, като по този начин създават нови възможности за развитие на конкурентна езикова индустрия в ЕС, която да се съобразява с нуждите на различните езикови общности в него;

г) да се погрижат инфраструктурните аспекти да бъдат включени във всички политики на ЕС, свързани с насърчаването на европейското многоезичие и изучаването на езици.

6. ЕФНИЕ предлага експертната си помощ на компетентните лица и институции за развитие и мониториране на политиките по отношение на това предизвикателство.

cs

Budapešťská rezoluce o lexikálních výzvách v mnohajazyčné Evropě

1. Evropská federace národních institucí pro jazyk vyzývá k celoevropské multilingvální jazykové infrastruktuře jakožto základnímu předpokladu pro skutečně mnohajazyčnou Evropu a její vícejazyčné občany.

2. Rozvoj moderní vysoce kvalitní lexikografické infrastruktury složené z dobrých (paralelních) korpusů, jedno-, dvou- a vícejazyčných slovníků a lexikálních databází, tezaurů, terminologických databází, wordnetů a srovnatelných lexikálních nástrojů a pomůcek je *conditio sine qua non* pro to, aby se evropští občané učili a užívali (cizí) jazyky, pro překlady a tlumočení i pro vícejazyčné zpracování textů technickými systémy a zařízeními.

3. Základní lexikální zdroje a jejich kvalitní sbírky by měly existovat aspoň pro všechny oficiální jazyky EU: mezi ně by měly patřit dvoujazyčné nástroje a pomůcky pro ty jazykové dvojice, které nejsou dostatečně vybaveny ze strany komerčně orientovaného průmyslu.

4. V důsledku multilingvního rozměru nezbytné lexikální infrastruktury, která přesahuje rámec každého jednotlivé jazykové oblasti či země, očekáváme, že EU sehraje aktivní úlohu při rozvoji infrastruktury oficiálního jazyka či jazyků, která bude dostupná v každém členském státu.

5. Z tohoto důvodu vyzývá Evropská federace národních institucí pro jazyk vlády členských zemí jakožto i Evropskou komisi a další relevantní entity:

   a) aby podporovaly rozvoj a dostupnost dvoujazyčných slovníků a srovnatelných digitálních nástrojů i online služeb pro všechny jazykové dvojice, pro něž existuje jasná potřeba v příslušném jazykovém společenství, a to nezávisle na komerčních argumentech pro produkování a marketing takových produktů,

   b) aby stimulovaly inovační technologie a metody, které využívají nových způsobů pojetí lexikálních pomůcek, včetně příležitostí, které poskytuje crowd-sourcing, a aby nabízely i významnou podporu pro relevantní expertní sítě a kooperativní projekty lexikálních ústavů v různých členských státech EU,

   c) aby prosazovaly partnerství mezi veřejnými a/nebo veřejnoprávními organizacemi a vytvářely tak nové příležitosti k rozvoji soutěživého jazykového průmyslu v EU, který si bude všímat skutečných potřeb různých jazykových komunit v EU,

   d) aby zajistily, že se tyto infrastrukturní aspekty včlení do politiky EU týkající se podpory evropského multi- a plurilingvismu a language-learningu.

6. EFNIL nabízí svou expertízu a pomoc tvůrcům politiky při rozvoji a monitorování takové politiky, která se s touto výzvou bude snažit vypořádat.

da

Budapestresolutionen om de leksikalske udfordringer I det mangesprogede Europa

1. *Den Europæiske Sammenslutning af Nationale Sproginstitutioner* (EFNIL) opfordrer til at der udvikles en mangesproget sproglig infrastruktur på europæisk niveau som en grundlæggende forudsætning for et ægte mangesproget Europa med flersprogede borgere.
2. Udviklingen af en moderne leksikografisk infrastruktur af høj kvalitet, bestående af gode (parallel)korpusser, en-, to- og flersprogede ordbøger og leksikalske databaser, synonymordbøger, terminologiske databaser, ordnetværker og sammenlignelige leksikalske redskaber og instrumenter, er en *conditio sine qua non* for europæiske borgeres tilegnelse og brug af (udenlandske) sprog, for oversættelse og tolkning og for mangesproget behandling af tekster ved hjælp af tekniske systemer.
3. Der bør findes grundlæggende leksikalske resurser og samlinger af god kvalitet for i det mindste alle de officielle EU-sprog, herunder tosprogede værktøjer og resurser til sprogpar som den kommercielt orienterede sprogindustri ikke tilgodeser i tilstrækkelig grad.
4. I betragtning af at den nødvendige leksikalske infrastruktur har en mangesproget dimension der går ud over rammerne for de enkelte sprogområder eller lande, forventes det at EU skal spille en aktiv rolle i udviklingen af infrastrukturer for det eller de officielle sprog der findes i hver enkelt medlemsstat.
5. Derfor opfordrer Den Europæiske Sammenslutning af Nationale Sproginstitutioner både regeringerne i medlemsstaterne, Europa-Kommissionen og andre relevante organer i EU til
   a) at fremme udviklingen og tilgængeligheden af tosprogede ordbøger og lignende digitale værktøjer og onlinetjenester for alle sprogpar som der er et klart behov for i deres respektive sprogsamfund, uafhængigt af kommercielle argumenter for produktion og afsætning af sådanne produkter;
   b) at stimulere innovative teknologier og metoder som drager fordel af nye måder til udvikle leksikalske systemer, herunder de muligheder som tilbydes af crowdsourcing, og at yde betydelig støtte til relevante ekspertnetværk og samarbejdsprojekter mellem leksikalske institutter i de forskellige medlemslande i EU;
   c) at fremme partnerskaber mellem offentlige organisationer og/eller offentlige og private organisationer og derved skabe nye muligheder for udvikling af en konkurrencedygtig sprogindustri i EU med udgangspunkt i de faktiske behov i de forskellige sprogsamfund i EU;
   d) at sikre at de infrastrukturelle aspekter integreres fuldt ud i alle EU-politikker der tager sigte på at fremme europæisk mange- og flersprogethed og sprogtilegnelse.
6. EFNIL tilbyder at stille sin ekspertise til rådighed for politiske beslutningstagere i udviklingen og overvågningen af politikker der tager denne udfordring op.

de

Budapester Resolution zu den lexikalischen Herausforderungen im vielsprachigen Europa

1. Die *Europäische Föderation nationaler Sprachinstitutionen* (EFNIL) empfiehlt eine europaweite vielsprachige linguistische Infrastruktur als Grundbedingung für ein wahrhaft vielsprachiges Europa und mehrsprachige Bürgerinnen und Bürger.
2. Der Aufbau einer modernen lexikographischen Infrastruktur von hoher Qualität aus guten (Parallel-)Korpora, ein-, zwei- und mehrsprachigen Wörterbüchern und lexikalischen Datenbanken, Thesauri, Terminologiedatenbanken, Wortnetzen und vergleichbaren lexikalischen Hilfsmitteln ist eine *conditio sine qua non* für das Sprachenlernen und den Sprachgebrauch der europäischen Bürgerinnen und Bürger, für Übersetzen und Dolmetschen und für die vielsprachige Textverarbeitung durch technische Systeme und Geräte für Übersetzerinnen und Übersetzer.
3. Grundlegende lexikalische Ressourcen und Sammlungen von guter Qualität sollte es zumindest für alle offiziellen Sprachen der EU geben, und hierzu sollten zweisprachige Hilfsmittel und Ressourcen für Sprachen gehören, die nicht ausreichend von der kommerziellen Sprachindustrie berücksichtigt werden.
4. Wegen der vielsprachigen Dimension der erforderlichen lexikalischen Infrastruktur, die über den Bereich jedes einzelnen Sprachgebiets oder Landes hinausgeht, wird von der EU erwartet, eine aktive Rolle in der Entwicklung dieser Infrastruktur aller offiziellen Sprachen, die für jeden Mitgliedstaat verfügbar ist, zu spielen.
5. Aus diesem Grund appelliert die *Europäische Föderation nationaler Sprachinstitutionen* (EFNIL) an die Regierungen der Mitgliedstaaten, die Europäische Kommission und andere Organe der EU:
   a) die Entwicklung und Verfügbarkeit von zweisprachigen Wörterbüchern, vergleichbaren digitalen Hilfsmitteln und Online-Diensten für alle Sprachen zu fördern, für die ein deutlicher Bedarf in den betreffenden Sprachgemeinschaften besteht, und dies unabhängig von kommerziellen Argumenten für die Erstellung und den Vertrieb solcher Produkte;
   b) innovative Technologien und Methoden anzuregen, die neue Wege für die Entwicklung lexikalischer Vorrichtungen nutzen, einschließlich der Möglichkeiten, die das *crowd-sourcing* bietet, sowie Expertennetzwerken und gemeinsamen Projekten lexikographischer Institute der verschiedenen Mitgliedstaaten der EU starke Unterstützung zu gewähren;
   c) Partnerschaften zwischen öffentlichen und/oder privaten Organisationen zu fördern, um so neue Möglichkeiten für die Entwicklung einer wettbewerbsfähigen Sprachindustrie in der EU zu schaffen, die von den tatsächlichen Bedürfnissen der verschiedenen Sprachgemein-schaften in der EU Kenntnis nimmt;

d) zu gewährleisten, dass die infrastrukturellen Aspekte in alle Maßnahmen der EU einbezogen werden, welche die europäische Viel- und Mehrsprachigkeit und das Sprachenlernen betreffen.

6. EFNIL bietet seine Fachkenntnisse an, um Entscheidungsträger/innen bei der Entwicklung und Prüfung von Maßnahmen zu unterstützen, welche diesen Anforderungen gerecht werden.

el

ΔΙΑΚΗΡΥΞΗ ΤΗΣ ΒΟΥΔΑΠΕΣΤΗΣ ΓΙΑ ΤΙΣ ΛΕΞΙΛΟΓΙΚΕΣ ΠΡΟΚΛΗΣΕΙΣ ΣΤΗΝ ΠΟΛΥΓΛΩΣΣΗ ΕΥΡΩΠΗ

1. Η *Ευρωπαϊκή Ομοσπονδία Εθνικών Φορέων για τη Γλώσσα* θεωρεί αναγκαία τη δημιουργία μιας πανευρωπαϊκής υποδομής για την ανάπτυξη της πολυγλωσσίας ως βασική συνθήκη για μια πραγματικά πολύγλωσση Ευρώπη και για πραγματικά πολλαπλόγλωσσους πολίτες.

2. Η ανάπτυξη μιας σύγχρονης, υψηλής ποιότητας λεξικογραφικής υποδομής, η οποία θα συγκροτείται με βάση ποιοτικά (παράλληλα) σώματα κειμένων, μονόγλωσσα, δίγλωσσα και πολύγλωσσα λεξικά και λεξιλογικές βάσεις δεδομένων, θησαυρούς, βάσεις δεδομένων ορολογίας, δίκτυα λέξεων [wordnets] και ανάλογα λεξιλογικά εργαλεία, αποτελεί αναγκαία προϋπόθεση για την εκμάθηση και χρήση (ξένων) γλωσσών από τους ευρωπαίους πολίτες, για τη μετάφραση και τη διερμηνεία, καθώς και για την πολύγλωσση επεξεργασία κειμένων μέσω τεχνικών συστημάτων και μέσων.

3. Βασικοί λεξικοί πόροι και ποιοτικές συλλογές δεδομένων θα πρέπει να υπάρχουν τουλάχιστον για όλες τις επίσημες γλώσσες της Ε.Ε., οι οποίες θα πρέπει να περιλαμβάνουν δίγλωσσα εργαλεία και πόρους για ζεύγη γλωσσών που δεν ικανοποιούν τις εμπορικές επιταγές της γλωσσικής βιομηχανίας.

4. Δεδομένης της πολυγλωσσικής διάστασης της αναγκαίας λεξιλογικής υποδομής, η οποία υπερβαίνει το πεδίο οποιασδήποτε μεμονωμένης γλωσσικής περιοχής ή χώρας, η Ε.Ε. αναμένεται να παίξει ενεργό ρόλο στην ανάπτυξη της υποδομής για την υποστήριξη της επίσημης γλώσσας (ή των επίσημων γλωσσών) κάθε κράτους-μέλους.

5. Για τον λόγο αυτό η Ευρωπαϊκή Ομοσπονδία Εθνικών Φορέων για τη Γλώσσα ζητά από τις κυβερνήσεις των κρατών-μελών καθώς και από την Ευρωπαϊκή Επιτροπή και τους άλλους σχετικούς φορείς της Ε.Ε.:

   α) να προωθήσουν την ανάπτυξη και τη διαθεσιμότητα δίγλωσσων λεξικών και αντίστοιχων ψηφιακών εργαλείων και διαδικτυακών υπηρεσιών για όλα τα ζεύγη γλωσσών που οι αντίστοιχες γλωσσικές κοινότητες έχουν ανάγκη, ανεξάρτητα από τις εμπορικές επιταγές για την παραγωγή, προώθηση και πώληση τέτοιων προϊόντων,

   β) να δώσουν κίνητρα για νεωτεριστικές τεχνολογίες και μεθόδους που αξιοποιούν τους νέους τρόπους προσέγγισης των λεξιλογικών εργαλείων, συμπεριλαμβανομένων των ευκαιριών που παρέχονται από εργαλεία πολλαπλών πηγών [crowdsourcing], και να παράσχουν ουσιαστική στήριξη σε συναφή δίκτυα ειδικών και σε προγράμματα συνεργασίας των ιδρυμάτων με λεξικολογικό αντικείμενο των χωρών-μελών της Ε.Ε., γ) να προωθήσουν συνεργασίες μεταξύ δημόσιων ή/και δημόσιων και ιδιωτικών φορέων, δημιουργώντας έτσι νέες ευκαιρίες για την ανάπτυξη μιας ανταγωνιστικής γλωσσικής βιομηχανίας στην Ε.Ε. η οποία λαμβάνει υπόψη τις πραγματικές ανάγκες των διάφορων γλωσσικών κοινοτήτων της,

δ) να διασφαλίσουν ότι ζητήματα υποδομής ενσωματώνονται πλήρως σε όλες τις πολιτικές της Ε.Ε. που αφορούν την προώθηση της ευρωπαϊκής πολυγλωσσίας, πολλαπλογλωσσίας και της εκμάθησης γλωσσών.

6. Η EFNIL θέτει την τεχνογνωσία της στην υπηρεσία των υπευθύνων για τη χάραξη πολιτικής τόσο για την ανάπτυξη όσο και για την παρακολούθηση συγκεκριμένων πολιτικών που θα ανταποκρίνονται σε αυτή την πρόκληση.

et

BUDAPESTI RESOLUTSIOON MITMEKEELSE EUROOPA LEKSIKAALSETE PROBLEEMIDE KOHTA

1. Euroopa Rahvuslike Keeleinstitutsioonide Föderatsioon (EFNIL) kutsub üles looma üleeuroopalist mitmekeelset keeletaristut kui põhitingimust tõeliselt mitmekeelse Euroopa ja mitmekeelsete kodanike jaoks.

2. Vältimatult vajaliku eeltingimusena (võõr-)keelte õppimiseks ja kasutamiseks Euroopa kodanike seas, kirjalikuks ja suuliseks tõlkeks ning tekstide mitmekeelseks töötlemiseks tehniliste süsteemide ja seadmete abil tuleb välja töötada tänapäevane kvaliteetne leksikograafiline taristu, mis koosneb kasulikest (paralleel-)korpustest, ühe-, kahe- ja mitmekeelsetest leksikonidest ja leksikaalsetest andmebaasidest, tesaurustest, terminibaasidest, Wordneti tüüpi andmebaasidest ning samalaadsetest keeletööriistadest.

3. Leksikaalsed põhiressursid ja kvaliteetsed kogud peaksid olemas olema vähemalt kõikide ELi ametlike keelte kohta. Need peaksid sisaldama kahekeelseid tööriistu ja ressursse selliste keelepaaride kohta, mille kasumlikkusele keskendunud keeletööstus on vajaliku tähelepanuta jätnud.

4. Vajamineva leksikaalse taristu mitmekeelsuse tõttu, mis väljub ühe piirkonna või riigi keelepiiridest, oodatakse, et EL osaleks aktiivselt iga liikmesriigi ametliku keele (ametlike keelte) taristu väljatöötamisel.

5. Seetõttu kutsub Euroopa Rahvuslike Keeleinstitutsioonide Föderatsioon (EFNIL) liikmesriikide valitsusi ning Euroopa Komisjoni ja teisi asjaomaseid ELi asutusi üles:
   a) edendama kahekeelsete sõnastike ning samalaadsete digitaalsete tööriistade ja veebiteenuste väljatöötamist ja kättesaadavaks tegemist kõigi keelepaaride jaoks, mille puhul keelekogukondades on niisuguste tööriistade järele tekkinud ilmne vajadus, olenemata selliste toodete tootmise ja turustamise kasumlikkusest;
   b) soodustama uuenduslikke tehnilisi lahendusi ja meetodeid, mis kasutavad ära kavandatavate leksikaalsete vahendite uusi võimalusi, kaasa arvatud ühistöö pakutavaid võimalusi, ning pakkuma olulist tuge asjaomastele asjatundjate võrgustikele ja ELi liikmesriikide keeleinstituutide koostööprojektidele;
   c) edendama partnerlust riiklike organisatsioonide ja/või riiklike ja eraorganisatsioonide vahel, luues seeläbi uusi võimalusi ELi erinevate keelekogukondade tegelikke vajadusi arvestava konkurentsivõimelise keeletööstuse väljaarendamiseks;
   d) tagama, et taristuga seotud aspektid lõimitakse täielikult kõikide ELi strateegiatega, mis on suunatud Euroopa mitme- ja paljukeelsuse ning keeleõppe edendamisele.

6. EFNIL püüab olla oma oskusteabega poliitikakujundajatele abiks kõnealuseid probleeme käsitlevate põhimõtete väljatöötamisel ja jälgimisel.

en

Budapest Resolution on the Lexical Challenges in Multilingual Europe

1. The *European Federation of National Institutions for Language* calls for a Europe-wide multilingual language infrastructure as a basic condition for a truly multilingual Europe and plurilingual citizens.
2. The development of a modern high-quality lexicographical infrastructure, consisting of good (parallel) corpora, mono-, bi-, and multilingual dictionaries and lexical databases, thesauruses, terminology databases, wordnets and comparable lexical tools and instruments is a *conditio sine qua non* for the learning and use of (foreign) languages by European citizens, for translation and interpretation and for the multilingual processing of texts by technical systems and devices.
3. Basic lexical resources and good quality collections should exist at least for all official languages of the EU: these should include bilingual tools and resources for language pairs that are not sufficiently catered for by the commercially oriented language industry.
4. Given the multilingual dimension of the necessary lexical infrastructure, which goes beyond the scope of any one language area or country, the EU is expected to play an active role in the development of the official language(s) infrastructure available in each Member State.
5. For this reason the European Federation of National Institutions for Language calls upon the governments of the Member States as well as the European Commission and other relevant bodies of the EU:
   a) to promote the development and availability of bilingual dictionaries and comparable digital tools and online services for all language pairs for which there is a clear need in their respective language communities, independent of commercial arguments for the production and marketing of such products,
   b) to stimulate innovative technologies and methods that take advantage of new ways of conceiving lexical devices, including the opportunities provided by crowd-sourcing, and to offer substantial support to relevant expert networks and co-operative projects of the lexical institutes of the various member states of the EU,
   c) to promote partnerships between public and/or public and private organisations, thus creating new opportunities for the development of a competitive language industry in the EU that takes notice of the actual needs of the various linguistic communities in the EU,
   d) to ensure that infrastructural aspects are fully integrated in all EU policies regarding the promotion of European multi-, plurilingualism and language-learning.
6. EFNIL offers its expertise to assist policy makers in the development and monitoring of policies that address this challenge.

fr

Résolution de Budapest sur les défis lexicaux dans une Europe multilingue

1. La *Fédération européenne des institutions linguistiques nationales* (*FEILIN*) plaide pour une infrastructure linguistique multilingue, à l'échelle européenne, condition essentielle à la constitution d'une Europe véritablement multilingue, composée de citoyens plurilingues.

2. La mise au point d'une infrastructure lexicographique moderne et d'excellence – constituée de (bons) corpus alignés, de dictionnaires et de bases de données lexicographiques bilingues et multilingues, de thésaurus, de bases de données terminologiques, d'outils permettant des comparaisons lexicales et sémantiques – est une condition *sine qua non* pour l'apprentissage et l'emploi des langues (étrangères) par les citoyens européens, la traduction, l'interprétation et le traitement multilingue de textes à l'aide de systèmes et de dispositifs techniques adaptés.

3. Des ressources lexicales de base et de bonne qualité devraient être disponibles au moins pour toutes les langues officielles de l'Union européenne: elles devraient comprendre des outils et des ressources bilingues pour des couples de langues que les priorités commerciales du secteur des industries de la langue ne permettent pas de prendre suffisamment en compte.

4. Compte tenu de son caractère multilingue, la portée de cette indispensable infrastructure linguistique dépasse l'aire géographique propre à une langue ou à un pays. Aussi, l'Union européenne se doit de jouer un rôle actif en mettant à disposition de chaque Etat membre une infrastructure concernant sa ou ses langues officielles.

5. Pour cette raison, la *Fédération européenne des institutions linguistiques nationales* appelle les gouvernements de chaque Etat membre comme la Commission européenne et les autres organismes concernés de l'Union européenne à:

   a) promouvoir la réalisation et la mise à disposition de dictionnaires bilingues et d'outils ou de services numériques en ligne comparables, pour les paires de langues faisant l'objet d'un besoin avéré aux yeux des communautés de locuteurs concernées. La réalisation et la promotion de tels outils doivent être exemptes de considérations commerciales.

   b) d'une part, encourager les technologies et les méthodes innovantes qui tirent parti des nouvelles façons de concevoir des dispositifs en matière de lexique (parmi ces nouvelles voies, les possibilités offertes par le “crowd sourcing”), d'autre part offrir un soutien conséquent aux réseaux d'experts concernés et aux projets coopératifs des organisations chargées des questions lexicales dans les différents Etats membres de l'Union européenne.

c) promouvoir des partenariats entre le secteur public et/ou des organismes publics ou privés, créant ainsi de nouvelles opportunités pour le développement d'une industrie de la langue compétitive et attentive aux besoins actuels des différentes communautés linguistiques dans l'Union européenne.
d) s'assurer que les aspects liés aux infrastructures sont bien pris en compte dans les politiques de l'UE relatives à la promotion du multi/plurilinguisme et de l'apprentissage des langues.

6. La FEILIN propose son expertise pour aider les décideurs dans la mise au point et le pilotage des politiques qui relèvent ce défi.

hr

Zaključak sa sjednice u Budimpešti o leksičkim izazovima višejezične Europe

1. Europsko udruženje nacionalnih instituta za jezike predlaže izgradnju europske višejezične lingvističke infrastrukture kao osnovnog temelja istinski višejezične Europe i višejezičnih građana.
2. Razvoj suvremene visokokvalitetne leksikografske infrastrukture, koja se sastoji od kvalitetnih (usporednih) korpusa, jednojezičnih, dvojezičnih i višejezičnih rječnika i leksičkih baza podataka, tezaurusa, terminoloških baza podataka, WordNet-ova i leksičkih alata za usporedbu nužan je za učenje (stranih) jezika, za prevođenje i tumačenje te za stručne sustave i alate koji se koriste za višejezičnu obradu tekstova.
3. Osnovni leksički izvori i kvalitetne zbirke morali bi postojati barem za sve službene jezike EU-a: tu bi se trebali podrazumijevati dvojezični alati i izvori za jezične parove koji u komercijalnoj jezičnoj industriji nisu dovoljno zastupljeni.
4. S obzirom na višejezičnu dimenziju prijeko potrebne leksičke infrastrukture, koja nadilazi sva pojedinačna jezična područja i zemlje, od EU-a se očekuje da aktivno sudjeluje u razvoju jezične infrastrukture u svakoj zemlji članici.
5. Europsko udruženje nacionalnih instituta za jezike poziva stoga Vlade zemalja članica kao i Europsku komisiju te ostala relevantna tijela EU-a na poduzimanje sljedećih koraka:
   a) promicanje razvoja i dostupnosti dvojezičnih rječnika te digitalnih alata i online servisa za usporedbu za sve jezične parove za koje postoji jasna potreba u pojedinačnim jezičnim zajednicama, neovisno o komercijalnim argumentima za proizvodnju i distribuciju tih proizvoda;
   b) poticanje uporabe inovativnih tehnologija i metoda koje koriste nove načine poimanja leksičkih alata, uključujući mogućnosti koje proizlaze iz crowdsourcinga i pružanje značajne potpore važnim stručnim mrežama i suradničkim projektima jezičnih instituta raznih država članica EU-a;
   c) promicanje suradnje između javnih i/ili javnih i privatnih organizacija, otvarajući na taj način nove mogućnosti za razvoj konkurentne jezične industrije u EU-u koja vodi računa o stvarnim potrebama raznih jezičnih zajednica unutar EU-a;
   d) integracija infrastrukture u politiku EU-a koja se odnosi na promicanje višejezičnosti u Europi te učenja stranih jezika.
6. EFNIL nudi svoju stručnost kako bi se stvaraocima politike pomoglo u stvaranju i praćenju smjernica koje bi pomogle u svladavanju tog izazova.

ga

RÚN BHÚDAIPEIST AR NA DÚSHLÁIN FOCLÓIREACHTA SAN EORAIP ILTEANGACH

1. Éilíonn *Cónaidhm Eorpach Institidiúidí Náisiúnta Teanga* infreastruchtúr ilteangach teanga ar fud na hEorpa mar bhunchoinníoll leis an Eoraip a bheith ilteangach go fíor agus le saoránaigh a bheith ilteangach.

2. Is *conditio sine qua non* i gcomhair foghlaim agus úsáid teangacha (iasachta) ag saoránaigh Eorpacha, i gcomhair aistriúcháin agus ateangaireachta agus i gcomhair próiseáil ilteangach téacsanna ag córais agus ag gléasanna teicniúla ná forbairt infreastruchtúr nua-aimseartha foclóireachta ar ardchaighdeán a bheith ann, ina bhfuil corpais mhaithe (chomhthreomhara), foclóirí agus bunachair foclóireachta, teasárais, bunachair théarmaí, líonraí focal agus uirlisí foclóireachta inchomparáide, atá aonteangach, dátheangach agus ilteangach.

3. Ba chóir bunacmhainní foclóireachta agus bailiúcháin ar ardchaighdeán a bheith ann i gcomhair, ar a laghad, gach teanga oifigiúil den AE: ba chóir go n-áireofaí leo seo uirlisí agus acmhainní dátheangacha do phéirí teanga nach ndéanann an tionscadal teanga atá dírithe ar an tráchtáil riar dóthanach orthu.

4. Ag cur san áireamh gné ilteangach an infreastruchtúir foclóireachta atá riachtanach, a théann thar réimse aon cheantair theanga nó tíre, táthar ag dréim leis an AE ról gníomhach a imirt i bhforbairt an infreastruchtúir i gcomhair teanga oifigiúil/ teangacha oifigiúla atá ar fáil i ngach Ballstát.

5. Ar an gcúis seo, éilíonn An Cónaidhm Eorpach um Institiúidí Teanga ar rialtais na mBallstát, chomh maith leis an gCoimisiún Eorpach agus comhlachtaí ábhartha eile den AE:

   a) forbairt agus infhaighteacht foclóirí dátheangacha agus uirlisí digiteacha agus seirbhísí ar líne inchomparáide a chur chun cinn do gach péire teanga mar a bhfuil riachtanas soiléir ann ina bpobail teanga faoi seach, gan bheann ar argóintí tráchtála ar son táirgeadh agus margaíocht táirgí mar seo;

   b) teicneolaíochtaí agus modhanna nuálaíocha a spreagadh, a bhaineann tairbhe as bealaí nua le gléasanna foclóireachta a cheapadh, lena n-áirítear na deiseanna a thugann sluafhoinsiú, agus tacaíocht shubstaintiúil a chur ar fáil do líonraí saineolaithe ábhartha agus tionscadail chomhoibriúla in institiúidí foclóireachta Bhallstáit éagsúla an AE;

   c) páirtíochtaí idir eagraíochtaí poiblí agus/nó poiblí agus príobháideacha a chur chun cinn, deiseanna nua a chruthú, mar sin, i gcomhair tionscadal teanga iomaíoch a fhorbairt san AE a thagann aird ar fhíor-riachtanais na bpobal éagsúil teanga san AE;

d) a chinntiú go bhfuil gnéithe infreastruchtúir go hiomlán comhtháite i ngach polasaí den AE a bhaineann le cur chun cinn na foghlama ilteangaí agus foghlaim teangacha.

6. Cuireann EFNIL a shaineolas ar fáil le cuidiú le lucht ceaptha beartais i bhforbairt agus monatóireacht beartas a thugann faoin dúshlán seo.

is

Budapest yfirlýsingin um tungumálatengdar áskoranir í fjölmála Evrópu

1. *Samtök evrópskra málræktarstofnana* (EFNIL) kallar eftir fjölmála stoðkerfi sem nái yfir Evrópu í heild. Það er grunnskilyrði fyrir raunverulega fjölmála Evrópu og fjöltyngi borgaranna.
2. Þróun nútímalegs hágæðagrunnvirkis orðabókarfræða, sem samanstandi af góðum (samsíða) textasöfnum, ein-, tví- og fjölmála orðabókum og orðasafnsgrunnum, hugtakaorðabókum, íðorðagrunnum, orðanetum og sambærilegum orðfræðitólum og verkfærum, er ófrávíkjanlegt skilyrði (*conditio sine qua non*) þess að Evrópubúar læri og noti (erlend) tungumál, fyrir þýðingar og túlkun og fyrir fjölmála textavinnslu með tölvukerfum og tækjum.
3. Undirtsöðuaðbúnaður fyrir máltækni og vönduð söfn ættu að vera til fyrir að minnsta kosti öll (opinber) tungumál Evrópusambandsins (ESB): til þessa ættu að teljast tvímála tól og hjálpargögn fyrir tungumálapör sem hinn markaðsmiðaði tungumálaiðnaður sinnir ekki nægjanlega.
4. Í ljósi þess hversu fjölmála hið nauðsynlega tungumálagrunnvirki þarf að vera sem yfirstígur umfang nokkurs eins tungumálasvæðis eða lands, er þess vænst að ESB taki að sér virkt hlutverk við að þróa grunnvirki opinbera tungumálsins (eða -málanna) sem stendur til boða í hverju aðildarríki.
5. Í ljósi þessa skorar EFNIL á ríkisstjórnir aðildarríkjanna og einnig Evrópuráðið og aðrar viðeigandi stofnanir ESB:
   a) að stuðla að þróun á og aðgengi að tvímála orðabókum og sambærilegum stafrænum tólum og vefþjónustu fyrir öll tungumálapör þar sem augljós þörf er fyrir slíkt í viðkomandi málsamfélögum, óháð viðskiptalegum rökum fyrir framleiðslu og markaðssetningu slíkra afurða.
   b) að örva og hvetja frumkvöðlatækni og aðferðir sem nýta sér nýjar leiðir við að hanna orðfræðileg tól, meðal annars þau tækifæri sem lýðvirkjun býður upp á, og að bjóða viðeigandi sérfræðinganetum og samvinnuverkefnum orðfræðistofnana hinna ýmsu aðildarríkja ESB umtalsverðan stuðning.
   c) að stuðla að samvinnu milli opinberra og/eða opinberra og einkarekinna stofnana og skapa þannig ný tækifæri fyrir þróun samkeppnishæfs tungumálaiðnaðar í ESB sem tekur mið af raunverulegum þörfum hinna ýmsu málsamfélaga innan ESB.
   d) að tryggja að grunnvirkishorf séu að fullu felld inn í alla stefnumörkun ESB sem varðar framgang evrópskrar fjöl- eða margtyngi og tungumálanáms.
6. EFNIL býður fram sérfræðiþekkingu sína við að aðstoða stefnumarkandi aðila við þróun og eftirlit með stefnum sem snerta þessa áskorun.

it

Risoluzione di Budapest sulle sfide lessicali nell'Europa multilingue

1. La Federazione Europea delle Istituzioni Linguistiche Nazionali auspica la creazione in tutti i paesi europei di infrastrutture linguistiche multilingui come condizione di base per una Europa veramente multilingue e per il plurilinguismo dei cittadini europei.
2. Lo sviluppo di infrastrutture lessicografiche moderne di alta qualità, costituite da corpora (paralleli), dizionari e database lessicali mono-, bi- e multilingui, thesauri, banche dati terminologiche, reti semantiche e da altre risorse e strumenti lessicali rappresenta una *conditio sine qua non* per l'apprendimento e l'uso delle lingue (straniere) da parte dei cittadini europei, per la traduzione e l'interpretazione e per il trattamento multilingue dei testi attraverso tecniche e strumenti specifici.
3. Risorse lessicali di base e raccolte di dati di buon livello dovrebbero essere disponibili almeno per tutte le lingue ufficiali della Ue e dovrebbero includere strumenti e risorse bilingui per coppie di lingue alle quali l'industria linguistica con finalità commerciali non provvede adeguatamente.
4. In considerazione della dimensione multilingue delle infrastrutture lessicali necessarie, che va al di là dell'ambito di qualsiasi singola area linguistica o paese, ci si aspetta che la Ue assuma un ruolo attivo nello sviluppo delle infrastrutture linguistiche relative alla/e lingua/e ufficiale/i disponibili in ciascun Stato Membro.
5. Pertanto la Federazione Europea delle Istituzioni Linguistiche Nazionali chiede ai governi degli Stati Membri, alla Commissione Europea e agli altri organi dell'Unione Europea di:
   a) promuovere lo sviluppo e la disponibilità di dizionari bilingui, di risorse digitali e di servizi online per tutte le coppie di lingue per le quali ciò si rende necessario nelle rispettive comunità linguistiche, senza riguardo per l'aspetto commerciale connesso con la produzione e la commercializzazione di questi prodotti;
   b) favorire tecnologie e metodologie innovative che traggano vantaggio dai nuovi modi di concepire le risorse lessicali, incluse le possibilità offerte dal crowdsourcing, e sostenere concretamente gruppi di esperti e progetti condivisi dei diversi istituti che operano nel settore del lessico nei vari stati membri della Ue;
   c) promuovere progetti comuni fra organizzazioni pubbliche e/o private in modo da creare nuove possibilità di sviluppo per una industria linguistica competitiva all'interno della Ue che tenga in considerazione le attuali necessità delle diverse comunità linguistiche della Ue;
   d) assicurare che gli aspetti relativi alle infrastrutture siano pienamente integrati in tutte le azioni politiche della Ue che mirano alla promozione del multilinguismo europeo, del plurilinguismo e dell'apprendimento delle lingue.
6. L'EFNIL offre la propria consulenza ai responsabili dello sviluppo e del monitoraggio delle politiche relative a questa sfida.

lv

Budapeštas rezolūcija par leksikas resursu un tehnoloģiju izaicinājumiem daudzvalodu Eiropā

1. *Eiropas Nacionālo valodu institūciju federācija* (EFNIL) aicina izveidot Eiropas mēroga daudzvalodu infrastruktūru kā pamata nosacījumu patiesi daudzvalodīgai Eiropai un daudzvalodīgiem pilsoņiem.

2. Modernas, kvalitatīvas leksikogrāfijas infrastruktūras izveide, kas sastāv no apjomīgiem (paralēliem) tekstu korpusiem, vienas valodas, divvalodu un daudzvalodu vārdu krājumiem un leksikas datubāzēm, tezauriem, terminoloģijas datubāzēm, *WordNet* leksiskajām datubāzēm un sastatāmiem leksikas rīkiem un instrumentiem, ir *conditio sine qua non* (obligāts nosacījums) Eiropas pilsoņu svešvalodu apguvei un izmantošanai, rakstiskajai un mutiskajai tulkošanai, tekstu apstrādei daudzās valodās, izmantojot valodu tehnoloģijas.

3. Katrā ES oficiālajā valodā ir nepieciešami konkrēti leksikas pamatresursi un kvalitatīvi leksikas kopumi: to vidū jābūt arī to valodu pāru divvalodu rīkiem un resursiem, kam komerciāli orientētajā valodas industrijā ir nepietiekams izmantojums.

4. Ņemot vērā nepieciešamās leksikas resursu un tehnoloģiju infrastruktūras daudzvalodu dimensiju, kas pārsniedz kādas valodas lietojuma teritorijas vai valsts robežas, ES ir jāuzņemas aktīva loma oficiālās valodas infrastruktūras izstrādē katrā dalībvalstī.

5. Šī iemesla dēļ Eiropas Nacionālo valodu institūciju federācija vēršas pie dalībvalstu valdībām, kā arī pie Eiropas Komisijas un citām ES iestādēm un aicina:
   a) veicināt divvalodu vārdnīcu un sastatāmo valodas digitālo rīku un tiešsaistes pakalpojumu pieejamību un izveidi visiem valodu pāriem, pēc kuriem ir acīmredzama nepieciešamība attiecīgajās valodas kopienās, neatkarīgi no šādu produktu izstrādes un tirgus komerciālajiem aspektiem;
   b) attīstīt inovatīvās tehnoloģijas un metodes, kuru pamatā ir jauni leksisko rīku lietojuma veidi, t. sk. izmantojot iespējas, ko piedāvā sabiedrība, un atbalstīt leksikoloģijas institūtu izveidotos ekspertu tīklus un sadarbības projektus dažādās ES dalībvalstīs;
   c) veicināt sadarbību starp sabiedriskajām un/vai sabiedriskajām un privātajām organizācijām, tādējādi sekmējot konkurētspējīga valodas sektora attīstību ES, kur būtu ņemtas vērā dažādo ES lingvistisko kopienu patiesās vajadzības;
   d) nodrošināt, ka infrastrukturālie aspekti tiek pilnībā iekļauti ES politikā, tā veicinot Eiropas daudzvalodību un valodu apguves procesus.

6. EFNIL piedāvā savas īpašās zināšanas, lai palīdzētu politikas veidotājiem šādas politikas veidošanas un uzraudzības procesā.

le

Resolutioun vu Budapest iwwert lexikalesch Changementer an engem méisproochegen Europa

1. D'European Federation of National Institutions for Language (EFNIL) fuerdert eng europawäit méisproocheg Sproocheninfrastruktur als elementar Viraussetzung fir e wierklech méisproochegt Europa a méisproocheg Bierger.

2. Den Opbau vun enger moderner qualitativ héichwäerteger lexikographescher Infrastruktur aus grëndlech zesummegestallte (parallelen) Korpora, aus eesproochegen, zwee- a méisproochege Lexika a lexikaleschen Datebanken, grad ewéi aus Thesauren, terminologeschen Datebanken, Wuertnetzer a vergläichbare lexikaleschen Instrumenter an Hëllefsmëttelen ass eng elementar Viraussetzung fir datt d'Bierger an Europa (friem) Sprooche léieren a gebrauchen, fir Aktivitéite wéi Iwwersetzen an Dolmetschen a fir e méisproochegt Verschaffen vun Texter mat der Hëllef vun technesche Systemer a Maschinnen.

3. Elementar lexikalesch Ressourcen a qualitativ héichwäerteg lexikalesch Sammlunge sollte wéinstens fir all déi offiziell Sprooche vun der Europäescher Unioun existéieren. Si sollten zweesproocheg Instrumenter a Ressourcë fir Sproochekoppelen ëmfaassen, déi vun der kommerziell orientéierter Sproochenindustrie net genuch ofgedeckt sinn.

4. Wéinst der méisproocheger Dimensioun vun der néideger lexikalescher Infrastruktur, déi iwwert de Beräich vun all Sproochgebitt oder Land erausgeet, gëtt erwaart, datt d'Europäesch Unioun beim Opbau vun der Infrastruktur fir déi offiziell Sprooch(en) an all Memberstaat eng aktiv Roll spillt.

5. Dofir fuedert d'European Federation of National Institutions for Language d'Regierunge vun de Memberstaten wéi och d'Europäesch Kommissioun an aner relevant Instanze vun der Europäescher Unioun op:
   a) d'Elaboratioun an d'Disponibilitéit vun zweesproochegen Dictionnairen a vergläichbaren digitalen Instrumenter an Online-Servicer fir all Sproochekoppel, fir déi an de respektive Sproochgemeinschaften e kloere Besoin do ass, ze promouvéieren, an zwar onofhängeg vu kommerziellen Argumenter a Bezuch op d'Produktioun an d'Commercialisatioun vun dëse Produiten;
   b) innovativ Technologien a Methoden ze stimuléieren, déi vun neie Weeër profitéieren fir lexikalesch Instrumenter ze entwéckelen, dorënner och d'Méiglechkeeten am Kader vum sougenannte Crowdsourcing, a wichteg Réseaue vun Experten a kooperative Projeten vun de lexikographeschen Instituter vun de Memberstate vun der Europäescher Unioun substantiell ze ënnerstëtzen;

c) d'Partnerschaften tëschent ëffentlechen an/oder ëffentlechen a privaten Organisatiounen ze promouvéieren an domat nei Méiglechkeete fir d'Entstoe vun enger kompetitiver Sproochenindustrie an der Europäescher Unioun ze schafen, déi deenen aktuelle Besoien vun de verschiddene Sproochgemeinschaften an der Unioun Rechnung droen;
d) dofir ze suergen, datt an alle politesche Moossnahmen vun der Europäescher Unioun a Bezuch op d'Promotioun vu Méi- a Villsproochegkeet wéi och vum Sproochunterrécht infrastrukturell Aspekter ëmfaassend mat abezu ginn.

6. D'EFNIL offréiert hir Expertise, fir de politeschen Décideuren dobäi ze hëllefen, politesch Approchen auszeschaffen an ze begleeden, déi sech mat dëser Erausfuerderung befaassen.

hu

Az EFNIL budapesti állásfoglalása a szókészlet kihívásaival kapcsolatban a többnyelvű Európában

1. A Nemzeti Nyelvi Intézetek Európai Szövetsége (EFNIL) széleskörű többnyelvű nyelvi infrastruktúra kialakítását szorgalmazza mint alapvető feltételét egy valóban soknyelvű Európa létrejöttének, ahol az állampolgárok is többnyelvűek.

2. Megbízható párhuzamos szövegkorpuszokra, egynyelvű, két-, ill. többnyelvű szótárakra és lexikai adatbázisokra, tezauruszokra, terminológiai adatbázisokra, fogalmi alapú lexikai adatbázisokra (wordnet) illetve ezekhez hasonló lexikai eszközökre épülő magas színvonalú szótári infrastruktúra kialakítása elengedhetetlen feltétele az EU állampolgárok idegennyelv-tanulásának és használatának, a fordításnak, tolmácsolásnak, valamint különböző technikai eszközök és szolgáltatások segítségével történő többnyelvű szövegfeldolgozásnak.

3. Kívánatos, hogy legalább az EU minden hivatalos nyelvén elérhetők legyenek az alapvető lexikai erőforrások és magas színvonalú nyelvi adathalmazok, köztük olyan nyelvpárokra épülő kétnyelvű eszközök és nyelvi erőforrások is, melyeket a kereskedelmi alapú nyelvi ágazat nem biztosít megfelelő mértékben.

4. Mivel a szükséges lexikai infrastruktúra többnyelvűsége átnyúlik bármely nyelvi és földrajzi országhatáron, az Európai Uniónak aktívan részt kell vennie minden egyes tagállam hivatalos nyelvi infrastruktúrájának kialakításában.

5. Mindezekre való tekintettel a Nemzeti Nyelvi Intézetek Európai Szövetsége felkéri a tagállamok kormányait, az Európai Bizottságot és egyéb az ügyben illetékes EU intézményt hogy:

   a) támogassák kétnyelvű szótárak valamint hasonló digitális eszközök és online szolgáltatások kifejlesztését és közzétételét minden olyan nyelvpárra, amelyekre egyértelműen szükség van a nyelveket használó közösségekben, az ilyen termékek gyártására és eladhatóságára vonatkozó kereskedelmi megfontolásoktól függetlenül.

   b) ösztönözzék olyan innovatív technológiák és módszerek fejlesztését, amelyek kiaknázzák a lexikai eszközök létrehozásának új módszereit, beleértve ezek közé az ún. crowdsourcing (közösség ötletgyűjtés) lehetőségeit is, továbbá nyújtsanak jelentős támogatást az érintett szakértői hálózatok valamint az EU különböző tagországainak szótárkészítéssel foglalkozó intézményei között létrejött együttműködési projektek számára.

   c) támogassák az együttműködést állami és magánszervezetek között, ezzel hozzájárulva az Európai Unióban egy olyan versenyképesebb nyelvi ágazat kialakításához, amely rugalmasan tudna alkalmazkodni az aktuális nyelvi közösségek nyelvi igényeihez.

d) biztosítsák, hogy az infrastrukturális szempontok integrált módon megjelenjenek az európai többnyelvűség és nyelvtanulás előmozdítását célzó valamennyi uniós politikában.

6. Az EFNIL szakértelmével segíti a politikai döntéshozókat a témával kapcsolatos politikai elképzelések kialakításában és a döntések ellenőrzésében.

nl

Resolutie van Budapest over de lexicale uitdagingen in een meertalig Europa

1. De *Europese Federatie van Nationale Taalinstellingen* pleit voor een breed-Europese meertalige taalinsfrastuctuur als een van de basisvoorwaarden voor een werkelijk meertalig Europa en voor meertalige burgers.

2. De ontwikkeling van een moderne lexicografische infrastructuur van hoge kwaliteit, bestaande uit goede (parallelle) corpora, eentalige, twee- en meertalige woordenboeken en lexicale databanken, thesauri, terminologische databanken, wordnetvoorzieningen en vergelijkbare lexicale tools en hulpmiddelen, is een *conditio sine qua non* voor het leren en gebruiken van (vreemde) talen door Europese burgers, voor vertaling en vertolking en voor meertalige tekst- en dataverwerking door technische voorzieningen en systemen.

3. Voor ten minste alle officiële talen van de Europese Unie moeten lexicale bronnen en collecties van goede kwaliteit beschikbaar zijn, ook voor taalparen die niet voldoende door de commerciële taalindustrie worden ondersteund.

4. Gegeven het meertalige karakter van de benodigde lexicale infrastructuur, die de verantwoordelijkheid van één land of taalgebied te boven gaat, wordt van de EU verwacht dat ze een actieve rol speelt in de ontwikkeling van een infrastructuur voor de officiële taal of talen binnen iedere Lid-Staat.

5. Daarom doet de Europese Federatie van Taalinstellingen een beroep op de regeringen van de Lid-Staten, evenals op de Europese Commissie en andere relevante instellingen van de EU om:
   a) De ontwikkeling en beschikbaarheid van tweetalige woordenboeken, van vergelijkbare digitale tools en van online diensten te bevorderen voor alle taalparen waaraan een duidelijke behoefte bestaat in de betreffende taalgebieden, ook als die uit commerciële overwegingen onvoldoende aantrekkelijk zijn;
   b) Innovatieve technologieën en methodes bevorderen, die gebruik maken van nieuwe mogelijkheden voor het opzetten van lexicale voorzieningen, o.a. de mogelijkheden van werken met crowd sourcing, en substantiële ondersteuning bieden aan relevante expertisenetwerken en samenwerkingsprojecten tussen de lexicografische instellingen van de verschillende Lid-Staten van de Europese Unie;
   c) Samenwerking en partnerships te bevorderen tussen publieke organisaties of tussen publieke en privaatrechtelijke organisaties om aldus nieuwe mogelijkheden voor een competitieve taalindustrie binnen de EU te bevorderen, gebruik makend van de feitelijke behoeften van de verschillende taalgemeenschappen in de Europese Unie.

d) Te verzekeren dat de infrastructurele elementen volledige geïntegreerd worden in het beleid van de EU betreffende de promotie van meertaligheid en het leren van talen binnen de EU.

6. EFNIL biedt haar expertise aan om beleidsmakers te ondersteunen met het ontwikkelen en volgen van beleid gericht op deze uitdagingen.

no – Bokmål

Budapest-Resolusjonen om de leksikalske utfordringene i det mangespråklige Europa

1. *Det europeiske forbundet for nasjonale språkinstitusjoner* (EFNIL) etterlyser en mangespråklig språkinfrastruktur for hele Europa som en grunnleggende forutsetning for et virkelig mangespråklig Europa og flerspråklige innbyggere.
2. Utvikling av en moderne leksikografisk infrastruktur av høy kvalitet bestående av gode (parallelle) korpus, en-, to- og mangespråklige ordbøker og leksikalske databaser, tesauruser, terminologidatabaser, ordnett og sammenlignbare leksikalske verktøy og instrumenter er en *conditio sine qua non* for læring og bruk av (fremmed) språk hos europeiske innbyggere, for oversettelse og tolking og for tekniske systemers og produkters mangespråklige analyse av tekster.
3. Grunnleggende leksikalske ressurser og samlinger av høy kvalitet bør i det minste finnes for alle de offisielle språkene i EU. De bør inkludere tospråklige verktøy og ressurser for språkpar som den kommersielt orienterte språkbransjen ikke sørger for.
4. Med utgangspunkt i at den nødvendige leksikalske infrastrukturen har en mangespråklig dimensjon som strekker seg lenger enn omfanget av en enkelt språkregion eller ett enkelt land, forventes det at EU spiller en aktiv rolle i utviklingen av infrastrukturen for det offisielle språket/de offisielle språkene i hver medlemsstat.
5. EFNIL ber derfor både myndighetene i medlemsstatene og Europakommisjonen og andre relevante EU-organer om
   a) å fremme utvikling og tilgjengeliggjøring av tospråklige ordbøker og sammenlignbare digitale verktøy og internettbaserte tjenester for alle språkpar det er et klart behov for i de respektive språksamfunnene, uavhengig av kommersielle argumenter for produksjon og markedsføring av slike produkter;
   b) å stimulere nyskapende teknologi og metoder som utnytter nye måter å lage leksikalske produkter på, blant annet mulighetene crowd-sourcing gir, og å tilby solid støtte til relevante ekspertnettverk og samarbeidsprosjekter hos de leksikalske instituttene i de ulike medlemsstatene i EU;
   c) å fremme partnerskap mellom offentlige og/eller offentlige og private organisasjoner og slik skape nye muligheter for utvikling av en konkurransedyktig språkbransje i EU som registrerer de faktiske behovene til de ulike språksamfunnene i EU;
   d) å sikre at infrastrukturelle aspekter integreres fullstendig i all EU-politikk for å fremme europeisk mangespråklighet, flerspråklighet og språklæring.
6. EFNIL tilbyr sin ekspertise til dem som skal utforme og følge opp politikk som tar fatt på denne utfordringen.

no – Nynorsk

Budapest-fråsegna om dei leksikalske utfordringane i det mangespråklege Europa

1. *Det europeiske forbundet for nasjonale språkinstitusjonar* (EFNIL) etterlyser ein mangespråkleg språkinfrastruktur for heile Europa som ein grunnleggjande føresetnad for eit verkeleg mangespråkleg Europa og fleirspråklege innbyggjarar.

2. Utvikling av ein moderne leksikografisk infrastruktur av høg kvalitet som består av gode (parallelle) korpus, ein-, to- og mangespråklege ordbøker og leksikalske databasar, tesaurusar, terminologidatabasar, ordnett og samanliknbare leksikalske verktøy og instrument, er ein *conditio sine qua non* for læring og bruk av (framand)språk hjå europeiske innbyggjarar, for omsetjing og tolking og for mangespråkleg analyse av tekstar i tekniske system og produkt.

3. Grunnleggjande leksikalske ressursar og samlingar av høg kvalitet bør i det minste finnast for alle dei offisielle språka i EU. Dei bør inkludere tospråklege verktøy og ressursar for språkpar som den kommersielt orienterte språkbransjen ikkje syter for.

4. Med utgangspunkt i at den naudsynte leksikalske infrastrukturen har ein mangespråkleg dimensjon som strekkjer seg lenger enn omfanget av ein einskild språkregion eller eit einskilt land, ventar ein at EU speler ei aktiv rolle i utviklinga av infrastrukturen for det offisielle språket/dei offisielle språka i kvar medlemsstat.

5. EFNIL bed difor både styresmaktene i medlemsstatane og Europakommisjonen og andre relevante EU-organ om

   a) å fremje utvikling og tilgjengeleggjering av tospråklege ordbøker og samanliknbare digitale verktøy og internettbaserte tenester for alle språkpar det er eit klart behov for i dei respektive språksamfunna, uavhengig av kommersielle argument for produksjon og marknadsføring av slike produkt;

   b) å stimulere nyskapande teknologi og metodar som utnyttar nye måtar å lage leksikalske produkt på, mellom anna dei moglegheitene crowd-sourcing gir, og å tilby solid støtte til relevante ekspertnettverk og samarbeidsprosjekt hjå dei leksikalske institutta i dei ulike medlemsstatane i EU;

   c) å fremje partnarskap mellom offentlege og/eller offentlege og private organisasjonar og slik skape nye moglegheiter for utvikling av ein konkurransedyktig språkbransje i EU som registrerer dei faktiske behova til dei ulike språksamfunna i EU;

   d) å sikre at infrastrukturelle aspekt blir fullstendig integrerte i all EU-politikk for å fremje europeisk mangespråklegheit, fleirspråklegheit og språklæring.

6. EFNIL tilbyr ekspertisen sin til dei som skal utforme og følgje opp politikk som tek fatt på denne utfordringa.

pl

Rezolucja budapeszteńska w sprawie wyzwań leksykalnych w wielojęzykowej Europie

1. Europejska Federacja Narodowych Instytucji Językoznawczych (EFNIL) opowiada się za ogólnoeuropejską wielojęzykową infrastrukturą języków, stanowiącą podstawowy warunek rzeczywistej wielojęzykowości Europy i wielojęzyczności jej obywateli.

2. Rozwój nowoczesnej, wysokiej jakości infrastruktury leksykograficznej, obejmującej porównywalne (paralelne) korpusy, jedno-, dwu- i wielojęzyczne słowniki i leksykalne bazy danych, tezaurusy, bazy terminologiczne, sieci wyrazowe oraz współmierne narzędzia i wyposażenie leksykalne, stanowi warunek sine qua non dla nauki (obcych) języków i używania ich przez obywateli Unii Europejskiej w celu przekładania, interpretowania i wielojęzykowego przetwarzania tekstów za pomocą systemów i urządzeń technicznych.

3. Podstawowe zasoby i zbiory leksykalne dobrej jakości powinny istnieć dla wszystkich (oficjalnych) języków UE: powinny one zawierać dwujęzyczne narzędzia i zasoby dla par językowych, które nie są dostatecznie obsługiwane przez komercyjnie zorientowany przemysł językowy.

4. Jeżeli wielojęzykowy wymiar niezbędnej infrastruktury leksykalnej wykracza poza możliwości jakiegokolwiek obszaru językowego lub kraju, oczekuje się, że UE odegra czynną rolę w rozwoju infrastruktury oficjalnych języków, dostępnej w każdym państwie członkowskim.

5. Z tego względu Europejska Federacja Narodowych Instytucji Językoznawczych wzywa rządy państw członkowskich, a także Komisję Europejską i inne odpowiednie organy UE:

   a) do popierania rozwoju i dostępności – dla wszystkich par językowych – dwujęzycznych słowników i współmiernych narzędzi cyfrowych, a także usług sieciowych, których wyraźnie potrzeba w ich społecznościach językowych, niezależnie od komercyjnych sporów co do produkcji i marketingu takich produktów;

   b) do pobudzania innowacyjnych technologii i metod, które korzystają z nowych sposobów pojmowania mechanizmów leksykalnych, łącznie z możliwościami jakie stwarza otwarta pomoc społeczna (crowd-sourcing) i do udzielania istotnego wsparcia stosownym sieciom eksperckim i projektom badawczym, opartym na współpracy instytutów leksykologicznych poszczególnych państw członkowskich UE;

   c) do popierania partnerstwa między instytucjami publicznymi oraz między publicznymi i prywatnymi, co stwarza nowe możliwości rozwoju w warunkach konkurencji dla przemysłu językowego w UE z uwzględnieniem faktycznych potrzeb różnych społeczności językowych w UE;

d) do zapewnienia, że infrastrukturalne aspekty zostaną w pełni zintegrowane z całą polityką UE, służącą promocji europejskiej wielojęzykowości, wielojęzyczności i nauki języków.

6. Europejska Federacja Narodowych Instytucji Językoznawczych (EFNIL) oferuje swoje doświadczenie, by pomóc decydentom w rozwijaniu i monitorowaniu strategii odpowiadających temu wyzwaniu.

pt

Resolução de Budapeste sobre os desafios lexicais na Europa multilingue

1. A *Federação Europeia das Instituições Nacionais para as Línguas* prescreve uma infraestrutura linguística multilingue pan-europeia como condição básica para uma Europa verdadeiramente multilingue e para o plurilinguismo dos cidadãos europeus.

2. O desenvolvimento de uma infraestrutura lexicográfica de alta qualidade, constituída por bons *corpora* (paralelos), dicionários e base de dados lexicais monolingues, bilingues e multilingues, *thesauri*, bases de dados terminológicas, wordnets e ferramentas e instrumentos de comparação lexical, é uma *conditio sine qua non* para a aprendizagem e o uso de línguas (estrangeiras) pelos cidadãos europeus, para a tradução e a interpretação, assim como para o processamento multilingue de textos por sistemas e dispositivos técnicos.

3. Devem existir recursos lexicais básicos e coleções de elevada qualidade para, pelo menos, todas as línguas oficiais da UE: estes devem incluir ferramentas e recursos bilingues para pares de línguas que não são suficientemente abrangidos pela indústria da língua com fins comerciais.

4. Dada a dimensão multilingue da infraestrutura lexical necessária, que ultrapassa o âmbito de qualquer área linguística ou país, espera-se que a UE desempenhe um papel ativo no desenvolvimento da infraestrutura de línguas oficiais disponível em cada Estado-Membro.

5. Por esta razão, a Federação Europeia de Instituições Nacionais de Língua apela aos governos dos Estados-Membros, assim como à Comissão Europeia e a outros organismos pertinentes da UE, para que:

   a) promovam o desenvolvimento e a disponibilização de dicionários bilingues, ferramentas digitais de comparação e serviços em linha para todos os pares de línguas para os quais existe uma clara carência nas respetivas comunidades linguísticas, independente de argumentos comerciais para a produção e *marketing* de tais produtos;

   b) estimulem tecnologias e métodos inovadores que tirem proveito de novas formas de conceber dispositivos lexicais, incluindo oportunidades oferecidas pelo *crowdsourcing* e que ofereçam um apoio substancial a redes relevantes especializadas e projetos cooperativos de institutos lexicais dos vários Estados-Membros da UE;

   c) promovam parcerias entre organizações públicas e/ou públicas e privadas, criando, assim, novas oportunidades para o desenvolvimento de uma indústria competitiva da língua na UE que tenha em conta as necessidades reais das diversas comunidades linguísticas na UE;

d) garantam que os aspetos infraestruturais estejam totalmente integrados em todas as políticas da UE que dizem respeito à promoção do multilinguismo, do plurilinguismo e da aprendizagem de línguas na Europa.

6. A EFNIL oferece o seu conhecimento especializado no apoio aos responsáveis pelo desenvolvimento e monitorização de políticas que respondam a este desafio.

sk

Budapeštianske uznesenie o lexikálnych výzvach vo viacjazyčnej Európe

1. *Európska federácia národných jazykových inštitúcií* sa zasadzuje za celoeurópsku multilingválnu jazykovú infraštruktúru ako základnú podmienku pre skutočnú viacjazyčnú Európu a plurilngválnych občanov.

2. Rozvoj modernej vysokokvalitnej lexikografickej infraštruktúry, ktorá by pozostávala zo spoľahlivých (paralelných) korpusov, jedno-, dvoj- a viacjazyčných slovníkov a lexikálnych databáz, tezaurov, terminologických databáz, wordnetov a porovnateľných lexikálnych nástrojov a zariadení, je *conditio sine qua non* pre učenie a používanie (cudzích) jazykov občanmi Európy, pre preklad a tlmočníctvo a pre viacjazyčné spracúvanie textov prostredníctvom technických systémov a zariadení.

3. Základné lexikálne zdroje a kvalitné súbory by mali existovať prinajmenšom pre všetky oficiálne jazyky EÚ: tie by mali zahŕňať bilingválne nástroje a zdroje pre dvojice jazykov, na ktoré sa dostatočne nezacielil komerčne orientovaný jazykový priemysel.

4. Vzhľadom na multilingválnu dimenziu nevyhnutnej lexikálnej infraštruktúry, ktorá presahuje rámec ktorejkoľvek jazykovej oblasti alebo krajiny, sa očakáva, že EÚ sa bude aktívne podieľať na rozvoji infraštruktúry oficiálneho jazyka (oficiálnych jazykov), dostupnej v každom členskom štáte.

5. Z uvedeného dôvodu Európska federácia národných jazykových inštitúcií vyzýva vlády členských štátov, ako aj Európsku komisiu a iné relevantné inštitúcie EÚ:
   a) podporovať rozvoj a dostupnosť dvojjazyčných slovníkov a porovnateľných digitálnych nástrojov a online služieb pre dvojice jazykov, ktoré sú dôležité pre príslušné jazykové komunity bez ohľadu na komerčné zdôvodnenia produkcie a marketingu takýchto produktov;
   b) stimulovať inovatívne technológie a metódy, ktoré využívajú nové spôsoby prezentácie lexikálnych nástrojov, vrátane možností získaných crowd-sourcingom, a ponúknuť zásadnú podporu relevantným expertným sieťam a spoločným projektom lexikálnych inštitúcií rozličných členských štátov v EÚ;
   c) podporovať partnerstvo medzi verejnými a/alebo verejnými a súkromnými organizáciami, a tak vytvárať nové príležitosti pre rozvoj konkurencieschopného jazykového priemyslu v EÚ, zohľadňujúceho aktuálne potreby rôznych jazykových komunít v EÚ;
   d) zaistiť, že infraštruktúrne aspekty sa plne integrujú do všetkých postupov EÚ týkajúcich sa podpory európskeho multilingvizmu a plurilingvizmu, ako aj výučby jazykov v Európe.

6. EFNIL ponúka svoju odbornú pomoc politickým činiteľom v rozvoji a monitorovaní postupov, ktorým je táto výzva adresovaná.

sl

Budimpeštanska resolucija o leksikalnih izzivih v večjezični Evropi

1. Evropska zveza državnih jezikovnih ustanov poziva k zagotavljanju vseevropske večjezične jezikovne infrastrukture kot poglavitnega pogoja za resnično večjezično Evropo in mnogojezične državljane.

2. Razvoj sodobne visokokakovostne leksikografske infrastrukture, ki jo sestavljajo dobri (vzporedni) korpusi, eno-, dvo- in večjezični slovarji in slovarske podatkovne zbirke, tezavri, terminološke podatkovne baze, semantični leksikoni (wordneti) in primerljiva leksikalna orodja in instrumenti, je osnovni pogoj za to, da se evropski državljani učijo in uporabljajo (tuje) jezike, za prevajanje in tolmačenje ter za večjezično obdelavo besedil s tehnološkimi sistemi in sredstvi.

3. Osnovni leksikalni viri in kakovostne zbirke bi morali obstajati vsaj za vse uradne jezike Evropske unije: to bi moralo vključevati dvojezična orodja in vire za jezikovne pare, ki jih komercialno usmerjena jezikovna industrija ni dovolj podprla.

4. Glede na večjezično razsežnost potrebne leksikalne infrastrukture, ki presega okvir samo enega jezikovnega območja ali države, se pričakuje, da bo EU imela aktivno vlogo pri razvoju infrastrukture uradnega jezika (uradnih jezikov) v vsaki državi članici.

5. Efnil zato poziva vlade držav članic kakor tudi Evropsko komisijo in druge pristojne organe držav EU:
   a) da podpirajo razvoj in razpoložljivost dvojezičnih slovarjev in primerljivih digitalnih orodij in spletnih storitev za vse jezikovne pare, za katere v njihovih jezikovnih skupnostih obstaja jasna potreba, neodvisno od ekonomskih argumentov za razvoj in trženje tovrstnih produktov;
   b) da spodbujajo inovativne tehnologije in metode, ki izkoriščajo prednosti novih načinov razvijanja leksikalnih pripomočkov, vključno z možnostmi, ki jih zagotavlja črpanje podatkov s pomočjo množic (crowd-sourcing), in da ponujajo precejšnjo podporo ustreznim strokovnim omrežjem in projektom sodelovanja leksikalnih inštitutov različnih držav članic EU;
   c) da spodbujajo partnerstvo med javnimi in/ali javnimi in zasebnimi organizacijami ter tako ustvarjajo nove priložnosti za razvoj konkurenčne jezikovne industrije v EU, ki bo upoštevala dejanske potrebe različnih jezikovnih skupnosti v EU;
   d) da zagotovijo, da bodo infrastrukturni vidiki v celoti vključeni v vse politike EU v zvezi s spodbujanjem več- in mnogojezičnosti ter učenja jezikov v Evropi.

6. Efnil ponuja svoje strokovno znanje kot pomoč nosilcem politik pri razvoju in spremljanju politik, ki se nanašajo na leksikalne izzive.

Contacts

Anna Dabrowska:	annadab@uni.wroc.pl
Claude Durand	Claude.Durand@ec.europa.eu
Patrick Hanks	patrick.w.hanks@gmail.com
Istvan Kenesei	kenesei@ny01.nytud.hu
Annette Klosa	klosa@ids-mannheim.de
Guðrún Kvaran	gkvaran@hi.is
Margit Langemets	margit@eki.ee
Willy Martin	w.j.r.martin@vu.nl
Christian Mattsson	Christian.Mattsson@sprakradet.se
Uwe Mohr	Uwe.Mohr@Bruessel.goethe.org
Pádraig Ó Mianáin	pomianain@forasnagaeilge.ie
Gábor Prószéky	proszeky@morphologic.hu
Georg Rehm:	georg.rehm@dfki.de
Cecilia Robustelli	cecilia.robustelli@unimore.it
Walery Pisarek	uwpisare@cyf-kr.edu.pl
John Simpson	john.simpson@oup.com
Gerhard Stickel:	stickel@ids-mannheim.de
Hans Uszkoreit:	hans.uszkoreit@dfki.de
Tamás Váradi	tavaradi@gmail.com
Jolanta Zabarskaitė	jolanta.zabarskaite@lki.lt

European Federation of National Institutions for Language (EFNIL): Members and associate member institutions

For detailed information on EFNIL and its members see www.efnil.org

Member institutions grouped by country

Austria	***Österreichisches Sprachen-Kompetenz-Zentrum***, Graz Austrian Centre for Language Competence
	Bundesministerium für Unterricht, Kunst und Kultur, Wien Federal Ministry for Education, Art, and Culture
Belgium	***Service de la langue française***, Bruxelles French Language Service
	Nederlandse Taalunie, Den Haag Dutch Language Union (Flanders and The Netherlands)
Bulgaria	***Българска академия на науките, Институт за български език***, Sofia Bulgarian Academy of Sciences, Institute for Bulgarian Language
Cyprus:	***Πανεπιστημίου Κύπρου,*** Nicosia University of Cyprus
Czech Republic	***Ústav Českého národního korpusu Univerzity Karlovy***, Praha Institute of Czech National Corpus, Charles-University
Denmark	***Dansk Sprognævn***, København Danish Language Council
Estonia	***Eesti Keelenõukogu***, Tallin Estonian Language Council
	Eesti Keele Instituut, Tallin Institute of the Estonian Language
Finland	***Kotimaisten kielten tutkimuskeskus / Forskningscentralen för de inhemska språken***, Helsinki/Helsingfors Research Institute for the Languages of Finland
France	***Délégation Générale à la langue française et aux langues de France***, Paris General Delegation for the French Language and the Languages of France

Germany	***Institut für Deutsche Sprache***, Mannheim Institute for the German Language
	Deutsche Akademie für Sprache und Dichtung, Darmstadt German Academy for Language and Literature
Greece	***Κέντρο Ελληνικής Γλώσσας***, Thessaloniki Centre for the Greek Language
Hungary	***Magyar Tudomános Akadémia, Nyalvtudományi Intézet***, Budapest Hungarian Academy of Sciences, Research Institute for Linguistics
Ireland	***Foras na Gaeilge***, Dublin (the all-island body for the Irish language)
Italy	***Accademia della Crusca***, Firenze (the central academy for the Italian language)
	CNR – Opera del Vocabolario Italiano, Firenze The Italian Dictionary
Latvia	***Valst valodas komisija***, Riga State Language Commission
	Valsts valodas aģentūra, Riga State Language Agency
Lithuania	***Lietviu Kalbos Institutas***, Vilnius Institute of the Lithuanian Language
	Valstybine Lietuviu Kalbos Komisija, Vilnius State Commission for the Lithuanian Language
Luxembourg	***Institut Grand-Ducal, Section de linguistique***, Luxembourg Grand Ducal Institute, Linguistic Section
	Conseil permanent de la langue luxembourgeoise, Luxembourg Permanent Council of the Luxembourgish language
Malta	***Kunsill Nazzjonali ta'l-Ilsien Malti*** National Council of the Maltese language
Netherlands/Belgium	***Nederlandse Taalunie***, Den Haag Dutch Language Union
Poland	***Rada Jezyka Polskiego***, Warszawa Council for the Polish Language

Portugal	***Instituto Camões***, Lisbõa (the institution for the promotion of Portuguese language and culture)
Romania	***Academia Româna, Institutul de Lingvistica***, Bucureşti Romanian Academy, Institute of Linguistics
Slovakia	***Jazykovedný ústav Ĺudovíta Štúra Slovenskej***, Bratislava Slovak Academy of Sciences, Ludovit Stúr Institute of Linguistics
Slovenia	***Ministrstvo za kulturo - Sektor za slovenski jezik***, Ljubljana Ministry of Culture, Section for the Slovenian language
Spain	***Real Academia Española***, Madrid Royal Spanish Academy
Sweden	***Språkrådet***, Stockholm The Swedish Language Council
United Kingdom	***Oxford English Dictionary***, Oxford ***The British Council***

Associate member institutions

Croatia:	***Institut za hrvatski jezik i jezikoslovlije***, Zagreb Institut of Croatian Language and Linguistics
Iceland	***Íslensk málnefnd***, Reykjavik Icelandic Language Council
Norway	***Språkrådet***, Oslo Norwegian Language Council

DUISBURGER ARBEITEN ZUR SPRACH- UND KULTURWISSENSCHAFT
DUISBURG PAPERS ON RESEARCH IN LANGUAGE AND CULTURE

Herausgegeben von
Ulrich Ammon, René Dirven und Martin Pütz

Band 1 René Dirven / Yvan Putseys (Eds.): A User's Grammar of English: Word, Sentence, Text, Interaction - Part A. The Structure of Words and Phrases. 1989.

Band 2 René Dirven / Richard A. Geiger (Eds.): A User's Grammar of English: Word, Sentence, Text, Interaction - Part B. The Structure of Sentences. 1989.

Band 3 René Dirven / Wolfgang Zydatiß / Willis J. Edmondson (Eds.): A User's Grammar of English: Word, Sentence, Text, Interaction - Parts C & D. The Structure of Texts / The Structure of Interaction. 1989.

Band 4 René Dirven: (Ed.): A User's Grammar of English: Word, Sentence, Text, Interaction - Compact Edition. 1989.

Band 5 Martin Pütz / René Dirven (Eds.): Wheels within Wheels. Papers of the Duisburg Symposium on Pidgin and Creole Languages. 1989.

Band 6 Ulrich Schmitz / Rüdiger Schütz / Andreas Kunz (Eds.): Linguistic Approaches to Artificial Intelligence. 1990.

Band 7 Friedrich Lenz: Organisationsprinzipien in mündlicher Fachkommunikation. 1989.

Band 8 Luc Van Doorslaer (Hrsg.): Niederländische Literatur im Spiegel niederländischer Kultur. Aufsätze zur Gastprofessur von Prof. Dr. Marcel Janssens (Universität Löwen) in Duisburg, Sommersemester 1988. 1990.

Band 9 Frank Lüschow / Marita Pabst-Weinschenk (Hrsg.): Mündliche Kommunikation als kooperativer Prozeß. Sprechwissenschaftliche Arbeitsfelder. Festschrift für Elmar Bartsch. 1991.

Band 10 Susanne Niemeier: Ein Fall im Medienvergleich: Film- und Fernsehversion von "A Streetcar Named Desire". Beitrag zur Annäherung an eine Mediensemiotik. 1990.

Band 11 Paul Kent Andersen: A new look at the passive. 1991.

Band 12 Richard Kremer: The efficiency of English language teaching in smaller countries: Denmark. Basic English language teaching in Denmark and its wider context. 1991.

Band 13 Frank Lüschow: Sprache und Kommunikation in der technischen Arbeit. 1992.

Band 14 Günter Kellermann / Michael D. Morrissey (Eds.): Diachrony within Synchrony: Language History and Cognition. Papers from the International Symposium at the University of Duisburg 26-28 March 1990. 1992.

Band 15 Wim Waumans (Hrsg.): Mit fremden Augen. Niederländisch: eine Sprache, verschiedene Kulturgemeinschaften. 1993.

Band 16 Eberhard Klein: Konditionalität in didaktischen und pädagogischen Grammatiken des Englischen. Prinzipien zur Erstellung von Lehr- und Lerngrammatiken. 1993.

Band 17 Xiaoan Zhu: "Wenn sich das Gras bewegt, dann muß auch der Wind blasen!" Studien zur Metapher in der deutschen politischen Pressesprache – unter besonderer Berücksichtigung der China-Berichterstattung. 1993.

Band 18 Fritz Ponelis: The Development of Afrikaans. 1993.

Band 19 Martin Pütz: Sprachökologie und Sprachwechsel. Die deutsch-australische Sprechgemeinschaft in Canberra. 1994.

Band 20 Heiner Pürschel (Ed.); Co-Editors: Elmar Bartsch, Peter Franklin, Ulrich Schmitz, Sonja Vandermeeren: : Intercultural Communication. Proceedings of the 17th Inter- national L.A.U.D. Symposium. Duisburg, 23-27 March 1992. 1994.

Band 21 Dominiek Sandra: Morphology in the reader's mental lexicon. 1994.

Band 22 René Dirven: Metaphor and Nation. Metaphors Afrikaners live by. 1994.

Band 23 Ralph Bisschops: Die Metapher als Wertsetzung. Novalis, Ezechiel, Beckett. 1994.

Band 24 René Dirven / Johan Vanparys (Eds.): Current Approaches to the Lexicon. A Selection of Papers Presented at the 18th LAUD Symposium, Duisburg, March 1993. 1995.

Band 25 Michael Schloßmacher: Die Amtssprachen in den Organen der Europäischen Gemeinschaft. Status und Funktion. 1996. 2., durchges. Aufl. 1997.

Band 26 Johan Vanparys: Categories and Complements of Illocutionary Verbs in a Cognitive Perspective. 1996.

Band 27 Hideaki Takahashi: Die richtige Aussprache des Deutschen in Deutschland, Österreich und der Schweiz nach Maßgabe der kodifizierten Normen. 1996.

Band 28 Angela Heidemann: The visualization of foreign language vocabulary in CALL. 1996.

Band 29 Kazuma Matoba: Referenzperspektive in Sprechakten. Ihre Funktion und Entwicklung in der deutschen und japanischen Sprache. 1997.

Band 30 Olaf Jäkel: Metaphern in abstrakten Diskurs-Domänen. Eine kognitiv-linguistische Untersuchung anhand der Bereiche Geistestätigkeit, Wirtschaft und Wissenschaft. 1997.

Band 31 Birgit Smieja / Meike Tasch (Eds.): Human Contact through Language and Linguistics. 1997.

Band 32 Martin Pütz (Ed.): The Cultural Context in Foreign Language Teaching. 1997.

Band 33 Andrea Gerbig: Lexical and Grammatical Variation in a Corpus. A Computer-Assisted Study of Discourse on the Environment. 1997.

Band 34 Helga Bister-Broosen: Sprachkontakte und Sprachattitüden Jugendlicher im Elsaß und in Baden. Vergleichende soziolinguistische Untersuchungen in Colmar (Frankreich) und in Freiburg und Müllheim (Deutschland). 1998.

Band 35 Helga Bister-Broosen (Hrsg.): Niederländisch am Niederrhein. 1998.

Band 36 Alicja Sakaguchi: Interlinguistik. Gegenstand, Ziele, Aufgaben, Methoden. 1998.

Band 37 Benjamin Biebuyck / René Dirven / John Ries (Eds.): Faith and Fiction. Interdisciplinary Studies on the Interplay between Metaphor and Religion. A Selection of Papers from the 25th LAUD-Symposium of the Gerhard Mercator University of Duisburg on 'Metaphor and Religion'. 1998.

Band 38 Ulrich Ammon (Hrsg.): Sprachförderung. Schlüssel auswärtiger Kulturpolitik. 2000.

Band 39 El Hadj Ibrahima Diop: Das Selbstverständnis von Germanistikstudium und Deutschunterricht im frankophonen Afrika. Vom kolonialen Unterrichtsfach zu eigenständigen Deutschlandstudien und zum praxisbezogenen Lernen. 2000.

Band 40 Herman M. Batibo / Birgit Smieja (Eds.): Botswana: The Future of the Minority Languages. 2000.

Band 41 Harald Haarmann: Die Kleinsprachen der Welt – Existenzbedrohung und Überlebenschancen. Eine umfassende Dokumentation. 2001.

Band 42 Dirk Scholten: Sprachverbreitungspolitik des nationalsozialistischen Deutschlands. 2000.

Band 43 Riana Roos Paola: Pro-active Language Teacher Education in a Multicultural Society. 2001.

Band 44 Angelika Daniel: Lernerwortschatz und Wortschatzlernen im bilingualen Unterricht. 2001.

Band 45 Edel O'Halloran: Ist Mode englisch? Französische und englische Einflüsse auf die deutsche Mode- und Gemeinsprache im 20. Jahrhundert. 2001.

Band 46 Maya Khemlani David (Ed.): Methodological and Analytical Issues in Language Maintenance and Language Shift Studies. 2002.

Band 47 Martin Praxenthaler: Die Sprachverbreitungspolitik der DDR. Die deutsche Sprache als Mittel sozialistischer auswärtiger Kulturpolitik. 2002.

Band 48 Ulrich Ammon / Grant McConnell: English as an Academic Language in Europe. A Survey of its Use in Teaching. 2002.

Band 49 Birgit Smieja: Language Pluralism in Botswana - Hope or Hurdle? A sociolinguistic survey on language use and language attitudes in Botswana with special reference to the status and use of English. 2003.

Band 50 Carlos Inchaurralde / Celia Florén (Eds.): Interaction and Cognition in Linguistics. 2003.

Band 51 Andreas Ross: Europäische Einheit in babylonischer Vielfalt. Die Reform des Sprachenregimes der Europäischen Union im Spannungsfeld von Demokratie und Effizienz. 2003.

Band 52 Michael Anton Böhm: Deutsch in Afrika. Die Stellung der deutschen Sprache in Afrika vor dem Hintergrund der bildungs- und sprachpolitischen Gegebenheiten sowie der deutschen Auswärtigen Kulturpolitik. 2003.

Band 53 Martin Pütz / JoAnne Neff-van Aertselear / Teun A. van Dijk: Communicating Ideologies. Multidisciplinary Perspectives on Language, Discourse, and Social Practice. 2004.

Band 54 Yuko Sugita: Gesprächserwartungen. Eine kontrastive Studie über die Gesprächsführung in deutschen und japanischen Telefonaten. 2004.

Band 55 Eithne B. Carlin: A Grammar of Trio. A Cariban Language of Suriname. 2004.

Band 56 Maya Khemlani David (Ed.): Teaching of English in Second and Foreign Language Settings. Focus on Malaysia. 2004.

Band 57 Rita Brdar-Szabó / Elisabeth Knipf-Komlósi (Hrsg.): Lexikalische Semantik, Phraseologie und Lexikographie. Abgründe und Brücken. Festgabe für Regina Hessky. 2004.

Band 58 Claudia Kunschak: Language Variation in Foreign Language Teaching. On the Road to Communicative Competence. 2004.

Band 59 Allan Turner: Translating Tolkien. Philological Elements in *The Lord of the Rings*. 2005.

Band 60 Markus Motz (Hrsg.): Englisch oder Deutsch in Internationalen Studiengängen? 2005.

Band 61 Birte Kellermeier-Rehbein: Areale Wortbildungsvarianten des Standarddeutschen. Beiuntersuchung zum *Variantenwörterbuch des Deutschen*. 2005.

Band 62 Maya Khemlani David / Hafriza Burhanudeen / Ain Nadzimah Abdullah (Eds.): The Power of Language and the Media. 2006.

Band 63 Vít Dovalil: Sprachnormenwandel im geschriebenen Deutsch an der Schwelle zum 21. Jahrhundert. Die Entwicklung in ausgesuchten Bereichen der Grammatik. 2006.

Band 64 Sara Hägi: Nationale Varietäten im Unterricht Deutsch als Fremdsprache. 2006.

Band 65 Albert Weideman / Birgit Smieja (eds.): Empowerment through Language and Education. Cases and Case Studies from North America, Europe, Africa and Japan. 2006.

Band 66 Iraide Ibarretxe-Antuñano / Carlos Inchaurralde / Jesús-M. Sánchez-García (eds.): Language, Mind, and the Lexicon. 2007.

Band 67 Roswitha Reinbothe: Deutsch als internationale Wissenschaftssprache und der Boykott nach dem Ersten Weltkrieg. 2006.

Band 68 Fredericka van der Lubbe: Martin Aedler and the *High Dutch Minerva*. The First German Grammar for the English. 2007.

Band 69 Frank Polzenhagen: Cultural Conceptualisations in West African English. A Cognitive-Linguistic Approach. 2007.

Band 70 Augustin Simo Bobda (ed.): Explorations into Language Use in Africa. 2008.

Band 71 Johannes Eckerth / Sabine Siekmann (eds.): Task-Based Language Learning and Teaching. Theoretical, Methodological, and Pedagogical Perspectives. 2008.

Band 72 Laura Sicola: *No, they won't 'just sound like each other'*. NNS-NNS Negotiated Interaction and Attention to Phonological Form on Targeted L2 Pronunciation Tasks. 2009.

Band 73 Gerhard Stickel (ed.): National and European Language Policies. Contributions to the Annual Conference 2007 of EFNIL in Riga. 2009.

Band 74 Daniel Klaaß: Untersuchungen zu ausgewählten Aspekten des Konsonantismus bei österreichischen Nachrichtensprechern. 2009.

Band 75 Javier Herrero Ruiz: Understanding Tropes. At the Crossroads between Pragmatics and Cognition. 2009.

Band 76 Javier Valenzuela / Ana Rojo / Cristina Soriano (eds.): Trends in Cognitive Linguistics. Theoretical and Applied Models. 2009.

Band 77 Maya Khemlani David / James McLellan / Shameem Rafik-Galea / Ain Nadzimah Abdullah (eds.): Code Switching in Malaysia. 2009.

Band 78 Gerhard Stickel (ed.): Language Use in Business and Commerce in Europe. Contributions to the Annual Conference 2008 of EFNIL in Lisbon. 2010.

Band 79 Geert Brône: Bedeutungskonstitution in verbalem Humor. Ein kognitiv-linguistischer und diskurssemantischer Ansatz. 2010.

Band 80 Olga Martynova: Sprachwahl in der deutsch-russischen Unternehmenskommunikation. 2010.

Band 81 Gerhard Stickel (ed.): National, Regional and Minority Languages in Europe. Contributions to the Annual Conference 2009 of EFNIL in Dublin. 2011.

Band 82 Harald Haarmann: Writing as Technology and Cultural Ecology. Explorations of the Human Mind at the Dawn of History. 2011.

Band 83 Beate Höhmann: Sprachplanung und Spracherhalt innerhalb einer pommerischen Sprachgemeinschaft. Eine soziolinguistische Studie in Espírito Santo / Brasilien. 2011.

Band 84 Gabriele Schmidt: Motives for Studying German in Australia. Re-examining the Profile and Motivation of German Studies Students in Australian Universities. 2011.

Band 85 Michael Szurawitzki: Der thematische Einstieg. Eine diachrone und kontrastive Studie auf der Basis deutscher und finnischer linguistischer Zeitschriftenartikel. 2011.

Band 86 Azirah Hashim / Maya Khemlani David / James McLellan: Text, Discourse and Society. Functional and Pragmatic Approaches to Language in Use. 2011.

Band 87 Gerhard Stickel / Tamás Váradi (eds.): Language, Languages and New Technologies. ICT in the Service of Languages. Contributions to the Annual Conference 2010 of EFNIL in Thessaloniki. 2011.

Band 88 Monika Reif: Making Progress Simpler? Applying Cognitive Grammar to Tense-Aspect Teaching. 2012.

Band 89 Jan Kruse: Das Barcelona-Prinzip. Die Dreisprachigkeit aller Europäer als sprachenpolitisches Ziel der EU. 2012.

Band 90 Maria-Antonia Kontostathi: Die Arbeit mit dem Europäischen Sprachenportfolio als Möglichkeit zum selbständigen Erarbeiten fremdsprachlicher Kompetenzen. 2012.

Band 91 Yu Chen: Verbessern chinesische Studierende ihre Sprechfertigkeit im Deutschen während des Fachstudiums in Deutschland? Eine empirische Untersuchung unter Berücksichtigung sozialer Aspekte. 2012.

Band 92 Jakob Haselhuber: Mehrsprachigkeit in der Europäischen Union. Eine Analyse der EU-Sprachenpolitik, mit besonderem Fokus auf Deutschland. Vollständige Dokumentation und Perspektiven für die Zukunft. 2012.

Band 93 Hans Wagener: Untergräbt Deutschland selbst die internationale Stellung der deutschen Sprache? Eine Folge der Förderung von Englisch im Bildungsbereich. 2012.

Band 94 G. Stickel / M. Carrier (eds.) · Language Education in Creating a Multilingual Europe. Contributions to the Annual Conference 2011 of EFNIL in London. 2012.

Band 95 Jun He: Die Auswirkungen der englischsprachigen Hochschullehre in Deutschland auf das Deutschlernen in China. 2013.

Band 96 Monika Reif / Justyna A. Robinson / Martin Pütz (eds.): Variation in Language and Language Use. Linguistic, Socio-Cultural and Cognitive Perspectives. 2013.

Band 97 Carla Figueira: Languages at War. External Language Spread Policies in Lusophone Africa. Mozambique and Guinea-Bissau at the Turn of the 21st Century. 2013.

Band 98 Siew Imm Tan: Malaysian English. Language Contact and Change. 2013.

Band 99 Gerhard Stickel / Tamás Váradi (eds.): Lexical Challenges in a Multilingual Europe. Contributions to the Annual Conference 2012 of EFNIL in Budapest. 2013.

www.peterlang.de

www.ingramcontent.com/pod-product-compliance
Ingram Content Group UK Ltd.
Pitfield, Milton Keynes, MK11 3LW, UK
UKHW041827100926
8556IPUK00002B/61

9 783631 643945